Introduction to Number Theory with Computing

R B J T Allenby and E J Redfern
School of Mathematics, University of Leeds

Edward Arnold
A division of Hodder & Stoughton
LONDON MELBOURNE AUCKLAND

First published in Great Britain 1989

Distributed in the USA by Routledge, Chapman and Hall, Inc.
29 West 35th Street, New York, NY 10001

British Library Cataloguing in Publication Data

Allenby, R.B.J.T.
Introduction to number theory with computing
1. Number theory
I. Title II. Redfern, E.J.
512′.7

ISBN 0-7131-3661-8

Typeset in 10/12 pt Times by J W Arrowsmith Ltd, Bristol.
Printed and bound in Great Britain for Edward Arnold, the educational, academic and medical publishing division of Hodder and Stoughton Limited, 41 Bedford Square, London WC1B 3DQ by J W Arrowsmith Ltd, Bristol

Preface

I have always thought of number theory as an experimental science and, even before the days of computers, Gauss and Ramanujan and others often treated it this way

Prof. Richard K Guy, in a letter, 86-09-10

As its title is meant to indicate, this book is first and foremost a book about number theory, in particular about those aspects of (elementary) number theory frequently to be found in 'first courses' in universities and other centres of higher education. Indeed the first author, on writing to several mathematics departments both in the UK and abroad, discovered a remarkable unanimity in what is regarded as being appropriate for such a course. A glance at the Contents will reveal what many of these items are. (In particular, one obvious candidate for a follow-up course, a proof of the prime number theorem, is not to be found here.)

Our title was deliberately chosen so as to avoid giving the impression that this is an introduction to number theory *and* to computing. In fact one of our aims was to produce a text which could be used in two ways—both *with* the computing element and also *without* it. Thus, if the reader wishes, any use of the computer may be eschewed. On the other hand we certainly wished to show such a reader how the number-theoretic horizon can open up if the computer is admitted as an aid to calculation. There are many examples of this in the text. Sometimes the computer exhibits a counterexample to a plausible conjecture and thereby saves many hours of calculation by hand or—even better—much aggravation in attempting to prove something which is false. On the other side of the coin, the massive amount of information which a computer can process quickly can, not infrequently, show up an underlying pattern which might otherwise, for paucity of examples, go unnoticed. Indeed, if the evidence seems convincing, proofs can be attempted with, possibly, a little more confidence. If nothing else, the computational power of the computer allows those of us of more modest ability—such as the two authors—to rub shoulders with geniuses of the past such as Euler and Gauss by allowing us easy access to the kind of empirical evidence which they had to accumulate by hand. (Interestingly enough, Dickson's amazing tome [1] on the history of the theory of numbers frequently describes those people whose (mainly pre-1900) work is being cited as 'computers'!)

Our title also carries with it the implication that, unlike the number-theoretic content, the computing element of this text does not begin *entirely* from scratch. Nevertheless many of the programs included in the book are pretty straightforward; in any case we assume that the reader will have no difficulty in entering them into his computer. It is then our hope that those with no previous programming experience will be sufficiently captivated to produce programs of their own—beginning, perhaps, with simple modifications of ours.

Those with a fair amount of programming experience will probably find little new from a programming point of view; our hope for them is that they be sufficiently enthralled by the number theory contained herein to direct their talents to making further discoveries of empirical relationships or counter-examples, as indicated above. (If further motivation is needed, note the stories concerning the 16-year-old Niccolo Paganini (Exercises 2.6) and the efforts of the 18-year-olds Laura Nickel and Curt Noll in Section 2.6.)

If there were a reader at whom the computing aspect of this book is chiefly aimed it would be one—and this would include many still at school—who is familiar with the rudiments of programming but has not so far found a subject of sufficient interest to which to apply it. For such people an excursion into number theory as presented here is just the ticket!

Of course, one of the most attractive features of the number theory presented in several of the chapters of this book is that, since the prerequisites are fairly few, almost everyone can join in the fun straight away. Nor is the computational side without its fascinating aspects. Apart from the problem of programming the computer so that it does what *you* want it to do, there is the interesting problem of constructing programs so that they run more efficiently. (Programs in this book are not always written with this efficiency in mind. Accordingly, you are left to try and improve any which take your fancy.) Of course one should try to avoid the attitude that every tedious task should be thrown at the computer without further ado.

Whilst no attempt has been made to give a systematic account of the history of number theory, the authors have tried to give the reader at least a feeling for the continuing development of the subject by mentioning names and ascribing dates where it seems to be of interest. In addition, potted biographies and portraits of some of the leading figures in this development are included.

There are, of course, many books already in print which deal with the subject matter discussed here, though many do not give much consideration to computing. A very readable book in this category, which is at the same level as this text, is that by Burton [2]. On the other hand, one which encourages use of the computer to introduce and consolidate number-theoretic ideas is Malm [3]. To learn about various (often unexpected) applications of the theory to the 'real' world one should consult [4] whilst a collection of fascinating open problems in *pure* number theory can be found in Guy's book [5]. For the history of the theory of numbers Dickson's 'History', referred to above, has to be delved into to be believed; if your interest in number theory is more modern, being aroused by the computing aspect, then Knuth's book [6], Volume II, is a must. References to other books and articles, many of which make for an enjoyable read, are to be found in the Bibliography.

A very brief word about the exercises, (computer) problems and programs. Appearing at the end of nearly every section, it is intended that the exercises be done *without* the aid of a computer. Naturally enough, the computer problems are (we hope) not *all* do-able by hand! The programs are presented in as near as possible a standard BASIC, the objective being to make them widely available. They have all been tested on a BBC microcomputer and should all run in a finite amount of time!

As is usual with a book of this kind, the authors find themselves wishing to thank a number of colleagues whose comments on the text have proved useful. In particular we should mention John McConnell and Bob Hart. However, our main thanks here go to the first author's research student, Lis Green, who, having chosen to attend the undergraduate course on which much of this book is based, volunteered to read the manuscript as a source of pleasure! The authors are also very much indebted to Prof. Dr Konrad Jacobs of the University of Erlangen-Nürnberg for supplying most of the photographs, to Alan Whittle, whose incredibly close attention to detail saved us from a number of embarrassments and to one of our undergraduates, Richard Warren, for a most timely remark.

On reading through this book you might make the (correct) inference that the greater part of the text was written by one of the authors whilst the majority of the programs are from the pen (or, rather, the computer) of the other. As each author is assuming that what is written in his section has, at least, the approval of the other, each author happily blames his co-author for any remaining transgressions! Perhaps the reader will be good enough to inform the offending author of any mistakes, discrepancies, oversights etc. which occur in his 'section' of the book. On the other hand both authors hope that the reader will get as much pleasure from consulting this book as they had in composing it. Have fun!

R B J T Allenby and E J Redfern
1988

Contents

Preface v

0 **Introduction** 1

0.1 Fascinating numbers 1
0.2 Well ordering 5
0.3 The division algorithm 7
0.4 Mathematical induction 10
0.5 The Fibonacci sequence 12
Portrait and biography of Fibonacci 12
0.6 A method of proof (reductio ad absurdum) 15
0.7 A method of disproof (the counterexample) 16
0.8 Iff 18

1 **Divisibility** 19

1.1 Primes and composites 19
1.2 The sieve of Eratosthenes 22
1.3 The infinitude of primes 25
1.4 The fundamental theorem of arithmetic 29
Portrait and biography of Hilbert 32
1.5 GCDs and LCMs 34
1.6 The Euclidean algorithm 37
1.7 Computing GCDs 40
1.8 Factorisation revisited 43

2 **More About Primes—A Historical Diversion** 47

2.1 A false dawn and two sorry tales 47
Portrait and biography of Dickson 50
2.2 Formulae generating primes 51
Portrait and biography of Dirichlet 53
2.3 Prime pairs and Goldbach's conjecture 56
2.4 A wider view of the primes. The prime number theorem 58
2.5 Bertrand's conjecture 67
Biography of Mersenne 70
2.6 Mersenne's and Fermat's primes 70

3 Congruences 76

3.1 Basic properties 76
3.2 Fermat's little theorem 82
Portrait and biography of Fermat 83
3.3 Euler's ϕ function 88
3.4 Euler's theorem 95
3.5 Wilson's theorem 97

4 Congruences Involving Unknowns 102

4.1 Linear congruences 102
4.2 Congruences of higher degree 109
4.3 Quadratic congruences modulo a prime 115
Portrait and biography of Lagrange 117
4.4 Lagrange's theorem 118

5 Primitive Roots 123

5.1 A converse for the FLT 123
5.2 Primitive roots of primes. Order of an element 125
Biography of Legendre 126
5.3 Gauss's theorem 132
5.4 Some simple primality tests. Pseudoprimes. Carmichael numbers 136
5.5 Special repeating decimals 142

6 Diophantine Equations and Fermat's Last Theorem 146

6.1 Introduction 146
6.2 Pythagorean triples 148
6.3 Fermat's last theorem 153
6.4 History of the FC 155
Portrait and biography of Germain 158
6.5 Sophie Germain's theorem 159
6.6 Cadenza 161

7 Sums of Squares 163

7.1 Sums of two squares 163
Portrait and biography of Mordell 166
7.2 Sums of more than two squares 169
7.3 Diverging developments and a little history 174

8 Quadratic Reciprocity 179

8.1 Introduction 179
8.2 The law of quadratic reciprocity 179
Portrait and biography of Euler 180

8.3	Euler's criterion	185
8.4	Gauss's lemma and applications	188
8.5	Proof of the LQR—more applications	193
	Portrait and biography of Jacobi	197
8.6	The Jacobi symbol	198
8.7	Programming points	200
9	**The Gaussian Integers**	202
9.1	Introduction	202
	Portrait and biography of Gauss	203
9.2	Divisibility in the Gaussian integers	205
9.3	Computer manipulation of Gaussian integers	209
9.4	The fundamental theorem	212
9.5	Generalisation. Two problems of Fermat	214
9.6	Lucas's test	221
10	**Arithmetic Functions**	224
10.1	Introduction	224
10.2	Multiplicative arithmetic functions	229
	Portrait and biography of Möbius	235
10.3	The Möbius function	235
10.4	Averaging—a smoothing process	240
11	**Continued Fractions and Pell's Equation**	249
11.1	Finite continued fractions	249
11.2	Infinite continued fractions	252
11.3	Computing continued fractions for irrational numbers	258
11.4	Approximating irrational numbers	261
11.5	iscfs for square roots and other quadratic irrationals	264
	Biography of Pell	267
11.6	Pell's Equation	267
11.7	Two more applications	272
12	**Sending Secret Messages**	277
12.1	A cautionary tale	277
12.2	The Remedy: the RSA cipher system	279
Appendices I	Multiprecision arithmetic	285
II	Table of least prime factors of integers	293
Bibliography		299
Index		303
Index of Notation		310

Programs

0.1 To find all integers $\leqslant 100\,000$ which are expressible in two distinct ways as the sum of two positive cubes 3
0.2 To transform an integer into its separate digits (base 10) 8
0.3 To check if a digital representation is palindromic 9
0.4 To find integers that are not expressible as the sum of r integers each raised to the power v 16

1.1 Determines if an integer $\geqslant 3$ is prime or finds its smallest factor if it is composite 20
1.2 Generation of a list of primes using Eratosthenes' Sieve 23
1.3 Modified Sieve of Eratosthenes program 24
1.4 To determine the prime factors of an integer N 27
1.5 Finds the prime factors and their exponents of an integer N 31
1.6 Calculation of gcd using the Euclidean algorithm 40
1.7 Calculation of gcd using only subtraction and division by two 41
1.8 Calculates gcd and expresses it as a linear combination of the two integers 42
1.9 Fermat's method of factorising 45
1.10 Factorisation using only the operations of addition and subtraction (based on Fermat's method) 45

2.1 Compact storage of prime lists 48
2.2 Numerical integration using Simpson's method 59
2.3 Determines the number of primes up to N by the Legendre formula 62
2.4 To produce the decimal representations of Mersenne numbers 73

3.1 Determination of b such that $a^m \equiv b \pmod{n}$. 78
3.2 Determination of $a^m \pmod{n}$ 79
3.3 To check possible factors (up to $2^{32}-1$) of Fermat or Mersenne numbers 86
3.4 Determination of $\phi(n)$. 92

4.1 Computes the solutions (if any) to the linear congruence $ax \equiv b \pmod{m}$. 104
4.2 To solve a system of simultaneous linear congruences 106
4.3 Solves the quadratic congruence $ax^2 + bx + c \equiv 0 \pmod{p}$ where p is prime 116

5.1 Finds the primitive roots (if any) of any given integer N 129
5.2 Finds the periodic decimal representation of $1/p$ working to base 10 143

6.1 To produce a list of primitive Pythagorean triples 150
6.2 To produce primitive Pythagorean triples in increasing magnitude of the even side between values of l (lower) and u (upper) 151

7.1 Expresses a given integer N as the sum of two squares 167
7.2 Finds all integers (less than some given integer N) that can be expressed as the sum of two squares 167

8.1 Calculation of the Legendre symbol using Gauss's lemma 192
8.2 Evaluation of the Jacobi Symbol 201

9.1 The division algorithm in $\mathbb{Z}[i]$ 209
9.2 Computation of the GCD in $\mathbb{Z}$ [i] 210
9.3 Computation in $\mathbb{Z}[i]$ of a linear combination expressing the GCD in terms of the original numbers 210
9.4 Factorisation of a Gaussian integer by trial division 211
9.5 The division algorithm in $\mathbb{Z}[\sqrt{d}]$ 219
9.6 Factorisation by trial division in $\mathbb{Z}[\zeta]$. 219

10.1 Calculation of $\tau(n)$ and $\sigma(n)$ 226

11.1 Conversion of a rational number to continued fraction form 250
11.2 Conversion of a finite continued fraction to a rational number 251
11.3 Calculation of convergents given the successive terms a_i in the continued fraction $[a_0; a_1, a_2, \ldots]$ 257
11.4 The continued fraction representation of any positive number 260
11.5 Continued fractions of quadratic irrationals 266
11.6 Factorisation using continued fractions 274

12.1 To encode a message using the RSA method 282
12.2 To decode a message using the RSA method 282

A1 Entry of long integers 285
A2 Display of long integers 286
A3 Multiprecision addition of the integers 286
A4 Multiprecision subtraction 287
A5 Multiprecision multiplication 288
A6 Multiprecision division 289

0 Introduction

0.1 Fascinating numbers

What is so fascinating about the positive integer* (i.e. whole number) 1729? The following story is told by the eminent British mathematician G. H. Hardy† in an obituary notice of the self-taught Indian genius Srinavasa Ramanujan‡. On visiting Ramanujan in hospital Hardy remarked that he had come in a taxi-cab whose licence number was 1729, a number he described as 'rather dull'. Ramanujan who, it has been said, thought of each positive integer as a personal friend replied, 'No, it is a very interesting number; it is the smallest number expressible as a sum of two [positive] cubes in two different ways'.

The above story encourages us to ask the reader 'Can you say anything interesting about the numbers* 30, 239, 341, 487, 945, 1093? If you work through this book you will find that you can! (And if you are still not convinced, you might care to find a flaw in the 'proof' (Exercise 0.2.3) that *all* positive integers are, in fact, fascinating!)

Of course, if the study of numbers involved nothing more than answering questions of the above kind, our subject, at least at a serious level, would not have had amongst its devotees some of the world's most powerful mathematicians. On the other hand, such numerological excursions are not wholly to be despised. Indeed an entire area of study of importance today, namely that concerning the Mersenne primes, arose out of philosophical speculations concerning numbers such as 6 $(=1+2+3)$ and 28 $(=1+2+4+7+14)$ which are the sums of their *proper divisors*—that is, positive divisors other than the number itself (see Chapter 2).

The numbers listed above are *answers* to just a few of the hoards of questions which arise quite naturally when an inquisitive person begins to look more closely at the integers, in particular the positive ones. Even if one restricts oneself to the *prime numbers* (see Definition 1.1.4) 2, 3, 5, 7, 11, 13, 17, 19, 23, 29, 31, 37, 41, 43, 47, 53, 59, 61, 67, 71, 73, 79, 83,... perfectly natural questions seem to pour forth in droves:

(i) Is each prime (from 3 on) less than twice its predecessor? (Or even less than $1\frac{1}{2}$ times it—from 13 onwards?)

* What is probably most fascinating about 1729 is that there is a fascinating story about it! Even without a calculator—but with some patience—anyone could discover its cubic properties. The properties which make some of the other numbers listed interesting are somewhat deeper.

† Godfrey Harold Hardy, 7 February 1877 - 1 December 1947.

‡ Srinavasa Ramanujan, 22 December 1887 - 26 April 1920.

(ii) Can gaps, as large as we please, be found between successive primes?
(iii) Are there infinitely many instances of pairs, such as 11, 13; 41, 43; 59, 61; ... of successive primes which differ by 2?

These questions illustrate one of the most attractive aspects of starting a study of the integers, that is, a study of the elementary *theory of numbers.* That aspect is the relative ease with which beginners can get a feeling of involvement in the subject by thinking up questions of the above types for themselves—and then trying to answer them! Indeed the writing of this book was partly stimulated by a young man from a local secondary school asking the first author the question: 'Is it true that every odd integer $\geqslant 3$ is either a prime or a sum of an odd prime and some power of 2?' (No matter that the question had essentially been posed 135 years before; the young man's delight in having found the problem for himself and in trying to answer it was obvious.)

On the other hand, one of the most intriguing features of number theory is the difference in the degree of difficulty often encountered in trying to answer questions which are equally easy to pose. For example, of (i), (ii), (iii) above, the answer to one must have been known to Adam and Eve(!), another took some nine years to answer whilst the third is still unresolved. [Can you decide which of (i), (ii), (iii) these comments refer to?]

One aim of this book is to introduce to you some of the undoubted delights that a study of the integers can provide even after only a relatively modest amount of preliminaries. We hope to get you involved in the subject, to encourage you to 'get your hands dirty' by experimenting for yourself, by making conjectures and then trying to verify (or disprove) them.

To help in amassing evidence to support (or destroy) a conjecture and also to help see any 'pattern' which might be present—as the great mathematician C. F. Gauss (see p. 203) did before conjecturing the celebrated prime number theorem—the modern number theorist has the computer at his disposal. [Of course, getting the computer to confirm that a specific assertion is valid for all positive integers up to, say, 10^{25}, by no means proves the assertion holds for all positive integers n (as computer problem 0.1.1 will emphasize). On the other hand, conjectures are disproved by finding *counterexamples* (see Section 0.7) and computers can be quite helpful in this regard. For instance, John Hill asserted (1727) that 139854276 ($=11826^2$) is the only perfect square which involves all nine non-zero digits once and once only.

We leave the reader to construct a computer program to prove John Hill wrong. However, we take the opportunity to register, even in this simple case, a note of caution which may not only save time but can make all the difference between solving a problem or not. *Think before you program.* Failing to do so is quite likely to generate programs that take a longer time to run and also cover redundant cases. For example, to investigate John Hill's claim we need only consider the squares of all the numbers between $[\sqrt{123\,456\,789}]$* and $[\sqrt{987\,654\,321}]$, the smallest and largest candidates. [Of course, you also have

* The notation $[x]$ is used (mathematically) to indicate the greatest integer not exceeding x.

to strike a balance between thinking time and the time you might expect your program to run. There is no point in thinking for a week to improve your program's running time by a few seconds.]

Likewise to confirm Moreau's assertion (1898) that there are precisely ten integers less than 100 000 which can be represented in more than one way as a sum of two positive cubes—and in particular to confirm Ramanujan's remark that 1729 is the least—there is little point in asking your computer to check the equality $x^3+y^3=z^3+t^3$ for each x, y, z, t in the range 1 to $\sqrt[3]{100\,000}$. Indeed, for *distinct* representations one may clearly suppose that x is the smallest of the four integers so that y is the largest. That is, we write into the program the inequalities $x<z\leq t<y$. The following program will then find Moreau's examples fairly quickly.

Program 0.1 *To find all integers ≤ 100 000 which are expressible in two distinct ways as the sum of two positive cubes*

```
10 FOR N=2 TO 74
20   FOR X=1 TO N/2
30     Y=N-X
40     FOR Z=X+1 TO Y-1
50       FOR T=Z TO Y-1
60          IF X^3+Y^3=Z^3+T^3 PRINT X,Y,Z,T,X^3+Y^3
70       NEXT T
80     NEXT Z
90   NEXT X
100 NEXT N
```

Lines 10, 20, 30 certainly ensure that each integer ≤100 000 expressible in the form x^3+y^3 is examined.

The program will run faster if we insert

```
35 U=X^3+Y^3
```

and change line 60 to

```
60 IF U=Z^3+T^3 PRINT X,Y,Z,T,U
```

It will run a bit quicker still if we amend *this* program by inserting

```
45 W=U-Z^3
```

and change line 60 to

```
60 IF W=T^3 PRINT X,Y,Z,T,U
```

From now on we shall not indicate possible variations in the programs presented. Rather we let the reader experiment for himself. Further variations to programs in the text can often be found in the programming problems suggested.

In many instances there is more than one algorithm for obtaining numerical solutions to a problem, so it is useful to determine, if possible, which might be the quickest. Many microcomputers have a version of BASIC which includes the facility to determine the time it takes to perform sets of statements in a program. Provided only the operations relating to the calculation are involved in these statements, then timing alternative sets of calculations gives us a practical way of determining the relative speed of two algorithms. Since this feature is not available in all BASICs we will not include it in any of our programs. Nevertheless, if one is available we recommend that you make use of it.

A second method is that of comparing the number (or more realistically the average number) of operations that it takes to perform a calculation. Here a useful rule to bear in mind when designing algorithms is that addition and subtraction are generally faster than multiplication and division while exponentiation (raising to a power) is yet more time consuming. Thus for example the first suggested alteration (including line 35 and altering line 60) to program 0.1 replaces $2(2n^3/3-11n^2/8+n/12)$ exponentiations by n for each value of n considered. Estimating the approximate number of operations in an algorithm is a whole subject in its own right, and we cannot pursue it in this text. For further details see [6] and [7].

As implied in the Preface we shall not expect the reader of this text to have access to a powerful computer. Indeed, for those problems for which a computer can usefully be used, we shall only assume that the reader has available a machine something akin to a 'home' microcomputer. (All the programs presented in the text have been developed and tested on a 32 K BBC microcomputer.) Accordingly all programs will be given in standard BASIC.

Finally we should point out that, although a main contention of this book is that the study of the integers is, quite simply, a whole lot of fun, its results are not without application. To mention just one: did Euler (see p. 180) know, in 1760, when he generalised a result of Fermat, (see p. 95, Section 3.4), that his result would, by 1979, be seen to hold the key (if you'll forgive the pun!) for producing apparently unbreakable codes?

Exercises 0.1

(*Warning*: Too strong a devotion to numerology may endanger your mathematical health!)

1 Prove that 11 is fascinating for the reason that it is the greatest integer not expressible as a sum of two (positive) composite integers. (*Note*—see Section 1.1—that 1 is not composite.)

2 Prove that 24 is fascinating for the reason that it is the greatest integer n for which $n!$ (factorial n) has exactly n decimal digits. [It is also the greatest integer n which is divisible by each integer not exceeding $\sqrt{n}$. (Exercise 2.5.4) At a deeper level it is the only integer n (>1) for which $1^2+2^2+\cdots+n^2$ is a square. An elementary proof of this fact is still sought.]

3 Show that 26 is fascinating, being the least non-palindromic integer whose square *is* palindromic. (n is *palindromic* if, in its decimal representation, it reads the same backwards as forwards. Examples are 1771, 35253.)

4 Show that 79 is fascinating being the smallest integer which is not expressible as a sum of less than 19 fourth powers. (For the relevance of this fact see Section 7.3.)

5 Show that 1444 is fascinating for being the least square which ends in three identical non-zero digits. (No square can end in *four* identical non-zero digits—prove it!)

Computer problems 0.1

1 Investigate whether there are any integers x and y such that (i) $x^2 = 13y^2 + 1$; (ii) $x^2 = 61y^2 + 1$. [We shall return to this type of problem later.]

2 Find an example of an integer expressible in two distinct ways as the sum of two fourth powers.

3 Write a program to prove John Hill wrong.

4 Write a program to find squares $\geqslant 1000$ which contain only two different digits such as 1444 ($= 38^2$), for example.

5 Write a program to find squares which use all 10 digits once and once only. [*Warning*: These numbers may be larger than some computers can handle directly. In this case you will need to use the multiple precision routines of Appendix I.]

6 Is there an $x > 1$ such that x and x^2
  (i) use precisely the *same* digits,
  (ii) use all ten digits once and once only between them?

7 Find Moreau's 10 integers. see top of page 3.

8 Find the least integer expressible in three ways as the sum of two positive cubes.

0.2 Well ordering

Before beginning our study of the integers we ought to set up some notation and assemble at least a few of the tools which will help us do the job better. (Despite Gauss's stricture that it is the notion rather than the notation which is important, good notation alone is often of tremendous benefit—witness, in particular, one of Gauss's own contributions, not only the notion but the very helpful notation of *congruence*, to the study of divisibility, in Chapter 3.)

Notation

Throughout we shall let $\mathbb{Z}$ denote the *set* (collection) *of all integers*:

$$\mathbb{Z} = \{\ldots, -2, -1, 0, 1, 2, 3, \ldots\}$$

where, as usual, we use curly brackets (braces) to enclose the *members* or *elements* of the set in question. The subset $\{1, 2, 3, \ldots\}$ comprising all the *positive integers* (also called the *natural numbers*) is denoted by the symbol $\mathbb{Z}^+$. As usual we signify this relationship by writing $\mathbb{Z}^+ \subset \mathbb{Z}$. The set of all *rational* (respectively, *real*) *numbers* will be denoted by $\mathbb{Q}$ (respectively $\mathbb{R}$).

We have already assumed that the reader is familiar with many of the symbols $=$, $\neq$, $<$, $\leqslant$, $>$, $\geqslant$, $\subset$, $\subseteq$, $\supset$, $\supseteq$ as applied to $\mathbb{Z}$, $\mathbb{Q}$ and $\mathbb{R}$ etc. We remind the reader that if a is any element of $\mathbb{Z}$ (or $\mathbb{Q}$ or $\mathbb{R}$) then $|a|$ is defined by:

$$|a| = \begin{cases} a & \text{if } a \geqslant 0 \\ -a & \text{if } a \leqslant 0. \end{cases}$$

Thus $|\frac{7}{3}| = \frac{7}{3}$, $|-2| = 2$, $|\mathrm{e} - \pi| = \pi - \mathrm{e}$.

We shall say that the set S is *non-empty* if it contains at least one element. The *empty set*, denoted by $\varnothing$, is thus the set $\{\ \ \}$ containing no elements.

An infinite set is often better described by indicating a property which characterises its elements. In particular we can define the set $\mathbb{N}$ of *non-negative integers* by

$$\mathbb{N} = \{a \colon a \in \mathbb{Z} \text{ and } a \geqslant 0\}.$$

Here, $a \in S$ is the notation for the statement 'the element a belongs to the set S'. Likewise the notation $a \notin S$ signifies that a is *not* an element of S. Thus $-\frac{5}{2} \in \mathbb{Q}$, $\frac{5}{3} \notin \mathbb{Z}$, $-4 \in \mathbb{Z}$, $\pi \notin \mathbb{Q}$.

Tools

One tool we cannot possibly do without is the

Well ordering principle (WO)
Let S be any non-empty set of non-negative integers (that is, $S \subseteq \mathbb{N}$, $S \neq \varnothing$). Then S contains a least member. That is, S contains a non-negative integer m such that, for all $s \in S$, we have $m \leqslant s$.

Example 0.2.1 Using the well-known expansion 3.14159265 . . . of the number π, consider the subset of non-negative integers in the list 3^2, $3^2 - 1^2$, $3^2 - 1^2 + 4^2$, $3^2 - 1^2 + 4^2 - 1^2, \ldots$ etc. According to WO this infinite (?) set of non-negative integers must contain a least member. It is not, perhaps, so completely obvious what this least number is. (Can you find it?)

Exercises 0.2

(From now on—more serious mathematics but still, we hope, fun!)

1 What is the smallest positive integer which can be expressed in the form:

(i) $3n^2-47n+71$ ($n \in \mathbb{Z}$); (ii) $105x+288y+150z$ where $x, y, z \in \mathbb{Z}$; (iii) $105x-288y+150z$ where $x, y, z \in \mathbb{Z}^+$ (Note: (ii), (iii) will be easier after you've completed Section 1.6).

2 Show that the WO principle is not applicable to $\mathbb{Q}^+$ by showing that the set of all positive rationals has no smallest member. Show that the set of all non-negative rationals *does* have a smallest member. Does the set of all rationals which are greater than $\sqrt{2}$ have a least member? Prove your assertion.

3 In [8] David Wells finds 39 to be the *least* uninteresting positive integer—so that, of course, it is very interesting indeed! This observation implies that if we apply the WO principle to the set, U say, of all (positive) uninteresting integers we find that U is the empty set. Consequently all integers are interesting—as is implicit in our earlier remarks!! Can this really be correct? Or is there a flaw in our proof?

4 Show that there is a least positive integer which is expressible in two distinct ways as the sum of two (positive or negative) cubes. (You are not asked to find it.)

Computer problem 0.2

1 Now find the integer mentioned in Exercise 0.2.4! Can you be sure you have got the smallest?

0.3 The division algorithm

How fundamental WO is can be judged by showing its use in deriving the intuitively 'obvious' result known as

The division algorithm (DA)
Let $a, b \in \mathbb{Z}$ be such that $b \neq 0$. Then there exist unique integers $m, r \in \mathbb{Z}$ such that $a = mb + r$ where $0 \leqslant r < |b|$.

Proof Consider the set $D = \{a + m|b|: m \in \mathbb{Z} \text{ and } a + m|b| \geqslant 0\}$. Then $D \neq \varnothing$, since on taking $m = |a|$ we find $a + m|b| = a + |a||b| \geqslant a + |a| \geqslant 0$. Now using the WO principle, D contains a smallest element r, say. Suppose $r = a + m_0|b| \geqslant 0$ where $m_0 \in \mathbb{Z}$. Then $r < |b|$. For, otherwise, (that is, if $r \geqslant |b|$) we should have $r = a + m_0|b| \geqslant |b|$, whence $a + (m_0 - 1)|b| \geqslant 0$, contradicting the choice of r as the smallest member of D. Thus $a = (-m_0)|b| + r$, where $0 \leqslant r < |b|$. Finally, if $b > 0$, we have $a = (-m_0)b + r$: if $b < 0$ we have $a = m_0 b + r$.

We leave the checking of the uniqueness of m and r to the exercises. □

We offer the following rather trivial examples.

Examples 0.3.1
(i) $a = 72$, $b = 13$. Then $72 = 5 \cdot 13 + 7$ so that $m = 5$ and $r = 7 (< 13)$.

(ii) $a=114$, $b=-27$. Then $114=(-4)\cdot(-27)+6$ so that $m=-4$ and $r=6$ $(<|-27|)$.

Notes 0.3.2

(i) In the DA we choose our notation, that is the letters m and r, carefully to remind ourselves that they represent *multiplier* and *remainder* respectively. Some authors refer to m as the *quotient* and correspondingly replace m by q. Generally we leave q free to represent a prime number.

(ii) The word 'algorithm' derives from the name of a 9th century Arabic mathematician Mohammed ibn Musa al-Khowarizmi. The meaning of the word has changed over the centuries but today it signifies a formal succession of definite procedures designed to produce, in a finite number of unambiguously determined steps, an answer to a problem under consideration. In particular each computer program in this book is based on an algorithm.

(iii) The DA is not badly named since it can be regarded as an algorithm rather than a mere existence theorem if we recast it as follows: Given a, b form $w(t)=a+(|a|-t)|b|$ for $t=0, 1, 2, \ldots, s$ where s is the least value of t making $w(t)$ negative. Then $m=s-1-|a|$ if $b>0$ whilst $m=|a|-s+1$ if $b<0$.

The determination of m and r for given values of a and b is simple from a computational viewpoint but it is perhaps useful to comment upon it at this point since it is at the basis of many programs to come. Many versions of BASIC include operators DIV and MOD which determine m and r directly. Thus `m = a DIV b` and `r = a MOD b`. However, since these operators are not always available, we shall use the INT function which gives the greatest integer not exceeding a given real value. That is INT(x) = [x] (see the footnote on p. 2). Using this we can determine m and r by

`m = INT(a/b)` and `r = a - INT(a/b)*b`

We illustrate their use in Program 0.2 which stores the digits of an integer N in an array A.

Program 0.2 *To Transform an integer into its separate digits (base 10)*

```
10 REM I is the number of digits
20 REM the digits are stored in reverse order in the array A
30 INPUT "Enter the number N",N
40 DIM A(10)
50 I=0
60 I=I+1
70     A(I) = N - INT(N/10)*10
80     N = INT(N/10)
90 IF N > 0 GOTO 60
```

We will need to handle integers represented in terms of their digits in several situations (for example see Problem 0.1.3). Here we offer a piece of program that checks whether or not a given integer is palindromic (see Exercise 0.1.3).

Program 0.3 *Check if a digital representation is palindromic*

```
100 REM the array A contains I digits
110 K=0
120 IF A(I-K) <> A(K+1) GOTO 170
130    K = K+1
140 IF K<= INT(I/2) GOTO 120
150 PRINT "The integer is palindromic"
160 GOTO 180
170 PRINT "The integer is not palindromic"
180 REM The next part of your program follows here
```

Exercises 0.3

1 Let $a=6183$, $b=17$. Write $a=mb+r$ where: (i) $m \in \mathbb{Z}$ and $0 \leqslant r < 17$; (ii) $m \in \mathbb{Z}$ and $-\frac{17}{2} \leqslant r < \frac{17}{2}$; (iii) $m \in \mathbb{Z}$ and r is a positive multiple of 10 which is less than 170. [Why 170?].

2 How many integers x are there which are such that $712 \leqslant x \leqslant 6173$ and x is divisible by 17?

3 Show that in the division algorithm the integers m and r are unique. Show that suitable m and r also exist and are unique, if instead, we insist that $-|b|/2 \leqslant r < |b|/2$.

4 Show that for each integer a we can write $a=6m+r$, where $m \in \mathbb{Z}$ and r is one of 66, 13, -4, 3, 100, 5003. Can you explain why this curious set of six 'remainders' works?

5 Use the division algorithm to show that each integer can be expressed in one of the forms $4k$, $4k+1$, $4k+2$, $4k+3$. Use this to prove that the square of each odd integer is of the form $8k+1$.

6 An integer whose only (decimal) digits are 1s (e.g. 11, 111, 1111, ...) is called a *repunit*. Show that no repunit (>1) can ever be a square.

Computer problems 0.3

1 Write a program to determine whether or not any given integer divides another (exactly).

2 Write a program to find the quotient and remainder in the division algorithm.

3 Write a program to find the quotient and remainder (and its sign) using the modified division algorithm suggested in Exercise 0.3.3.

4 Write a program to check whether an integer is even or odd.

5 Find examples of non-palindromes with palindromic squares.

6 Are there any palindromic numbers whose squares use (i) all 9 non-zero digits; (ii) all 10 digits?

0.4 Mathematical induction

The WO principle can be shown* to be logically equivalent to the much better known

Principle of mathematical induction (PMI)
Let S be a non-empty subset of $\mathbb{Z}^+$ such that both (i) and (ii) hold where (i) $1 \in S$ and (ii) *If* $k \in S$ *then* $k+1 \in S$. Then $S = \mathbb{Z}^+$.

Note 0.4.1 The PMI has often been dynamically illustrated by considering an infinite sequence of dominoes $d_1, d_2, \ldots$ If the dominoes are placed so that (i) d_1 can be knocked over and (ii) for each $i \geq 1$ *if* d_i falls *then* d_{i+1} also falls, then all the dominoes will get knocked over.

As an application of the PMI we prove

Theorem 0.4.2 For each $n \in \mathbb{Z}^+$, $1^3 + 2^3 + \cdots + n^3 = (n(n+1)/2)^2$.

Proof The desired result is trivially true if $n = 1$: the left-hand side equals 1^3, the right-hand side $(2/2)^2$. So we now suppose the result valid for $n = k$ and try to establish it in case $n = k+1$. Thus we suppose $1^3 + 2^3 + \cdots + k^3 = (k(k+1)/2)^2$. We then add $(k+1)^3$ to each side. Since the right-hand side is now

$$\begin{aligned}(k(k+1)/2)^2 + (k+1)^3 &= ((k+1)/2)^2(k^2 + 4(k+1)) \\ &= ((k+1)/2)^2(k+2)^2\end{aligned}$$

we see that the claimed equality also holds if $n = k+1$. The PMI then tells us that the above equality does hold for each $n \in \mathbb{Z}^+$. □

We shall occasionally require the following principle which can also be shown* to be equivalent to PMI and hence to WO.

The second principle of mathematical induction (PMI2)
Let S be any non-empty subset of $\mathbb{Z}^+$ such that both (i) and (ii) hold where (i) $1 \in S$ and (ii) *If* $1, 2, \ldots, k \in S$ *then* $k+1 \in S$. Then $S = \mathbb{Z}^+$.

As an example not without interest, especially with computing in mind, we offer

Example 0.4.3 Each positive integer n can be expressed as a sum $2^{\alpha_0} + 2^{\alpha_1} + \cdots + 2^{\alpha_t}$, where $t \geq 0$ and $0 \leq \alpha_0 < \alpha_1 < \cdots < \alpha_t$.

For, let S be the set of all positive integers for which the stated result holds. Taking $t = 0$ and $\alpha_0 = 0$ shows that $1 \in S$. Now suppose $1, 2, \ldots, k \in S$ and consider the integer $k+1$ where $k \geq 1$. Let 2^β be the largest power of 2 such that $2^\beta \leq k+1$. If $k+1 = 2^\beta$ the desired result clearly holds. Otherwise $0 < k+1-2^\beta \leq k$ which implies that $k+1-2^\beta \in S$. Thus $k+1-2^\beta = 2^{\gamma_0} + 2^{\gamma_1} + \cdots + 2^{\gamma_r}$ where $0 \leq r$ and $0 \leq \gamma_0 < \gamma_1 < \cdots < \gamma_r$. Then $k+1 = 2^{\gamma_0} + 2^{\gamma_1} + \cdots + 2^{\gamma_r} + 2^\beta$ where $y_r < \beta$. [Why?]

* See, for example, p. 17 of RFG (see the end of the Bibliography).

Note 0.4.4 Minor variants of PMI and PMI2 in which the 'starting value' 1 in step (i) is replaced by some other integer k, say, and the conclusion $S=\mathbb{Z}^+$ is replaced by the conclusion that $S=\{n: n\in\mathbb{Z} \text{ and } n\geqslant k\}$, are used fairly often. See, for example, Exercises 0.4.3, 0.4.4 and Theorem 1.1.5.

Exercises 0.4

1 Prove by induction that $\sum_{k=1}^{n} k^2 = n(n+1)(2n+1)/6$.

2 Try to prove, using PMI, that $\sum_{i=1}^{n} k^2 = n(n+1)(n^2-n+3)/6$. Where does your proof fail? (After all the equality holds for $n=1$ and $n=2$.)

3 Prove, for all $n\in\mathbb{N}$, that $2.5^{4n+1}+3.8^{4n}$ is divisible by 13.

4 Prove that $(2n)!/(n!)^2<2^{2n}/5$ for all $n\geqslant 10$.

5 Prove that if a is an odd integer then, for all integers $n>0$, $a^{2^n}-1$ is a multiple of 2^{n+2}.

6 For each positive integer n and each integer r $(0\leqslant r\leqslant n)$ define $\binom{n}{r}$ to be the rational number $n!/r!(n-r)!$ (where $0!$ is defined to be 1). Prove that for $1\leqslant t\leqslant n$,

$$\binom{n}{t}+\binom{n}{t-1}=\binom{n+1}{t}.$$

Show that $\binom{1}{0}$ and $\binom{1}{1}$ are both integers.

Suppose that $\binom{n}{r}$ has been proved to be an integer for each $n\leqslant k$ and for each r such that $0\leqslant r\leqslant n$. Prove by induction that $\binom{k+1}{r}$ is an integer for each r such that $0\leqslant r\leqslant k+1$. Hence prove, by induction, that $\binom{n}{r}\in\mathbb{Z}^+$ for each pair of integers n, r where $n\geqslant 1$ and $0\leqslant r\leqslant n$. Deduce that the product of any r consecutive positive integers is divisible by $r!$

7 Use the previous exercise to show that if $n=n_1+n_2+\cdots+n_r$ where each $n_i\in\mathbb{N}$, then $n!/(n_1!n_2!\cdots n_r!)\in\mathbb{Z}^+$.

Computer problems 0.4

1 Is 10 the smallest (positive) value of n for which the inequality in Exercise 0.4.4 holds?

2 Find the value, for $n=1,2,3,4,5$, of $n(n-1)(n^2-5n+18)/24$. Make a conjecture involving 2^{n-1}. Try to prove this conjecture by induction. Evaluate the formula for $n=6,7$. Reformulate your conjecture, if necessary, and try to prove it now.

0.5 The Fibonacci sequence

Definition by induction

As well as being able to call upon mathematical induction to help us *prove* theorems, we can also ask it to help us make definitions. Within the theory of numbers one of the more important of these definitions, both historically and from a practical point of view, is that of the *Fibonacci sequence* as given below. The sequence was introduced by Fibonacci, also known as Leonardo of Pisa, in his book *Liber Abaci*, written in 1202, via the problem outlined in Exercise 0.5.1. Amongst other things the Fibonacci sequence, which has so many delightful properties of its own that there exists a research journal devoted to its study, has played a prominent role in determining the primeness or compositeness of some astronomically large numbers. (See Section 9.6)

Leonardo Fibonacci *c1170–1240*

Picture by courtesy of M. R. Schroeder: *Number Theory in Science and Communication*, Springer (1986).

Fibonacci was born in Pisa and is, accordingly, sometimes referred to as Leonardo of Pisa or Leonardo Pisano. Like many fathers, Fibonacci's expected his son to follow in his footsteps. And indeed he did, but more from the arithmetic point of view than the mercantile. In learning the 'art of calculation', Fibonacci, in his travels in Egypt, Sicily, Greece and Syria, made the acquaintence of the Hindu–Arabic methods.

Around 1200 Fibonacci returned to Pisa. Two years later he published the *Liber Abaci.* For the next quarter century his writings, five of which survive, promoted calculations using the 'new Indian numerals' including applications to commerce—whilst also including, for those with purer mathematical tastes, problems of an algebraic and geometric flavour.

The *Liber Abaci*, which was rewritten in 1228, contains sections on Roman and Indian numerals and on finger counting. Later chapters are devoted first to commercial calculations and then to puzzles and recreational mathematics—including the 'rabbit problem' (see Exercise 0.5.1.)

Fibonacci deals, via numerous examples, with approximating square roots, cube roots and, later, with problems on volumes in which he takes π to be $3\frac{1}{7}$. Later in the *Practica Geometricae* he obtains the value 3.141818 using Archimedes' 96-sided polygonal representation of the circle. In *Flos*, Fibonacci considers, amongst other things, the equation $x^3+2x^2+10x=20$. Showing that there is no rational solution he gives an approximate solution using the sexagesimal number system. In *Liber Quadratorum*, a work on indeterminate analysis, Fibonacci emerges as a major number theorist. He mentions the 'sums of squares' formula (see Lemma 7.1.1) and discusses the problem of finding numbers h (each called a *congruum*) such that both x^2+h and x^2-h are squares for some x. He shows that each congruum is necessarily a multiple of 24 and can never be a square.

Fibonacci appears as the lone mathematical beacon of his time in Europe. On the number-theoretic stage he had no real successor until Bachet and Fermat followed, aided by Bachet's translation of Diophantus' *Arithmetica*.

Definition 0.5.1 Let $u_1=1$, $u_2=1$ and for each integer $n\geqslant 3$ set $u_n=u_{n-1}+u_{n-2}$. The sequence $u_1, u_2, u_3, \ldots$ (that is 1, 1, 2, 3, 5, 8, 13, 21, 34, 55, ...) is called the *Fibonacci sequence.*

We leave some of the more elementary, yet delightful, properties to the exercises and warn, instead, that not everything in the garden is quite as rosy as it might first appear. There is a logical difficulty in the so-called' recursive' definitions of the above kind which we will leave the interested (or worried?) reader to look up for himself. (See, for example, [A]*.) The reader who is keener to get to the computer might care to investigate Computer Problem 0.5.2.

Exercises 0.5

1 The Fibonacci sequence was introduced by Fibonacci via the following problem. Pairs of rabbits (one male, one female) produce, on the last day of each month from the second month onwards, a pair of rabbits which themselves produce offspring in the same way. If on 1 January one pair of new born rabbits is put in a (large!) hutch, how many pairs of rabbits will there be on the first day of each succeeding month assuming that none of the rabbits dies? (Figure 0.1 should be self-explanatory.) A. Girard† was the first (1625) to state that the number of pairs on the first day of month n is given by the term u_n of the Fibonacci sequence. Prove this!

2 There are many relationships which hold between the terms of the Fibonacci sequence. The following is only a minute sample.

(i) $u_1+u_2+\cdots+u_n=u_{n+2}-1$;
(ii) $-u_1+u_2-\cdots+(-1)^n u_n=(-1)^n u_{n-1}-1$;
(iii) $u_n^2-u_{n-1}u_{n+1}=(-1)^{n-1}$;
(iv) $u_{m+n}=u_{m-1}u_n+u_m u_{n+1}$;

* This symbolism refers to the list of papers in the bibliography.
* Albert Girard, 1595 – 8 December 1632.

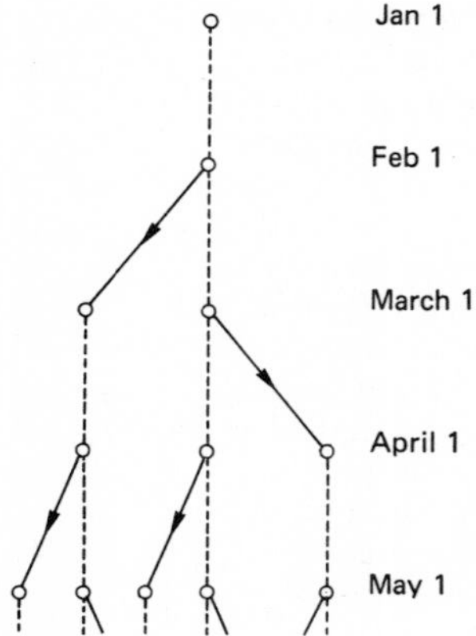

Fig. 0.1

(v) $\sqrt{5}u_n = \left(\frac{1+\sqrt{5}}{2}\right)^n - \left(\frac{1-\sqrt{5}}{2}\right)^n$; $u_n > \left(\frac{1+\sqrt{5}}{2}\right)^{n-2}$ if $n \geqslant 3$;

(vi) $u_n = \binom{n-1}{0} + \binom{n-2}{1} + \cdots + \binom{n-j-1}{j}$ where $j = \left[\frac{n-1}{2}\right]$, the greatest integer not exceeding $\frac{n-1}{2}$;

(vii) Expand $P(x) = (1-x-x^2)^{-1}$ as $1 + (x+x^2) + (x+x^2)^2 + \cdots$ and collect like powers together. Show that $xP(x) = \sum u_n x^n$. Thus $xP(x)$ is called a *generating function* for the Fibonacci sequence;

(viii) Show that if $5|n$ then $5|u_n$. Is the converse true? That is, if $5|u_n$ is it necessary that $5|n$?

3 The Lucas sequence is defined by $L_1 = 1$ and for $n \geqslant 2$ by $L_n = u_{n+1} + u_{n-1}$. Write down the first twenty terms. Show that, for each $n \geqslant 3$, $L_n = L_{n-1} + L_{n-2}$ and that $L_n = u_{2n}/u_n$ for all $n \geqslant 1$.

Computer problems 0.5

1 Write a program to generate the terms u_n in the Fibonacci sequence and the ratio $\frac{u_{n+1}}{u_n}$. Show that the ratio appears to approach the value $(1+\sqrt{5})/2$ (cf. Exercise 11.2.3(b)). Do your calculations give you enough confidence to try and prove it?

2 Investigate the sequences a_n defined by:

(i) $a_1 = 1$, $a_2 = 1$, $a_n = a_{n-a_{n-1}} + a_{n-a_{n-2}}$ (if $n \geqslant 3$); [see D. Hofstadter [B] and [5] p. 129].

(ii) $a_1 = 1$, $a_2 = 1$, $a_3 = 1$, $a_n = a_{n-a_{n-1}} + a_{n-a_{n-3}}$ (if $n \geqslant 4$).

3 Generate the sequence defined by $b_1 = 1$, $b_2 = 2$ and, for $n \geqslant 3$, b_n is the least integer greater than b_{n-1} that cannot be expressed as the sum of two or more *consecutive* terms of the sequence, $b_1, b_2, \ldots, b_{n-1}$. What do you observe? (See [5], p. 129.)

4 Let $c_1 = 2$, $c_2 = 3$ and when $c_1, c_2, \ldots, c_n$ are defined, form all possible expressions $c_i c_j - 1$, $1 \leqslant i < j \leqslant n$, placing the values in the sequence so that the whole sequence is in increasing order of magnitude. Write a program to generate the sequence. (See [5], p. 130.)

0.6 A method of proof (*reductio ad absurdum*)

During the remainder of this book we shall make many assertions (called lemmas, theorems and corollaries) which will be supported by arguments purporting to be 'proofs'. We shall, in general, be happy to let the reader decide if our proofs are logically watertight. However, one method stands out as worthy of special mention: the method of *reductio ad absurdum.* This method attempts to prove that a given assertion A, say, is valid by showing that the negation of A is untenable. Perhaps the most often used example showing *reductio* in action is that proving

Theorem 0.6.1 $\sqrt{2}$ is not a rational number.

Proof We suppose, to the contrary, that $\sqrt{2}$ *is* a rational number. That is, we assume that $\sqrt{2} = a/b$ for suitable $a, b \in \mathbb{Z}$. Clearly we may suppose that a/b is in its 'lowest terms', in other words that a, b have no common divisor >1 in $\mathbb{Z}$. Squaring up we get $2 = a^2/b^2$, that is $a^2 = 2b^2$. This means that a^2, and hence a, is an even integer. We can therefore write $a = 2m$ for some integer m. It follows that $2b^2 = a^2 = (2m)^2 = 4m^2$ and hence that $b^2 = 2m^2$. But this implies that b^2, and hence b, is even. Consequently, from the assumption that $\sqrt{2} = a/b$—with a, b in 'lowest terms'—we have deduced that a, b are, in fact, both even!

It follows (if our *argument* is logically sound!) that the only thing that can give rise to this absurd deduction is our assumption that $\sqrt{2}$ is rational. Thus $\sqrt{2}$ *can't* be rational. □

Exercises 0.6

1 Prove that $\sqrt{3}$ is not rational. Where does your proof break down if you try to adapt it to proving that $\sqrt{4}$ is not rational?

2 Prove *directly* that if a is an odd integer then a^2 is also odd. [*Hint*: $a^2 = (2m+1)^2$ for some $m \in \mathbb{Z}$].

Prove, by *reductio*, that if a is an integer with a^2 odd, then a is odd. (That is, assume a is even and obtain a contradiction.)

3 Prove that $\mathbb{Z}^+$ satisfies the *Archimedean property*: given $a, b \in \mathbb{Z}^+$ there exists $n \in \mathbb{Z}^+$ such that $na > b$. [*Hint*: assuming the desired result false we see that $\{b - na: n \in \mathbb{Z}\}$ is a set of non-negative integers which, by WO, has a least member.]

0.7 A method of disproof (the counterexample)

Consider the assertions:

(i) each positive integer a is a sum of four (non-negative) integer squares: $a = x^2 + y^2 + z^2 + t^2$ with $x, y, z, t \in \mathbb{N}$.

(ii) each positive integer b is a sum of eight (non-negative) integer cubes: $b = \alpha^3 + \beta^3 + \gamma^3 + \delta^3 + \kappa^3 + \lambda^3 + \mu^3 + \nu^3$ with $\alpha, \beta, \gamma, \delta, \kappa, \lambda, \mu, \nu \in \mathbb{N}$.

As it happens, the first statement is true (see Theorem 7.2.4) although a computer check even up to, say, $a = 10^{100}$ would be insufficient to prove the assertion *for every a*. (For all you would then know the assertion may not be valid for $a = 10^{100} + 1$.) On the other hand the second statement is false: all that is required to confirm this is a single instance of a number not so expressible. Such an instance, showing that an assertion is not *universally* valid, is called a *counterexample*. Computers can be quite useful in looking for counterexamples (as you will no doubt agree if you have done Computer Problem 0.1.3). In this case resort to a computer is not really essential since the smallest such counterexample, 23, is soon found. In fact there is only one other positive integer not expressible as a sum of 8 (non-negative) integer cubes (see [C]). Program 0.4 will find it for you fairly easily (but note once again that not finding any more counterexamples less than $a = 10^{100}$ will *not* prove our claim that these are the only two).

Program 0.4 expresses an integer N as $\sum_{i=1}^{r} x_i^v$, where $x_1, x_2, \ldots, x_r$ is a non-increasing sequence of integers and v is a fixed positive integer, if such an expression exists. By restricting the search to a set of realistic values we can check whether N can be expressed in this way for large values of r very quickly. (Exercise 0.1.4, for example, can be easily confirmed.) [We must of course be careful to ensure that every possibility is considered.]

While the program presented here is fairly complex it illustrates how some careful thought can result in a search for possible solutions being restricted to a minimal set of possibilities. [You might like to consider how to tackle the problem before looking in detail at the program presented here.]

Program 0.4 *To find integers that are not expressible as the sum of r integers each raised to the power v*

```
10 INPUT "Enter the number of terms and the power",r,v
20 DIM P(r)
30 FOR A = 1 TO 1000
40 FOUND=FALSE
50 S=0
60 FOR j= 1 TO r
```

```
 70   P(j)=0
 80 NEXT j
 90 k=0
100  i=k+1
110 REM find a non-increasing sequence of r integers
120 REM whose sum of vth powers is not greater than A
130   IF i>r GOTO 290
140 REM find the integer whose vth power is the greatest less than A-S
150      j=0
160         j=j+1
170      IF (j+1)^v <= A-S GOTO 160
180      IF i=1 GOTO 210
190 REM avoid increasing sequences
200      IF j>P(i-1) THEN j=P(i-1)
210      P(i)=j
220      S=S+j^v
230      i=i+1
240      IF A=S FOUND=TRUE
250   IF FOUND GOTO 490
260   GOTO 130
270 REM If a sequence has not been found reduce one of the terms by one
280 REM to try other sequences
290            k=1 : IF k< r THEN k=k+1
300 REM if terms are identical only reduce the last one
310            IF k>=r-1 GOTO 350
320        IF P(k)=0 GOTO 350
330           k=k+1
340        IF P(k)<=P(k+1) AND k<r-1 GOTO 330
350        IF P(k)>0 GOTO 390
360          k=k-1
370        GOTO 350
380 REM reduce the chosen term in the existing sequence by one
390        P(k)=P(k)-1
400        S=0
410        FOR j=1 TO k
420          S=S+P(j)^v
430        NEXT j
440 REM once we have chosen our term all remaining terms are set to zero
450     IF k=r GOTO 470
460     FOR J=k+1 TO r : P(J)=0 : NEXT J
470     IF NOT(FOUND) AND P(1)>0 GOTO 100
480     IF FOUND GOTO 510
490       PRINT A;" cannot be expressed as ";r;" ";v;"th powers"
500     GOTO 520
510       PRINT A;" " : FOR J=1 TO r : PRINT ;P(J);" " : NEXT J
520 NEXT A
```

Exercises 0.7

1 Find a counterexample to the assertion that the integer $2^{2^n}+3$ is prime for each positive integer n.

2 Charles de Bouvelles (1470–1553) asserted that, for each positive integer n, at least one of $6n-1$ and $6n+1$ is a prime. Find an example to prove him wrong.

Computer problems 0.7

1 Show that the assertion, that no term of the Fibonacci sequence is divisible by 100, is false.

2 Find a counterexample to the assertion that if p is an odd prime then the term u_p of the Fibonacci sequence is also a prime.

3 (L. Collatz) Let a be any odd integer greater than 1. Define the sequence $a_0, a_1, \ldots$ by $a_0 = a$, $a_{k+1} = a_k/2$ (if a_k even), $a_{k+1} = 3a_k + 1$ (if a_k odd). It is conjectured that for each a there is an a_k such that $a_k = 1$. No counterexample is known. You could try to find one. If $3a_k + 1$ is replaced by $3a_k - 1$ what limiting cycles (i.e. repeating subsequences) arise?

0.8 Iff

Finally, it is worth considering a small point relating to economy of presentation and to precision of statements. Let a be an integer and consider the (valid) assertion: if a is even then a^2 is even, (briefly; a even $\Rightarrow a^2$ even). The converse of this statement is also true: if a^2 is even then a is even, (briefly; a^2 even $\Rightarrow$ a even). The equivalence of these two conditions (i) a even; (ii) a^2 even, can be described economically by the single assertion

a is even *if and only if* a^2 is even. (Briefly a even $\Leftrightarrow$ a^2 even).

The expression 'if and only if'—abbreviated to 'iff'—is also of use in making definitions more watertight. For example, one should really say that 'The integer m is even iff m is an integer multiple of 2'. The 'definition': 'the integer m is even if m is an integer multiple of 2' does leave open the possibility that a certain number might be called even even(!) if it is not a multiple of 2.

1
Divisibility

1.1 Primes and composites

We begin our study proper with two easy definitions.

Definition 1.1.1 Let $a, b \in \mathbb{Z}$. We say that b *is divisible by* a, or that a *divides* b, if there exists $c \in \mathbb{Z}$ such that $ac = b$. We then call a a *factor* or *divisor* of b and b a *multiple* of a and write $a|b$. If a *doesn't* divide b we write $a \nmid b$.

Examples 1.1.2 $7|42$, $-9|18$, $3 \nmid 8$, $0|0$, $4|0$, $0 \nmid 4$.

Notes 1.1.3
(i) We insist that $c \in \mathbb{Z}$. Thus $2 \nmid 1$ (in $\mathbb{Z}$) since, in $\mathbb{Z}$, there is no c such that $2c = 1$.
(ii) 0 is the only integer which is divisible by 0.

An integer n (other than $-1, 0, 1$) which can be expressed as the product of two integers l, m, neither of which is -1 or 1, is called *composite*. Thus 15 $(=3\cdot 5=(-5)\cdot(-3)$ etc.) and $-11\,021$ $(=(-103)\cdot(107)=103\cdot(-107)$ etc.) are composite. The remaining integers (other than $-1, 0, 1$) which are thus 'multiplicatively indecomposable' are the *primes*. They are the multiplicative 'building blocks' for $\mathbb{Z}$ (see Theorem 1.4.1). Formally

Definition 1.1.4 The integer p is *prime* iff (i) $p \neq -1, 0, 1$ and (ii) the only divisors of p in $\mathbb{Z}$ are $-1, 1, -p$ and p. (The reason for excluding $-1, 0, 1$ is given in Note 1.4.5.)

Thus the first few (positive)* primes are: 2, 3, 5, 7, 11, 13, 17, 19, 23, 29, 31, 37, 41, 43, 47, 53, 59, 61, 67, 71, 73, 79, 83, . . . , 181, 191, 193, 197, 199, 211, . . . , 1259, 1277, . . . , $76\cdot 3^{139}-1$, $76\cdot 3^{139}+1$, ...

We have earlier (pp. 1, 2) posed three questions concerning the prime numbers. We (and you!) can easily extend the list:

(iv) Is there a general 'formula'—of a type like x^2+x+41, say—which always produces a prime whenever we substitute the integers $1, 2, 3, \ldots$ for x?
(v) Do there exist infinitely many primes ending in a 1? (or a 3, 7 or 9 for that matter? Or a 5?)

* According to our definition $-2, -3, -5, \ldots$ also qualify as primes. Allowing this is useful in certain parts of algebra and number theory (see RFG and Chapter 9 here). Until Chapter 9 we shall use the word 'prime' to signify a positive prime in $\mathbb{Z}$.

(vi) Is each even integer from 6 onwards the sum of two (odd) primes ?

Which of these problems is easy and which (if any) is hard? The answer is . . . see Theorem 2.2.1, Theorem 2.2.2 and Section 2.3 respectively.

Before we answer any of the questions we've raised concerning the primes, we shall show how we can augment the above list of primes fairly painlessly.

First note that to show that an integer is composite we only have to find a smaller number ($\geqslant 2$) which divides it. The following result, which also helps us answer a question even more fundamental than those already posed, shows that we may restrict ourselves to looking for *prime* divisors.

Theorem 1.1.5 (Euclid Book 7)* Let $a \in \mathbb{Z}$, $a \geqslant 2$. Then a is divisible by some prime number.

Proof If a itself is prime then, since $a|a$, we have nothing more to prove. This is the case if $a = 2$ which we make the starting point of a proof by the induction principle PMI2. So we now suppose the desired result true for all integers $2, 3, 4, \ldots, k$ and let $a = k+1$. Now either $k+1$ is prime, in which case there is nothing more to be proved—or it isn't(!) In this latter case we can write $k+1 = l \cdot m$, where $1 < l \leqslant m < k+1$. By the inductive hypothesis there is at least one prime p dividing l (and at least one dividing m). We infer that $p|k+1$ (by Exercise 1.1.1). □

We can go further: in looking for prime divisors of an integer n we may clearly restrict our search to those primes p which are no bigger than $\sqrt{n}$. For, if $n = l \cdot m$, we surely can't have both l and m greater than $\sqrt{n}$. Putting this another way:

Theorem 1.1.6 Let $n \geqslant 2$ be an integer divisible by no prime $\leqslant \sqrt{n}$. Then n itself is prime. □

Despite the above emphasis on *prime* divisors, the simplest, if most naive way, of computing whether or not a given integer N is prime is to check *all* the integers up to $\sqrt{N}$, to see whether any of them is a factor of N. (Checking division only by primes first requires the *finding* of the primes not exceeding $\sqrt{N}$.) Making a trivial improvement on this observation, the following program tests N for primeness by dividing by 2 and all the odd numbers greater than 2 and less than or equal to $\sqrt{N}$.

Program 1.1 *Determines if an Integer ≥ 3 is Prime or finds its smallest factor if it is composite*

```
10 INPUT "enter the number N ",N
20 REM * check if the number is even *
30 p=2
40 f = N/2
```

* Euclid (fl. c300 BC). His famous 'Elements' contains substantial amounts of number theory as well as geometry.

```
50 IF f = INT(f) GOTO 180
60 REM * If number is odd and less than 9 then it is prime *
70 IF N < 9 GOTO 160
80 p = 1
90 REM * check possible factors up to √N *
100 REM * stopping when the first is found *
110  p = p + 2
120    f = N/p
130    IF f = INT(f) GOTO 180
140  IF p < SQR(N) GOTO 110
150    REM * if no factors are found then N is PRIME *
160    PRINT N;" is prime "
170  STOP
180    PRINT N;" is composite ";p;" is a factor"
190  STOP
```

Exercises 1.1

Let $a, b, c, d, m, n, z \in \mathbb{Z}$

1 Show that (i) If $a|b$ and $b|c$ then $a|c$; (ii) If $a|b$ and $a|c$ then $a|mb+nc$.

2 Suppose $a|b$ and $c|d$. Prove, or give a counterexample to, each of the assertions: (i) $a+c|b+d$; (ii) $ac|bd$.

3 Prove that: (i) If $3|a^2+b^2$ then $3|a$ and $3|b$; (ii) If $5|a^2+b^2+c^2$ then $5|a$ or $5|b$ or $5|c$.

4 Luca Paciuolo (1494) claimed that $1+2+2^2+\cdots+2^{26}$ is a prime. Prove him wrong by finding a factor of it. [*Hint*: $x^3-1=(x-1)(x^2+x+1)$.]

5 Show (as Cataldi* did in 1588) that if a^n-1 is a prime (where $a \geqslant 2$ and $n \geqslant 2$) then $a=2$ and n is prime.

6 Show that if 2^n+1 is an odd prime then $n=2^t$ for some integer $t \geqslant 0$.

7 Prove that if n^4+4 is a prime then $n=1$ or -1. [*Hint*: Try n^2+2n+2 as a factor.]

8 Check—by hand—using the √ divisor test, which of the integers $64k+1$ ($k=1, 2, \ldots, 10$) are prime. (This is of great historial significance—see Section 3.2.)

9 Determine, by hand, which of 1357, 3579, 5791, 7913, 9135, if any, are primes.

10 Show that if p is the smallest prime divisor of n and if $p>\sqrt[3]{n}$, then n/p is also a prime. Factorise, by hand, 1937.

Computer problems 1.1

1 Find out what is the largest number that your computer can test in Program 1.1 before numerical errors occur.

* Pietro Antonio Cataldi, 15 April 1552 – 11 February 1626.

2 Modify Program 1.1 to generate a list of primes up to a given integer N. (In particular try $N = 1000, 2000, 3000$.)

3 In Program 1.1 we test for factors by dividing by 2 and every odd integer. Modify this approach by testing for divisibility by 2, 3 and 5 and then succeeding odd integers with alternating gaps of 2 and 4 (i.e. we test for division by 2, 3, 5, 7, 11, 13, 17, 19, 23, 25, . . .). We are thus omitting testing for divisibility by multiples of 3. Compare the speed of this program with that of Program 1.1.

4 In Problem 3 can you introduce a further modification to the list of possible divisors to omit multiples of 5?

5 Store the primes generated by your program from Problem 2 or 3 in a file on a storage device. Modify Program 1.1 so that it tries only primes read from this file as possible divisors. (If you do not have a disk drive or cassette on which to store files you can read the primes from a DATA statement.)

1.2 The sieve of Eratosthenes

For one method of painlessly supplying a list of *all* the primes up to a given not-too-large integer N we can thank Eratosthenes* of Cyrene who lived through much of the third century B.C. Eratosthenes was well versed in many subjects; in particular he tried to study geography from a more mathematical point of view. Perhaps his greatest achievement was his determination of the circumference of the earth as being approximately 29 000 miles.

To find all primes up to, say, 100, Eratosthenes advocated a method to 'sieve' out all these primes as follows. Begin by writing down all the integers from 2 to 100 and circling the first of these. Then strike out† all subsequent multiples of 2, as indicated. Next, circle the first of the integers not yet struck out—in this case 3. Now strike out all multiples of 3 from 6 onwards and circle the first remaining number namely, now, 5. Continuing in this way the primes $\leqslant 100$ are revealed as being the numbers not struck out.

②	③	4	⑤	6	⑦	8	9	10	11	12	13	14	15	16	17	18	19	20
21	22	23	24	25	26	27	28	29	30	31	32	33	34	35	36	37	38	39	40
41	42	43	44	45	46	47	48	49	50	51	52	53	54	55	56	57	58	59	60
61	62	63	64	65	66	67	68	69	70	71	72	73	74	75	76	77	78	79	80
81	82	83	84	85	86	87	88	89	90	91	92	93	94	95	96	97	98	99	100

* Eratosthenes, 276 - 195 B.C.

† We place a bar above each number, the height of the bar indicating at which stage the number was eliminated, to make our table more readable.

This method is especially easy to use on a computer—it was also employed, with modification, by D. N. Lehmer, early this century, in determining the primes up to 10 006 721. The neatest way to handle this on a computer is to store the numbers 2 to n in an array. Then as a number is identified as being a composite, the value in that position of the array is replaced by zero to signify that it is no longer in the list. Once all the composites have been deleted we simply display the non-zero terms in the array. Program 1.2 will determine the primes less than L quickly (for moderately large L) using the Sieve of Eratosthenes.

Program 1.2 *Generation of a list of primes using Eratosthenes Sieve*

```
 10 INPUT "Enter the value of the maximum integer",L
 20 DIM A(L)
 30 FOR I=1 TO L
 40   A(I)=I
 50 NEXT I
 60 FOR M=2 TO SQR(L)
 70   FOR N=M TO L/M
 80     A(M*N)=0
 90   NEXT N
100 NEXT M
110 FOR K=2 TO L
120      IF A(K)<>0 PRINT K;
130 NEXT K
```

Note that, in the 'sieve' method described above, as soon as the first circled integer (i.e. prime) k, say, which is greater than $\sqrt{n}$ appears, the striking out process can be stopped, all circled and unstruck numbers being primes. For, all multiples of such a k which are less than n will necessarily be of the form tk where $t<\sqrt{n}$ (since $k>\sqrt{n}$) and will therefore already have been struck out at least once. For the same reason, on striking out multiples of (the prime) k, one need not always begin at $2k$, but rather with $k \cdot k$, $(k+1) \cdot k, \ldots$ since smaller multiples of k will already have been dealt with. These observations are already built into Program 1.2.

As we pointed out earlier, one should always keep an eye open for refinements which will cut down computing time. In addition there will be instances when we should also try to reduce the amount of storage that a program uses. For instance, in finding all primes less than some integer n, we can, taking hints from above, clearly restrict out attention to the *odd* integers less than n since 2 is the only even prime. Program 1.3 illustrates how these modifications can be made and how the storage space that the method uses can be reduced. (It should be noted that the operations that enable us to reduce the storage do increase the time taken but the modified program performs the calculations in less than one third of the time taken by Program 1.2.) Obviously if our array A uses all the available computer memory, then Program 1.3 can generate a longer list of primes than can Program 1.2. Computer Problem 1.2.1 suggests how time and space usage can be improved yet further.

Program 1.3 *Modified sieve of Eratosthenes program*

```
 10 INPUT "Enter the value of the largest integer required",L
 20 DIM A(INT(L/2))
 30 K=0
 40 FOR I=3 TO L STEP 2
 50   K=K+1
 60   A(K)=I
 70 NEXT I
 80 FOR M=3 TO SQR(L) STEP 2
 90   FOR N=M TO L/M STEP 2
100     A(INT(M*N/2))=0
110   NEXT N
120 NEXT M
130 FOR K=1 TO INT(L/2)
140   IF A(K)<>0 PRINT A(K);
150 NEXT K
```

If you modify the above method to locate all primes between 370 270 and 370 370 you will find that there . . . aren't any! In addition, Exercise 1.2.1, in answering question (ii) of Section 0.1, tells us that sequences, as long as you wish, of successive composite numbers *do* exist. Does this imply that the supply of prime numbers eventually dries up? A very convincing (?) argument that it *does* is supplied by the observation that the bigger an integer is the more smaller ones there are which could possibly divide it. (Note that if the list of primes does terminate then all our questions concerning the primes—except the *first*—become meaningless.)

Exercises 1.2

1 Show that, for each integer $n \geqslant 2$, $n!+2, n!+3, \ldots, n!+n$ constitutes a sequence of $n-1$ consecutive composites. Use this to find an example of 6 successive composites. Find the least positive integer k such that $k, k+1, \ldots, k+5$ are all composite.

2 Show that for $n \geqslant 4$, all integers from $n!-n$ to $n!+n$ inclusive with the possible exception of $n!-1$ and $n!+1$ are composite.

3 Find positive integers n so that, of the integers $n!-1$ and $n!+1$, (i) each is prime; (ii) each is composite, (iii) one is prime and one is composite.

4 Find positive integers n so that, of the integers $n!-n-1$ and $n!+n+1$, (i) each is prime; (ii) each is composite; (iii) one is prime and one is composite.

5 Why can no three successive odd numbers, except 3, 5, 7, all be primes?

Computer problems 1.2

1 Modify Program 1.2 to consider (i) only odd integers that are not multiples of 3; (ii) to omit multiples of 5 as well.

Compare the running time required by the programs to produce the primes up to $N = 1000$, 2000 and 3000 with those of the programs in the text and also with those of Problem 1.1.3.

Extend the value of N as far as possible for each of the programs to obtain the maximum number of primes that your computer can find in each case.

2 Write a program to determine the gaps between successive primes and to produce a table of the value of N at which the first gap of size x occurs.

Using the modified sieve program with 32K of available memory you should be able to get as far as gaps of about 30. Are there likely to be gaps corresponding exactly to every even integer?

3 Modify Program 1.2 to produce a list of the primes between two given integers. Use your program to produce a list of the primes in each block of 1000 integers up to 100 000 recording the number of primes found in each block.

4 Find the first occurrence of (i) 50; (ii) 100 consecutive composites. [*Hint*: You will need to modify Program 1.3 to allow consideration of successive ranges of integers.]

5 *Lucky numbers* (see [5]) are generated by the following sieving process. From the list of integers delete the even numbers. Apart from 1 the first remaining number is 3. Strike every third member of those remaining. The next number remaining is 7 so we strike out every 7th term in the remaining sequence. Continuing in this way we are left with a set of numbers called the lucky numbers. Write a program to perform such a sieving process to generate the lucky numbers.

6 Write a program to compare the nth Fibonacci number u_n, the nth lucky number l_n and the nth prime p_n. If you observe any apparent patterns investigate with proofs or counterexamples whether the pattern persists or eventually breaks down.

1.3 The infinitude of primes

In fact it was Euclid who first established that the sequence of primes is endless by proving the following beautiful theorem.

Theorem 1.3.1 (Euclid Book 9) 'The prime numbers are more than any assigned multitude of prime numbers'—that is, there exist infinitely many primes.

Proof (by the method of *reductio ad absurdum*) Suppose, to the contrary, that there exist only finitely many primes. Denote them by* $p_1(=2), p_2(=3), \ldots, p_t$. Form the number $N = p_1p_2 \cdots p_t + 1$. By Theorem

* We retain our restriction that primes are positive.

1.1.5, N is divisible by some prime p, say. But $p_1, p_2, \ldots, p_t$ is a list of *all* the primes—and so p must be one of them, $p = p_i$, say. Then $p_i | N$ and $p_i | N-1$. Consequently (Exercise 1.1.1(ii) $p_i | N-(N-1)$, i.e. $p_i | 1$. But this is absurd, by definition of primeness. Thus the supposition that there are only finitely many primes has led to a contradiction. Hence there must be infinitely many. □

To emphasise once again the curious difference that can exist in the methods of the solutions required for seemingly identical problems let us consider the following.

Once one knows there exist infinitely many primes, one is soon led to omit 2 and split the rest into two camps; those leaving remainder 3 on division by 4 and those leaving remainder 1:

Type $4k+3$: 3 7 11 * 19 23 * 31 * * 43 ...
Type $4k+1$: 5 * 13 17 * * 29 * 37 41 ...

We then ask, quite naturally: Are there infinitely many primes in each list?

It turns out that the answer is 'yes', although it seems harder to prove this fact for the primes in the second row than for those in the first. (See Theorems 1.3.5 and 3.5.8.) Again, all odd primes greater than 3 are of the form $6k+1$ or $6k+5$ [why?]. Here, too, one can prove that there are infinitely many of each type, the proof for the latter type again yielding fairly easily (Exercise 1.3.6). On splitting the primes amongst the four classes $8k+1$, $8k+3$, $8k+5$ and $8k+7$, however, not even the infinitude of the $8k+7$ type primes is very easy to establish (see Theorem 8.4.6).

All this suggests several questions, in fact infinitely many questions! namely: Given any two non-zero integers a, b does there exist in the arithmetic progression $am+b$ ($m = 0, 1, 2, \ldots$) an infinitude of primes? Clearly we shall have to demand that a and b have no divisor in common which is greater than 1 (Exercise 1.3.5). But what then?

In fact we are just 152 years late in asking this question. P. G. L. Dirichlet* answered it completely in 1837. Which way? We leave you with bated breath—or invite you to find out via the index!

To return to the problem of the $4k+3$ primes. It turns out that we require the following fundamental result before we can copy Euclid's argument in Theorem 1.3.1.

Theorem 1.3.2 Let $a \in \mathbb{Z}$, $a \geq 2$. Then we may write $a = q_1 q_2 \cdots q_m$ where each of the q_i is a prime.

Proof (Using PMI2) If $a = 2$ the desired conclusion clearly holds, (with $m = 1$ and $q_1 = 2$). So now suppose the claimed result is true for all the integers $2, 3, \ldots, k$ and suppose that $a = k+1$. If $k+1$ is prime there is nothing more to prove. If $k+1 = u \cdot v$ is composite where $1 < u \leq v < k+1$ then, by induction,

* See p. 53.

each of u, v is expressible as a product of primes. Hence so too is $k+1$ and the desired result is true using PMI2. □

As trivial examples we offer

Examples 1.3.3 $12=2\cdot2\cdot3$; $555,555=3\cdot5\cdot7\cdot11\cdot13\cdot37$;
$123\,456\,789=3\cdot3\cdot3607\cdot3803$.

Notes 1.3.4

(i) In Theorem 1.3.2 no assertion is made that the q_i are distinct. Example 1.3.3 provides two such instances.

(ii) Nor does Theorem 1.3.2 assert that $q_1q_2\cdots q_m$ is the *only* way of expressing a as a product of primes. (However Theorem 1.4.1 below *does*—essentially—make this assertion.)

(iii) The factorisation $3\cdot3\cdot3607\cdot3803$ of $123\,456\,789$ is easily checked. It can be found using the following program

Program 1.4 *To determine the prime factors of an integer N*

```
 10 INPUT "ENTER N",N
 20 P = 2
 30 REM Remove the factor 2
 40   F = N/P
 50     IF F = INT(F) GOTO 170
 60     IF N < 9 GOTO 140
 70     IF P=2 THEN P=3
 80 REM test for factors in the set of odd numbers
 90     F = N/P
100       IF F = INT(F) GOTO 170
110       P=P+2
120     IF P <= SQR(N) GOTO 90
130 REM Display the last factor
140     IF N<> 1 PRINT N
150     STOP
160 REM display the factor found and set N equal to the remainder
170     PRINT P;
180     N = F
190  GOTO 40
200 END
```

Using Theorem 1.3.2 we now prove, at last,

Theorem 1.3.5 There are infinitely many primes of the form $4k+3$.

Proof Suppose to the contrary, that there exist only finitely many primes of the form $4k+3$ and let them be $p_1(=3), p_2(=7), \ldots, p_t$. Form the number $N=4(p_1p_2\cdots p_t)-1$. By Theorem 1.3.2, we may write $N=q_1q_2\cdots q_m$ where the q_i are primes. Now each q_i must be odd [why?] and hence of the form $4k+1$ or $4k+3$. Furthermore not all of the q_i can be of the form $4k+1$ since the product of any two (and hence any number of) numbers of the form $4k+1$ is again a number of the same form (Exercise 1.3.4), and yet N is a number of the form $4k+3$. Thus at least one of the q_i is a $4k+3$ prime and is, consequently, one of the p_j [why?]. But then p_j divides both N and $N+1$ [why?] and hence their difference $(N+1)-N$, i.e. 1. This contradiction establishes the theorem. □

We shall show later, by a different approach, that there are infinitely many primes of the form $4k+1$. In the meantime here is a

Problem

Can the above proof be adapted to show this? If not, try to identify any major sticking point.

Exercises 1.3

1 Improve Euclid's argument to read: For each $n \geqslant 2$, $p_{n+1} \leqslant p_1 p_2 \cdots p_n - 1$. Show, for $n \geqslant 1$, that $p_n \leqslant 2^{2^{n-1}}$.

2 Show that for $n \geqslant 3$ there exists a prime p such that $n < p < n!$ [*Hint*: Apply Euclid's argument to the number $n!-1$.]

(The estimates in Exercises 1 and 2 are terrible! For vast improvements see Section 2.5.)

3 Show that $p_1 p_2 \cdots p_n + 1$ is never a square. [*Hint*: An odd square must be of the form $4k+1$.] Can it ever be a cube?

4 Show that a product of two integers of the form $4k+1$ is another of the same form.

5 Let $a, b > 0$. Show that if a, b have a common divisor $d > 1$, then the arithmetic progression $am+b$ ($m = 0, 1, 2 \ldots$) contains at most one prime.

6 Prove, in the style of Theorem 1.3.5, that there exist infinitely many primes of the form $6k+5$. [*Hint*: Assume not. Form $N = 6(p_1 p_2 \cdots p_t) - 1$ where the p_i are all the $6k+5$ type primes.] Identity where your argument breaks down if you try to adapt it to proving the existence of infinitely many primes of the form $8k+7$. [*Hint*: $3.5 = 15$(!).]

Computer problems 1.3

1 Let $\pi_{4,j}(n)$ denote the number of primes of the form $4k+j$ ($j=1$ or 3) which are less than or equal to n. Using the most efficient of the programs developed above or by simply reading primes from a list you have saved on your storage device, calculate the difference $\pi_{4,3}(n) - \pi_{4,1}(n)$ for various n up to 10 000. Make a conjecture. Try to prove it. Run your programs for higher values of n to test your conjecture further. (For some related pretty pictures see [20].)

2 Modify your program for Problem 1 to examine the behaviour of the number of $6k-1$ and $6k+1$ primes. Consider likewise the number of $8k+1$, $8k+3$, $8k+5$ and $8k+7$ primes, up to various limits.

3 Amend Program 1.4 so that (i) only integers that are not multiples of 3 are considered; (ii) primes read from a file are considered.

4 For each of the integers 5 123 471, 1 234 567, 82 994 123, 5 739 281, 7 682 947, 71 264 357, 5 739 877, 7 000 001, 5 256 929, 6 348 751 find out the time it takes your computer to determine (i) whether the integer is prime; (ii) all of its factors if it is composite.

5 For each of the following numbers compare the time it takes to *check* that each of the factors is prime with the time it takes to *find* the factors given only their product: $6521 \times 7193 = 469\,055$, $9137 \times 9697 = 8\,860\,148$, $10\,313 \times 9833 = 10\,140\,772$.

6 Write a program to determine the fraction of primes in intervals of size 200 about the integers $N = 100, 300, 500, \ldots, 5000$. Compute also the values of functions such as $1/N$, $1/\exp(N)$, $1/\log(N)$ and $1/\log(\log(N))$ and comment on the suitability of any of these functions as possible approximations to the density of primes as N increases.

1.4 The fundamental theorem of arithmetic

Theorem 1.3.2 and Example 1.3.3 leave open the possibility that a given number may be expressible as a product of primes in *two or more distinct ways.* We tidy this point up with

Theorem 1.4.1 (*The Fundamental Theorem of Arithmetic*) Let $a = q_1 q_2 \cdots q_m$, as in Theorem 1.3.2 and suppose also that $a = r_1 r_2 \cdots r_n$ where the q_i and r_j are (positive) primes. Then $m = n$ and the q_i and r_j can be paired off so that the paired primes are equal. In other words the representation of a as a product of (positive) primes is (essentially) unique.

Proof (Using WO) If a ($\geqslant 2$) is an integer possessing distinct (that is, non-pairable) prime decompositions we shall call such an integer 'nasty'. Let $\mathcal{N}$ be the set of all nasties. Suppose $\mathcal{N} \neq \varnothing$. Since $\mathcal{N} \subset \mathbb{N}$ we can then use the W.O. principle to deduce that $\mathcal{N}$ has a smallest member b, say. Thus $b = q_1 q_2 \cdots q_m = r_1 r_2 \cdots r_n$, where we may assume $q_1 \leqslant q_2 \leqslant \cdots \leqslant q_m$ and $r_1 \leqslant r_2 \leqslant \cdots \leqslant r_n$, is the smallest nasty. If $q_1 = r_1$ we can write $b/q_1 = q_2 \cdots q_m = r_2 \cdots r_n$. Since b/q_1 is not nasty (that is, $b/q_1 \notin \mathcal{N}$, why not?) we can conclude that $m-1 = n-1$ and that the q_i and r_j ($2 \leqslant i \leqslant m, 2 \leqslant j \leqslant n$) pair off as equals. Hence $m = n$ and all the qs and rs pair off as claimed. We may therefore suppose that $q_1 \neq r_1$ and that, WLOG,* $q_1 < r_1$. In this case consider

* Without Loss of Generality. Roughly speaking this means: We need only show you the proof in this particular case. All other cases can be dealt with in an identical manner with only the most trivial modifications.

$c = b - q_1 r_2 \cdots r_n = (r_1 - q_1) r_2 \cdots r_n = u_1 u_2 \cdots u_k r_2 \cdots r_n$, where $(r_1 - q_1) = u_1 u_2 \cdots u_k$ the u_i being primes. But $c = q_1(q_2 \cdots q_m - r_2 \cdots r_n) = q_1 v_1 \cdots v_l$, likewise, where the v_i are primes. Since $c < b$ these factorisations for c are (essentially) unique. However $q_1 \nmid (r_1 - q_1)$ [why not?] and so $q_1 \neq u_s$ for each s, $1 \leqslant s \leqslant k$. Hence $q_1 = r_j$ for some $j \geqslant 2$. But this is impossible since $q_1 < r_1 \leqslant r_j$. We conclude that no nasty integers exist and our theorem is proved. □

Note 1.4.2 We include the word 'essentially' in the statement of Theorem 1.4.1 since we are perfectly happy to consider decompositions such as 2·2·5·3 and 5·2·3·2 of 60, for example, as being 'the same'.

Notation 1.4.3 If, in the decomposition $a = q_1 q_2 \cdots q_m$, the distinct primes $p_1, p_2, \ldots p_t$ occur, and if α_1 of the q_i are equal to p_1, α_2 of the q_i are equal to p_2 etc, we can write $a = q_1 q_2 \cdots q_m$ more economically as $a = p_1^{\alpha_1} p_2^{\alpha_2} \cdots p_t^{\alpha_t}$, where α_i is called the *exponent* of p_i in a. Note that $\alpha_1 + \alpha_2 + \cdots + \alpha_t = m$ and that, because of Theorem 1.4.1, a determines the p_i and the α_i uniquely. As an example we have

Example 1.4.4 (briefly)

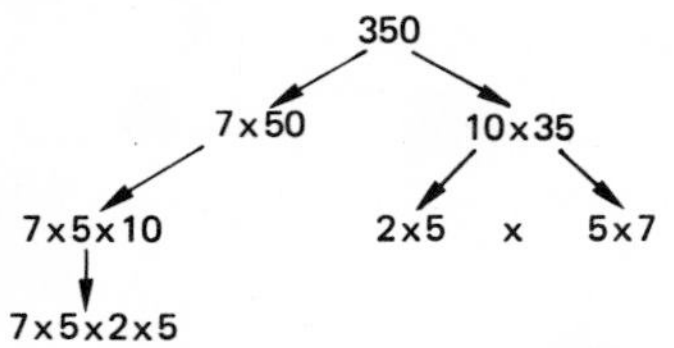

so that each decomposition yields $350 = 2 \cdot 5^2 \cdot 7$.

Notes 1.4.5

(i) The reason for excluding 1 from being a prime is now apparent. In any decomposition into a product of primes we could, if 1 were taken as a prime, slip in as many copies of 1 as we wished and would then lose the (essential) uniqueness of the decomposition. Similar remarks will apply to -1 when we extend our definition of 'primes' later—and, of course, 0 is of no use as a factor of any number (other than 0 itself!).

(ii) It will often be convenient, see Exercises 1.4.5 and 1.4.7 for example, to be able to write $a = p_1^{\alpha_1} \cdots p_i^{\alpha_i} \cdots p_t^{\alpha_t}$ even if $p_i \nmid a$. This is easily achieved by allowing $\alpha_i = 0$ in such cases. (What aspects of uniqueness of decomposition are lost? Does it matter?)

The following program displays the prime factors and their exponents for a given integer *N*.

Program 1.5 *Determines the prime factors and their exponents of an integer N*

```
 10 DIM G(25),M(25)
 20 K=0
 30 D=1
 40 INPUT "ENTER N",N
 50 P = 2
 60 REM Remove the factor 2
 70   F = N/P
 80     IF F = INT(F) GOTO 290
 90     IF N < 9 GOTO 160
100     IF P=2 THEN P=3
110 REM test for factors in the set of odd numbers
120     F = N/P
130       IF F = INT(F) GOTO 290
140       P=P+2
150     IF P <= SQR(N) GOTO 120
155 REM store the last factor
160     IF N=1 GOTO 230
170     IF N=D GOTO 210
180       K=K+1
190       G(K)=N
200       GOTO 230
210     M(K)=M(K)+1
220 REM display the factors and their exponents
230     FOR I=1 TO K
240       PRINT ".";G(I);
250       IF M(I)>1 THEN PRINT "^";M(I);
260     NEXT I
270     STOP
280 REM store new factor or increase power of the previous one
290     IF P=D GOTO 350
300       K=K+1
310       G(K)=P
320       M(K)=1
330       D=P
340     GOTO 360
350     M(K)=M(K)+1
360     N = F
370   GOTO 70
```

Warning

Theorem 1.4.1 should not be regarded as stating the obvious. Indeed there are perfectly sensible number systems in which the analogue of Theorem 1.4.1 is false! An example to satisfy the reader on this point, at least temporarily, is given in Exercise 1.4.1.

Exercises 1.4

1 Let H be the set $\{4k+1: k \in \mathbb{Z}, k \geqslant 0\}$. A number h in H is called a Hilbert* prime (briefly H-prime) iff: (i) $h \neq 1$ and (ii) *if* $h = \alpha\beta$ with $\alpha, \beta \in H$ *then* either $\alpha = 1$ or $\beta = 1$. Find the first ten H-primes. Find H-primes a, b, c, d such that $693 = a \cdot b = c \cdot d$ and yet a, b, c, d are all different.

* After David Hilbert who used the example for expository purposes.

Is every prime of the form $4k+1$ in $\mathbb{Z}$ an H-prime? Do there exist infinitely many H-primes which are not primes in $\mathbb{Z}$?

Show that, by augmenting H by adjoining the set of positive integers of the form $4k+3$, we obtain H as a subset of a larger set H^+ in which factorisation *is* unique. Factorise 693 in H^+. (We meet this idea again later in Section 9.5.)

David Hilbert *(23 January 1862 - 14 February 1943)*
Hilbert was born at Königsburg, now Kaliningrad, the son and grandson of judges. After being Privatdocent at Königsburg from 1886 to 1892 he succeeded Hurwitz there as professor in 1892. In 1895 he obtained the chair at Göttingen, a position he held until his retirement in 1930.

Although Hilbert's mathematical interests were wide ranging he preferred to work on one subject at a time, investigate it thoroughly, and then forget it! In this way he was able to contribute profound results to many areas of mathematics. The approximate dates of his main interests were: up to 1892, algebraic invariant theory; 1892–1899, algebraic number theory; 1898–1903, foundations of geometry; 1899–1905, calculus of variations and the Dirichlet principle; 1901–1912, integral equations. From 1912 to 1917 he was occupied with the mathematical foundations of physics; from 1917 until the end of his life he devoted himself to logic. There was little overlap: except (!) for his solution of Waring's problem, he published no work on number theory after 1899.

His outstanding textbooks include the *Report on the theory of algebraic number fields* (1895–1897) and his *Foundations of Geometry* (1899), in which he fully axiomatised Euclid's geometry, replacing the many intuitive steps remaining in Euclid's work with formal deductions.

Hilbert believed that for a science to thrive, it was essential for it to supply an abundance of problems for researchers to work on. At the International Congress of Mathematicians in 1900 Hilbert presented his famous list of 23 difficult but inspiring problems to which he believed mathematicians should address themselves. Several of these remain unsolved to this day.

After his death Hilbert was given the accolade of 'the greatest mathematician of the 20th century'. It seems very likely that he will remain so.

---

2 Find an integer n such that each of $n, n+1, n+2$ is a product of exactly two primes (not necessarily distinct). Show that there can be no similar sequence comprising *four* consecutive integers.

3 Let a, b be positive integers such that $a+b \mid a \cdot b$. Show that there must exist a prime p which divides both a and b. [*Hint*: $a+b \mid ab$ and $a+b \mid a(a+b)$.]

4 For which positive integers n does $\sum_{i=1}^{n} i \mid \prod_{i=1}^{n} i$? [*Hint*: $\sum_{i=1}^{n} i = n(n+1)/2$.]

5 Show that if $b = p_1^{\beta_1} p_2^{\beta_2} \cdots p_t^{\beta_t}$ and $a \mid b$, then $a = p_1^{\alpha_1} p_2^{\alpha_2} \cdots p_t^{\alpha_t}$ where, for $1 \leq i \leq t$, we have $0 \leq \alpha_i \leq \beta_i$.

6 Prove—or give counterexamples to—the assertions:

(i) $a^2 \mid b^2 \Rightarrow a \mid b$;
(ii) $a^2 \mid b^3 \Rightarrow a \mid b$;
(iii) $a^n \mid b^{n+1}$ for $n = 1, 2, 3, \ldots \Rightarrow a \mid b$.

7 Prove that if $x, y \in \mathbb{Z}$, if $0 < x < y$ and if $x^y = y^x$, then $x = 2$ and $y = 4$. [*Hint*: Write $x = p_1^{\alpha_1} \cdots p_t^{\alpha_t}$, $y = p_1^{\beta_1} \cdots p_t^{\beta_t}$ and equate various exponents.]

8 Prove that each positive rational number (other than 0, 1) is expressible uniquely in the form $p_1^{\alpha_1} p_2^{\alpha_2} \cdots p_n^{\alpha_n}$, where the p_i are distinct primes and the α_i are integers (positive or negative).

Computer problems 1.4

1 Let $\tau(n)$ denote the number of (positive) factors and $\sigma(n)$ the sum of all the (positive) factors of the positive integer n. Write a program to compute $\tau(n)$ and $\sigma(n)$ and produce a table of results for $n = 2$ to 100 (say). Do you notice any interesting patterns?

2 Find instances of four consecutive integers each having the same number of prime factors (including repetitions).

3 Write a program to determine the percentage of integers in a given interval that have one, two, three, ... prime factors. How do the percentages change as the numbers considered become larger? Explore both the number of distinct factors and the total number of factors. How does the average number of factors over an interval change as we increase the size of the integers considered?

4 (i) Find primes of the form n^2+1. Do you think there are infinitely many? (ii) Find primes which *divide* numbers of the form n^2+1. Do you think there are infinitely many? (See Chapter 2.)

5 Modify Program 1.5 to produce decompositions of H-numbers into H-primes (see Exercise 1.4.1).

1.5 GCDs and LCMs

Theorem 1.4.1 has implications for the calculation of the *greatest common divisor* (*gcd*) of each given pair of integers (not *both* zero).

Definition 1.5.1 Let a, b be integers. An integer c such that $c|a$ and $c|b$ is called a *common divisor* of a and b. If d is an integer such that

(i) $d|a$ and $d|b$;

and

(ii) *if* $c|a$ and $c|b$ *then* $c|d$,

we call d a *greatest common divisor** of a and b.

Note 1.5.2 If d is a gcd of a and b then so is $-d$ and they are the only two gcds of a and b (Exercise 1.5.1). The positive member of the pair is denoted by (a, b).

Examples 1.5.3

(i) The divisors of 98 are 1, 2, 7, 14, 49 and 98 (and their negatives); the divisors of 308 are 1, 2, 4, 7, 11, 14, 22, 28, 44, 77, 154, 308 (and negatives). Clearly ± 1, ± 2, ± 7, ± 14 are their common divisors, 14 and -14 being the two greatest common divisors. That is $(98, 308) = 14$.

(ii) $(-72, 45) = 9$;

(iii) $(261\,360, 357\,742) = (2^4 \cdot 3^3 \cdot 5 \cdot 11^2, 2^2 \cdot 3^4 \cdot 11 \cdot 101) = 2^2 \cdot 3^3 \cdot 11$
$= 1188$;

(iv) For all a, b (not both zero) we have $(a, b) = (|a|, |b|)$. This means that we can always restrict attention to positive a and b.

Note 1.5.4 By definition, a gcd is a common divisor which is a multiple of every common divisor. We might, more naturally, have defined *the* gcd of a and b to be their numerically largest common divisor. With this definition the gcd of a and b would coincide with (a, b) as defined above (Exercise 1.5.14). However, Definition 1.5.1 is better later when we shall be dealing with numbers in which a simple use of the idea of 'largest' is not available.

Example 1.5.3(iii) illustrates

Theorem 1.5.5 If $a = p_1^{\alpha_1} p_2^{\alpha_2} \cdots p_r^{\alpha_r}$, $b = p_1^{\beta_1} p_2^{\beta_2} \cdots p_r^{\beta_r}$ (where, if $p_i \nmid a$, we set $\alpha_i = 0$—see Note 1.4.5(ii), then $(a, b) = p_1^{\gamma_1} p_2^{\gamma_2} \cdots p_r^{\gamma_r}$, where γ_i is $\min\{\alpha_i, \beta_i\}$—the smaller of α_i and β_i $(1 \leq i \leq r)$.

We leave a formal proof of this to the reader. □

* Also called highest common factor (hcf).

There is a notion which we shall call upon later and which is 'dual' to that of gcd, as given by

Definition 1.5.6 Let a, b be integers (not both zero). An integer n such that $a|n$ and $b|n$ is called a *common multiple* of a and b. If m is an integer such that

(i) $a|m$ and $b|m$

and

(ii) *if* $a|n$ and $b|n$ *then* $m|n$,

we call m a *least common multiple* (lcm) of a and b.

If m is an lcm so is $-m$. We denote the positive one by $[a, b]$.

It is easy to check—we leave them to the reader—the following facts relating to lcms.

Theorem 1.5.7

(i) If $a = p_1^{\alpha_1} \cdots p_r^{\alpha_r}$, $b = p_1^{\beta_1} \cdots p_r^{\beta_r}$ then $[a, b] = p_1^{\gamma_1} \cdots p_r^{\gamma_r}$, where $\gamma_i = \max\{\alpha_i, \beta_i\}$, $1 \leq i \leq r$.

(ii) $[a, b](a, b) = ab$; $(a, b)|[a, b]$. □

Theorems 1.5.5 and 1.5.7(i), whose proofs make full use of Theorem 1.4.1, seem to indicate that to find (a, b) and $[a, b]$ we only need to factorise both a and b. Section 1.6 will show that we don't *have* to work ourselves quite so hard.

Exercises 1.5

1 Prove that if d is a gcd of integers a and b then so is $-d$. Furthermore these are the only two gcds of a and b.

2 Show that if p is a prime and if $(p, a) > 1$, then $p|a$.

3 Show that: (i) if $(a, b) = 1$ and $c|a+b$, then $(a, c) = (b, c) = 1$; (ii) if $k \neq 0$ $(k \in \mathbb{Z})$, then $(ka, kb) = |k|(a, b)$.

4 Give proofs or counterexamples to the following assertions: (i) if $(a, b) = (c, d)$, then $(a^2, b^2) = (c^2, d^2)$; (ii) if $(a, b) = (k, l) = 1$, where $a < b < k < l$, then $(ka + lb, la + kb) = 1$; (iii) $(a^2, b^2) = (a, b)^2$.

5 Let $d = (a, b)$. Prove $(a/d, b/d) = 1$. Prove or give a counterexample to: (i) $(a/d, b) = 1$; (ii) if $a|bc$, then $a/d|c$.

6 Suppose $a, b \in \mathbb{Z}$ with $(a, b) = 1$. If $ab = c^3$ can one deduce that a, b are both cubes? If $ab = d^2$ can one infer that a, b are both squares? (Careful! You are *not* told $a, b \in \mathbb{Z}^+$.)

7 From the equality $a = mb + r$ deduce that $(a, b) = (b, r)$.

8 (i) Show that if a, b, c are all non-zero then $(a,(b, c))=((a, b), c)$. Thus we can unambiguously denote such an expression by (a, b, c). (ii) Setting $d=(a, b, c)$ show that: *if* $e|a$, $e|b$ and $e|c$, *then* $e|d$. (Since $d|a$, $d|b$ and $d|c$ from (i) we can rightly call (a, b, c) *the positive gcd of* a, b, c. The extensions to more than three integers is made similarly.) (iii) Find integers a, b, c such that $(a, b, c)=1$ and yet (a, b), (b, c) and (c, a) are all greater than 1.

9 Find all common divisors of 1848 and 840.

10 Show that if $(m_1, m_2)=1$ and if $d|m_1m_2$, then $d=d_1d_2$ where $d_1|m_1$ and $d_2|m_2$.

11 Show that if $a, b, n \in \mathbb{Z}$ and $(b, n)=1$ then exactly one of $a+b$, $a+2b, \ldots a+nb$ is divisible by n. [*Hint*: If none of these has remainder 0 on division by n, then there must be a pair with the same (non-zero) remainder. The difference of these two is divisible by n. But this is impossible.] Deduce that one of 2151, 3151, 4151, 5151, 6151, 7151, 8151 is divisible by 7. Which?

12 If $(a, b)>1$ must we have $(a+1, b+1)=1$? Given $a>b>0$ must there exist a $k>0$ such that $(a+k, b+k)=1$?

13 (i) If $c|ab$ must it be true that $c|(c, a)(c, b)$? Prove or give a counter-example. (ii) Is $(ab, c)=(a, c)(b, c)$ for all $a, b, c>0$? If not, can you determine when it *is* true? (iii) Prove that if $(a, c)=(b, c)=1$ then $(ab, c)=1$. (iv) Prove that if $c|ab$ and $(b, c)=1$ then $c|a$. (v) Prove that if $a|c$ and $b|c$ and $(a, b)=1$ then $ab|c$. (vi) Prove that if $n, k \in \mathbb{Z}^+$ and $n=(r/s)^k$ where $(r, s)=1$, then $s=\pm 1$. Deduce that if $\sqrt[k]{n}=r/s$ then n is the kth power of an integer.

14 Let us define the *numerically largest divisor* of two integers a, b (not both zero) to be that integer g which satisfies: (i) g is a common divisor of a and b and (ii) $g>c$ for each other common divisor of a and b. Prove that $g=(a, b)$ as defined previously.

15 Find: (i) $[2^2 3^3 5^5, 2^5 3^2 5^3]$; (ii) $[3243, 2047]$.

16 Find integers a, b—other than 18 and 540—such that $(a, b)=18$ and $[a, b]=540$.

17 Prove that $[a, b]$ is the least positive integer which is a multiple of a and of b. (Cf. Exercise 14 above.)

18 Is $[a,[b, c]]=[[a, b], c]$ for all $a, b, c \in \mathbb{Z}^+$? (Cf. Exercise 8(i) above.)

19 Extend the definition of lcm to sets of 3 and more (positive) integers. (Cf. Exercise 8 above.) Is $[a, b, c](a, b, c)=abc$ for all $a, b, c \in \mathbb{Z}^+$? If not, can you find the correct formula?

20 (Lambert* 1769) Suppose $a, b, d, m \in \mathbb{Z}^+$ are such that $a|d^m-1$, $b|d^n-1$ and $(a, b)=1$. Show that $ab|d^{[m,n]}-1$.

* Johann Heinrich Lambert, 26 August 1728 - 25 September 1777.

21 Prove that for all $a, b, c \in \mathbb{Z}^+$ we have $([a, b], c) = [(a, c), (b, c)]$ and its 'dual' $[(a, b), c] = ([a, c], [b, c])$.

Computer problem 1.5

1 Write a program to determine the gcd and lcm of two integers a and b by factoring a and b and using Theorems 1.5.5 and 1.5.7.

1.6 The Euclidean algorithm

As intimated at the end of Section 1.5, there is a method which enables us to find (a, b) without factoring either a or b; it is, to boot, more efficient! The method involves the repeated use of the division algorithm and appears as proposition 2 of Euclid's 7th book. We call it

The Euclidean algorithm (EA)
Let $a, b \in \mathbb{Z}$ with $b \neq 0$. Proceed by the following steps:

Step (0): set $r_0 = |a|$, $r_1 = |b|$.
Step (i): Find $m_1, r_2 \in \mathbb{Z}$ such that $r_0 = m_1 r_1 + r_2$, where $0 \leqslant r_2 < r_1$.
Step (ii): Find $m_2, r_3 \in \mathbb{Z}$ such that $r_1 = m_2 r_2 + r_3$, where $0 \leqslant r_3 < r_2$.
Step (iii): Find $m_3, r_4 \in \mathbb{Z}$ such that $r_2 = m_3 r_3 + r_4$, where $0 \leqslant r_4 < r_3$

⋮

and generally

⋮

Step (l): Find $m_l, r_{l+1} \in \mathbb{Z}$ such that $r_{l-1} = m_l r_l + r_{l+1}$ where $0 \leqslant r_{l+1} < r_l$.

Now the sequence $r_1 > r_2 > \cdots (\geqslant 0)$ is a decreasing sequence of non-negative integers. Hence, for some integer f, we must have $r_{f+1} = 0$. In that case we have

Step ($f-1$): Find $m_{f-1}, r_f \in \mathbb{Z}$ such that $r_{f-2} = m_{f-1} r_{f-1} + r_f$, where $0 \leqslant r_f < r_{f-1}$.
Step (f): Find $m_f, r_{f+1} \in \mathbb{Z}$ such that $r_{f-1} = m_f r_f + r_{f+1}$, where $0 = r_{f+1}$.

Now, starting from step (i), it is not difficult to check (Exercise 1.5.7) that $(r_0, r_1) = (r_1, r_2)$ and, from subsequent steps, that similarly, $(r_1, r_2) = (r_2, r_3) = \cdots = (r_f, r_{f+1})$. But, clearly, $(r_f, 0) = r_f$. Hence $(a, b) = r_f$, where r_f may be identified as 'the last non-zero remainder in the repeated DA'

To cement these ideas let's give

Example 1.6.1 Find (30 031, 16 579).

Now $30\,031 = 1.16\,579 + 13\,452$

$$
\begin{aligned}
16\,579 &= 1 \cdot 13\,452 + 3127 \\
13\,452 &= 4 \cdot 3127 + 944 \\
3127 &= 3 \cdot 944 + 295 \\
944 &= 3 \cdot 295 + 59 \\
295 &= 5 \cdot 59 + 0.
\end{aligned}
$$

Hence 59 is the (positive) g.c.d. of 30 031 and 16 579.

If we read the above equalities 'backwards' we get a pleasant surprise.

Theorem 1.6.2 Given $a, b \in \mathbb{Z}$ (not both zero), there exist integers s, t such that $(a, b) = sa + tb$.

Proof From step $(f-1)$ we can write $(a, b) = r_f = r_{f-2} - m_{f-1}r_{f-1}$. Using step $(f-2)$ we may write $r_{f-1} = r_{f-3} - m_{f-2}r_{f-2}$ and hence (a, b) in terms of r_{f-2} and r_{f-3}. Continuing in this way back to step (i) we finish up expressing r_f in terms of a and b, as asserted. □

Example 1.6.3 From Example 1.6.1 we get

$$\begin{aligned} 59 &= 1\cdot 944 - 3\cdot 295 = 1\cdot 944 - 3\cdot(3127 - 3\cdot 944) \\ &= 10\cdot 944 - 3\cdot 3127 = 10\cdot(13\,452 - 4\cdot 3127) - 3\cdot 3127 \\ &= 10\cdot 13\,452 - 43\cdot 3127 = 10\cdot 13\,452 - 43\cdot(16\,579 - 13\,452) \\ &= 53\cdot 13\,452 - 43\cdot 16\,579 = 53\cdot(30\,031 - 16\,579) - 43\cdot 16\,579 \\ &= 53\cdot 30\,031 - 96\cdot 16\,579. \end{aligned}$$

Notes 1.6.4

(i) The coefficients 53 and -96 are by no means uniquely determined (Exercise 1.6.4).

(ii) Although it tells us how to obtain the integers s and t, the proof of Theorem 1.6.2 is rather 'messy'. A beautifully elegant proof of Theorem 1.6.2 can be given by calling upon the WO principle (see Exercise 1.6.3). One snag with this elegant proof is that it is, for all practical purposes, an existence proof—that is, it shows that the integers s and t always exist but doesn't immediately tell you how to find them in any particular case.

As presented, the EA and Theorem 1.6.2 do not indicate the most efficient way of obtaining (a, b) as a linear combination of a and b. In order to find this linear combination our method requires us to save *all* the m_i, r_i which arise in using the EA in order to use them 'backwards' as in Example 1.6.3. In using the computer it would be more efficient to use the m_i, r_i as we find them, rather than store them. Such a method exists. It is based on the fact that each r_i is expressible as a linear combination $r_k = s_k a + t_k b$ of a and b and the deduction (from this and step (k) above, where we have $r_{k+1} = r_{k-1} - m_k r_k$) that $s_{k+1}a + t_{k+1}b = (s_{k-1}a + t_{k-1}b) - m_k(s_k a + t_k b)$. That is:

Theorem 1.6.5 Let a, b be positive integers. Define $s_0 = 1$, $t_0 = 0$; $s_1 = 0$, $t_1 = 1$ and, for $k \geqslant 1$: $s_{k+1} = s_{k-1} - m_k s_k$, $t_{k+1} = t_{k-1} - m_k t_k$. If r_f is the last non-zero remainder in the Euclidean algorithm, then $(a, b) = s_f a + t_f b$. □

The reader might also be interested to learn that one can, at the outset, put an upper bound on the number of steps required to complete the Euclidean algorithm. The Frenchman Gabriel Lamé*, whom we shall meet again in Chapter 6, used (1844) the Fibonacci sequence to show that the number of steps required is no more than five times the number of digits in the smaller of the two given numbers. A proof is outlined in Exercise 1.7.1.

Theorem 1.6.2 has several useful consequences. One, which we shall use immediately, is

Corollary 1.6.6 Let $a, b \in \mathbb{Z}$ be such that $(a, b) = 1$. Then there exist $s, t \in \mathbb{Z}$ such that $sa + tb = 1$. In particular, if p is a prime and $p \nmid a$, then $(a, p) = 1$ and there exist $u, v \in \mathbb{Z}$ such that $ua + vp = 1$. □

In this connection it is useful to make

Definition 1.6.7 If $a, b \in \mathbb{Z}$ and $(a, b) = 1$ we say that a and b are *coprime* (or *relatively prime*).

Example 1.6.8 55 555 and 7811 are coprime. (Note that neither number is itself a prime.)

Exercises 1.6

1 Find (37 129, 14 659)—first by factoring each number and then by using the Euclidean algorithm. [Which method is quicker?]

2 Show that, for all $n \in \mathbb{Z}$, $(5n+2, 12n+5) = 1$.

3 Prove that each pair a, b of integers, not both zero, has a gcd—as follows. (i) Let S be the set $\{sa + tb : s, t \in \mathbb{Z}\}$. (ii) Show that S contains positive integers and hence a least one. Call the least one d. (iii) Let $w \in S$. Write $w = md + r$ where $0 \leqslant r < d$. Show that $r\ (= w - md) \in S$. (iv) Deduce that $r = 0$ and hence that $d \mid w$. (v) Show that $a, b \in S$— so that $d \mid a$ and $d \mid b$ by (iv). (vi) Note that $d = s_0 a + t_0 b$ for certain $s_0, t_0 \in \mathbb{Z}$ and deduce that if $c \mid a$ and $c \mid b$ then $c \mid s_0 a + t_0 b = d$. (vii) Deduce that $d = (a, b)$.

4 Prove that if $d = (a, b) = sa + tb = ua + vb$, then $u = s + kb/d$ and $v = t - ka/d$ for some integer k.

5 Show that if $(a, b) = sa + tb$, then s and t can both be chosen such that $|s| \leqslant |b|$ and $|t| \leqslant |a|$.

6 Show that if $(a, b) = sa + tb$, then $(s, t) = 1$.

7 Given that $sa + tb = 1$ prove, or give a counterexample to, the assertions (i) $(sa, tb) = 1$; (ii) $(st, ab) = 1$; (iii) $(sb, at) = 1$.

8 Let $a < 0 < b$ be given integers. In writing $(a, b) = sa + tb$ is it always possible to choose both s, t to be (i) primes; (ii) squares?

* Gabriel Lamé, 22 July 1795 - 1 May 1870.

9 Given that $a, b, c > 0$, show that there are only a finite number of positive integers x, y such that $ax + by = c$.

10 Find the general solution—if there is a solution—of the linear equations: (i) $51x + 39y = 11\,111$; (ii) $51x + 39y = 6$; (iii) $138x + 238y = 338$; (iv) $918x + 534y = 424$.

Is there a solution to (iii) for which $0 \leqslant x \leqslant 50$?

11 (From Euler's *Algebra* [9]) (i) Divide 100 into two parts such that one part is divisible by 11 and the other by 7. (ii) Two women have together 100 eggs. One says 'When I count my eggs by eights I have an overplus (!) of 7'. The other says 'If I count mine by tens I have the same overplus of 7'. How many eggs had each?

12 Given $a, b > 0$ with $(a, b) = 1$, show that for each integer $n \geqslant (a-1)(b-1)$ the equation $xa + yb = n$ is soluble using non-negative integers x, y. Show that for precisely half of the integers t from 0 to $(a-1)(b-1)-1$ inclusive the equation is soluble with $x, y \geqslant 0$. [*Hint*: Suppose $a < b$. The representable integers are $0, a, 2a, \ldots; b, b+a, \ldots; 2b, 2b+a, \ldots, (a-1)b, (a-1)b+a, \ldots$. Deduce that the number of non-representable integers is $[b/a] + [2b/a] + \cdots + [(a-1)b/a]$. To evaluate this see Lemma 8.5.2.]

13 Show that $ax + by + cz = d$ has a solution in integers iff $(a, b, c) \mid d$. Find $s, t, u \in \mathbb{Z}$ such that $(105, 150, 288) = 105s + 150t + 288u$.

1.7 Computing GCDs

The algorithm (EA) described above gives us an easy-to-program method for obtaining the gcd of two numbers which we present below.

Program 1.6 *Calculation of gcd using the Euclidean Algorithm*

```
10 INPUT a,b
20 PRINT "GCD of ";a;" and ";b;" is ";
30   r=a - INT(a/b)*b
40   a=b
50   b=r
60  IF r<> 0 GOTO 30
70 PRINT;a
80 END
```

We do not need to ensure that $a > b$. Why not? Do we need $a, b > 0$?

From the above discussion we see that the number of times the loop is repeated is less than 5 times the number of digits in the smaller number. It can also be shown ([10], p. 60) that if $a > b$, then the average number of division steps required is $1.94 \log_{10} b$. Thus as b increases the number of operations increases. Once we reach numbers beyond those which our computer can handle naturally, the cost of this division increases greatly compared to the cost of addition and subtraction (see Appendix I). It is therefore useful to present an alternative method based on subtraction which, while slightly less efficient for small numbers, is much quicker in handling larger ones.

The method is based on the following observations concerning the gcd of two positive integers a and b.

(i) If a and b are both even then $(a, b) = 2(a/2, b/2)$ (Exercise 1.5.3(ii)).
(ii) If a is even and b odd then $(a, b) = (a/2, b)$.
(iii) If $a > b$ then $(a, b) = (a - b, b)$.
(iv) If a and b are both odd then $|a - b|$ is even.

The program based on these observations is

Program 1.7 *Calculation of gcd using only subtraction and division by two*

```
 10 INPUT a,b
 20 PRINT "gcd of ";a;" and ";b;" is ";
 24 a=ABS(a):b=ABS(b):REM why ?
 25 REM Remove the common power of 2
 30 m = 1
 40 IF a/2<>INT(a/2) OR b/2<>INT(b/2) GOTO 90
 50    a = a/2
 60    b = b/2
 70    m = m * 2
 80 GOTO 40
 90    IF a/2 = INT (a/2) THEN a = a/2
100    IF b/2 = INT (b/2) THEN b = b/2
110    IF a>b THEN a=a-b ELSE IF b>a THEN b = b-a
120    IF a<>b GOTO 90
130 PRINT ;a*m
140 END
```

The second computational problem relating to the positive gcd of two given numbers a and b is that of representing (a, b) as a linear combination of a and b. One way of performing the computation is to store the quotients and remainders obtained at each stage of the iteration used to determine the gcd and then use these to construct the linear combination as illustrated in Example 1.6.3. This method would require us to estimate at the outset the amount of storage needed for the quotients and remainders which occur. Lamé's result above gives us an upper bound for the dimension and BASIC allows us to declare this dynamically in the program by first determining the number of digits in the smaller number before declaring the dimension. (Of course this increases with the size of the numbers. Furthermore, the number of operations required for storing and recovering the numbers also increases.) We can avoid all these problems by using Theorem 1.6.5 which presents us with an algorithm for constructing the linear combinations as we proceed; it only requires two arrays of size three whatever the size of the numbers involved!

Program 1.8 *Calculates gcd and expresses it as a linear combination of the two integers*

```
10 REM gcd(a,b) and linear combination in single step
20 DIM a(3),b(3)
30 INPUT x,y
40 a(1)=1
50 a(2)=0
60 a(3)=x
70 b(1)=0
80 b(2)=1
90 b(3)=y
100   q=INT(a(3)/b(3))
110   FOR i=1 TO 3
120      r=a(i) - q*b(i)
130      a(i)=b(i)
140      b(i)=r
150   NEXT
160 IF b(3)<>0 GOTO 100
170 PRINT "The GCD is ";ABS(a(3));
175 IF a(3)=-ABS(a(3)) THEN x=-x : y=-y
180 PRINT ;" and equals ";a(1);"*";x;"+";a(2);"*";y
190 END
```

Exercises 1.7

1 Using the notation of Section 1.6, that is, with $r_0=|a|$, $r_1=|b|$ and r_f the last non-zero remainder and with u_n being the nth term of the Fibonacci sequence, prove Lamé's theorem as follows: Show (i) $r_f \geqslant 1 = u_2$; (ii) $r_{f-1} \geqslant 2r_f \geqslant 2u_2 = u_3$. Now use induction together with the inequality $r_{f-k} \geqslant r_{f-(k-1)} + r_{f-(k-2)}$ to show, for $0 \leqslant i \leqslant f-1$, that $r_{f-i} \geqslant u_{i+2}$.

Deduce that $|b| = r_1 \geqslant u_{f+1}$.

Using Exercise 0.5.2(v), show that $u_{f+1} > \alpha^{f-1}$, where $\alpha = (1+\sqrt{5})/2$. Deduce that $\log_{10}|b| > (f-1)\log_{10}\alpha > (f-1)\cdot\frac{1}{5}$ so that $f \leqslant 5\log_{10}|b|$, as claimed.

2 Show that the number of divisions in applying the Euclidean algorithm to the pair of numbers u_{n+2}, u_{n+1} of the Fibonacci sequence is exactly n.

Computer problems 1.7

1 Calculate the gcd of 73 524 913 and 5 739 877 using (i) your program for problem 1.5.1, (ii) Program 1.6 and (iii) Program 1.7. Which is quickest? Try other numbers to see if one program is always faster than each of the others.

2 Modify the gcd program so that it also calculates the lcm $[a, b]$ of two integers.

3 Write a program to determine whether or not two integers are coprime. Modifying the program so that it generates two non-equal random integers between 2 and 100 000, estimate the proportion of pairs of integers that are coprime.

4 Use the relation in Exercise 1.5.8 to write a program to compute the gcd of an arbitrary list of positive integers.

5 Write a program to express the gcd of an arbitrary list of positive integers as a linear combination of the integers in that list.

1.8 Factorisation revisited

We use Corollary 1.6.6 to establish a property which characterises the primes in $\mathbb{Z}$.

Theorem 1.8.1

(i) (Euclid Book 7) Let p be a prime and let $a, b \in \mathbb{Z}$ be such that $p|ab$. Then $p|a$ or $p|b$ (or both*).

(ii) Conversely: if n $(\neq -1, 0, 1) \in \mathbb{Z}$ and if, whenever $n|ab$, we are forced to deduce that $n|a$ or $n|b$ (or both*) then n must be prime.

Proof

(i) Let a, b, p be as given. If $p|a$ there is nothing left to prove. So suppose that $p \nmid a$. Now the only divisors of p are $-1, 1, -p$ and p and, of these, only -1 and 1 also divide a. Thus $(a, p) = 1$. From Corollary 1.6.6 we deduce the existence of $s, t \in \mathbb{Z}$ such that $sa + tp = 1$. It follows that $sab + tpb = b$. But $p|ab$ (given) and $p|tpb$ (clearly!). Hence $p|sab + tpb$. That is, $p|b$.

We have therefore shown that either $p|a$ or, failing that, $p|b$—as required.

(ii) (by *reductio*) Let us assume that n $(\geqslant 2)$ is *not* a prime. Then $n = kl$ (where $1 < k < n$ and $1 < l < n$) is composite. But then $n|kl$ and yet $n \nmid k$ and $n \nmid l$. This contradicts the given property of n. Hence the assumption that n is composite is false. Thus n is prime—as required. □

Notes 1.8.2

(i) Theorem 1.8.1 is a vital ingredient in a more direct proof of Theorem 1.4.1 given below.

(ii) Theorem 1.8.1 easily extends to: Let p be a prime and let $a_1, a_2, \ldots, a_n \in \mathbb{Z}$. If $p|a_1a_2 \cdots a_n$, then $p|a_i$ for some i $(1 \leqslant i \leqslant n)$.

The more direct (and more transparent—but less pretty) proof of Theorem 1.4.1 then goes, very informally, as follows.

Suppose

$$a = q_1q_2 \cdots q_m = r_1r_2 \cdots r_n \qquad (*)$$

* In mathematics 'or' is always assumed to include the possibility of both occurrences. (Thus if at your maths professor's house you are asked 'white wine or red?' you should—even if you drink only white or drink only red or if you want wine but don't mind which— reply 'yes please'. Of course, you might end up with a glass of the 'wrong' colour or conceivably with a glass of each!)

where the q_i and r_j are primes and where, WLOG*, we may as well suppose that $q_1 \leqslant q_2 \leqslant \cdots \leqslant q_m$ and $r_1 \leqslant r_2 \leqslant \cdots \leqslant r_n$. Since $q_1 | q_1 q_2 \cdots q_m$ we see that $q_1 | r_1 r_2 \cdots r_n$. By Note 1.8.2(ii), $q_1 | r_i$ for some i $(1 \leqslant i \leqslant n)$. Since r_i is a (positive) prime and since q_1 is positive and not equal to 1 we see that $q_1 = r_i$ for some i. Likewise $r_1 = q_j$ for some j $(1 \leqslant j \leqslant m)$. Hence $q_j = r_1 \leqslant r_i = q_1$ and we are forced to deduce that $q_j = q_1$ and consequently $q_1 = r_1$.

From equation (*) we can infer, by cancellation of q_1 $(= r_1)$ from each side, that $q_2 q_3 \cdots q_m = r_2 r_3 \cdots r_n$.

In a like manner we can now show that $q_2 = r_2$, $q_3 = r_3$, etc. We then easily deduce that $m = n$ and that the qs and rs can be paired off as Theorem 1.4.1 claims.

The problem of factoring a given number a, or checking it is prime, is one that has long concerned all those, not only mathematicians, with an interest, theoretical or practical, in whole numbers. And the advent of rapid computing devices has not really allieviated the problem. It's just that the numbers which cause the problems are nowadays that little bit bigger! Indeed the transmission of top secret messages is aided by the fact that the present-day computer (and its programmer) has only marginally less difficulty† in factoring a 200-digit number than Father Marin Mersenne estimated he would have in checking the primeness of a given number of 15 to 20 digits.

Here is a scheme for factorising invented by the 'father of modern number theory' Pierre de Fermat. Not only is it interesting from a historical point of view but, although in its original form it can be quite inefficient, a modification of it has recently been revived for use in computer factorisations.

We suppose N to be any odd integer. [If N were even we could repeatedly factor by 2 until an odd integer results.] If N factorises, $N = uv$, say, where $u \leqslant v$ are both odd, then setting $x = (1/2)(v+u)$, $y = (1/2)(v-u)$ we find that $N = x^2 - y^2$, in other words $y^2 = x^2 - N$.

Starting with the smallest integer k for which $k \geqslant \sqrt{N}$ evaluate $x^2 - N$ for $x = k, k+1, k+2, \ldots$ successively. When some value s, say, of x yields a perfect square t^2, say, then N factorises as $(s-t)(s+t)$ as required. [Must we reach such an s?] So far we have not really said much—but here is Fermat's observation which made it all worth while. Fermat noticed that no square number ever ends in a 2, 3, 7 or 8. Thus if, for a given value of x, $x^2 - N$ ends in one of these digits, we may immediately pass on to the next value of x. Even this step can be performed other than naively. Namely, instead of working out $k^2 - N$, $(k+1)^2 - N$, $(k+2)^2 - N, \ldots$ etc. one needs only to add, successively, to the initial value $k^2 - N$ the integers $2k+1, 2k+3, 2k+5, \ldots$.

[The method of allowing all x for which $x^2 - N$ ends in 2, 3, 7 or 8 to fall through the net is another example of 'sieving'.]

Fermat advertised his method by showing that $2027651281 = 44021 \cdot 46061$, an example no doubt specially cooked for the occasion, the factors soon being found since they are fairly close to one another. Nevertheless the moral is

* See p. 29.

† Taking several million years as against 'all of time'.

again clear—even with a computer to hand. You can often save yourself (computer) time if you apply a little brainpower first. [See in particular Theorem 3.2.3 and Computer Problem 6.1.1.]

Program 1.9 uses Fermat's method, without making use of the sieving idea, to factor N. We note once again that this method works best in cases when two factors are of similar size—in the worst possible situation we would need to try as many as $(N+1)/2-\sqrt{N}$ integers.

Program 1.9 *Fermat's method of factorising*

```
 10 INPUT N
 20 K=INT(SQR(N))+1
 30 Y=K*K-N
 40 D=1
 50 IF INT(SQR(Y))=SQR(Y) GOTO 110
 60   Y=Y+2*K+D
 70   D=D+2
 80 IF SQR(Y)<N/3 GOTO 50
 90 PRINT "no factors found "
100 STOP
110 X=SQR(N+Y)
120 Y=SQR(Y)
130 PRINT " Two factors are ",(X-Y)," and ",(X+Y)
```

The final program we offer in this chapter uses an alternative algorithm, based on Fermat's method, and shows how factors can be obtained using addition and subtraction rather than the square root used in line 50. Fermat checked x^2-N at each step to see whether it was a perfect square using a similar observation to the above but involving the last two digits of x^2-N. In the program below we have replaced this by computing both x and y and considering whether $r=x^2-y^2-N$ is zero. If r is positive we increase the value of y while if it is negative we increase the value of x. In the program we use a to represent $2x+1$ and $b=2y+1$. Thus once we have a value of $r=0$ then $(a-b)/2$ represents the smaller factor of N.

Program 1.10 *Factorisation using only the operations of addition and subtraction (based on Fermat's method)*

```
 10 REM factorisation using division.
 20 REM set up the initial values
 30 INPUT N
 40 a=2*INT(SQR(N))+1
 50 b=1
 60 r=INT(SQR(N))^2-N
 70 IF r <= 0 GOTO 110
 75 REM reduce r and increase a
 80     r = r-b
 90     b = b+2
100   GOTO 70
110   IF r = 0 GOTO 150
115 REM increase r and increase b
120   r = r + a
130   a = a + 2
140   GOTO 70
150 PRINT "Two factors are ";INT((a-b)/2);" and ";N/INT((a-b)/2)
```

Exercises 1.8

1 Prove that if p is prime and if $p|a^n$, then $p^n|a^n$. Show that the same conclusion may not be drawn if p is not a prime. Nor is the conclusion necessarily true in the H-numbers of Exercise 1.4.1. [*Hint*: Try 9 and 21^2.]

2 Prove that if p is a prime and if $1 \leqslant r \leqslant p-1$, then $p \left| \binom{p}{r} \right.$.

3 Let $n \in \mathbb{Z}^+$. Find the gcd of the set

$$\binom{n}{1}, \binom{n}{2}, \ldots, \binom{n}{n-1}$$

of binomial coefficients. [See Exercise 1.5.8(ii). *Hint*: Experiment with values of n up to 20 or 25, if necessary, in order to find the pattern.]

4 Find all possible remainders when a square is divided by 100. (Note that n^2, $(100-n)^2$, $(50+n)^2$, $(50-n)^2$ all have the same remainder. So one need only take $0 \leqslant n \leqslant 25$. [If you want to work this out on your computer feel free to do so!]

5 Work out, by hand, which of the following, if any, are perfect squares: 1248, 124 816, 1 2481 632, 1 234 567, 139 854 276, 31 415 926 535, 2 718 281 828 459.

6 Is 194489672241689 a fourth power?

Computer problems 1.8

1 Factorise, by Fermat's method: (i) 8 496 167; (ii) 60 096 559; (iii) 24 498 431. Compare the speed of factorising with methods considered earlier in the text.

2 Factorise, by Fermat's method, the integer $N = 123\,456\,789$ (i) directly; (ii) after searching for small prime factors of N—say up to 100. Compare running times of (i) and (ii) using this and other N.

3 Factorise, by any means you wish, (i) 110 450 171; (ii) 593 505 099.

2

More about primes —a historical diversion

2.1 A false dawn and two sorry tales

Perhaps in part because of their fundamental role in the multiplicative theory of the integers, but possibly even more due to their enigmatic distribution amongst the integers, the primes have long been a source of fascination. As we have seen, it is easy to pose questions about primes: this chapter supplies some more. Some of these questions now have answers; others are as far away as ever from being answered.

One can't be sure when each of the six (numbered) problems so far raised was first posed. The qualities of primeness and compositeness were distinguished by the Pythagorean Philolaus in the 5th century B.C. According to [1]*, the Chinese of the same period knew that for each prime p, $p|2^p-1$. ([1] also reports* that they claimed, conversely—and wrongly!—that if n is a positive integer such that $n|2^{n-1}-1$ then n is prime. You may care to try and find the smallest composite integer n for which $n|2^{n-1}-1$ and, before rushing to your computer, learn that this example was discovered in 1820.)

In trying to discover any general 'pattern' which will help us probe more deeply into the (infinite) set of all primes, one's first efforts would be to identify the first few hundred, then few thousand primes by calculation or from tables already constructed. Such tables have long existed: in connection with his investigations into numbers of the form 2^p-1, Cataldi had, by 1588, produced a list of all the primes up to 750. Eighty years later a table of primes up to 100 000, which was used by Euler in his work on the same problem, had been prepared by Brancker. Just over 100 years after that, tables of primes up to 400 000 were available and in 1909, D. N. Lehmer produced the list of primes up to 10 000 000 refered to earlier. Of course, computers have diminished the usefulness of such printed lists.

Two rather sad stories about prime tables concern those produced by an Austrian school teacher A. Felkel in 1776 and by J. P. Kulik, a professor in Prague, *circa* 1860. Felkel had produced a manuscript table up to 2 000 000 but, as few people purchased the first part (up to 408 000), almost the entire edition was used in the manufacture of cartridges for use in the war against Turkey! Kulik spent 20 years of his life preparing his tables up to 100 000 000.

* Claims refuted by Joseph Needham in Volume 3, page 54, of his 'Science and Civilisation in China', published by Cambridge University Press.

Occupying over 4000 pages in 8 volumes it never emerged from its manuscript form.

When using a computer to explore conjectures it is often useful to have to hand a list of primes rather than to generate them during the investigation. Storing them in the computer memory will of course considerably reduce the amount of storage available for the rest of the program. We need therefore to balance the number of primes that are stored against our main objective. We know that to test N for primeness we only need primes up to $\sqrt{N}$. Using alternate gaps of 2 and 4 after the first three primes (see Computer Problem 1.1.3) we can generate, using Eratosthenes' sieve, with an array size of 5000, all the 1754 primes up to 14 993 and hence test the primeness of integers up to $(14\,993)^2 = 224\,790\,049$. So, even if only the primes are read into any subsequent program, we will still, of course, require about $\frac{1}{3}$ of the memory available on a 32 K computer.

It is possible (Problem 1.2.3) to modify Program 1.2 so that it generates all the primes between given integers m and n $(m < n)$. Hence we can fairly easily produce lists of the primes in any range within the bounds of the largest integer our computer can handle. Nevertheless the storage problem still remains critical if we retain the information *in the form generated by the sieve program.*

Changing the original array generated by the sieve so that it consists of 0s and 1s (1 indicating a prime) and chopping this binary sequence into subsequences of length m—the value of m depending on the size of integers that your computer can cope with—we can store the original long binary sequence as a much more compact sequence of decimal numbers. For example the BBC and other small microcomputers, because of the way they store integers, work with binary subsequences of length 32 which means we store in a single location

Program 2.1 *Compact storage of Prime lists*

```
160 REM Array A has the value 1 to indicate a prime and zero otherwise
170 REM Its dimension is L
180 S=2
190 R=0
200 N=0
210   P=2^31
220   FOR I=S TO S+30
225     P=P/2
230     IF A(I)<>0 THEN N = N+P
250   NEXT I
251 REM The next 3 statements controls how many numbers
252 REM are displayed on each line
255   R=R+1
256   IF R=6 THEN PRINT:R=1
260   PRINT ;N;
270   S=S+31
280 IF S+30 < L GOTO 200
```

numbers up to 2^{31}. Program 2.1 does this and produces Table 2.1, which represents all the 1754 primes up to 14 993.

Table 2.1 Primes stored as converted binary numbers. Each number represents a binary code of 31 digits.

2145113837	528928107	505665878	1914574057	758277843
1650887700	1452650023	745088149	1261474206	568451172
1296257677	1295204842	705055058	449913069	1906312520
303996179	1950649164	1639663639	14967978	96766216
798052449	1084613938	155685254	1916862884	478620440
191389090	1355885570	77283468	319855791	659331144
1846596289	312772715	6603554	1182871680	951143553
1895880113	1180796162	166732883	1516397613	352903524
1249993780	210182544	929235460	986723368	1753695106
19713203	343942730	547500122	1100004358	337985806
1783697516	151120993	2429092	978552172	1628572954
1342839076	552604001	675831818	1390602263	59605078
604014329	93487568	52775478	1824686472	538184722
1750386835	304351020	1093355722	1385605408	336337184
75732673	285486163	440598918	839356588	557056411
694325636	604313092	1093170326	1074829464	809517378
92497045	456240225	54577968	1481048160	353438657
576242689	109120069	1688733785	136737803	126160914
1233139248	1342317880	153194722	1117365573	1417872153
842535937	843415662	147996741	46318755	579608690
79929424	1421066474	337924864	138785092	421552848
828527010	1647354212	1094716419	23358593	845776930
55805028	1317290128	117686854	281027593	1412573955
51807250	604022120	743443600	1385173030	832598276
1728188428	1487160720	406999312	1478014217	25185027
134748464	1646266181	634394642	1356212628	100782128
231740640	43027658	840978624	474583429	87370010
1112820998	1413556512	1631659149	142609719	36263996
55607341	168191328	105157122	1176174724	414197074
571609220	1116022848	1306735627	1092911504	568387888
50357772	169050368	188940866	46141728	1889550731
424427809	70629382	12195972	282252595	69568780
1291887825				

Note. Only the numbers 2, 3, 5 followed by the odd integers separated by alternate gaps of 2 and 4 are stored. Thus 2145113837 corresponds to the binary sequence 1111111101101111010110111101101 which in turn represents the primeness of the integers 2, 3, 5, 7, 11, 13, 17, 19, 23, 25, 29, 31, 35, 37, 41, 43, 47, 49, 53, 55, 59, 61, 65, 67, 71, 73, 77, 79, 83, 85, 89. The next number contains the information on the integers 91, 95, 97 etc.

When we need to use the primes we can first regenerate the binary code using the following

```
400 FOR I=1 TO 31
410    B(32-I)=NUMBER MOD 2
420    NUMBER = NUMBER DIV 2
430 NEXT I
```

Exercises 2.1

Leonard Eugene Dickson *(22 January 1874 – 17 January 1954)*

Picture by courtesy of the American Mathematical Society.

Dickson was born in Independence, Iowa, a descendant of one William Dickson who had emigrated from Londonderry, Northern Ireland to Londonderry, New Hampshire in the eighteenth century. Whilst serving as a chemist with the Texas Geological Survey he attended the University of Texas taking a bachelor's degree in 1893 and a master's a year later. He continued with postgraduate study at the University of Chicago, gaining, in 1896, the first Ph.D. awarded in mathematics by that institution. Following periods at the Universities of Leipzig, Paris, California and Texas, he returned to Chicago in 1900, becoming a full professor in 1910.

One of the most productive of all mathematicians, Dickson wrote over 250 research papers and 18 books. He also found time to supervise some 55 research students! Having long desired to research in the theory of numbers, the 1600 page *History of the Theory of Numbers* was, according to Dickson himself, written in order that he might better acquaint himself with all that had been written on the subject! Given his dedication to the subject it is even more surprising that, on reaching the age of 65, in 1939, the supply of research papers stops abruptly and completely! Perhaps this apparent sudden disengagement from mathematics left him more time to pursue his main recreations which included bridge, tennis and billiards.

1 Dickson ([1] Vol. I p. 91) reports that Leibniz* 'proved' (1680/1) that if n isn't prime then $2^n - 2$ is not divisible by n. He wrote $n = pm$ where p is the smallest prime dividing n and asserted that $n \nmid \binom{n}{p}$ so that not all the terms in

* Gottfried Wilhelm Leibniz, 1 July 1646 – 14 November 1716.

the expansion of $(1+1)^n-2$ are multiples of n. He then deduced the (invalid) result claimed. Criticise this proof.

2 It appears ([1] Vol. I p. 93) that G. Levi (1892) believed that the positive integer n is prime or composite according as it is or is not a divisor of $10^{n-1}-1$. Excluding the trivially false cases $n=2$, $n=5$ and $n=9$ show that Levi's belief is still false. (And then see Theorem 5.4.4.)

Computer problems 2.1

1 Using Program 1.3 generate tables of primes for ranges up 100 000. Convert the resulting binary sequence into decimal form and store for later use.

2 A. Korselt (1899) believed that $645|2^{644}-1$. Is this correct? (It is not difficult to check this by hand after reading Section 3.2.)

2.2 Formulae generating primes

Perhaps the first question which arises on looking at tables of primes is: Is there an easy formula which will generate some or all of the primes—but only primes—amongst the integers? Despite the encouragement of finding, as Euler did, that $f(x)=x^2+x+41$ yields a prime number for each x for which $0 \leqslant x \leqslant 39$ (note that $f(40)$ is composite), one easily proves Theorem 2.2.1 below. (Note yet another triumph for *reductio ad absurdum.*)

But first let us observe a rather surprising pattern which arises if we print the integers greater than or equal to 41 in an anticlockwise spiral with 41 at its centre. Continuing from

←	51	50
43	42	49
44	41	48
45	46 →	47

and eliminating the composites we get Fig. 2.1.

It seems that all the terms on the NW–SE diagonal are primes! Is this always* the case? We invite you to extend the spiral as far as your computer will allow. (You will need to use a graphics mode replacing the primes by some kind of small 'marker' if you are to obtain a similar picture for integers much in excess of 500.)

Theorem 2.2.1 (Goldbach 1752†, Euler 1762) No non-constant polynomial in x with integer coefficients can yield a prime number‡ for each integer value

* In fact you have just been told the answer to this question!!
† Christian Goldbach, 18 March 1690–20 November 1764.
‡ For ease of exposition and to get a result more general than we otherwise would, we here admit −2, −3, −5 . . . etc. as primes—as well as the usual 2, 3, 5, . . . etc. (See footnote on page 19).

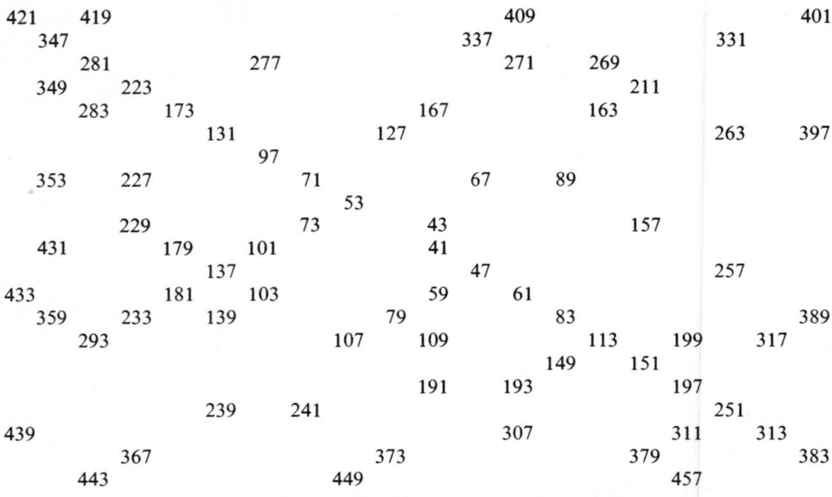

Fig. 2.1. The primes from 41 to 457 in their 'spiral' positions.

of x (nor even for each integer x greater than or equal to some fixed integer N, say).

Proof Suppose $f(x)=a_nx^n+a_{n-1}x^{n-1}+\cdots+a_1x+a_0$ $(n>0,\ a_n\neq 0)$ were such a polynomial. Then $f(N)=a_nN^n+a_{n-1}N^{n-1}+\cdots+a_1N+a_0$ is a prime p, say. For each integer t,

$$\begin{aligned} f(N+tp)&=a_n(N+tp)^n+a_{n-1}(N+tp)^{n-1}+\cdots+a_1(N+tp)+a_0\\ &=f(N)+p\cdot F(t)=p\cdot(1+F(t)) \end{aligned}$$

where $F(t)$ is a polynomial in t having integer coefficients. Since, by assumption, $f(N+tp)$ is prime, it follows that $f(N+tp)=p$ (or $-p$) for each t. But this means that the polynomial $F(t)$ of degree n becomes 0 (or -2) for infinitely many different values of t. Exercise 2.2.2(i) asks you to show that this is impossible. □

In fact no polynomial of degree $\geqslant 2$ in a single variable is known which actually yields infinitely many primes. In particular, such questions as: Are there infinitely many primes of the form n^2+1? remain unanswered. (Curiously enough it has been proved (see [5] page 5) that on infinitely many occasions n^2+1 is the product of no more than two primes.)

On the other hand reducing the degree to 1 or increasing the number of variables beyond 1 changes the picture somewhat. For the case of degree 1 we have Dirichlet's result—as promised in Section 1.3.

Theorem 2.2.2 (Dirichlet 1837) Let a, b be positive integers such that $(a, b)=1$. Then the polynomial $f(x)=ax+b$ is prime for infinitely many positive (integer) values of x. □

The proof of this is hard! See, for example, [11]. [In particular there are infinitely many (positive) primes of each of the forms $4k+1$, $6k+1$, $8k+1$, $8k+3$, $8k+5$, $8k+7$, results we (or you!) will prove separately later.]

Peter Gustav Lejeune Dirichlet *(13 February 1805 – 5 May 1859)*
Dirichlet was born in Duren, Germany. As a young man he attended a Jesuit college where one of his teachers was Georg Simon Ohm, the physicist. In 1822, the presence in Paris of Laplace, Legendre, Fourier, Cauchy and others induced him to go there. In particular he found the work of Fourier appealing; later, in 1829, he was to contribute an important theorem concerning the representation of functions by Fourier series. (In the course of his work on Fourier series Dirichlet replaced the rather hazy notion of 'function' then in use by a definition which is essentially that we use today.)

But initially Dirichlet's first love was number theory. He read and reread Gauss's *Disquisitiones*, even keeping a copy under his pillow at night! His first paper (1825) dealt with the impossibility of solving equations of the form $x^5+y^5=Az^5$. Legendre, using the same method, found a complete proof of Fermat's conjecture for the case $n=5$ shortly afterwards.

In 1828 Dirichlet moved to Berlin to teach mathematics at the military academy. In 1831 he was made a member of the Berlin Academy of Sciences. And also in that year he got married—to Rebecca Mendelsohn–Bartholdy, a sister of the composer.

In 1837 he wrote a paper in which he used methods of analysis to prove a result (Theorem 2.2.2) about the integers. He also wrote on Pell's equation and solved completely the problem of the units of the ring of integers of an algebraic number field. 1842 saw him writing a paper in which he enunciated his famous 'pigeon-hole principle'.

Dirichlet was, however, not just a pure mathematician. In 1830 he worked on the problem of the temperature distribution of heat in a thin bar, given the temperatures at its ends. Further work in applied mathematics resulted in 1850 in the emergence of the 'Dirichlet problem': Find a function $V(x, y, z)$, say, which satisfies Laplace's equation in a given region of space given, also, the value of V on the boundary of this region.

Although a shy man, Dirichlet was an excellent teacher and expositor. A contribution for which he will long be remembered is his *Vorlesungen über Zahlentheorie*, published after his death by his pupil Dedekind.

There is a story that, at the 50th anniversary celebrations of the award of Gauss's doctorate, Gauss was about to light his pipe with a page from the original *Disquisitiones*. Dirichlet, appalled by this, grabbed the page from Gauss and treasured it the rest of his life.

Dirichlet (1840) also proved that if a, $2b$, c have no common divisor greater than 1 then the quadratic form $ax^2+2bxy+cy^2$ represents an infinite number of primes. More recently (1970), in answering an old question of Hilbert's, there have been constructed polynomials $P(x, y, \ldots)$ in several variables and with integer coefficients which are such that *each positive* value of P is a prime and, furthermore, all positive primes occur as values taken by P.

Other ways of attempting to generate primes have been suggested. In 1947 W. H. Mills proved that there is a real number a such that $[a^{3^n}]$ is prime for each positive integer n. Unfortunately, Mills could only prove that such an a exists—he couldn't give its value. There are even (non-silly) functions f for which $f(n)$ is the nth prime p_n. (See for example, [11], p. 101, and [D].) Unfortunately these too are of little use for computing extensive lists of primes. Yet other ways of obtaining primes have been raised earlier in this book. For example, in Theorem 1.3.1 we considered the integers $N=p_1p_2\cdots p_t+1$ where $p_1, p_2, \ldots p_t$ are the first t primes. One soon notes that for $t=1, 2, 3, 4, 5$ the corresponding value of N is prime. Is N prime infinitely often? No-one knows. Indeed for $p_k \leqslant 1031$ the only values of p_k for which N is prime are 2, 3, 5, 7, 11, 31, 379, 1019 and 1021. See [5], p. 6, and [E].

A similar question can be asked about $n!+1$. Is it prime infinitely often? Again, no-one knows. (On the other hand, as Exercise 1.2.1 shows, each such $n!+1$ comes perilously close to a whole succession of composites whilst Theorem 3.5.1 shows that it is *composite* infinitely often.)

Exercises 2.2

1 (Escott 1899) Show that $n^2-79n+1601$ is prime for $n=0, 1, \ldots, 79$. [*Hint*: In x^2+x+41 replace x by $n-40$.]

2(i) Show that a polynomial $f(x)$ of degree $n(\geqslant 1)$ cannot take the same value, v, say, for infinitely many different values of x. [In fact it can't even take the same value for $n+1$ distinct values of x—see RFG, Exercise 1.11.5].
(ii) Show that the polynomial $f(x)$ of Theorem 2.2.1 is certainly composite for infinitely many values of x.

3 Let $f(x, y)$ be a polynomial ($\neq$ constant) in the two variables x, y with integer coefficients. Prove that $f(a, b)$ cannot be prime for all integer pairs a, b. Given that

$$f(x, y) = x^2y^2 - 3x^2y + xy^2 + 2y^3 + 4x^2 - 3xy + 6y^2 - 32y + 43,$$

find positive a and b such that $f(a, b)$ is composite.

4 It is unknown whether or not n^2+2 is prime infinitely often. Show however that, for each *prime* $p \geqslant 5$, p^2+2 is composite.

5 Show that $2^{1002}+1$ is composite. [*Hint*: $(2^{2n+1}+2^{n+1}+1)(2^{2n+1}-2^{n+1}+1)=$?]

6 Show that for each positive integer k the arithmetic progression $am+b$ contains a succession of k or more *consecutive* terms all of which are composite. [Use Exercise 1.2.1]

7 Let $a, d, c \in \mathbb{Z}$ such that $(a, d) = 1$ and $c \neq 0$. Show, without using Theorem 2.2.2, that there are infinitely many $n \in \mathbb{Z}$ such that $(a+dn, c) = 1$.

8 Given $k \in \mathbb{Z}$ show that there exists a prime p such that each of $p \pm 1$, $p \pm 2, \ldots, p \pm k$ is composite. [*Hint*: (i) Choose a prime $q > k+1$ and form

$$a = (q-k)(q-k+1) \cdots (q-2)(q-1)(q+1)(q+2) \cdots (q+k).$$

Show $(a, q) = 1$. (ii) In the sequence $\{am+q: m \in \mathbb{Z}^+\}$ let p be any prime. Show that this p solves the problem.]

Computer problems 2.2

1(i) Find the percentage of primes of the form x^2+x+41 for x lying in the ranges 0–100, 0–200, 0–300, ..., 0–1000. Is there an N for which less than half the integers $\{x^2+x+41: 0 \leqslant x \leqslant N\}$ are primes?
(ii) Can you find any other positive integers A such that x^2+x+A is prime for each x such that $0 \leqslant x \leqslant A-2$.

2 Repeat Problem 1 using x^2+ax+b for other values of a and b. Can you find values of a and b which improve on the performance of x^2+x+41? [Cf. [12], p. 19.]

3 Repeat Problem 1(i) for the function $|2x^2-199|$.

4 Chabert (1844) stated that $3n^2+3n+1$ represents many primes for n small. Investigate this claim.

5 Write a program to check if N is prime where $N = p_1p_2 \cdots p_k + 1$ and $p_1, \ldots, p_k$ are the first k primes. Run the sequence as far as possible on your computer. Once you have reached the limit of your computer's arithmetic accuracy use multiprecison arithmetic to extend the sequence as far as your time and patience allow!

6 Does the sequence $2+1=3, 2\cdot3+1=7, 2\cdot3\cdot7+1=43, \ldots$ produce many primes?

7 Find all instances of four *consecutive* primes, below 2000, which are in arithmetic progression.

8 There is a sequence of seven primes in a.p. with gap of 150 between each successive pair. Can you find this sequence? (G. Lemaire, 1909).

9 Write a computer program to display the points (x, y) of the plane where $-4 \leqslant x \leqslant 4$, $-4 \leqslant y \leqslant 4$ printing 'P' or 'C' at the 'point' (x, y) according as the corresponding value of the polynomial of Exercise 2.2.3 has prime or composite value.

2.3 Prime pairs and Goldbach's conjecture

Apart from the trivial instance 2, 3 of a pair of primes differing by 1, the smallest possible difference between successive primes is, of course, 2. Examples of such prime pairs, also called *twin primes* are:

$$3, 5; 5, 7; \ldots; 41, 43; \ldots 1639494(2^{4423}-1)-1,$$
$$1639494(2^{4423}-1)+1; \ldots (!),$$

this last-named pair having been discovered by Keller in 1983.

We know (Euclid knew) that there are infinitely many primes. Are there infinitely many prime pairs? No-one knows. But at least one thing is known for sure. Even if there are infinitely many prime pairs there is a 'smaller infinity' of them than the infinity of all primes! This is merely a provocative way of registering the following remarkable fact. If one forms the sequence of reciprocals $\frac{1}{3}, \frac{1}{5}, \frac{1}{7}, \frac{1}{11}, \ldots$ of the odd primes then, by adding together sufficiently many of these terms one can obtain a total greater than any preassigned number* (see Exercise 2.3.5). On the other hand, the sum $\frac{1}{3}+\frac{1}{5}+\cdots+\frac{1}{17}+\frac{1}{19}+\frac{1}{29}+\cdots$ of the reciprocals of those primes which are members of prime pairs (note that $\frac{1}{23}$ is the first term 'missing' from the sum) never exceeds 2[F]†. In fancy language: the infinite series $\Sigma 1/p$ is *divergent* if p runs over all (odd) primes and *convergent*‡ if p runs over all members of prime pairs. In fact one can show that there is some constant C such that

$$\log\log t - C < \sum_{\substack{p \leqslant t \\ p \text{ prime}}} \frac{1}{p} < \log\log t + C$$

for all t (see, for example, [13], p. 326) a result we shall call upon very briefly later.

* You may care to calculate how many terms of $\Sigma\, 1/p$ are required to get the sum beyond, say, 3.
† Assuming the validity of a plausible conjecture of Hardy and Littlewood which estimates the number of such pairs less than any given number x.
‡ This is Brun's Theorem (1919). [Viggo Brun 13 October 1885 – 15 August 1978].

Closely related to the problem of prime pairs is perhaps the most famous of all unproven assertions concerning the primes, namely Goldbach's conjecture: *Each even integer greater than* 2 *is expressible as a sum* $p+q$ *of two primes.* In 1937 the Russian Vinogradov proved that every sufficiently large* odd integer is the sum of three primes (so that every large enough even integer is the sum of (at most) four primes). More recently (1973) Chen Jing-Run has shown that every large enough even integer is of the form $p+q$ or $p+rs$ where p, q, r and s are primes.

Exercises 2.3

1 When is the next occurrence of a twin prime pair of years? [1949, 1951 was the last such pair.]

2 Show that if p, q are twin primes then (except for $p=3, q=5$) $p+q$ is a multiple of 12 and $pq+1$ is a perfect square. (Can $pq+1$ be a perfect cube?)

3 Show that there is only one value of $n \in \mathbb{Z}^+$ for which n, $n+2$ and $n+4$ are all primes.

4 Given 3 primes in arithmetic progression, the first not being 3, show that their common difference is divisible by 6. (Lagrange† 1771). Try the equivalent problem with 3 replaced by 5, then by 7 (after suitably amending the difference of 6).

5 Show that $\sum(1/p)$ is divergent as follows.

(i) For $n \in \mathbb{Z}$, $n \geq 2$, show that

$$\begin{aligned}\textstyle\prod_{p \leq n}(1-1/p)^{-1} &= \textstyle\prod_{p \leq n}(1+1/p+1/p^2+\cdots)\\ &> \sum_{k=1}^{n}(1/k) > \int_1^{n+1}\frac{1}{x}\,dx = \log(n+1);\end{aligned}$$

(ii) For $-\frac{1}{2} \leq x < 0$, $\log(1+x)-2x$ is positive. Hence for each $p \geq 2$, $-2/p < \log(1-1/p)$;

(iii) $\sum_{p \leq n}(2/p) > \sum_{p \leq n}\log(1-1/p)^{-1}$

$$= \log \textstyle\prod_{p \leq n}(1-1/p)^{-1} > \log\log(n+1).$$

6 Prove that each integer greater than 6 is a sum of two relatively prime positive integers neither of which is 1. [*Hint*: $4n=(2n-1)+(2n+1)$, $4n+2=(2n-1)+(2n+3)$.]

7 ([G]) Prove that each even integer greater than 38 is a sum of two positive odd composites. [*Hint*: Express each number of the form $10k$ as $15+(10k-15)$. Do the same for numbers of the form $10k+2$, $10k+4$, $10k+6$ and $10k+8$.]

* $\geq 3^{3^{15}}$, for example (see [5], p. 58).
† See p. 117.

8 Prove that each positive integer is a sum of distinct Fibonacci numbers.

9 Prove that Goldbach's conjecture is equivalent to: Each integer greater than 5 is a sum of three primes.

Computer problems 2.3

1 Find primes p such that $p, p+2, p+6$ are all primes and primes p such that $p, p+4, p+6$ are all primes.

2 Conjecture: Given even n, there exist infinitely many pairs of primes p, q such that $p-q=n$. Find instances where $p-q=100$.

3 Explore the following conjectures where $\alpha(\geqslant 3)$ and $a(\geqslant 0)$ belong to $\mathbb{Z}$.

(i) α odd $\Rightarrow \alpha =$ prime or prime $+2^a$ (De Polignac conjecture)
(ii) α odd $\Rightarrow \alpha =$ prime $+2a^2$ (Goldbach conjecture to Euler 1752)
(iii) $\alpha = p + a^2$ ($p=1$ or prime)
(iv) $\alpha = p + a^\beta$ ($p=1$ or prime, $\beta \geqslant 2$)
(v) Lagrange (1775): Each odd $\alpha > 5$ is $p+2q$ (p, q both primes). Confirm this as far as you feel able.
(vi) If α is of the form $4k+2$ then α is the sum of two $4k+1$ type primes. (Goldbach conjecture to Euler 1742).

4 Find primes p such that $p-k!$ is composite for all k such that $k! < p$. (It is unknown if there are infinitely many such primes; [5], p. 6.)

5 Test Goldbach's conjecture for various large N—you might just find a counterexample!

6 Test the following extended conjecture of Goldbach for various values of N. Each even integer $N \geqslant 8$ is a sum of *distinct* primes.

7 Write a program to determine as accurately as you can the value of $\sum(1/p)$ where the summation is over all primes that are members of prime pairs.

2.4 A wider view of the primes. The prime number theorem

If the behaviour of the primes is too chaotic to identify precisely where each is hiding, perhaps we can smooth out the local irregularities by asking how the collection of primes behaves 'globally'—for example: How often do primes put in an appearance, *on average*? After extensive calculations Legendre* (1798) and Gauss† (1793 according to a letter he wrote 50 years later), suggested

* See p. 126.
† See p. 203.

answers which took the best part of a century to confirm. We begin with

Definition 2.4.1 For each positive real* number x we define $\pi(x)$ to be the number of primes from 1 to x inclusive.

Thus $\pi(1000) = 168$ whilst $\pi(3.14159) = 2$.

From information of the kind registered in the first two columns of the table on p. 60 Legendre and Gauss (aged 16), respectively, formulated† just before 1800,

Conjecture L: Let $L(x) = \dfrac{x}{\log x - 1.08366}$. Then $\pi(x)$ is approximately $L(x)$.

Conjecture G: Let $G(x) = \displaystyle\int_2^x \frac{dt}{\log t}$. Then $\pi(x)$ is approximately $G(x)$.

Conjecture G expresses an approximation to the number of primes up to x in the form of an integral. The integrand, $1/\log t$ in this case, represents the proposed 'density' of the primes. To obtain an approximate value for $G(x)$ we can use a numerical integration method such as Simpson's‡ which estimates $\int_a^b f(x)\,dx$ by

$$(h/3)[f(a)+4f(a+h)+2f(a+2h)+4f(a+3h)+\cdots$$
$$+2f(a+(n-2)h)+4f(a+(n-1)h)+f(a+nh)].$$

where h represents the length of each of the even number, n, of small intervals into which the interval $[a, b]$ is broken. The following lines of BASIC will calculate the integral between bounds U and L for any function *FNA* defined before the statements are used.

Program 2.2 *Numerical integration using Simpson's method*

```
 980 REM  the following statement, defining the function to be
 981 REM  integrated must appear earlier in the program
 985 REM         DEF FNA(V)=1/LN(V)
 990 REM the values of N, the number of intervals,
 995 REM L and U, the limits of integration, must also be defined
1000 H=(U-L)/N
1005 X=LOW
1010 I=FNA(L)+FNA(H)
1020 FOR J=1 TO N-1
1025    X=X+H
1030    IF J - INT(J/2)*2 = 0 GOTO 1060
1040       I=I+4*FNA(X)
1050    GOTO 1070
1060       I=I+2*FNA(X)
1070 NEXT J
1080 I=I*H/3
1090 REM Return to the main part of the program
1100 REM I contains the result of the integration
```

* For what follows it is more convenient to define $\pi(x)$ for all $x \in \mathbb{R}^+$ rather than merely for all $x \in \mathbb{Z}^+$.

† Here $\log x$ denotes the log of x to base e.

‡ Thomas Simpson 20 August 1710 – 14 May 1761.

Table 2.2 Comparing $L(x)$, $G(x)$ and $\pi(x)$ for small values of x.

x	$\pi(x)$ = Number of primes $\leqslant x$	G	error	L	error
100	25	29	4	28	3
500	95	100	5	97	2
1 000	168	177	9	172	4
2 000	303	314	11	307	4
3 000	430	442	12	437	7
4 000	550	564	14	555	5
5 000	669	683	14	673	4
6 000	783	799	16	788	5
7 000	900	913	13	901	1
8 000	1007	1025	18	1012	5
9 000	1117	1136	19	1122	5
10 000	1229	1245	16	1231	2
50 000	5133	5166	33	5136	3
100 000	9592	9629	37	9588	−4

Note: Although the error for G is growing in absolute terms the relative error is decreasing.

By varying the function *FNA* used in Simpson's method other attempts to approximate $\pi(x)$ can be made. (What alternatives merit consideration? What form should a potential function take?)

In terms of limits both conjectures G and L become

$$\textit{Conjecture PNT}: \quad \lim_{x\to:\infty} \frac{\pi(x)}{x/\log x} = 1.$$

In fact conjecture PNT was turned into a theorem, since known as the prime number theorem, by the Frenchman J. Hadamard* and the Belgian Ch.-J. de la Vallée Poussin† simultaneously in 1896. Their proof is too deep to include here. However Erdos and Selberg obtained a (non-trivial) proof using only elementary concepts in 1949.

As can be seen from the table, Gauss's approximation to $\pi(x)$ is a very good one—at least over the range shown—which appears always to overestimate, if only just, the true value of $\pi(x)$. Appearances, however, can be deceptive: the value $G(x)-\pi(x)$—which is positive across the range indicated—is nonetheless known to change sign infinitely many times as x increases. An estimate for the value of x at which the first change of sign takes place was given by S. Skewes in 1933 as being 'less than $10^{10^{10^{34}}}$'. (Earlier versions of [14] credited this as 'the greatest number appearing naturally in mathematics'.)

Of course we can only remark how good an approximation to $\pi(x)$ Gauss's function is if we are certain of the exact value of $\pi(x)$ for the listed values of x. How can we be sure of these values? Apart from merely finding the primes less than x and then counting them, at best a thankless task, we could employ

* Jacques Hadamard, 8 December 1865 – 17 October 1963.
† Charles-Jean-Gustave-Nicolas de la Vallée Poussin 14 August 1866 – 2 March 1962.

Theorem 2.4.2 (Legendre 1798) For each integer $N \geq 1$

$$\pi(N) - \pi(\sqrt{N}) + 1 = N - \sum_{p_i \leq \sqrt{N}} \left[\frac{N}{p_i}\right] + \sum_{p_i < p_j \leq \sqrt{N}} \left[\frac{N}{p_i p_j}\right] - \sum_{p_i < p_j < p_k \leq \sqrt{N}} \left[\frac{N}{p_i p_j p_k}\right] + \cdots$$

where $p_1, p_2, \ldots$ are the primes not exceeding $\sqrt{N}$ and $[t]$ is the greatest integer not exceeding the real number t.

Proof For each prime p_i, $[N/p_i]$ is the number of integers less than or equal to N which are divisible by p_i. If we were to subtract these quantities (for each $p_i \leq \sqrt{N}$) from N we would have the exact number of integers between 1 and N not divisible by any prime less than or equal to $\sqrt{N}$—except that we would have counted twice all those N divisible by two or more such primes.

If we added these back again—that's the term

$$\sum_{p_i < p_j \leq \sqrt{N}} \left[\frac{N}{p_i p_j}\right]$$

—we would have obtained the number of integers between 1 and N not divisible by any pair of distinct primes less than or equal to $\sqrt{N}$—except that we would now have counted twice those integers between 1 and N which are divisible by three of the primes p_i. Continuing the argument in this way yields the formula above. □

Legendre used the above theorem to find $\pi(10^6)$ in 1830 but his answer was marginally farther away from the true value than that given by the (incorrect) prime tables then available! This emphasises the complexity of the calculations involved for large values of N; for this and reasons of speed and economy other methods have been sought. Of course by ignoring even numbers one can halve the work by using the formula

$$\pi(N) - \pi(\sqrt{N}) + 1 = \langle N/2 \rangle - \sum_{p_i \leq \sqrt{N}} \langle N/(2p_i) \rangle + \sum_{p_i < p_j \leq \sqrt{N}} \langle N/(2p_i p_j) \rangle - \sum_{p_i < p_j < p_k \leq \sqrt{N}} \langle N/(2p_i p_j p_k) \rangle + \cdots$$

where the p_i are again the odd primes not exceeding $\sqrt{N}$ and $\langle t \rangle$ is the nearest integer to t-taking the larger value if t is an integer and a half. (For a proof of this and for further improvements see [24] and [20].)

As an example let us take $N = 100$ so that $\pi(\sqrt{N}) = 4$. By Legendre's theorem

$$\pi(100) - 4 + 1 = 100 - [100/2] - [100/3] - [100/5] - [100/7] + [100/2\cdot 3] + [100/2\cdot 5] + \cdots + [100/5\cdot 7] - [100/2\cdot 3\cdot 5] - \cdots - [100/3\cdot 5\cdot 7] + [100/2\cdot 3\cdot 5\cdot 7]$$

i.e. $$\pi(100)-3=100-(50+33+20+14)+(16+10+7+6+4+2)-(3+2+1+0)+0=22.$$

Using the second formula we obtain

$$\begin{aligned}\pi(100)-4+1=&\langle 100/2\rangle-\langle 100/2\cdot 3\rangle-\langle 100/2\cdot 5\rangle-\langle 100/2\cdot 7\rangle\\ &+\langle 100/2\cdot 3\cdot 5\rangle+\langle 100/2\cdot 3\cdot 7\rangle\\ &+\langle 100/2\cdot 5\cdot 7\rangle-\langle 100/2\cdot 3\cdot 5\cdot 7\rangle\end{aligned}$$

i.e. $\pi(100)-3=50-(17+10+7)+(3+2+1)-0=22$. Thus $\pi(100)=25$.

Subsequently other formulae have been given for evaluating $\pi(N)$ for large N. These formulae, whilst generally requiring less running time and storage space (in the computer) than previous ones, tend to require knowledge of $\pi(x)$ for at least some values of x beyond $\sqrt{N}$ (as required by Legendre's method). We present here a program based on Legendre's result and leave the reader to consider the improvement suggested above and other methods.

Program 2.3 *Determines the number of primes up to N by the Legendre formula*

```
 10 REM  A contains the primes up to SQR(N)
 20 REM NP is the number of primes up to SQR(N)
170 ANS=INT(N)
175 REM subtract the number of integers divisible by single primes
180 FOR I=1 TO NP
190   ANS=ANS-INT(N/A(I))
200 NEXT I
205 REM Adjust for integers divisible by two or more primes
210 SIGN=-1
220 FOR R=2 TO NP
230   K=1
240   SIGN=SIGN*-1
250   SUM=0
255 REM set u the first r values A(1)...A(r)
260   INDEX(1)=1
270   FOR J=2 TO R
290     INDEX(J)=INDEX(J-1)+1
300   NEXT J
310   J=R
320   GOTO 420
325 REM set up the suffixes for the next product
330     IF INDEX(J)=NP-R+J GOTO 390
340       INDEX(J)=INDEX(J)+1
350         IF J=R GOTO 420
360         J=J+1
370         INDEX(J)=INDEX(J-1)+1
380       GOTO 350
390     J=J-1
400     IF J=0 GOTO 500
410     GOTO 330
415 REM Calculate product and add the number of primes divisible by
416 REM that product to sum
420   PROD=1
430   FOR I=1 TO R
440     PROD=(PROD*A(INDEX(I)))
```

```
450    NEXT I
455 REM once the product is >N
456 REM there is no need to include higher value primes
460    IF PROD>N AND SUM=0 GOTO 500
470    IF PROD>N J=J-1 GOTO 330
480    SUM=SUM+INT(N/PROD)
490    GOTO 330
495 REM correct the answer by
496 REM the number of integers divisible by r primes
500    ANS=ANS+SUM*SIGN
510 NEXT R
520 PRINT "Up to ";N;" there are ";ANS+NP-1;" primes
```

The first real progress on the above conjectures L and G was made in 1852 by the Russian P. L. Tchebychef*. He proved

Theorem 2.4.3 If $\lim_{x\to\infty} \dfrac{\pi(x)}{x/\log x}$ exists and is equal to L then $L=1$. □

He also proved

Theorem 2.4.4 There exist constants c and C such that, for each real $x \geqslant 2$, $cx/\log x < \pi(x) < Cx/\log x$. □ (The proof is given below.)

Although in Theorem 2.4.4 Tchebychef could show that for large x he could take $c=0.921$ and $C=1.106$ he was unable to convert either theorem in to a full proof of the PNT. Nevertheless as Theorem 2.4.4 is not too difficult to establish, let's have a look at a proof of it now. A key role in this proof is played by a result about binomial coefficients!

Theorem 2.4.5 Let $n \geqslant 1$ be an integer and let p be a prime $\leqslant 2n$. Define α_p by $p^{\alpha_p} \leqslant 2n < p^{\alpha_p+1}$.

Then (i) $\displaystyle\prod_{n<p\leqslant 2n} p \,\Big|\, \binom{2n}{n}$ and (ii) $\displaystyle\binom{2n}{n} \,\Big|\, \prod_{p\leqslant 2n} p^{\alpha_p}$.

Proof (i) is immediate: each prime p such that $n<p\leqslant 2n$ clearly divides $(2n)!$ and not $(n!)^2$. For (ii) we use the fact (Exercise 2.4.1) that the exponent of the highest power of p which divides $(2n)!$ is

$$\left[\frac{2n}{p}\right]+\left[\frac{2n}{p^2}\right]+\cdots+\left[\frac{2n}{p^{\alpha_p}}\right]=\sum_{m=1}^{\alpha_p}\left[\frac{2n}{p^m}\right].$$

Likewise the exponent of the highest power of p which divides $(n!)^2$ is

$$2\sum_{m=1}^{\alpha_p}\left[\frac{n}{p^m}\right]$$

* Pafnuty Lvovich Tchebychef, 16 May 1821 - 8 December 1894.

(why the same α_p?). Hence the exponent of the highest power of p dividing $\binom{2n}{n}$ is

$$\sum_{m=1}^{\alpha_p}\left(\left[\frac{2n}{p^m}\right]-2\left[\frac{n}{p^m}\right]\right)\leqslant\sum_{m=1}^{\alpha_p}1=\alpha_p.\text{ (See Exercise 2.4.1.)}\quad\square$$

We use this immediately to prove

Corollary 2.4.6 Let $n\geqslant 1$ be an integer. Then

(i) $n^{\pi(2n)-\pi(n)}<\binom{2n}{n}\leqslant(2n)^{\pi(2n)}$;

(ii) (a) $\pi(2n)-\pi(n)\leqslant\dfrac{2n\log 2}{\log n}$ if $n\geqslant 2$

(b) $\dfrac{n\log 2}{\log 2n}\leqslant\pi(2n)$.

Proof (i) follows immediately from Theorem 2.4.5. Since, in (i),

$$n^{\pi(2n)-\pi(n)}<\prod_{n<p\leqslant 2n}p$$

whilst, in (ii), $\prod_{p\leqslant 2n}p^{\alpha_p}\leqslant\prod_{p\leqslant 2n}2n=(2n)^{\pi(2n)}$.

To prove (ii) we first observe that

$$2^{2n}=(1+1)^{2n}=\binom{2n}{0}+\binom{2n}{1}+\cdots+\binom{2n}{n}+\cdots+\binom{2n}{2n}>\binom{2n}{n}$$

whilst

$$\binom{2n}{n}=\frac{2n(2n-1)\cdots(n+1)}{n(n-1)\cdots 1}\geqslant 2^n.$$

Consequently, taking logs in (i), we have

$$(\pi(2n)-\pi(n))\log n\leqslant\log\binom{2n}{n}\leqslant\pi(2n)\log 2n.$$

It follows that $(\pi(2n)-\pi(n))\log n\leqslant\log 2^{2n}=2n\log 2$ whilst $n\log 2=\log 2^n\leqslant\pi(2n)\log 2n$ as claimed. $\square$

We can now give the

Proof of Theorem 2.4.4 Let x be any real number $\geqslant 2$ and let $2n$ be the greatest *even* integer not greater than x (so that $n\geqslant 1$). By Corollary 2.4.6(ii) (b):

$$\pi(x)\geqslant\pi(2n)\geqslant\frac{n\log 2}{\log 2n}=\frac{4n\log 2}{4\log 2n}\geqslant\frac{(2n+2)\log 2}{4\log 2n}>\frac{x\log 2}{4\log x}.$$

To prove the other inequality, first let y be any real number ≥ 4 and let $2n$ be the *least* even integer not less than y (so that $n \geq 2$, whence $n/2 \geq 1$). We then have

$$2n-2 < y \leq 2n \text{ so that } \pi(y/2) \geq \pi(n-1) \geq \pi(n)-1.$$

By Corollary 2.4.6(ii)(a)

$$\begin{aligned}\pi(y)-\pi(y/2) \leq \pi(2n)-\{\pi(n)-1\} &\leq \frac{2n \log 2}{\log n}+1 < \frac{(y+2)\log 2}{\log (y/2)}+1\\ &= \frac{2(y+2)\log 2}{\log (y^2/4)}+1\\ &\leq \frac{3y \log 2}{\log y}+1 \text{ (since } y \geq 4) \leq \frac{(7/2)y \log 2}{\log y},\end{aligned}$$

as is easily checked. Consequently

$$\begin{aligned}\pi(y)\log y-\pi(y/2)\log (y/2) &= \{\pi(y)-\pi(y/2)\}\log y+\pi(y/2)\log 2\\ &\leq (7/2)y \log 2+(y/2)\log 2 = 4y \log 2\end{aligned} \qquad (*)$$

Now let x be any real number ≥ 4 and write $2^{j+2} \leq x < 2^{j+3}$, where j is a non-negative integer. From $(*)$, we have, since $x/2^j \geq 4$,

$$\begin{aligned}
&\pi(x)\log x &&-\pi(x/2)\log (x/2) &&\leq 4x \log 2\\
&\pi(x/2)\log (x/2) &&-\pi(x/4)\log (x/4) &&\leq 4(x/2)\log 2\\
&\quad\vdots && \quad\vdots && \quad\vdots\\
&\pi(x/2^j)\log (x/2^j) &&-\pi(x/2^{j+1})\log (x/2^{j+1}) &&\leq 4(x/2^j)\log 2.
\end{aligned}$$

Adding we get $\pi(x)\log x-\pi(x/2^{j+1})\log (x/2^{j+1}) < 8x \log 2$. Consequently

$$\begin{aligned}\pi(x)\log x &< 8x \log 2+\pi(x/2^{j+1})\log (x/2^{j+1})\\ &\leq 8x \log 2+2\log 4 = (8x+4)\log 2 \leq 9x \log 2\end{aligned}$$

(since $x \geq 4$), an equality which is true for $2 \leq x \leq 4$ by inspection.

We have thus shown that for, $x \geq 2$, $\dfrac{\log 2}{4}\dfrac{x}{\log x} < \pi(x) < 9\log 2 \cdot \dfrac{x}{\log x}$ □

Exercises 2.4

1(i) Prove that the highest power p^α of the prime p dividing $n!$ is given by $\alpha = [n/p]+[n/p^2]+\cdots+[n/p^k]$, where $p^k | n$ and $p^{k+1} \nmid n$. Find the number of zeros at the end of 100!

(ii) Prove that for positive integers a, b we have $0 \leq \left[\dfrac{2a}{b}\right]-2\left[\dfrac{a}{b}\right] \leq 1$.

2 Use Theorem 2.4.4 to show, that, for each real $x \geq 2$, and for each $\varepsilon > 0$,

$$\frac{\pi(x(1+\varepsilon)) - \pi(x)}{x/\log x} > \frac{c(1+\varepsilon)}{1+F(\varepsilon, x)} - C,$$

where $F(\varepsilon, x) = \log(1+\varepsilon)/\log x$. Now suppose ε is such that $c(1+\varepsilon) - C = \delta > 0$. Show that, provided x is large enough,

$$\frac{c(1+\varepsilon)}{1+F(\varepsilon, x)} - C > \frac{\delta}{2}.$$

Deduce that, provided x is large enough, there is necessarily a prime between x and $x(1+\varepsilon)$.

3 Use Exercise 2 and the PNT to prove that for each $\varepsilon > 0$, there exists an integer $N(\varepsilon)$ such that for $x > N(\varepsilon)$ there is necessarily a prime lying between x and $x(1+\varepsilon)$. Deduce, in particular that, provided n is large enough, $p_{n+1} < (1+\varepsilon)p_n$, p_n being the nth prime.

4 Let $c = (\log 2)/4$ and $C = 9 \log 2$, as in Theorem 2.4.4. Show that, in this case, the ε of Exercise 2 must be chosen to be >35. Deduce that, provided x is large enough, there is necessarily a prime between x and $36x$(!) [For substantial improvements see Section 2.5.]

5 Use the PNT to show that if r is any positive real number then a sequence of primes $p(n)$ $(n = 1, 2, 3, \ldots)$ can be found for which $\lim_{n\to\infty} p(n)/n = r$.

6 Show that for each positive integer n there exists an integer N which is expressible as a sum of two odd primes in at least n distinct ways. [*Hint*: For x large enough $\log x < x^{1/4}$. Hence $\pi(x) > cx^{3/4}$. Put $\pi(x) = t+1$. Thus the t (odd) primes $\leq x$ can be combined into at least $t(t+1)/2$ sums—each no greater than $2x$. Spreading these $t(t+1)/2$ sums over the even integers in the range $[4, 2x]$ it appears that at least one such integer* must be represented as a sum in at least $t(t+1)/2x$ ways. Since c is fixed and $t+1 > cx^{3/4}$, it is easy to choose x big enough to make $t(t+1)/2x > n$.]

Computer problems 2.4

1 Using Program 2.3, check the values of the functions $\pi(x)$ and $x/(\log x - 1)$ over various ranges of x. Modify program 2.3 to use the method, which ignores even numbers, suggested in the text. Compare the speed of the two programs as x increases.

2 Count prime pairs in intervals of size 1000 up to 10 000. How does the percentage in successive intervals change? Compare the number of pairs of twin primes less than x with the function $x/(\log x)^2$.

* This is a somewhat informal use of Dirichlet's pigeon-hole principle. See p. 107.

3 If $(a, b)=1$ then the set $\{an+b: n=1, 2\ldots\}$ contains an infinite number of primes (Theorem 2.2.2). By considering values of b between 1 and a such that $(a, b)=1$ what can you discover about the density of primes within each arithmetic progression?

2.5 Bertrand's conjecture

As well as proving Theorem 2.4.4 Tchebychef was able to resolve an intriguing conjecture posed 9 years earlier by the Frenchman J. Bertrand*, namely

Conjecture
Let $n \geqslant 2$ be an integer. Then there exists a prime p such that $n<p<2n$. (Bertrand himself checked this conjecture up to 3 000 000, not quite so arduous a task as you might at first imagine (the proof can be given in two lines)—though still fairly formidable at the time. In fact Tchebychef was able to show that, provided x is large enough, then there exists a prime between n and $(1+\frac{1}{5})n$. As Exercise 2.4.3 shows, the full PNT enables one to do even better.)

In proving the conjecture we use the following very interesting result.

Theorem 2.5.1 Let $n \geqslant 2$ be an integer. Then $\prod_{p \leqslant n} p<4^n$, where p signifies a prime.

Proof The result is clearly true for $n=2$ and 3. Clearly, if we prove it for $n=2m-1$, an odd integer, then it is trivially also true for $n=2m$. So suppose the theorem proved for all odd $n \leqslant 2t-1$ and suppose $n=2t+1$.

Clearly $\dfrac{(2t+1)!}{t!(t+1)!}$ is divisible by each prime p such that $t+2 \leqslant p \leqslant 2t+1$. Also, from

$$2^{2t+1}=(1+1)^{2t+1}=\binom{2t+1}{0}+\cdots+\binom{2t+1}{t}+\binom{2t+1}{t+1}+\cdots+\binom{2t+1}{2t+1}$$

we deduce that

$$\binom{2t+1}{t}=\binom{2t+1}{t+1}<(1/2)\cdot 2^{2t+1}.$$

Consequently

$$\prod_{p \leqslant 2t+1} p \leqslant \binom{2t+1}{t} \prod_{p \leqslant t+1} p<2^{2t}\cdot 4^{t+1}=4^{2t+1}$$

as required. □

* Joseph Louis Francois Bertand, 11 March 1822 – 5 April 1900.

Next we need another result on binomial coefficients, namely

Lemma 2.5.2 Let $n \geqslant 4$ be an integer and let p be a prime such that $\frac{2}{3}n < p \leqslant n$. then $p \nmid \binom{2n}{n}$.

Proof

(i) Since $2n < 3p$ we see that p and $2p$ are the only multiples of p less than or equal to $2n$.

(ii) Since $n \geqslant 4$, $p > \frac{8}{3} > 2$. Hence $p^2 | (2n)!$ and $p^3 \nmid (2n)!$

(iii) Since $p \leqslant n$ we have $p^2 | (n!)^2$.

Hence $p \nmid \binom{2n}{n}$. □

We now give the

Proof of Bertrand's conjecture The conjecture is valid for $n = 2$ and 3. Suppose it is false for some $n \geqslant 4$. Using the notation of Theorem 2.4.5 we can write

$$\binom{2n}{n} \Bigg| \prod_{p \leqslant 2n} p^{\alpha_p}, \qquad \text{where } p^{\alpha_p} \leqslant 2n < p^{\alpha_p + 1} \tag{$*$}$$

Thus, if $\alpha_p \geqslant 2$, we conclude that $p \leqslant \sqrt{2n}$, so that at most $[\sqrt{2n}]$ of the primes in $(*)$ have exponent 2 or more. Furthermore, by Lemma 2.4.2 and our supposition, $\binom{2n}{n}$ has no prime factor greater than $2n/3$. This implies that

$$\binom{2n}{n} \leqslant \prod_{p \leqslant \sqrt{2n}} p^{\alpha_p} \cdot \prod_{q \leqslant 2n/3} q. \tag{$**$}$$

On the other hand, by the by now customary kind of argument,

$$4^n = (1+1)^{2n} < (2n+1)\binom{2n}{n} \tag{$***$}$$

From $(**)$ and $(***)$ we deduce that, for $n \geqslant 4$,

$$\begin{aligned} 4^n < (2n+1)\binom{2n}{n} < 4n^2\binom{2n}{n} &\leqslant 4n^2 \prod_{p \leqslant \sqrt{2n}} p^{\alpha_p} \prod_{q \leqslant 2n/3} q \\ &\leqslant 4n^2 \cdot (2n)^{[\sqrt{2n}]} \cdot 4^{2n/3}. \end{aligned}$$

Consequently,

$$4^{n/3} \leqslant 4n^2 \cdot (2n)^{[\sqrt{2n}]} \leqslant (2n)^{\sqrt{2n}+2}.$$

But this inequality is false for all $n \geq 507$ (take logarithms!). To check Bertrand's conjecture is valid up to that point it suffices to list the following sequence of primes: [Can you see why?] 3, 5, 7, 13, 23, 43, 83, 163, 317, 631* □

Because of the relative ease with which Bertrand's conjecture was established it is interesting that the following problem remains unsolved: Is there for each sufficiently large integer n a prime lying between n^2 and $(n+1)^2$? (For n^3 and $(n+1)^3$ the answer is known to be positive! [H]).

Exercises 2.5

1 Use Bertrand's conjecture to show that $p_n \leq 2^n$, p_n being the nth prime. (C.f. Exercise 1.3.1.)

2 Use Bertrand's conjecture to prove that: (i) for $n > 1$ and $t > 1$ the equation $x^t = n!$ has no solution in $\mathbb{Z}$; (ii) if $x, y, m, n \in \mathbb{Z}^+$ and if $(x!)^m = (y!)^n$ then $x = y$ and $m = n$; (iii) for no positive integer n is $1/2 + 1/3 + \cdots + 1/n$ an integer.

Can you prove (iii)—or (ii) for that matter—without† using Bertrand?

3 Prove that, for each $n > 6$, n can be expressed as a sum of (one or more) distinct primes. [*Hint*: show that each x with $7 \leq x \leq 19$ can be so expressed using no prime greater than 11 and then that each x with $20 \leq x \leq 32$ can be so expressed using no prime greater than 13. Try to continue in this way, introducing primes 17, 19, 23, etc and using Bertrand's conjecture.]

4. Use Bertrand's conjecture to prove *Bonse's inequality*: For $n \geq 5$, $p_n^2 < p_1 p_2 \cdots p_{n-1}$. Deduce that 24 is the largest integer which is divisible by all integers not exceeding its square root.

5 Show that $\prod_{N<p\leq 2N}^{p} p < 4^N$. $\left(\textit{Hint}: \text{Use } \prod_{N<p\leq 2N} p \leq \binom{2N}{N}.\right)$

Computer problems 2.5

1 Legendre conjectured that for n sufficiently large there is always a prime between n and $n + \sqrt{n}$. Investigate how large N must be for this to appear to hold for all $n \geq N$.

2 Use Bonse's inequality (above) to prove that 30 is the largest integer N such that: if $(N, n) = 1$ and if $1 < n < N$, then n is prime. (Use theory to show that such an N exists. Then, if necessary, tidy up using the computer.)

* 509 would suffice here, but if you continue far enough (i.e. up to 6 000 000) in this way you will have Bertrand's proof! The difficulty comes, of course, in finding the last few primes in the list.
† (ii) appears to be hard if use of Bertrand's conjecture is forbidden.

Marin Mersenne *(8 September 1588–1 September 1648)*
Born in Oize, Maine, France, Mersenne entered the Jesuit college at La Flèche in 1604. He remained there until 1609 before studying theology at the Sorbonne. In 1611 he joined the Order of Minims, moving, in 1619, to the Minim convent in Paris where he remained—except for brief excursions—for the rest of his life.

From the point of view of science, Mersenne's main accomplishment was his taking on the role of 'scientific information centre', corresponding with many of the intellectuals of the day and holding meetings in his quarters. At one such gathering, in 1647, Pascal first met Descartes. Some 18 years after his death this 'academy' had become the Académie des Sciences.

Mersenne's theological stance encouraged belief that only God knew *for certain* how or why things happened: man could only answer enquiry by experiment. For mortals absolute certainty about the world was not possible. After initial articles of theological content, Mersenne chose as his domain of (experimental) enquiry questions relating to vision and (musical) sound. His first work on vibrating strings was done c1623; in a work of 1647 he summarised his contributions. In particular, he observed that the intensity of sound is inversely proportional to the distance from the source and that the velocity of sound is independent of pitch and loudness. He was also the first—before Galileo—to discover that the frequency of swing of a pendulum is inversely proportional to the square root of its length.

On his death a friend described him as 'A man of simple innocence with a pure heart and without guile.'

2.6 Mersenne's and Fermat's primes

Finally, returning to sequences, we come to what are probably the two most famous (special) sequences as far as questions concerning the primes which appear amongst them are concerned. As we have intimated earlier, philosophers of the early Christian and pre-Christian eras were much concerned with the mystical and religious significance of the positive integers. Particular attention was paid to the so-called *perfect numbers* (see the exercises below) such as 6 and 28, each of which, as indicated previously, is equal to the sum of its proper divisors. The perfection of The Creation was 'proved' by observing that God took just 6 days to create Heaven and Earth and that the Moon circles the Earth in 28*.

In fact Euclid had previously proved (Elements, Book 9) that if $p=1+2+2^2+\cdots+2^{k-1}=2^k-1$ is a prime, then $2^{k-1}\cdot p$ is a perfect number (Exercise 2.6.1).

Thus interest was aroused early on in primes of the form 2^k-1. Now it is not difficult to check (cf. Exercise 1.1.5) that if 2^k-1 is prime then k itself must be prime. The converse is, however, not true, the number $2^{11}-1=2047=$

* The fact that the first author lives at a house numbered 6 whilst his parents live at one numbered 28 offers more substantial evidence, of course!

23·89 providing the smallest counterexample—first noted as late as 1536. By 1588 Cataldi was able to show that $2^{13}-1$, $2^{17}-1$ and $2^{19}-1$ are all primes simply by trying each prime divisor less than their respective square roots. He went on to assert that 2^k-1 is also prime when $k=23$, 29, 31 and 37. The first and last of these assertions were dismissed around 1640 by Pierre de Fermat (see Application 3.2.5(i)) when he proved both $2^{23}-1$ and $2^{37}-1$ to be composite. (If you want to see these and similar numbers in decimal form use Program 2.4 below.)

In 1644 a Franciscan friar, Father Marin Mersenne (opposite) who ran a kind of mathematical information service, corresponding with many of the important mathematicians of his day, made the amazing assertion that, for $p \leqslant 257$, 2^p-1 is prime when—and only when—$p=2$, 3, 5, 7, 13, 17, 19, 31, 67, 127 and 257. (Because of this the number 2^n-1 is nowadays denoted by M_n and is referred to as the *nth Mersenne number*.)

In 1732 Euler showed that M_{29} is composite and in 1772 he confirmed Cataldi's and Mersenne's statement concerning M_{31} (see Section 3.2). Cataldi's $2^{19}-1$ had stood as the largest known prime for about 200 years.

A burst of pessimism followed, in 1811, when Barlow* asserted that 'M_{31} is the greatest [prime] that will ever be found.' 'Eternity' was reached some 65 years later when the French mathematician Edouard Lucas showed that

$$M_{127}=170\,141\,183\,460\,469\,231\,731\,687\,303\,715\,884\,105\,727$$

is a prime whilst Mersenne's M_{67} is, in fact, composite. Within 11 years M_{61} had joined Mersenne's list as had M_{89} and M_{107} by 1914.

A lovely story concerning M_{67} is described by Eric Temple Bell† in [15]. First we note the apparently curious fact that, although Lucas had genuinely proved M_{67} to be composite, no-one actually knew any of its proper factors! (How could this be? See Theorem 9.6.1.) At the October, 1903, meeting of the American Mathematical Society Professor F. N. Cole‡ was to give a talk 'On the factorisation of large numbers'. Cole's 'talk' proceeded by his calculating $2^{67}-1$, longhand, on one half of a blackboard and by evaluating, longhand, on the other half the product $193\,707\,721 \times 761\,838\,257\,287$. The resulting numbers were equal! Cole resumed his seat to prolonged applause having said . . . nothing! Bell says Cole told him, later, that the calculation had taken him 'Three years of Sundays'. Nowadays, such a computation, on a fairly standard mainframe computer, may take in the order of 1/10 of a second!

M_{127} remained the largest number known to be prime for 75 years with Ferrier's $(2^{148}+1)/17$ just squeezing in as the largest prime found 'by hand' before R. Robinson (and computer) in 1952 showed that M_{521}, M_{607}, M_{1279}, M_{2203}, M_{2281} (the latter being a number of 687 digits) are all primes. (Mersenne's assertions had been cleared up by 1947. Of the 55 primes less

* Peter Barlow, October 1766 - 1 March 1862.

† Eric Temple Bell, 7 February 1883 - 21 December 1960.

‡ Frank Nelson Cole, 20 September 1861 - 26 May 1926.

than 258 he had made a mistake with only five, incorrectly including M_{67} and M_{257} and excluding M_{61}, M_{89}, and M_{107}.)

Table 2.3 Mersenne primes currently known.*

p	Number of digits	Discoverer	Date
2	1	Known to Euclid	
3	1	Known to Euclid	
5	2	Known to Euclid	
7	3	Known to Euclid	
13	4	Unknown	1456
17	6	Cataldi	1588
19	6	Cataldi	
31	10	L. Euler	1772
61	19	I. M. Pervouchine	1883
89	27	R. E. Powers	1911
107	33	R. E. Powers and E. Fauquemberg	1914
127	39	E. Lucas	1876
521	157	R. Robinson (SWAC computer)	1952
607	183	R. Robinson (SWAC computer)	
1 279	386	R. Robinson (SWAC computer)	
2 203	664	R. Robinson (SWAC computer)	
2 281	687	R. Robinson (SWAC computer)	
3 217	969	H. Riesel (BESK computer)	1957
4 253	1 281	A. Hurwitz (IBM-7090)	1961
4 423	1 332	A. Hurwitz (IBM-7090)	1961
9 689	2 917	D. Gillies (ILLIAC II)	1963
9 941	2 993	D. Gillies (ILLIAC II)	
11 213	3 376	D. Gillies (ILLIAC II)	
19 937	6 002	B. Tuckerman (IBM 360-91)	1971
21 701	6 533	L. Nickel & C. Noll (CDC-CYBER-174)	1978†
23 209	6 987	C. Noll (CDC-CYBER-174)	1979
44 497	13 395	H. Nelson & D. Slowinski (CRAY-1)	1979
86 243	25 962	D. Slowinski (CRAY-1)	1982
132 049	39 751	D. Slowinski (CRAY-IMP)	1983
216 091	65 050	D. Slowinski (CRAY-XMP)	1985

* Since compiling this table Colquitt and Welch have found another $2^{110\,503}-1$.
† Laura Nickel and Curt Noll were aged 18 at the time of their record-breaking discovery!

One final note. Whilst the above makes it obvious that we do not know of infinitely many M_p which are prime, we do not even know if there are infinitely many still to be found. Accordingly it is even more curious that, amongst those M_p, it is not known if infinitely many are composite!

Just as famous as Mersenne's primes are those of Fermat. His amazing ability at spotting universal relationships between numbers and solutions to particular problems was matched only by his apparent unwillingness to give any detailed indication of his methods of procedure. Many results he states, often in letters to friends, with confidence but no proof. One place where his initial assertions later gave way to doubts involves his claim that each number $F_n = 2^{2^n} + 1$, where n is any non-negative integer, is a prime* Indeed $F_0 = 3$,

* For $2^k + 1$ to be prime it is necessary for k to be a power, 2^n, of 2 (Exercise 1.1.6).

$F_1=5$, $F_2=17$, $F_3=257$, $F_4=65\,537$, are all primes: but Fermat couldn't confirm $F_5=2^{32}+1=4\,294\,967\,297$ nor any larger F_n to be prime. For F_5 this is not too surprising since, in 1732, Euler showed that F_5 is *not* prime—indeed it is divisible by 641 (!). Now Euler spent many hours involved in mathematical computations but he certainly wasn't going to spend time dividing F_5 by 3, 5, 7, 11, . . . and all the primes up to $\sqrt{F_5}$. In fact the first number he tried as a possible divisor of F_5 was . . . 193(!); and 641 was his fifth choice! So Euler must have shown F_5 is not prime in less than 10 minutes! The message here is, once again, that these mathematicians didn't just charge headlong into unthinking calculations; they often first, or simultaneously, constructed a theory to lighten their load. Some of their ideas and those of their successors are the subject matter of the rest of this book.

As regards later F_n, no prime F_n has been found. Indeed F_n is known to be composite for all n such that $5 \leqslant n \leqslant 21$ as well as for some larger n. Hardy and Wright [16] have even offered a plausible argument suggesting only finitely many of the remaining F_n are prime.

As n increases the Fermat and Mersenne numbers obviously soon exceed the largest number that a computer can accurately hold. (On the second author's BBC Micro F_5 and M_{31} are the first offenders). To work with these larger numbers we need to use an array in which the *digits that make up the number* are stored. This can be done as follows for Mersenne numbers M_n.

Program 2.4 *Program to produce the decimal representations of Mersenne numbers*

```
 10 INPUT N
 70 DIM F(100)
 80 F(1)=1
 90 NF=1
100 FOR I=1 TO N
110    FOR J=1 TO NF
120       F(J)=F(J)*2
125    NEXT J
126    FOR J=1 TO NF
130       F(J+1)=F(J+1) + F(J) DIV 10
140       F(J)=F(J) MOD 10
150    NEXT J
160    IF F(NF+1)<>0 NF=NF+1
200 NEXT I
210 F(1)=F(1)-1
```

To display the numbers the array is printed out in reverse order since the first position in the array contains the units etc.

```
220 FOR K=NF TO 1 STEP -1
230 PRINT;F(K);
240 NEXT K
```

To generate the Fermat numbers F_n we need to use

```
20 P=1
30 FOR I=1 TO N
40 P=P*2
50 NEXT I
```

and replace the N in line 100 by P. We also need to add 1 in line 210 rather than subtract it.

Exercises 2.6

1 Prove that if $2^p - 1$ is a prime then $n = 2^{p-1}(2^p - 1)$ is perfect. (Later—Theorem 10.2.7—we shall prove that every *even* perfect number is of this kind. Show that this implies that each even perfect number ends in a 6 or an 8 (indeed 28).)

2 Robert Recorde* claimed 130 816 is a perfect number. Prove him wrong. $[130\,816 = 2^8(2^9 - 1)]$

3 (J. Broscius 1652) Show that each perfect number is of the form $1 + 2 + \cdots + k$ for suitable $k \in \mathbb{Z}$.

For each positive integer n let $\sigma(n)$ denote the sum of all the positive divisors of n including n itself. Then n is called *abundant* or *deficient* according as $\sigma(n) > 2n$ or $\sigma(n) < 2n$ (and *perfect* if $\sigma(n) = 2n$).

4 Check the numbers from 2 to 50 for abundancy or deficiency. Prove that each proper multiple of a perfect or abundant number is abundant and every proper divisor of a perfect number is deficient (Jordanus c. 1200). (Surely these assertions raise a few questions in your minds?)

5 Prove that, with one exception, the product pq of two primes is deficient (Bachet†, c. 1620).

The pair m, n of integers is an *amicable pair*‡ if $\sigma(m) = m + n = \sigma(n)$.

6 Show that 220 and 284 form an amicable pair. Show (Thabit ben Korrah 9th Century) that $2^n pq$ and $2^n r$ form an amicable pair if $p = 3 \cdot 2^n - 1$, $q = 3 \cdot 2^{n-1} - 1$, $r = 9 \cdot 2^{2n-1} - 1$ are odd primes. (Fermat found a second pair—put $n = 4$ in Thabit's formula—and Euler found some 60 more. In 1866 the 16-year-old Nicolo Paganini found a pair, both less than 1500, which Euler had missed. Computer problem 2.6.4 invites you to find this pair. Paganini didn't reveal his method. Whether or not there are infinitely many amicable pairs is unknown although it has recently been proved that $\sum (1/m)$ is convergent if m runs over all members of amicable pairs—see [5], p. 31—and note a similar result for prime pairs in Section 2.3.)

7 Mersenne asserted that $2^p - 1$ will be prime if p is a prime of the form $2^{2^n} + a$, where $a = 1$ or 3. Prove him wrong.

8 Prove that, for $n \in \mathbb{Z}$ and $n \geq 2$, $2^n - 1$ is never a perfect square. (It is not known if $2^p - 1$, where p is prime, is square free. (Guy [5] reports D. H. Lehmer

* Robert Recorde, c. 1510 - 1588.

† Claude Gaspar Bachet de Meziriac, 9 October 1581 - 26 February 1638.

‡ Dickson [1] reports that in 1000 A.D. an Arabic writer related how he had 'tested the erotic(!) effect' of giving someone the number 220 to eat whilst he himself ate the larger number 284 (!) This appears to substantiate our warning at the head of Exercises 0.1.

as saying that anyone lucky enough might just solve this problem so that, maybe, 'happiness is just around the corner'.)

9 Prove that (i) if $m<n$ then $(2^{2^m}+1, 2^{2^n}+1)=1$ [*Hint*: if $a^{2^m}=\alpha d-1$ then $a^{2^n}=\beta d+1$.)
(ii) $(2^a-1, 2^b-1)=2^{(a,b)}-1$. [*Hint*: From $a=mb+r$ deduce that $2^a-1=M(2^b-1)+(2^r-1)$ for suitable $M\in\mathbb{Z}$.]
Deduce the infinitude of primes in $\mathbb{Z}$ both from (i) and from (ii).

10 For each of the following sequences find the least n for which the nth term is composite.
(i) $\{2^{2^n}+3\}$; (ii) $\{2^{2^n}+5\}$; (iii) $\{2^{2^n}+7\}$, where $n\in\mathbb{Z}^+$.

11 Show that, for each $k\geqslant 0$, $F_{k+1}=F_1F_2\cdots F_k+2$.

Computer problems 2.6

1 Print out $2^{23}-1$ and $2^{37}-1$ on the computer. Can you see obvious factors? [If not, marvel at Fermat's achievement!]

2 Many early authors repeated without proof the assertions:

(i) there exists one perfect number between 10^n and 10^{n+1} for each integer $n\geqslant 0$.
(ii) perfect numbers end alternately in 6 and 8.
Show that both are wrong!

3 Find all the abundants $\leqslant 500$. Charles de Bouvelles (c. 1509) claimed that not all abundant numbers are even by citing 45 045. Since he also believed 511 to be prime you'd better check he is right. Is there a smaller odd abundant number?

4 Find the pair of amicable numbers ($\leqslant 1500$) discovered by Paganini.

5 Find all amicable pairs a, b with $a<b$ and $a<6233$. [This was achieved by Dickson in 1913.]

6 Thomas Taylor (1823) called numbers m, n *imperfectly amicable* if the sums of the proper divisors of m and n are equal, that is if $\sigma(m)-m=\sigma(n)-n$.

Find as many pairs of such numbers as you can. Would you suspect the existence of infinitely many such pairs? (cf. the bracketed remarks of Exercise 2.6.6.) [*Hint*: Exercise 2.4.6 might help.]

3

Congruences

3.1 Basic properties

Faced with the problem of showing that $2^{2^5}+1$ is divisible by 641, most of us (if no calculators were available) would take a deep breath, get on with it, by long division, and end up showing that

$$2^{2^5}+1=4\,294\,967\,297=641\times 6\,700\,417.$$

Faced with the problem of showing that 341 is a factor of $2^{340}-1$ (and thus refuting the 'Chinese' assertion mentioned at the start of Chapter 2) most of us would probably just give up, unless we thought of using an idea which was employed by some 17th and 18th century mathematicians—and, indeed, by some over 2000 years earlier—and which was put into workable form by Carl Friedrich Gauss in his influential book *Disquisitiones Arithmeticae* ([17] 1801). The idea, that of employing a kind of 'arithmetic of remainders', was formalised by Gauss as follows:

Definition 3.1.1 Let n be an integer. Integers x and y are *congruent for the modulus* n (briefly, *congruent modulo* n) if and only if their difference $x-y$ is divisible by n. We write this as $x\equiv y \pmod n$. Otherwise x and y are *incongruent modulo* n, written $x\not\equiv y \pmod n$.

The following examples are trivial; less obvious ones will arise as we develop the theory.

Examples 3.1.2 $8\equiv 22 \pmod 7$; $7\equiv -5 \pmod 4$; $-112\not\equiv -72 \pmod{12}$; $78\equiv 0 \pmod 6$.

Notes 3.1.3

(i) It is easily seen that $x\equiv y \pmod n$ iff x, y leave the same remainder r (where $0\leqslant r<n$) on division by n. (Assuming $n\neq 0$. See Exercise 3.1.3(i).)

(ii) In Definition 3.1.1 we could allow n to be negative. But since each integer divisible by $-n$ is also divisible by n—and because of the triviality of the cases $n=0$ and $n=1$ (see Exercise 3.1.3)—we shall assume from now on that $n\geqslant 2$.

(iii) If, using the division algorithm, we write $a=mb+r$, where $0\leqslant r<|b|$, we see that $a\equiv r \pmod b$. In particular, $b|a$ when and only when $a\equiv 0 \pmod b$. This indicates how congruences can be useful in checking if one integer is divisible exactly by another (see Example 3.1.8(iii), (iv) below). Indeed problems concerning division—in some ways the most unpleasant of the four arithmetical operations in $\mathbb{Z}$—can be solved, using congruences, without employing a single division!

Before being able to expand on our opening remarks, we shall make some easy deductions from Definition 3.1.1.

Proposition 3.1.4 Let n, a, b, c be integers. Then (i) $a \equiv a \pmod{n}$; (ii) if $a \equiv b \pmod{n}$ then $b \equiv a \pmod{n}$; (iii) if $a \equiv b \pmod{n}$ and $b \equiv c \pmod{n}$ then $a \equiv c \pmod{n}$.

Proof of (iii) The congruence $a \equiv b \pmod{n}$ is equivalent to the assertion $n | a-b$. Likewise, from $b \equiv c \pmod{n}$ we may deduce that $n | b-c$. But then $n | (a-b)+(b-c)$, i.e. $n | a-c$. Translated into the language of congruences this says $a \equiv c \pmod{n}$, as claimed. □

We leave the proofs of (i) and (ii) as exercises.

The usefulness of the notion of congruence begins to emerge after we combine it with the operations of arithmetic. We have

Proposition 3.1.5 Let n, a, b, c, d, k be integers such that $a \equiv b \pmod{n}$ and $c \equiv d \pmod{n}$. Then (i) $a+c \equiv b+d \pmod{n}$; (ii) $a-c \equiv b-d \pmod{n}$; (iii) $ac \equiv bd \pmod{n}$; (iv) $a+k \equiv b+k \pmod{n}$; (v) $ka \equiv kb \pmod{n}$.

Proof
(i) From $a \equiv b \pmod{n}$ and $c \equiv d \pmod{n}$ we deduce that $n | a-b$, $n | c-d$ and then $n | (a-b)+(c-d)$. Consequently $n | (a+c)-(b+d)$; in other words $a+c \equiv b+d \pmod{n}$.
(iii) Using a slightly different approach: what we're given implies that $a = b+sn$ and $c = d+tn$ for suitable integers s and t. But then $ac = bd + n(sd+tb+nst)$. This tells us immediately that $n | ac-bd$, that is $ac \equiv bd \pmod{n}$. □

Note 3.1.6 These congruences generalise easily to the cases of many summands and factors. For example, if $a_i \equiv b_i \pmod{n}$ for each i, $1 \leqslant i \leqslant s$, then

$$\sum_{i=1}^{s} a_i \equiv \sum_{i=1}^{s} b_i \quad \text{and} \quad \prod_{i=1}^{s} a_i \equiv \prod_{i=1}^{s} b_i \pmod{n} \text{ etc.}$$

As important deductions from Proposition 3.1.5 we have, immediately,

Corollary 3.1.7 Let $a \equiv b \pmod{n}$. Then (i) for every positive integer t, $a^t \equiv b^t \pmod{n}$. (ii) More generally, if $f(x)$ is a polynomial with integer coefficients, then $f(a) \equiv f(b) \pmod{n}$. □

To illustrate the usefulness of these ideas, elementary though they be, we offer

Examples 3.1.8

(i) *Problem* Find the remainder r such that $0 \leqslant r < 13$ when 99^{99} is divided by 13.

Solution $99 \equiv 8 (\mathrm{mod}\ 13)$. Therefore $(99)^2 \equiv 8^2 \equiv -1 (\mathrm{mod}\ 13)$. It follows that $99^{99} = (99^2)^{49} \cdot 99 \equiv (-1)^{49} \cdot 8 \equiv -8 \equiv 5 (\mathrm{mod}\ 13)$. Thus $r = 5$.

(ii) *Problem* Find the remainder r such that $0 \leqslant r < 68$ when 3^{75} is divided by 68.

Solution Working modulo 68 we have: $3^1 \equiv 3$; $3^2 \equiv 9$; $3^4 \equiv 81 \equiv 13$; $3^8 \equiv 169 \equiv 33$; $3^{16} \equiv 33^2 \equiv 1089 \equiv 1$. Then $3^{75} = 3^{64} \cdot 3^8 \cdot 3^2 \cdot 3 \equiv 1 \cdot 33 \cdot 9 \cdot 3 \equiv 7$.

(Note the economy in thinking of 75 as $64+8+2+1$—i.e. as a sum of powers of 2. One doesn't need to undertake 74 successive multiplications by 3 reducing each time by 68.)

We now deal with the problems mentioned at the start of the chapter.

(iii) (Euler 1732) $641 | 2^{2^5}+1$. For, working modulo 641, we have: $640 = 5 \cdot 2^7 \equiv -1$. Then $5^4 \cdot 2^{28} \equiv (-1)^4 \equiv 1$. But $5^4 \equiv -16 = -(2^4)$.

Hence $-(2^{32}) \equiv 1$. This does it. (If nothing else the use of congruences makes Euler's claim easier to check than it would be by long division. However, before the reader thinks that congruences will solve all our problems very easily he should note that the congruence concept only helped to *verify* Euler's claim, it did not *suggest* that 641 would be a good number to try.)

(iv) $341 | 2^{340}-1$. We first note that $2^{10}-1 = 1023 = 3 \cdot 11 \cdot 31$. Thus $2^{10} \equiv 1 (\mathrm{mod}\ 11)$ and $2^{10} \equiv 1 (\mathrm{mod}\ 31)$. It follows that $(2^{10})^{34} \equiv 1 (\mathrm{mod}\ 11)$ and $(2^{10})^{34} \equiv 1 (\mathrm{mod}\ 31)$. This means that 11 and 31 each divide $2^{340}-1$. But then, since $(11, 31) = 1$, so does their product 341 (Exercise 1.5.13(v)).

(v) Congruences can also be useful in problems of the following kind: Does either of the equations $x^2 - 15y^2 + z^2 = 7$ and $y^2 = x^3 + 7$ have a solution in integers x, y, z? We shall not consider these now but leave them for you to ponder until later.

Note 3.1.9 These examples confirm that congruence arithmetic is remarkably like ordinary arithmetic. Indeed it was this similarity which led Gauss to introduce the notation $\equiv$.

To calculate $b (0 \leqslant b < n)$ such that $a^m \equiv b (\mathrm{mod}\ n)$ is a simple matter using a computer. By reducing modulo n after every multiplication we are always working with numbers between 0 and n^2. This allows us to handle much larger numbers than would be possible if we calculated a^m *before* reducing modulo n.

Program 3.1 *Determination of b such that* $a^m = b \bmod n$

```
10 INPUT "Enter the values of a,m and n ",a,m,n
20 PRINT a;"^";m;" is congruent to ";
30 b = 1
40 x = a - INT(a/n) * n
```

```
 50 FOR i=1 TO m
 60    b = b * x
 70    b = b - INT(b/n) * n
 80 NEXT
 90 PRINT ;b;" modulo ";n
100 END
```

In Program 3.1 the multiplication operation is repeated m times.

As suggested in Example 3.1.8(ii) the program can be greatly improved by using the binary representation of the power. Using a variation of that method, but one that is just as efficient, we can for example calculate x^{13} using only five multiplications, calculating the partial results x, x^2, x^3, x^6, x^{12} and x^{13}. In general we express the power in its binary form, e.g. $13 = 1101$, square and multiply by x for each 1 (ignoring the first) and simply square for each 0. Thus to calculate x^{13} we use the sequence of operations SMSSM. From a programming point of view it is simpler to work in reverse since then we do not have to convert the decimal number to a binary sequence in advance. We proceed as follows:

(1) set $b = 1$
(2) set $m = m/2$
(3) If m is not an integer multiply b by x
(4) set $m = \mathrm{INT}(m)$
(5) If $m = 0$ stop—b contains the required result
(6) square x and go to (2)

This method was known in India before 200 B.C. but does not seem to have been referred to outside India until 952 A.D. (by al-Uglîdisî of Damascus). (If we replace the operation of multiplication by that of addition and we use 0 rather than 1 as a starting point, then the algorithm produces mx. The result is a method of multiplying two numbers using only the operations of halving, doubling and adding. It was used by the Egyptians as early as 1800 B.C. and by peasants in nineteenth century Russia. It is sometimes referred to as Russian multiplication.)

Returning to the problem of calculating $a^m \pmod n$ Program 3.2 uses the above squaring and multiplying technique and is, consequently faster than Program 3.1. (You may care to determine by how much.)

Program 3.2 *Determination of a^m mod n*

```
 10 INPUT "Enter the values of a,m and n ",a,m,n
 20 PRINT a;"^";m;" is congruent to ";
 30 b = 1
 40 x = a - INT(a/n)*n
 50 t = m/2
 60    IF t = INT(t) GOTO 80
 70       b = x*b -INT(b*x/n)*n
 80    m = INT(t)
 90    IF m = 0 GOTO 120
100       x = x*x - INT(x*x/n)*n
110 GOTO 50
120 PRINT ;b;" modulo ";n
```

Congruences also help us establish certain useful divisibility tests, 1500 years old or more, some of which may already be known to the reader. For example we pose the

Question
Is the number $N = 381\,752\,263\,715\,876\,513$ divisible by 9?

Solution
Since $3+8+1+7+5+2+2+6+3+7+1+5+8+7+6+5+1+3=80$ and since $9 \nmid 80$ we deduce that N is *not* divisible by 9.

Why does this work? Well, let N be any integer. Write N in the form $N = a_n \cdot 10^n + a_{n-1} \cdot 10^{n-1} + \cdots + a_1 \cdot 10 + a_0$, where the a_i belong to the set $\{0, 1, 2, 3, 4, 5, 6, 7, 8, 9\}$. Now, modulo 9, $10 \equiv 1$, $10^2 \equiv 1^2 = 1$, and generally $10^k \equiv 1$. Consequently $N \equiv a_n + a_{n-1} + \cdots + a_0$. It follows that $9 | N$ when and only when $a_n + a_{n-1} + \cdots + a_0 \equiv 0 (\text{mod } 9)$—which is the case when and only when $9 | a_n + a_{n-1} + \cdots + a_0$.

Note 3.1.10 This technique is known as the principle of *casting out nines.* Similar but generally unusable rules are available for each modulus. Those for division by 2, 4, 5, 10 are essentially trivial. That for division by 11 is similar to that for 9 (see Exercise 3.1.12).

Division on congruences

So far we have not confirmed that congruences obey the same laws for division as do the integers. The main reason for this omission is that, in general, *they don't.* That is, from $kx \equiv ky (\text{mod } n)$, $k \not\equiv 0$, one cannot, in general, infer that $x \equiv y (\text{mod } n)$. For example, $2 \times 8 \equiv 2 \times 2 (\text{mod } 4)$ and yet $8 \not\equiv 2 (\text{mod } 4)$.

Returning to the old notation illustrates the cause of the trouble—and suggests the remedy. From $n | k(x-y)$ we wish to infer that $n | x-y$. Clearly we can only be *certain* of this conclusion if no divisor of n can cancel out any divisor of k. That is, $n | x-y$ will follow from $n | k(x-y)$ provided we know that $(k, n) = 1$. More generally, suppose $(k, n) = d$ so that $k = \alpha d$, $n = \beta d$ with $(\alpha, \beta) = 1$ for suitable α, β (see Exercise 1.5.5). Then, from $n\gamma = k(x-y)$ we get $\beta\gamma = \alpha(x-y)$. Since $(\alpha, \beta) = 1$ we must deduce that $\beta | x-y$ (Exercise 1.5.13(iv)). We therefore have

Theorem 3.1.11 Let $kx \equiv ky (\text{mod } n)$ and let $d = (k, n)$. Then $x \equiv y (\text{mod } n/d)$. □

And, as an important consequence,

Corollary 3.1.12 Let $kx \equiv ky (\text{mod } p)$ where p is a prime and $p \nmid k$. Then $x \equiv y (\text{mod } p)$. □

Exercises 3.1

1 List, as economically as you can, 100 solutions—if any exist at all—of the congruences: (i) $3x \equiv 13 (\bmod 23)$; (ii) $4x \equiv 14 (\bmod 24)$; (iii) $5x \equiv 15 (\bmod 25)$.

2 (i) Show that $a \equiv b (\bmod n)$ iff a and b leave the same remainder (in the range 0 to $n-1$) on division by n.
(ii) Complete the proof of Proposition 3.1.4.

3 Show that: (i) $a \equiv b (\bmod 0)$ iff $a = b$; (ii) $a \equiv b (\bmod 1)$ for all $a, b \in \mathbb{Z}$.

4 Suppose that $a \equiv b (\bmod n)$. (i) Show that $(a, n) = (b, n)$. Deduce that a and n are coprime iff b and n are coprime. (ii) Show that if $m|n$ then $a \equiv b (\bmod m)$.

5 Show that if $a \equiv b (\bmod m)$, if $a \equiv b (\bmod n)$ and if $(m, n) = 1$, then $a \equiv b (\bmod mn)$.

6 (a) Show that if n is prime and if $a^2 \equiv b^2 (\bmod n)$, then $a \equiv \pm b (\bmod n)$. Show, by means of a counterexample, that this result no longer necessarily holds if n is composite.
(b) Is it true, given $a^2 \equiv b^2 (\bmod n)$ and $a^3 \equiv b^3 (\bmod n)$, that one may always deduce $a \equiv b (\bmod n)$?

7 Working modulo 10 show, for each $n \geq 2$, that $F_n = 2^{2^n} + 1$ ends in a 7.

8 Prove that for each odd positive integer a and for each $n \in \mathbb{Z}^+$, we have $a^{2^n} \equiv 1 (\bmod 2^{n+2})$.

9 Find the remainder r $(0 \leq r < 17)$ on dividing 13^{15} by 17.

10 Show that $2^{83} - 1$ is composite by showing it to be divisible by 167. [*Hint*: Write $2^{83} = 2^{64} \cdot 2^{16} \cdot 2^2 \cdot 2$ or use $83 = 1010011$ and the alternative method suggested after Program 3.1.]

11 Show that $3^{90} \equiv 1 (\bmod 91)$.

12 Show that the number $a_n 10^n + a_{n-1} 10^{n-1} + \cdots + a_1 10 + a_0$ is divisible by 11 iff $a_n - a_{n-1} + \cdots + (-1)^n a_0$ is divisible by 11. Is 1357 902 468 divisible by 11, or not?

13 Develop similar tests for division by 1001 and 111. Noting that $1001 = 7 \cdot 11 \cdot 13$ and that $111 = 3 \cdot 37$, devise tests for divisibility by 7, by 13 and by 37.

14 Without performing the division, test 17 418 609 for divisibility by 7, by 9, by 11, by 13, by 99, by 117.

15 Prove that $9|81\,725 - 52\,718$. Generalise this example as far as you can.

16 Apply 'casting out nines' to the following three numbers to confirm that the asserted equality is wrong: $67247 \times 9673 = 650\,470\,231$. Given that only the fifth digit in the product is wrong, correct it.

17 In 1659 Fermat asserted that no prime number of the form $3n-1$ can be expressed in the form x^2+3y^2. Prove him right. [*Hint*: show that $3n-1 \equiv x^2+3y^2 \pmod 3$ is impossible.]

18 Let n, α be integers $\geqslant 2$. Show that $n-1 \mid n^\alpha - 1$ but that $(n-1)^2 \nmid n^\alpha - 1$ if $\alpha \leqslant n-2$.

Computer problems 3.1

1 Write a program which, for a given value of n, produces a table of values of $a^m \pmod n$ for $1 \leqslant a < n$ and $1 < m < 20$. After examining the tables produced for $n < 15$ make a conjecture concerning those values of n for which there is an a such that each k $(1 \leqslant k < n)$ is congruent to some power of a.

2 Write a program which computes for each a $(1 < a < n)$, the smallest power a^m such that $a^m \equiv 1 \pmod n$ or else informs you that no such power exists. Trying various values of n (say all $n \leqslant 30$) see if you can discover any underlying pattern. Test any conjecture by trying further values of n.

3 Write a program to calculate $(n-1)! \pmod n$. Is there any pattern to the values of n which divide $(n-1)!$? Make a conjecture. Can you prove it?

4 Write an alternative version of Program 3.2 based on the method of Example 3.1.8(ii). (That is, (i) determine the binary expansion of m; (ii) calculate successive powers of x multiplying b by only those represented by a 1 in that expansion.)

5 Modify Program 3.2 to evaluate x^n and record the number of multiplications. For $100 \leqslant n \leqslant 1000$ work out the average number of operations in blocks of 100 and compare with the value of $\log n$.

6 Write a program which calculates x^n by factoring n into primes $n = q_1 q_2 \cdots q_k$ and then calculating $(\cdots((x^{q_1})^{q_2})\cdots)^{q_k}$. Is this method more efficient than those suggested above?

7 For each prime p (say $3 \leqslant p \leqslant 61$) find the first few terms of the Fibonacci sequence which are divisible by p. Do you see a pattern in these results? [Edouard Lucas* did and he used it to prove that $2^{127}-1$ is a prime. See Section 9.6.]

3.2 Fermat's little theorem (FLT)

The result, already noted as being 'known' to the ancient Chinese, that $p \mid 2^{p-1}-1$ whenever p is an odd prime, was (re)discovered by Fermat in 1640 whilst investigating perfect numbers. A few months later he stated in a letter to Frenicle†, the following generalisation: 'Every prime number measures (i.e.

* Francois-Edouard-Anatole Lucas, 1842 - 3 October 1891. He died shortly after being struck, accidentally, at a banquet, by a piece of broken pottery.
† Bernard Frenicle de Bessy, 1605(?) - 17 January 1675.

divides), infallibly, one of the powers minus unity, in any progression and the exponent of this power is a divisor of the given prime number minus one . . . '. In easier terms this becomes

---

Pierre de Fermat *(20 August 1601 - 12 January 1663)*
Fermat was born near Toulouse, his father being a prosperous leather merchant and his mother coming from a family of high social standing. It was therefore a fairly natural step for Fermat to pursue studies in law in which he obtained a degree from the University of Orleans in 1631. In May of that year he was appointed to a position in the high court in Toulouse and became entitled, as had been his mother, (nee Claire de Long) to include the 'de' in his name.

Most of what we know about Fermat comes from letters he wrote from 1636 onwards, the year he began corresponding with Mersenne and Roberval. Fluent in Italian, Spanish, Latin and Greek—he enjoyed writing poetry in Latin and Spanish—he persued mathematics as a hobby. (In *Men of Mathematics* Bell calls him the 'Prince of amateurs'.)

Serious mathematical study seems to have begun around 1629 when, along with several contemporaries, he became interested in reconstructing Apollonius's 'Plane loci', a lost work referred to by Pappus. The upshot was his 'discovery', independently of Descartes, of analytic geometry. He is also regarded as a co-founder, along with Pascal, of the theory of probability and his work on maxima and minima ($f''(a)<0$ for a maximum and $f''(a)>0$ for a minimum) encouraged Laplace to credit him with the discovery of the differential calculus. Out of his work on optics arose the principle now named after him.

The influence of most of Fermat's work on his contemporaries seems to have been slight and of that for which he is most famous, concerning number theory, just about non-existant. (It might have been greater if he had agreed to publish his findings but this aspect of communication he shunned.) However his influence on later generations, in particular in his insistence on seeking all *integer* solutions rather than just one possibly *rational* solution led to the 'rebirth', [26] p. 2, of modern number theory, Fermat being designated its 'father'.

For an extensive account of Fermat's (and Euler's) life and work see [26].

Theorem 3.2.1 (*Fermat's little theorem*) Let p be a prime and a any positive integer such that $p \nmid a$. Then $p | a^{p-1} - 1$. In Gauss's notation: $a^{p-1} \equiv 1 (\text{mod } p)$.

Whilst Fermat offered to send his correspondent a proof of Theorem 3.2.1, Leibniz had already written one down, before 1683, in a manuscript which came to light only after his death. The first of several proofs given by Euler appeared in 1736. Our proof follows Euler's first.

Proof of Theorem 3.2.1 (by induction on a). Actually we shall prove an equivalent version of the statement, namely: For *all* a, $a^p \equiv a (\text{mod } p)$. (See Exercise 3.2.1.)

In case $a = 1$ the result claimed is trivially true: $1^p \equiv 1 (\text{mod } p)$. So now suppose the result claimed is already known to be true for $a \leqslant n$ and take a to be $n+1$. By the binomial theorem $(n+1)^p = n^p + \binom{p}{1} n^{p-1} + \cdots + \binom{p}{p-1} n + 1$. Now by Exercise 1.8.2 each of the binomial coefficients—except the first and last—is a multiple of p. Consequently, working modulo p, we have

$$(n+1)^p \equiv n^p + 0 + 0 + \cdots + 0 + 1 \equiv n + 1$$

since $n^p \equiv n (\text{mod } p)$ by the induction hypothesis. But this establishes the validity of the statement of the theorem at step $n+1$ and so PMI tells us the result is valid for all a. □

As a very primitive first application of Theorem 3.2.1 we have:

Examples 3.2.2

(a) $3^{30} \equiv 1 (\text{mod } 31)$—by FLT. Hence $3^{330} \equiv 1^{11} \equiv 1 (\text{mod } 31)$. It follows that $3^{340} = 3^{330} \cdot 3^{10} \equiv 3^{10} \equiv 25 \not\equiv 1 (\text{mod } 31)$.

(b) Let a be any integer such that $(a, 561) = 1$. Then $3 \nmid a$, $11 \nmid a$, $17 \nmid a$. By FLT, $a^2 \equiv 1 (\text{mod } 3)$, $a^{10} \equiv 1 (\text{mod } 11)$, $a^{16} \equiv 1 (\text{mod } 17)$. Hence $a^{560} \equiv 1^{280} = 1 (\text{mod } 3)$; $a^{560} \equiv 1^{56} = 1 (\text{mod } 11)$; $a^{560} \equiv 1^{35} = 1 (\text{mod } 17)$. Since 3, 11, 17 are primes we see that $a^{560} \equiv 1 (\text{mod } 3 \cdot 11 \cdot 17)$, i.e. $a^{560} \equiv 1 (\text{mod } 561)$.

561 is what is called a *Carmichael number.* We shall look more closely at such numbers in Section 5.4.

Digging a bit deeper, FLT is very useful for demolishing a belief held for some time by Fermat himself, namely, that for each $n \in \mathbb{N}$, the number $F_n = 2^{2^n} + 1$ is a prime.

Indeed suppose that p is a prime dividing $2^{2^n} + 1$. Then $2^{2^n} \equiv -1 (\text{mod } p)$ and $2^{2^{n+1}} = (2^{2^n})^2 \equiv 1 (\text{mod } p)$. Let $d = (2^{n+1}, p-1) = \alpha \cdot 2^{n+1} + \beta(p-1)$ for suitable $\alpha, \beta \in \mathbb{Z}$ (using Theorem 1.6.2). Then

$$2^d = 2^{2^{n+1} \cdot \alpha + (p-1)\beta} = (2^{2^{n+1}})^\alpha \cdot (2^{p-1})^\beta \equiv 1^\alpha 1^\beta (\text{mod } p).$$

Since $d | 2^{n+1}$, $d = 2^\gamma$ for some γ such that $0 \leqslant \gamma \leqslant n+1$. Hence $2^{2^\gamma} \equiv 1 (\text{mod } p)$, whilst $2^{2^n} \not\equiv 1 (\text{mod } p)$. Since $(2^{2^t})^2 = 2^{2^{t+1}}$ for each integer t, we see that we cannot have $\gamma \leqslant n$. It follows that $\gamma = n+1$. Consequently, from $2^{n+1} = d$ and $d | p-1$ we have $p - 1 = k \cdot 2^{n+1}$ for some $k \in \mathbb{Z}^+$. We therefore have (where did we use the FLT?)

Theorem 3.2.3 Each prime factor of $F_n = 2^{2^n} + 1$ is of the form $2^{n+1}k + 1$ where $k \in \mathbb{Z}^+$. □

In particular, the prime divisor of $2^{2^5} + 1$ are all of the form $64k + 1$. The first five such primes are those not struck out in ~~65~~, ~~129~~, 193, 257, ~~321~~, ~~385~~, 449, ~~513~~, 577, 641, ... Thus Euler had to try only five *possible* prime divisors of F_5 before proving it composite.

It is very odd that Fermat missed this result since he had given, fairly early in his career, a test for finding factors of the Mersenne numbers $M_n = 2^n - 1$.

Theorem 3.2.4 (Fermat 1640) Let $r > 2$ be a prime. Each prime divisor of $M_r = 2^r - 1$ is of the form $2kr + 1$.

Proof Let p be a prime divisor of M_r. Then $p | 2^r - 1$, that is $2^r \equiv 1 (\text{mod } p)$. Also by Theorem 3.2.1, $2^{p-1} \equiv 1 (\text{mod } p)$.

Let $d = (r, p-1) = \alpha r + \beta(p-1)$ for suitable α, β in $\mathbb{Z}$. It follows that $2^d = (2^r)^\alpha (2^{p-1})^\beta \equiv 1^\alpha \cdot 1^\beta = 1 (\text{mod } p)$. Since M_r is odd we see that $p > 2$; since $p | 2^d - 1$ we infer that $d > 1$. Because r is a prime and $d > 1$ we have $r | p - 1$. Consequently $p - 1 = sr$ for some $s \in \mathbb{Z}^+$. Finally, $p - 1$ is even and r is odd. Hence s is even, $s = 2k$, say, as claimed. □

Applications 3.2.5

(i) (Fermat 1640) (a) $2^{23} - 1$ is not a prime. (Indeed $47 | 2^{23} - 1$.) (b) $2^{37} - 1$ is not a prime. (Indeed 223 ($= 6 \cdot 37 + 1$) divides M_{37}.)

(ii) (Euler 1732) $2^{29} - 1$ is not a prime. (What is its least prime divisor?)

Fermat's findings well and truly knock Cataldi's claim (Section 2.6), that M_{23}, M_{29}, M_{31} and M_{37} are *all* primes, on the head. And yet as late as 1752 Euler admitted he didn't know the status of M_{31}. By 1772 he'd got it! M_{31} is indeed prime and it became the record holder, a position it was to keep for 104 years.

How was Euler able to prove this? Of course he could have used Theorem 3.2.4 which would have told him that each prime divisor of $2^{31} - 1$ is of the form $62t + 1$. And indeed he did use it! But he further halved the work required of him by combining it with another result he had known for 30 years, namely:

Theorem 3.2.6 Each odd prime divisor of a number of the form $x^2 - 2y^2$, where $(x, y) = 1$, is necessarily of the form $8k + 1$ or $8k - 1$. □

Later he was to conclude that, conversely, each prime of the form $8k \pm 1$ is expressible in the form $x^2 - 2y^2$. We shall prove these assertions in Chapter 8.

Using Theorems 3.2.4 and 3.2.6 Euler could immediately infer

Theorem 3.2.7 Each prime divisor of M_{31} is of the form $248k + 1$ or $248k + 63$.

Proof Let q be a prime divisor of $2^{31}-1$. Then, of course, q divides $2^{32}-2=x^2-2y^2$, where $x=2^{16}$ and $y=1$. Consequently q is of the form $8k\pm 1$. But q is also of the form $62t+1$. Setting $t=4u+v$ where $v=0$, 1, 2 or 3, we find that $q=62(4u+v)+1$, that is $q=248u+w$, where $w=1$ or 63 or 125 or 187.

Now $248u+125=8(31u+15)+5$ and $248u+187=8(31u+23)+3$, neither of which is of the form $8k\pm 1$. Hence $q=248u+1$ or $248u+63$. □

By dividing $2^{31}-1$ by all the primes which are of these two forms and also less than $\sqrt{M_{31}}=46\,340.95$, Euler established the primality of M_{31}.

We have already described how Fermat and Mersenne numbers can be stored in decimal form on a computer (Program 2.4). The more important computational aspect lies in finding possible factors.

Since we can look for factors of the integer N amongst all integers no greater than $\sqrt{N}$ we can essentially handle all possible factors of N up to $2^{32}-1$* without having to store them in an array. Thus we can check all possible factors in numbers up to F_5 and M_{64}. For numbers beyond these we can still check possible factors in the range $1<x<2^{32}-1$, without resorting to full multiprecision division routines described in Appendix I, using Program 3.3. This divides the number, stored in the array F, by the denominator, D, using long division. It produces the resultant quotient in an array Q and the remainder in the variable N. Obviously if N is zero, then D is a factor of F.

Program 3.3 *Program to check possible factors (up to $2^{32}-1$) of Fermat or Mersenne numbers*

```
390 REM D contains a possible factor
400 N = 0
410 FOR I = NF TO 1 STEP -1
420      N = N * 10 + F(I)
430      Q(I) = INT(N/D)
440      N = N - INT(N/D)*D
450 NEXT I
460 IF N <> 0 GOTO 530
470      PRINT D; "    ";
480      FOR I= NF TO 1 STEP -1
490          PRINT ;Q(I);
500      NEXT I
510      PRINT N
520 GOTO next operation as factor is found
530 PRINT D; " is not a factor"
540 REM Set up the next possible factor
```

* The limit here is machine dependent and may vary depending on the computer that you have available.

Exercises 3.2

1 Prove that the FLT is equivalent to the assertion: for *all* $a\in\mathbb{Z}$, $a^p\equiv a(\text{mod } p)$. (Cf. Theorem 3.2.1.)

2 Show that for each positive integer n, $n^5/5+n^3/3+n^2/2+29n/30$ is an integer.

3 Show that for each positive integer a, $a^{61} \equiv a(\text{mod } 1001)$.

4 For $k \geqslant 2$ define $f_1(x) = x$ and $f_k(x) = x^{f_{k-1}(x)}$. Prove that $10 | f_4(7) - f_3(7)$. [*Hint*: work modulo 5.]

5 Let p and q be distinct primes. Show that $p^{q-1} + q^{p-1} \equiv 1(\text{mod } pq)$.

6 Show that for each odd prime p, $(p-1)2^{p-1}+1$ and $(p-2)2^{p-2}+1$ are each divisible by p. [You should already be asking the next question. The answer is 'no'!]

7 Show that, if $n > 1$, then $2^n \not\equiv 1(\text{mod } n)$.

8 Let p be an odd prime. Prove that $J_p(n) = 1^n + 2^n + \cdots + (p-1)^n$ is congruent to 0 or -1 modulo p according as $n = p$ or $p-1$. To what is $J_p(n)$ congruent, modulo p, if: (i) $n = p+1$; (ii) $n = p-2$? (Cf. Exercise 5.2.16.) [The question as to whether $J_q(q-1) \equiv -1(\text{mod } q)$ implies that q be prime appears to be unanswered as yet.]

9 Show that if $a, b \in \mathbb{Z}^+$ and if p is a prime such that $p | a^p - b^p$, then $p^2 | a^p - b^p$.

10 In 1732 Euler stated—but couldn't prove—that $p \nmid a$ and $p \nmid b$ together imply $p | a^{p-1} - b^{p-1}$. Prove this for him.

11 In 1742 Goldbach asserted that $(a+b)^n - a^n - b^n$ is divisible by n for each composite n. Euler claimed that $2^{35} - 2$ is divisible by neither 5 nor 7. Prove Euler correct. Prove Goldbach's assertion *is* correct if n is prime.

12 For distinct primes p and q show that if $a^p \equiv a(\text{mod } q)$ and $a^q \equiv a(\text{mod } p)$, then $a^{pq} \equiv a(\text{mod } pq)$. Deduce that if $(a, pq) = 1$, then $a^{pq-1} \equiv 1(\text{mod } pq)$. [The eminent physicist Sir James Jeans* noted (1897) that $(a, p, q) = (2, 11, 31)$, $(2, 19, 73)$, $(2, 31, 331)$—amongst others—satisfied the first two and hence the final congruence.]

13 (Lucas 1891.) Show that if $(2^{p-1}-1)/p$ is a perfect square then $p = 3$ or 7. [*Hint*: from $2^{p-1} - 1 = p\alpha^2$ deduce that one of $2^{(p-1)/2}+1$, $2^{(p-1)/2}-1$ is an odd perfect square. These conditions are the only possible for $p = 7$, 3 respectively.]

14 Show that each prime, except 2 and 5, is a divisor of infinitely many integers all of whose (decimal) digits are 9s. Prove the same result for repunits (see Exercise 0.3.6). Deduce that each integer has a multiple whose decimal form contains only 0s and 1s.

15 For each odd prime p and for each a such that $0 \leqslant a \leqslant p-1$ prove that $\binom{p-1}{a} \equiv (-1)^a(\text{mod } p)$.

* James Hopwood Jeans, 11 September 1877 - 16 September 1946.

16 Prove Euler's result of 1747 that if $(a, b) = 1$ then each (prime) factor of the number $a^{2^n} + b^{2^n}$ is either 2 or of the form $2^{n+1}k + 1$. [*Hint*: Let p be an odd prime dividing $a^{2^n} + b^{2^n}$. Show that $p \nmid a$ and $p \nmid b$. If $cb \equiv 1 (\mathrm{mod}\ p)$, then $(ac)^{2^n} + 1 \equiv 0 (\mathrm{mod}\ p)$. Now use the proof of Theorem 3.2.3.]

Computer problems 3.2

1 Is 341 the smallest composite n such that $2^{n-1} \equiv 1 (\mathrm{mod}\ n)$? Find the next three such n. Find the first three n for which $3^{n-1} \equiv 1 (\mathrm{mod}\ n)$.

2 For some time it was believed that $2^{p-1} \equiv 1 (\mathrm{mod}\ p^2)$ was not possible for a prime p. Find the first such p. Is $3^{p-1} \equiv 1 (\mathrm{mod}\ p^2)$ for this prime? (Results of this kind are relevant in a study of Fermat's last theorem. See Chapter 6.)

3 Can $2^{n-1} \equiv 1 (\mathrm{mod}\ n^2)$ hold for n composite?

4 Find pairs of primes p, q such that $2^{p-1} \equiv 1 (\mathrm{mod}\ q)$ and $2^{q-1} \equiv 1 (\mathrm{mod}\ p)$.

5 We know that if p is an odd prime, then $2^{p-1} \equiv 1 (\mathrm{mod}\ p)$ and therefore (Exercise 3.1.6) $2^{(p-1)/2} \equiv \pm 1 (\mathrm{mod}\ p)$. By calculating $2^{(p-1)/2} (\mathrm{mod}\ p)$ for various values of p can you find any pattern in the occurrence of the results $+1$ and -1?

6 Using Theorem 3.2.3 and Programs 2.4 and 3.3, find as many factors of the Fermat numbers F_n as possible.

7 Using Theorem 3.2.4 and Programs 2.4 and 3.3, write a program to check the Mersenne numbers for primeness and confirm as many as possible without resorting to multiprecision routines. (You should be able to confirm, for example, that 2351 and 4513 divide M_{47} (Winsheim 1751) and 439 divides M_{71} (Euler 1732).)

8 Show that 6 700 471 is prime.

9 Fermat's interest in factorising numbers of the form $a^n - 1$ soon had him wanting to factorise numbers of the form $a^m + 1$ (since if $n = 2m$ then $a^n - 1 = (a^m + 1)(a^m - 1)$.) Fermat asked: Given a, and a prime p, when is there an m such that $p | a^m + 1$? Try (from experimental evidence) to characterise those primes which divide—don't divide—integers of the form $3^m + 1$, $5^m + 1$.

10 How many primes had Euler to divide M_{31} by (according to Theorem 3.2.7) in order to confirm that M_{31} is prime?

3.3 Euler's ϕ function

120 years after Fermat had announced Theorem 3.2.1 and 24 years after Euler had first published a proof, Euler offered his generalisation of the FLT. In doing so he introduced the following very important number-theoretic function.

Definition 3.3.1 For each positive integer n let $\phi(n)$ denote the number of integers t such that

(i) $1 \leq t \leq n$ and (ii) $(t, n) = 1$.

This function $\phi: \mathbb{Z}^+ \to \mathbb{Z}^+$ is called *Euler's ϕ-function.*

Examples 3.3.2

(i) $\phi(1) = 1$;
(ii) $\phi(10) = 4$;
(iii) $\phi(2560) = 1024$;
(iv) $\phi(p) = p - 1$ whenever p is a prime;
(v) If $\alpha \in \mathbb{Z}^+$ then $\phi(2^\alpha) = 2^{\alpha-1}$.

Problem Calculate $\phi(15\,481)$. Does it help you to know that $15\,481 = 137 \times 113$ the factors being prime? We shall see in Chapter 12 how your enemies *not* knowing such factorisations is a great help in keeping secret messages secret!

How can we calculate $\phi(15\,481)$ or even $\phi(2560)$? Obviously we could simply count! But first we establish a bit more theory. The following 'reduction' theorem helps a lot.

Theorem 3.3.3 (Euler 1760) Let $n = p_1^{\alpha_1} p_2^{\alpha_2} \cdots p_t^{\alpha_t}$, where the p_i are distinct primes. Then $\phi(n) = \phi(p_1^{\alpha_1})\phi(p_2^{\alpha_2}) \cdots \phi(p_t^{\alpha_t})$. $\square$ (The proof is Theorem 3.3.7 + Theorem 3.3.8.)

In order to prove this it is useful to introduce the following definitions.

Definition 3.3.4 Let n be a positive integer.

(i) A *complete residue system* (*c.r.s*)* *modulo n* is any set $r_1, r_2, \ldots, r_n$, of n integers such that each integer x is congruent to one and only one of the r_i.
(ii) A *reduced residue system* (*r.r.s*)* *modulo n* is any set $s_1, s_2, \ldots, s_k$ of k integers each coprime to n such that each integer x *which is coprime to n* is congruent to one and only one of the s_i.

It is not difficult to see that complete and reduced residue systems exist for each n.

Examples 3.3.5

(i) Each of $\{0, 1, 2, 3, 4, 5, 6, 7, 8, 9\}$ and $\{0, 11, 22, 33, 44, 5, -4, -103, 48, -601\}$ is a c.r.s modulo 10.
(ii) Each of $\{1, 3, 7, 9\}$, $\{81, 3, 47, -11\}$, $\{101, 103, 107, 109\}$† is a r.r.s modulo 10.

Notes 3.3.6

(i) It follows immediately from Definition 3.3.4 that in neither kind of residue system can any two distinct elements be congruent modulo n.

* We adopt c.r.s.s, r.r.s.s for the plurals.
† This suggests Exercise 3.3.23.

(ii) The number of elements in *each* reduced residue system modulo n is $\phi(n)$. (Exercise 3.3.21.)

Now to give the proof of Theorem 3.3.3. The following result is essentially it.

Theorem 3.3.7 Let U, V be positive integers such that $(U, V)=1$. Then $\phi(UV)=\phi(U)\phi(V)$.

Proof Let $X=\{x_1, x_2, \ldots, x_{\phi(U)}\}$ be an r.r.s. modulo U and $Y=\{y_1, y_2, \ldots, y_{\phi(V)}\}$ an r.r.s. modulo V. Consider the set $G=\{Vx_i+Uy_j: x_i \in X, y_j \in Y\}$. We first show that no two of these integers are congruent modulo UV. For, if $Vx_i+Uy_j \equiv Vx_k+Uy_l \pmod{UV}$ then UV, and hence also U and V, divide $V(x_i-x_k)+U(y_j-y_l)$. It then follows that $U \mid V(x_i-x_k)$ and that $V \mid U(y_j-y_l)$. Since $(U, V)=1$ we deduce (Exercise 1.5.13(iv)) that $U \mid x_i-x_k$ and $V \mid y_j-y_l$, i.e. $x_i \equiv x_k \pmod U$ and $y_j \equiv y_l \pmod V$. Since X, Y are reduced residue systems modulo U, V respectively, Note 3.3.6(i) above tells us that $x_i=x_k$ and $y_j=y_l$. It follows immediately that the Vx_i+Uy_j—there are $\phi(U)\phi(V)$ of them—are pairwise incongruent modulo UV. We leave the reader to check that each Vx_i+Uy_j is coprime to UV.

The only question remaining is: Is each integer a such that $(a, UV)=1$ congruent to one of the Vx_i+Uy_j? Well, since $(U, V)=1$ we know (Corollary 1.6.6) that there exist integers x and y such that $yU+xV=1$. But then we also have $(y, V)=(x, U)=1$ [why?] and, further, $(ay, V)=(ax, U)=1$ since $(a, V)=(a, U)=1$ [why?]. It follows that there are $x_i \in X$ and $y_j \in Y$ such that $ay \equiv y_j \pmod V$ and $ax \equiv x_i \pmod U$, that is, $ax=x_i+rU$, $ay=y_j+sV$ for suitable $r, s \in \mathbb{Z}$. But then

$$a=a(yU+xV)=(ay)U+(ax)V=y_jU+x_iV+(s+r)UV.$$

Consequently $a \equiv Vx_i+Uy_j \pmod{UV}$, as required. □

To complete the proof of Theorem 3.3.3 we need the following immediate generalisation:

Theorem 3.3.8 Let $U=U_1U_2 \cdots U_t$ where $(U_i, U_j)=1$ for each pair $\{i, j\}$. Then $\phi(U)=\phi(U_1)\phi(U_2)\cdots\phi(U_t)$. □

We can get a different formulation of Theorem 3.3.3 with almost no effort using

Theorem 3.3.9 Let p be a prime. Then $\phi(p^\alpha)=p^{\alpha-1}(p-1)=p^\alpha(1-1/p)$.

Proof Count! [The only positive integers $\leqslant p^\alpha$ which are *not* coprime to p^α are $p, 2p, 3p, \ldots, p^2, \ldots, p^\alpha-p, p^\alpha$.] □

We can now rewrite Theorem 3.3.3 as

Theorem 3.3.10 Let $n = p_1^{\alpha_1} p_2^{\alpha_2} \cdots p_t^{\alpha_t}$ where the p_i are distinct primes. Then

$$\phi(n) = p_1^{\alpha_1 - 1}(p_1 - 1) p_2^{\alpha_2 - 1}(p_2 - 1) \cdots p_t^{\alpha_t - 1}(p_t - 1)$$
$$= n\left(1 - \frac{1}{p}\right)\left(1 - \frac{1}{p_2}\right) \cdots \left(1 - \frac{1}{p_t}\right). \quad \square$$

Using this result we arrive at last, but very easily, at

Examples 3.3.11
(i) $\phi(2560) = \phi(2^9 \cdot 5) = 2560(1 - \frac{1}{2})(1 - \frac{1}{5}) = 1024.$
(ii) $\phi(15481) = \phi(137)\phi(113) = 136 \cdot 112 = 14\,232.$

One very useful consequence of Theorem 3.3.7 (it is an essential part of Theorem 5.2.7) is the following intriguing equality!

Theorem 3.3.12 Let n be any positive integer. Then $\sum_{d|n} \phi(d) = n$. ($\sum_{d|n}$ means that the sum is taken over all divisors d of n.)

Proof We proceed using the second principle of mathematical induction. Now it is trivial to observe that the result claimed is true for $n = 1$. So let us suppose it is valid for all $n \leq N - 1$ and let us consider the case $n = N$. We write $N = p^\alpha M$ where $(p, M) = 1$, p being a prime divisor of N. Suppose we let d run over all the divisors of M. Then the divisors of N are easily seen to be all the $d, pd, p^2 d, \ldots, p^\alpha d$. It follows that

$$\sum_{\delta|N} \phi(\delta) = \sum_{d|M} \{\phi(d) + \phi(pd) + \cdots + \phi(p^\alpha d)\}.$$

By Theorem 3.3.7 we know that, for each i, $\phi(p^i d) = \phi(p^i)\phi(d)$. [Why can we use 3.3.7?] Consequently,

$$\sum_{\delta|N} \phi(\delta) = \sum_{d|M} \phi(d)\{1 + (p-1) + p(p-1) + \cdots + p^{\alpha-1}(p-1)\}$$
$$= \sum_{d|M} \phi(d) p^\alpha$$
$$= p^\alpha \sum_{d|M} \phi(d)$$
$$= p^\alpha M = N,$$

as required. $\square$

Example 3.3.13 With $n = 18$ we have:

$$\phi(1) + \phi(2) + \phi(3) + \phi(6) + \phi(9) + \phi(18) = 1 + 1 + 2 + 2 + 6 + 6 = 18,$$

as it should be!

Euler's function is for ever appearing in number-theoretic arguments. Later we shall meet a theoretical—sometimes practical—application in the theory of linear congruences (see Example 4.1.3(ii)). It also appears in de la Vallée Poussin's version of the prime number theorem:

Suppose a and b are integers such that $(a, b) = 1$. Let $\pi_{a,b}(x)$ denote the number of primes no greater than x in the arithmetic progression $\{an + b: 0 \leq n\}$. Then

$$\lim_{x\to\infty} \frac{\pi_{a,b}(x)}{x/\log x} = \lim_{x\to\infty} \frac{\pi_{a,b}(x)}{\pi(x)} = \frac{1}{\phi(a)}.$$

This means, for instance, that in the four $(=\phi(8))$ arithmetic progressions $8k+1, 8k+3, 8k+5, 8k+7$ the primes are approximately equally distributed. (As an amusing digression on this see Problem 1.3.2.).

To compute $\phi(n)$ the naive method is simply to count the integers from 1 to n that are coprime to n. This can be done using the following program, which uses Euclid's algorithm.

Program 3.4 *Determination of $\phi(n)$*

```
 10 INPUT "Enter the value of n ",N
 20 P = 0
 30 FOR T = 1 TO N
 40    A = N
 50    B = T
 60    R = A - INT(A/B)*B
 70      A = B
 80      B = R
 90    IF R<>0 GOTO 60
100    IF A = 1 THEN P = P + 1
110 NEXT T
120 PRINT P
```

However, using Theorem 3.3.10, we can achieve the result much more quickly using the following lines after Program 1.5, which stores the k prime factors in the array G.

```
261 P = N1
262 FOR I = 1 TO K
263    P = P*(1-1/G(I))
264 NEXT I
265 PRINT P
```

ϕ also makes an appearance in questions such as: What is the probability that two integers are coprime? (see Problem 1.7.3) or: What is the probability that a randomly given integer will be square-free? (see for example, [4]). And finally, as observed earlier, ϕ has 'gone public' introducing itself (at an admittedly rather trivial level) to a wider audience via its connection with so called 'unbreakable' codes. See Chapter 12.

Exercises 3.3

1 (i) Find $\phi(5000)$: (ii) Find the greatest prime divisor of $\phi(100!)$

2 (i) Find the least integer n such that $\phi(n) \geqslant 1000$ and all the integers n such that $\phi(n) = 1000$.
(ii) Given $\phi(n) = n/2$, find n.

3 Prove that the equation $\phi(x) = a$ has, for each $a \in \mathbb{Z}^+$, a finite number of solutions x—possibly none. Find all such x when $a = 2, 3, 4, 5, 6, 7, 8, 9, 10$.

4 Show that if $\phi(x) = 4k + 2 (k > 0)$ then $x = p^\alpha$ or $2p^\alpha$, where p is some prime of the form $4t + 3$. Show that $\phi(x) = 14$ has no solution. Find the next even a for which $\phi(x) = a$ has no solution.

5 Show that if $a\phi(a) = b\phi(b)$, then $a = b$. Is it true that if $a\phi(b) = b\phi(a)$, then $a = b$?

6 Carmichael* conjectured—indeed originally believed he had proved—that if $a = \phi(n)$ then there exists $m \neq n$ such that $a = \phi(m)$. Prove the conjecture true if a is of the form $4k + 2$.

7 Prove that there are infinitely many n for which $\phi(n)$ is (i) a square; (ii) twice an odd square. What about $\phi(n) = 3t^2$ with $(3, t) = 1$? For which n is $\phi(n) = 2^\alpha$ for some α?

8 Find the least n such that: (i) $\phi(n) < n/4$; (ii) $\phi(n) < n/8$.

9 Show that if Goldbach's conjecture is true then so is Erdos's, namely: To each positive integer n there correspond integers u, v such that $2n = \phi(u) + \phi(v)$.

10 Prove that $\sum_{d|n} \phi(d) = n$ as follows: (i) Write down all the fractions $1/n, 2/n, \ldots, n/n$: (ii) write each in 'lowest terms', that is, in the form a/b with $(a, b) = 1$: (iii) show that r/s appears in the new list iff $s|n$ and (except for n/n) r is less than and coprime to s: (iv) For each s dividing n count the number of fractions in the list with denominator s.

11 Show that $\phi(n) = n - 1$ iff n is prime. It is not known if $\phi(n)|n - 1$ implies that n is prime. But one can at least prove that, if $\phi(n)|n - 1$ and n is composite, then n is square-free and is a product of at least three distinct primes. [*Hint*: If $p^2|n$, then $p|\phi(n)$. If $n = pq$, then $(p-1)(q-1)|(p-1)q + q - 1$.]

12 Show that if $\phi(n)|n$ then $n = 2^k$ or $2^k 3^j$.

13 Show that if $d|n$ then $\phi(d)|\phi(n)$.

14 Prove that $\sqrt{n/2} \leqslant \phi(n) \leqslant n$ and that if n is composite then $\phi(n) \leqslant n - \sqrt{n}$. [*Hint*: (i) $p^{k-1}(p-1) > p^{k-1}\sqrt{p} \geqslant p^{k/2}$ if p is odd and $k \geqslant 1$; (ii) If $p|n$ then $\phi(n) \leqslant n(1 - 1/p)$.]

* Robert Daniel Carmichael, 1 March 1879 - 2 May 1967.

15 (Cauchy* 1840) Prove that if $n \geq 3$ then $\sum_{a \leq n; (a,n)=1} a = n\phi(n)/2$. [*Hint*: $(a, n) = 1$ iff $(a, n-a) = 1$.]

16 Prove that there are infinitely many primes as follows: Let $p_1, p_2, \ldots, p_t$ be them all and set $M = p_1 p_2 \cdots p_t$. Then prove that $\phi(M) = 1$ and yet $\phi(M) = M(1 - 1/p_1) \cdots (1 - 1/p_t)$. [Make sure your argument isn't circular—that is, it doesn't depend upon the fact that there *are* infinitely many primes.]

17 Given the positive integer n, show that the number of pairs $\{a, b\}$ for which $1 \leq a \leq n$, $1 \leq b \leq n$ and $(a, b, n) = 1$ is

$$n^2\left(1 - \frac{1}{p_1^2}\right)\left(1 - \frac{1}{p_2^2}\right) \cdots \left(1 - \frac{1}{p_k^2}\right)$$

$p_1, \ldots, p_k$ being the distinct primes dividing n.

18 Show that, for each integer $k \geq 1$, the equation $\phi(x) = \phi(x+k)$ has at least one solution.

19 Show that $0, 2, 2^2, 2^3, \ldots, 2^{16}$ is not a c.r.s. modulo 17. What about the set $\{0, 3, 3^2, \ldots, 3^{16}\}$? Find an integer k such that the set $\{0, k, k^2, \ldots, k^{22}\}$ forms a c.r.s. modulo 23.

20 For which m is $1^2, 2^2, \ldots, m^2$ a c.r.s. modulo m? Is there an $n > m \geq 2$ for which $1^2, 2^2, \ldots, m^2$ is an r.r.s. modulo n?

21 Show that the number of integers in *each* r.r.s. modulo m is $\phi(m)$.

22 Give a c.r.s. modulo 17 comprising multiples of 4.

23 Is there, for each integer $m \geq 2$, an r.r.s. comprising only primes?

24 Let $\{r_i : 1 \leq i \leq m\}$ be a c.r.s. and $\{s_i : 1 \leq i \leq \phi(m)\}$ an r.r.s. modulo m, let a be any integer and b an integer such that $(b, m) = 1$. Prove, or give counterexamples to, each of the following assertions: (i) $\{a + r_i : 1 \leq i \leq m\}$ is a c.r.s.; (ii) $\{a + s_i : 1 \leq i \leq \phi(m)\}$ is an r.r.s. (iii) $\{br_i : 1 \leq i \leq m\}$ is a c.r.s.; (iv) $\{bs_i : 1 \leq i \leq \phi(m)\}$ is an r.r.s.

25 (a) If $\{r_i\}$ is a c.r.s. modulo m prove that $\sum_{i=1}^{m} r_i \equiv 0 \pmod{m}$ provided m is odd. Is $\prod_{i=1}^{m} r_i \equiv 0 \pmod{m!}$?
(b) Let $\{s_i\}$ be an r.r.s. modulo m. For which $m \geq 2$, is $\sum_{i=1}^{\phi(m)} s_i \equiv 0 \pmod{m}$? Prove that $(\prod_{i=1}^{\phi(m)} s_i)^2 \equiv 1 \pmod{m}$.

26 Let p be a prime. Show that $1^k, 2^k, \ldots, (p-1)^k$ form an r.r.s. modulo p if $(k, p-1) = 1$.

Computer problems 3.3

1 Find values of n such that $\phi(n) = \phi(n+1)$ (Guy [5] identifies values up to 975.) Do you think there are infinitely many?

* Augustin-Louis Cauchy, 21 August 1789 - 22 May 1857.

2 Burton ([2]) says that $n=5186$ is such that $\phi(n)=\phi(n+1)=\phi(n+2)$. Is it the first? Can you find any others?

3 Gather experimental evidence about the following conjectures:

(i) Carmichael—For each n there exists $m \neq n$ such that $\phi(m)=\phi(n)$.
(ii) D. H. Lehmer—If $\phi(n) \mid n-1$ then n is prime.

4 Find the greatest integer n such that $\phi(n) \leqslant 1000$. (This might need a bit of thought.)

3.4 Euler's theorem

Let us now return to Euler and his generalisation of FLT.

Theorem 3.4.1 (Euler 1760) Let a, m be any positive integers such that $(a, m)=1$. Then $a^{\phi(m)} \equiv 1 (\bmod m)$.

Note that if we put $m=p$, then the FLT results. The following proof is essentially due to Ivory* (1806) and Horner† (1826). (For Euler's original proof see Exercise 3.4.7.)

Proof Let $r_1, r_2, \ldots, r_{\phi(m)}$ be an r.r.s. modulo m and consider the integers $ar_1, ar_2, \ldots, ar_{\phi(m)}$. These integers are each coprime to m, (Exercise 1.5.13(iii)) and are pairwise incongruent. (For: from $ar_i \equiv ar_j (\bmod m)$ we deduce by Theorem 3.1.11 that $r_i \equiv r_j (\bmod m)$ and hence that $r_i = r_j$ so that $ar_i = ar_j$.)

Thus the list $ar_1, ar_2, \ldots, ar_{\phi(m)}$ is a list of $\phi(m)$ numbers, each coprime to m and incongruent, mod m, in pairs. The $ar_i (1 \leqslant i \leqslant \phi(m))$ are therefore, congruent mod m to the $r_j (1 \leqslant j \leqslant \phi(m))$—possibly in a rearranged order. It follows that

$$ar_1 \cdot ar_2 \cdots ar_{\phi(m)} \equiv r_1 \cdot r_2 \cdots r_{\phi(m)} (\bmod m),$$

that is,

$$a^{\phi(m)} r_1 \cdot r_2 \cdots r_{\phi(m)} \equiv r_1 \cdot r_2 \cdots r_{\phi(m)} (\bmod m)$$

which, since $(r_1 \cdot r_2 \cdots r_{\phi(m)}, m)=1$ [why?], reduces to $a^{\phi(m)} \equiv 1 (\bmod m)$ by Theorem 3.1.11 as claimed. □

To help the reader get to grips with this we offer

Example 3.4.2 Modulo 18 one set of residues is given by $\{1, 5, 7, 11, 13, 17\}$. In particular $\phi(18)=6$. Taking $a=7$ we get, mod 18,

$$7 \cdot 1 \equiv 7; \quad 7 \cdot 5 \equiv 17; \quad 7 \cdot 7 \equiv 13; \quad 7 \cdot 11 \equiv 5; \quad 7 \cdot 13 \equiv 1; \quad 7 \cdot 17 \equiv 11.$$

* James Ivory, 17 February 1765 – 21 September 1842.
† William George Horner, 1786 – 22 September 1837.

This leads to: $7\cdot 1\cdot 7\cdot 5\cdot 7\cdot 7\cdot 7\cdot 11\cdot 7\cdot 13\cdot 7\cdot 17\equiv 7\cdot 17\cdot 13\cdot 5\cdot 1\cdot 11$,

i.e. $$7^6\cdot 1\cdot 5\cdot 7\cdot 11\cdot 13\cdot 17\equiv 1\cdot 5\cdot 7\cdot 11\cdot 13\cdot 17$$

so that $7^6\equiv 1 \pmod{18}$. As an elementary, but amusing, application of Theorem 3.4.1 we give

Example 3.4.3 What are the last two digits of the integer 123^{123}?

We work mod $100=2^2\cdot 5^2$. Note that $\phi(100)=100(1-\frac{1}{2})(1-\frac{1}{5})=40$. We then get $123^{40}\equiv 1 \pmod{100}$ whence $123^{120}\equiv 1^3\equiv 1 \pmod{100}$. Consequently, mod 100, $123^{123}\equiv 123^3\equiv 23^3=20^3+3\cdot 20^2\cdot 3+3\cdot 20\cdot 3^2+3^3\equiv 27\cdot(20+1)=567\equiv 67$. The last two digits are therefore 67.

Exercises 3.4

1 Find the last two digits of 654^{321} and the last *three* of 103^{406}.

2 Prove that if $(m, n)=1$ then $m^{\phi(n)}+n^{\phi(m)}\equiv 1 \pmod{mn}$. (Cf. Exercise 3.2.5.)

3 (Laplace* 1776) Prove Euler's theorem directly from Fermat's as follows. Given m, let $p^\alpha | m$, where p is a prime and let a be such that $(a, m)=1$.

(i) Note that $a^{p-1}=1+kp$;
(ii) Deduce that $a^{(p-1)p^{\alpha-1}}=1+k_1p^\alpha$ for some integer k_1;
(iii) Deduce that $a^{\phi(m)}\equiv 1 \pmod{p^\alpha}$ and then that $a^{\phi(m)}\equiv 1 \pmod{m}$.

4 (Sauer 1905) Show that if $(a, k)=(b, k)=(a-b, k)=1$ then, setting $f=\phi(k)$,

$$a^f+a^{f-1}b+a^{f-2}b^2+\cdots+ab^{f-1}+b^f\equiv 1 \pmod{k}.$$

[*Hint*: $a^{f+1}-b^{f+1}\equiv a-b \pmod{k}$.]

5 (Lewi ben Gersen 1288–1344) Prove that if $m>2$ then neither equation (i) $3^m+1=2^n$ nor (ii) $3^m-1=2^n$ has a solution in integers. [*Hint*: (i) $2^n\equiv 1 \pmod 9 \Rightarrow 6|n$. Then $2^n\equiv 1 \pmod 7$. (ii) $n>4$. Hence $3^m\equiv 1 \pmod{16}$. Then $4|m$ so that $3^m\equiv 1 \pmod 5$.]

6 Let $a\geqslant 2$ be an integer and let n be a positive integer. Show that $n|\phi(a^n-1)$. [*Hint*: $a^n\equiv 1 \pmod{a^n-1}$.]

7 Prove Theorem 3.4.1 as Euler did as follows. Let $a, m\in\mathbb{Z}^+$ with $(a, m)=1$. Let h be the least positive integer such that $a^h\equiv 1 \pmod m$. [Prove there is such an h without using Theorem 3.4.1.] If $S_1=\{a^k: 1\leqslant k\leqslant h\}$ accounts for all r in an r.r.s. modulo m, then $h=\phi(m)$—end of proof [why?]. If not, there exists b such that $(b, m)=1$ and $b\not\equiv a^k (1\leqslant k\leqslant h)$. Consider the set $S_2=\{ba^k: 1\leqslant k\leqslant h\}$. Show S_1 and S_2 together form a set of $2h$ distinct members of some r.r.s. modulo m. If these residues do not constitute an entire r.r.s., there exists c such that $(c, m)=1$ and $c\not\equiv a^k$, $c\not\equiv ba^k$.

* Pierre-Simon Laplace, 28 March 1749 – 5 March 1827.

Consider $S_3 = \{ca^k : 1 \leq k \leq h\}$, etc. Show that, continuing in this way, we find $th = \phi(m)$ for some t. This does it—why?

Computer problem 3.4

1 Write a program to check Euler's theorem numerically for $1 \leq n \leq 100$, say.

3.5 Wilson's theorem

Let us, for the moment, return to something a little simpler. As we have already implied, many results of number theory were first 'established' empirically. That relying too heavily on empirical evidence can be dangerous is well demonstrated by tackling Problem 0.1.1 and reading Theorem 11.6.2. But one result where empirical evidence was soon supported by unquestionable proof was in the following theorem, discovered, presumably on numerical evidence alone, by one John Wilson* and reported, without proof, in the book *Meditationes Arithmeticae* by the English mathematician Edward Waring† (1770)—although a manuscript written by Leibniz in 1682 also contains a proof. A proof of *Wilson's theorem*, as it is called, was given almost immediately by the French mathematician Lagrange and Wilson (almost immediately) took to the law, subsequently becoming a judge and a knight! (There must be a moral here if only one could see it!)

Wilson had asserted that, for each prime p, $[(p-1)!+1]/p$ is an integer. In congruence notation this becomes

Theorem 3.5.1 Let p be a prime. Then $(p-1)! \equiv -1 (\text{mod } p)$. □ (Proof below.)

One method of proof, due to Gauss who, it appears, plugged up the holes in a proof by F. von Schaffgotsch, can be discovered by generalising the principles of the following specific example.

Example 3.5.2 Mod 17 we have: $2 \cdot 9 \equiv 1$, $3 \cdot 6 \equiv 1$, $4 \cdot 13 \equiv 1$, $5 \cdot 7 \equiv 1$, $8 \cdot 15 \equiv 1$, $10 \cdot 12 \equiv 1$, $11 \cdot 14 \equiv 1$, whilst, trivially, $1 \cdot 1 \equiv 1$ and $16 \cdot 16 \equiv (-1)(-1) \equiv 1$. This means that

$$2 \cdot 9 \cdot 3 \cdot 6 \cdot 4 \cdot 13 \cdot 5 \cdot 7 \cdot 8 \cdot 15 \cdot 10 \cdot 12 \cdot 11 \cdot 14 \equiv 1^7$$

and consequently

$$\begin{aligned} &1 \cdot 2 \cdot 3 \cdot 4 \cdot 5 \cdot 6 \cdot 7 \cdot 8 \cdot 9 \cdot 10 \cdot 11 \cdot 12 \cdot 13 \cdot 14 \cdot 15 \cdot 16 \\ &\quad \equiv 1 \cdot 1^7 \cdot 16 \equiv -1. \end{aligned}$$

We can immediately give the proof for general p.

* John Wilson, 6 August 1741 – 18 October 1793.
† Edward Waring, 1736 – 15 August 1798.

Proof of Theorem 3.5.1 Since we wish to consider the numbers $2, 3, \ldots, p-2$ we are forced to assume that $p \geq 5$—the separate proofs for $p=2$ and $p=3$ we leave to the reader. We show that these $p-3$ integers pair off into products each of which is congruent to 1 (mod p).

To do this let a be any integer such that $2 \leq a \leq p-2$. Then $(a, p)=1$. Therefore there exist integers r, s such that $ra+sp=1$. It follows that $ra \equiv 1 (\text{mod } p)$. Writing $r=mp+t (0 \leq t < p)$ by the division algorithm we see that $ta \equiv 1 (\text{mod } p)$. Now we can't have $t=0$ nor $t=1$ [why not?]. Nor can we have $t=p-1$, because $(p-1)a \equiv 1 (\text{mod } p)$ leads to $a \equiv -1 (\text{mod } p)$, which is an impossibility since $2 \leq a \leq p-2$.

Next we show that a cannot be paired with more than one r in the range 2 to $p-2$. Indeed, if $ar_1 \equiv ar_2 (\text{mod } p)$ for $2 \leq r_1 < r_2 \leq p-2$ we'd have $r_1 \equiv r_2 (\text{mod } p)$ [why?]. But this is impossible [why?].

Finally we note that no integer a is paired with itself. For, if $a^2 \equiv 1 (\text{mod } p)$ we'd have $p | a^2-1$, that is, $p | (a-1)(a+1)$. Since p is a prime this would imply that either $p | a-1$ or $p | a+1$. But each of these is impossible since $2 \leq a \leq p-2$.

We thus deduce that, given p, the $p-3$ numbers $2, 3, \cdots, p-2$ can be paired off to yield products congruent to 1 modulo p. We then find, immediately, that $1 \cdot 2 \cdots (p-2)(p-1) \equiv 1 \cdot 1^{(p-3)/2} \cdot -1 \equiv -1 (\text{mod } p)$ as required. □

In fact, as noted by Lagrange, the converse of Wilson's theorem is also true (see Exercise 3.5.9).

Theorem 3.5.3 Let $n \in \mathbb{Z}$ be such that $n \geq 2$. If $n | (n-1)!+1$ then n is a prime. □

This is marvellous! Theorems 3.5.1 and 3.5.3 tell us that an integer n is prime if and only if.... The only trouble is ... well, you try and check, using Theorem 3.5.3, that, for example, 101 is prime. Even working modulo 101 the evaluation of 100! is somewhat duanting!

Nevertheless Wilson's theorem is useful in allowing us to glean information about integers which can be represented as the sum of two squares. Before reading Chapter 7 you might like to gather empirical evidence by doing computer Problem 3.5.3.

In this connection we have the following theorem which is a very weak version of Theorem 7.1.4 and yet is also a cornerstone in its proof.

Theorem 3.5.4 (Euler 1749) Let p be a prime. If $p=2$ or if $p \equiv 1 (\text{mod } 4)$ then the congruence $x^2 \equiv -1 (\text{mod } p)$ can be solved for x.

Proof. If $p=2$ then surely $x=1$ will suffice. So suppose that p is a prime of the form $4k+1$. Applying Wilson's theorem with $p=4k+1$ we get

$$1 \cdot 2 \cdot 3 \cdots (2k)(2k+1) \cdots (4k-2)(4k-1)(4k) \equiv -1 (\text{mod } p). \qquad (*)$$

Now, modulo p, $2k \equiv -(2k+1)$, $(2k-1) \equiv -(2k+2), \ldots, 2 \equiv -(4k-1)$, $1 \equiv -(4k)$. Consequently (*) can be written

$$1 \cdot 2 \cdot 3 \cdots (2k) \cdot (2k)(2k-1) \cdots 3 \cdot 2 \cdot 1 \cdot (-1)^{2k} \equiv -1(\bmod p),$$

that is, $\{(2k)!\}^2 \equiv -1(\bmod p)$, in other words $p \mid 1+x^2$ (where $x=(2k)!$). □

Note 3.5.5 Euler proved this not long after Wilson was born! How did he do it? See the footnote to Exercise 8.3.5—and the proof of Theorem 7.1.2.

The converse of Theorem 3.5.4 is also true.

Theorem 3.5.6 (Fermat 1640; Proved by Euler 1742) Let p be a prime such that the congruence $x^2 \equiv -1(\bmod p)$ can be solved for x. Then $p=2$ or $p \equiv 1(\bmod 4)$.

Proof The claim is that, if $p \neq 2$, then p is necessarily of the form $4k+1$. So let us suppose that p is of the form $4k+3$. Further let a be a solution of the given congruence. Now $a^{4k+2} \equiv 1(\bmod p)$—by FLT. On the other hand $a^2 \equiv -1(\bmod p)$ (given!) and hence $a^{4k+2} \equiv (-1)^{2k+1} \equiv -1(\bmod p)$. These two assertions about a^{4k+2} are clearly incompatible; the consequence is that p cannot be of the form $4k+3$. □

Part of Theorem 3.5.6 can also be stated nicely as follows.

Corollary 3.5.7 Let n be an integer and let p be an odd prime dividing $1+n^2$. Then p is necessarily of the form $4k+1$. □

This corollary enables us to answer the very natural question raised earlier (see the end of Section 1.3) with

Theorem 3.5.8 There are infinitely many primes of the form $4k+1$.

Proof Suppose to the contrary that there are only finitely many primes of the form $4k+1$. Let them be $p_1(=5)$, $p_2(=13), \ldots, p_t$ say. Form the integer $N=4(p_1 p_2 \cdots p_t)^2+1$ and express N as a product $q_1 q_2 \cdots q_r$ of primes each of which is odd [why?]. By Corollary 3.5.7 we deduce that each q_i is of the form $4k+1$. In particular q_i must be one of the p_j. The usual finish—q divides both N and $N-1$ and hence 1, contradiction—completes the proof. □

A little problem which sticks out like a sore thumb. Do we *really* need that multiplying factor 4? Can't we omit it? What do you think?

Corollary 3.5.7 proves useful on many an occasion, for example in the solving of so-called Diophantine equations. As an appetiser for later, perhaps you might try to prove, as was first achieved in 1877, that the equation

$x^3+17=y^2$ has no solutions in integers. Corollary 3.5.7 can help whereas your computer certainly can't. Good luck!

Exercises 3.5

1 By copying Example 3.5.2 check Wilson's theorem in the case of $p=23$.

2 Show that if $0<k<p$ then $(p-k)!(k-1)!\equiv(-1)^k(\text{mod } p)$.

3 Show that if $(p-1)!+1=p^\alpha$ for some α, then $p=2, 3$ or 5. [*Hint*: If $p>5$ then $(p-1)!$ is divisible by 2, $(p-1)/2$ and $p-1$ and hence by $(p-1)^2$. But $(p-1)^2 \nmid p^\alpha-1$ if $\alpha\leqslant p-2$ by Exercise 3.1.18.]

4 Show that if $\{[(p-1)/2]!\}^2+1=p^\alpha$ for some α then $p=5$.

5 Show that for each prime p of the form $4k+3$, $[(p-1)/2]!\equiv\pm1(\text{mod } p)$.

6 Leibniz (1682) proved that if p is an odd prime then $(p-2)!\equiv1(\text{mod } p)$. Show that this is equivalent to Wilson's theorem. Find a prime factor of $17!-1$.

7 Prove that p, $p+2$ are twin primes iff $4\{(p-1)!+1\}+p\equiv0(\text{mod } p(p+2))$.

8 Use Wilson's theorem to prove that

$$1^2 3^2\cdots(p-2)^2\equiv2^2 4^2\cdots(p-1)^2$$
$$\equiv(-1)^{(p+1)/2}(\text{mod } p) \text{ for each odd prime } p.$$

9 Prove Theorem 3.5.3. [*Hint*: If n is composite then $n=n_1n_2$ with $n_1, n_2<n$.]

10 What is the *smallest* prime dividing $(p-1)!+1$, p being a prime?

11 Show that the function $f(n)=n!+1$ is composite for infinitely many n. [Cf. the remark about $p_1p_2\cdots p_t+1$ in Section 2.2.]

12 Find (by hand) the least x such that $29|1+x^2$. Are there infinitely many x (infinitely many *prime* x) for which $29|1+x^2$?

13 (Bouniakovsky* 1830) Prove that $\{(p-1)!\}^{p^{n-1}}\equiv-1(\text{mod } p^n)$, p being an odd prime.

14 Show, for $n\geqslant10$, that $1!+2!+\cdots+n!$ is a multiple of 99.

15 Let p be a prime and a be an integer.

Show that: (i) If $p=2$ or $p\equiv1(\text{mod } 4)$ then $x^2\equiv-a^2(\text{mod } p)$ can be solved for x; and conversely: (ii) If $x^2\equiv-a^2(\text{mod } p)$ can be solved for x and if $(a, p)=1$, then either $p=2$ or $p\equiv1(\text{mod } 4)$.

16 Let p be an odd prime and let each of $\{r_i\}$ and $\{s_i\}$ $(1\leqslant i\leqslant p)$ be a c.r.s. modulo p. Show that $\{r_is_i\colon 1\leqslant i\leqslant p\}$ is *not* a c.r.s. modulo p.

* Viktor Yakovievich Bouniakovsky, 16 December 1804 – 12 December 1889.

Computer problems 3.5

1 A prime p is called a Wilson prime if $(p-1)! \equiv -1 \pmod{p^2}$. Find the first three Wilson primes.

2 For primes less than 50 check whether $\{((p-1)/2)!\}^2 \equiv -1 \pmod{p^2}$. Make a conjecture! Now run your program further.

3 Run a program to try to determine which integers are expressible as sums of two integer squares.

4

Congruences involving unknowns

4.1 Linear congruences

In a Chinese work on arithmetic, written about 100 A.D., Sun-Tsu gave a rule which would determine a number having remainders 2, 3 and 2 when divided by 3, 5 and 7 respectively. Using the congruence notation of the previous chapter we see that Sun-Tsu was asking for an integer x such that, simultaneously, $x \equiv 2(\text{mod } 3)$, $x \equiv 3(\text{mod } 5)$, $x \equiv 2(\text{mod } 7)$. That is, we are required to solve (simultaneous) equations involving congruences. Subsequent writers have also posed similar problems (see Exercises 4.1.7 and 4.1.8). How can we solve them?

To begin at the beginning, it would seem sensible to consider first the single equation $ax \equiv b(\text{mod } m)$ where a, b, m are given integers and x is to be determined. One small preliminary. If x is a solution of $ax \equiv b(\text{mod } m)$, then so also, trivially, is $x + tm$ for each integer t. Accordingly, to make sense of the expression 'the number of solutions of $ax \equiv b(\text{mod } m)$' we shall count solutions x_1, x_2 as 'different' when and only when $x_1 \not\equiv x_2(\text{mod } m)$. In other words, the 'number of solutions' is to be the number of distinct solutions in any complete residue system modulo m. The following is then easily established.

Theorem 4.1.1 Let a, b, m be integers with $m > 0$ and set $d = (a, m)$. Then

(i) If $d \nmid b$ the congruence $ax \equiv b(\text{mod } m)$ has no solution.
(ii) If $d | b$ the congruence $ax \equiv b(\text{mod } m)$ has d (pairwise incongruent) solutions.

In particular if x_0 is one solution, then the rest are

$$x_0 + m/d, x_0 + 2m/d, \ldots, x_0 + (d-1)m/d.$$

Proof
(i) Suppose x_0 is a solution of $ax \equiv b(\text{mod } m)$. Then $ax_0 = b + mt$ for some integer t. Thus $ax_0 - mt = b$. But $d|a$ and $d|m$. Hence $d|b$. Put another way: if $d \nmid b$ there can be no solution x_0.
(ii) Suppose $d|b$; say $b = wd$. We know from Theorem 1.6.2 that there exist integers u, v such that $au + mv = d$. But then $a(wu) + m(wv) = wd = b$. Thus $a(wu) \equiv b(\text{mod } m)$ so that wu will solve the given congruence. Put $x_0 = wu$.

From $ax_0+m(wv)=b$ we deduce immediately that

$$a\left(x_0+\frac{m}{d}z\right)+m\left(wv-\frac{a}{d}z\right)=b,$$

z being an integer. We claim that, for $z=0, 1, \ldots, d-1$, the integers $x_0+(m/d)z$ are pairwise incongruent modulo m. Indeed, if $x_0+(m/d)i \equiv x_0+(m/d)j \pmod m$ where $0 \leq i < j \leq d-1$, we would have $(m/d)i \equiv (m/d)j \pmod m$. Then, by Theorem 3.1.11 we would have $i \equiv j[\bmod m/(m/d)]$, i.e. $i \equiv j \pmod d$.

But this is impossible since $1 \leq i < j \leq d-1$. We have thus exhibited at least d different solutions. Do these account for them all?

Let x_1 be any solution of $ax_1 \equiv b \pmod m$. Then $ax_1 \equiv b \equiv ax_0 \pmod m$, so that $a(x_1-x_0)=my$ for suitable $y \in \mathbb{Z}$. Setting $a=\alpha d$ and $m=\beta d$ we have $\alpha(x_1-x_0)=\beta y$, where $(\alpha, \beta)=1$ (by Exercise 1.5.5). It follows that $\beta | x_1-x_0$, i.e. $x_1-x_0=s\beta$ for suitable $s \in \mathbb{Z}$. That is, $x_1=x_0+(m/d)s$. Finally, if we write $s=kd+r$, where $0 \leq r < d$, we see that

$$x_1=x_0+mk+(m/d)r \equiv x_0+(m/d)r \qquad \pmod m,$$

as required. □

A useful consequence is

Corollary 4.1.2 If a, b, m are as above and if $(a, m)=1$ then the congruence $ax \equiv b \pmod m$ has precisely one solution. □

Examples 4.1.3

(i) From $8x \equiv 5 \pmod{27}$ we obtain $80x \equiv 50 \pmod{27}$, that is $-x \equiv -4 \pmod{27}$ and so $x \equiv 4 \pmod{27}$.

(ii) Rather than proceeding as if by magic, we can proceed mechanically. Recalling Euler's result (Theorem 3.4.1) we can multiply each side of the given congruence by $8^{\phi(27)-1}$, that is, by 8^{17} to obtain $8^{17} \cdot 5 \equiv 8^{18}x \equiv x \pmod{27}$. Now 8^{17}—modulo 27—is easily evaluated as $8^{16} \cdot 8$. Indeed, modulo 27, $8^2 \equiv 10$, $8^4 \equiv 10^2 \equiv 19$, $8^8 \equiv 19^2 \equiv 10$ and so $8^{16} \equiv 19$. From this $8^{17} \equiv 152 \equiv 17$ and so, finally, $8^{17} \cdot 5 \equiv 85 \equiv 4$—as obtained previously.

(iii) Now let us solve the congruence $28x \equiv 4 \pmod{244}$. Here d, as in Theorem 4.1.1, is equal to $(28, 244)=4$. So we try to solve, instead, the congruence $7x \equiv 1 \pmod{61}$. This is not, perhaps, so easy to do by guesswork (as in (i) above) nor is the idea of finding 7^{59} [why 7^{59}?] so palatable. So what can we do? One answer is to use the Euclidean algorithm on the pair $7, 61$. Doing this we find

$$\begin{aligned} 61 &= 8 \cdot 7+5,\\ 7 &= 1 \cdot 5+2,\\ 5 &= 2 \cdot 2+1. \end{aligned}$$

Working back leads to $1=1\cdot 5-2\cdot 2=3\cdot 5-2\cdot 7=3\cdot 61-26\cdot 7$. Consequently, modulo 61, we have $7\cdot(-26)\equiv 1$, that is, $7\cdot 35\equiv 1 \pmod{61}$. Thus $x=35$ (and, indeed each integer $35+61t$) is a solution of the congruence $7x\equiv 1 \pmod{61}$ and hence also of $28x\equiv 4 \pmod{244}$. From Theorem 4.1.1 it then follows that a complete set of (pairwise) incongruent solutions for the given congruence is $35+61s$, where $s=0, 1, 2$ and 3.

Note 4.1.4 In (iii) there was no need to divide through the congruence first by (28, 244). Indeed if the gcd of a and m is not easy to determine by inspection it may be necessary to apply the Euclidean algorithm to find it! Note that if we'd done that in the above example we would have finished up with $4=3\cdot 244-26\cdot 28$. That is we'd have found both (28, 244) and the solution $x=-26$ at the same time.

Obviously one approach to finding any solutions of the linear congruence $ax\equiv b \pmod m$ is to search over all possible values of x between 0 and $m-1$. For each such value of x we can calculate the value of $ax \pmod m$ and if this equals b we have a solution. For large m this is clearly going to be very slow.

The method employed in Example 4.1.3(iii) shows, immediately, that the problem of solving $ax\equiv b \pmod m$ is equivalent to that of writing down the general solution, in integers, of the linear equation $ax+my=b$. For, if $ax+my=b$, then certainly $ax\equiv b \pmod m$. On the other hand, if $ax\equiv b \pmod m$, then there must be an integer y such that $ax+my=b$. Program 4.1 uses Euclid's algorithm in this way and is a modification of Program 1.8. (The changes to the earlier program are indicated in italics.)

Program 4.1 *Computes the solutions (if any) to the linear congruence ax ≡ b (mod m)*

```
 10 DIM a(3),b(3)
 20 INPUT "a,b and m",a1,b1,m
 30 IF a1 = 1 GOTO 270
 40 x=a1:y=m
 50 a(1)=1:a(2)=0:a(3)=x
 60 b(1)=0:b(2)=1:b(3)=y
 70 IF b(3) = 0 GOTO 170
 80    q=a(3) DIV b(3)
 90    FOR i=1 TO 3
100       r=a(i) - q*b(i)
110       a(i)=b(i)
120       b(i)=r
130    NEXT i
140 GOTO 70
150 REM a(3) contains the GCD while a(1) and a(2) are the coefficients
160 REM in the linear combination
170 REM Check if there is a solution
180 IF b1 MOD a(3) = 0 GOTO 210
190   PRINT "a solution does not exist"
200   END
210 REM a solution exists therefore we display the values
220   PRINT "The solutions are"
230   FOR i= 1 TO a(3)
```

```
240       s = (a(1)*b1+i*m)/a(3) : s=s-INT(s/m)*m
245       PRINT s;
250    NEXT i
260 END
270 PRINT b1-INT(b1/m)*m
280 END
```

Note that to construct the solutions we only need one coefficient, $a(1)$, of the linear combination. Hence we can make the program more efficient by only computing $a(1)$ and $a(3)$. We leave readers to make this modification themselves.

Equations of the type $ax + by = c$ were considered by Aryabhatta in the fifth century and by later workers of the same general period. They and their solution were 'rediscovered' by Bachet around 1610 (see Exercise 4.1.4).

We can now return to Sun-Tsu's problem or, rather, the following generalisation of it.

Theorem 4.1.5 Let $m_1, m_2, \ldots, m_r$ be positive integers such that $(m_i, m_j) = 1$ for $i \neq j$. Then the system of simultaneous congruences

$$x \equiv b_1(\text{mod } m_1),\ x \equiv b_2(\text{mod } m_2), \ldots, x \equiv b_r(\text{mod } m_r)$$

has a solution which is, moreover, unique modulo $m_1 m_2 \cdots m_r$.

Proof Set $M = m_1 m_2 \cdots m_r$. For each i put

$$M_i = M/m_i = m_1 m_2 \cdots m_{i-1} m_{i+1} \cdots m_r.$$

Since $(m_i, m_j) = 1$ we have $(M_i, m_i) = 1$ for each i. It follows (Corollary 1.6.6) that, for each i, there exist integers c_i, t_i such that $c_i M_i + t_i m_i = 1$, that is, $c_i M_i \equiv 1(\text{mod } m_i)$. But then $c_i M_i b_i \equiv b_i(\text{mod } m_i)$ whilst $c_i M_i b_i \equiv 0(\text{mod } m_j)$ if $j \neq i$ [why?]. Consequently, setting $x_0 = \sum_{k=1}^{r} c_k M_k b_k$, we see that $x_0 \equiv c_i M_i b_i \equiv b_i(\text{mod } m_i)$ for each i, as required.

To show that this solution is unique modulo M, suppose x_1 is another solution. Then for $i = 1, \ldots, r$ we have $x_0 \equiv b_i \equiv x_1(\text{mod } m_i)$. This means that $m_i | x_1 - x_0$ for each i. Since the m_i are pairwise coprime we deduce immediately (Exercise 1.5.13(v)) that $m_1 m_2 \cdots m_r | x_1 - x_0$, that is $x_1 \equiv x_0(\text{mod } M)$. □

Now to solve Sun-Tsu's problem* (at last!).

Since $(3, 5) = (5, 7) = (7, 3) = 1$, Theorem 4.1.5 is available. In the above notation we have $M = 3 \cdot 5 \cdot 7 = 105$, $M_1 = 35$, $M_2 = 21$, $M_3 = 15$, so that we want c_1, c_2, c_3 such that $35c_1 \equiv 1(\text{mod } 3)$, $21c_2 \equiv 1(\text{mod } 5)$, $15c_3 \equiv 1(\text{mod } 7)$. Clearly we may take $c_1 = 2$, $c_2 = 1$ and $c_3 = 1$. Since $b_1 = 2$, $b_2 = 3$ and $b_3 = 2$ we set $x_0 = 2 \cdot 35 \cdot 2 + 1 \cdot 21 \cdot 3 + 1 \cdot 15 \cdot 2 = 233$. Therefore the unique x in the range $0 \leq x < M$ is $233 - 210$, that is $x = 23$.

Note 4.1.6 Essentially this method of solution was offered by Sun-Tsu and described by several later authors including Yih-Hing (a priest who died in

* Page 102.

717 A.D. and who found uses for his work in problems arising in astronomy), Euler (1734) and Gauss in the *Disquisitiones.* Because of Sun-Tsu's contributions Theorem 4.1.5 is usually called the *Chinese remainder theorem.*

Actually, Sun-Tsu's problem can be solved by a somewhat more direct and naive attack. Since we require $x \equiv 2 (\text{mod } 3)$ we *must* take $x = 2 + 3u$ where $u \in \mathbb{Z}$. Since we also want $x \equiv 3 (\text{mod } 5)$ we *must* have $2 + 3u \equiv 3 (\text{mod } 5)$. This implies that $3u \equiv 1 (\text{mod } 5)$, in other words $u \equiv 2 (\text{mod } 5)$. Consequently $u = 2 + 5v$ for some $v \in \mathbb{Z}$. It follows that $x = 2 + 3u = 8 + 15v$. Finally we require $x \equiv 2 (\text{mod } 7)$, that is $8 + 15v \equiv 2 (\text{mod } 7)$, in other words $v \equiv -6 \equiv 1 (\text{mod } 7)$. Hence $x = 8 + 15(1 + 7w) = 23 + 105w$, from which we conclude that $x = 23$ is one solution of Sun-Tsu's problem.

The proof of the Chinese remainder theorem is constructive and presents us with an algorithm for solving the problem. However, it is a fairly simple task (cf. Exercise 4.1.10) to generalise the set-up in Theorem 4.1.5 so that we can solve systems of congruences of the form $a_i x \equiv b_i (\text{mod } m_i) (1 \leq i \leq r)$. Program 4.2 is based on the algorithm suggested by the proof of Theorem 4.1.5 but solves the more general problem. It uses parts of Program 4.1.

Program 4.2 *To solve a system of simultaneous linear congruences*

```
 10 INPUT "How many congruences ?",k
 20 DIM a1(k),b1(k),m1(k),c(k),s(k),t(k)
 30 INPUT "enter values of a(k),b(k),m(k) "
 40 FOR i=1 TO k
 50   INPUT a1(i),b1(i),m1(i)
 60 NEXT i
 70 DIM a(2),b(2)
 80 REM ***********************************************
 81 REM IF a1(j) <> 1
 82 REM  Solve the system a1(j)*X≡b1(j) MOD m1(j) using
 83 REM the method of program 4.1 at line 3000
 84 REM store the answers in c(j)
 85 REM ************************************************
 90 FOR j=1 TO k
100   IF a1(j)<> 1 GOTO 130
110     c(j)=b1(j) MOD m1(j)
120   GOTO 170
130   a(1)=1:a(2)=a1(j)
140   b(1)=0:b(2)=m1(j)
150   GOSUB 3000
160   c(j)=(a(1)*b1(j)/a(2)+m1(j)/a(2)) MOD m1(j)
170 NEXT j
180 m=1
190 FOR i = 1 TO k
200   m=m*m1(i)
210 NEXT i
211 REM *****************************************
212 REM Solve the congruence t(j)*X≡1 MOD m1(j)
213 REM using the method of program 4.1 at line 3000
214 REM Store the answer in s(j)
215 REM *****************************************
220 FOR j= 1 TO k
230   t(j)=m/m1(j)
240   a(1)=1:a(2)=t(j)
```

```
 250    b(1)=0:b(2)=m1(j)
 260    GOSUB 3000
 270    s(j)=a(1)+m1(j)/a(2)
 280 NEXT j
 285 REM Construct the final solution
 290 x=0.0
 300 FOR j=1 TO k
 310    x=x+c(j)*s(j)*t(j)
 320 NEXT j
 330 PRINT"solution",x-INT(x/m)*m
 340 END
3000 REM Subroutine to solve linear congruence
3010    q=a(2) DIV b(2)
3020      FOR i=1 TO 2
3030        r=a(i) - q*b(i)
3040        a(i)=b(i)
3050        b(i)=r
3060      NEXT
3070    IF b(2)<>0 GOTO 3010
3080 RETURN
```

Before we pass to congruences of higher degree we mention one result concerning congruences of degree one with two unknowns. As well as being useful later* it is interesting in its own right perhaps because it is slightly unexpected, and its proof highlights a rather trivial, but fundamental principle of mathematics, namely

Dirichlet's pigeon-hole principle
If k objects are placed in l boxes and $k > l$ then some box will contain at least two objects.

With this we can prove

Lemma 4.1.7 (Thue's† lemma) Let a, m be integers such that $m \geqslant 2$ and $(a, m) = 1$. Then the congruence $ax \equiv y \pmod{m}$ has a solution x_0, y_0 for which $0 < |x_0| \leqslant \sqrt{m}$ and $0 < |y_0| \leqslant \sqrt{m}$.

Proof Let $s = [\sqrt{m}] + 1$. Consider the set $S\{ax - y: 0 \leqslant x < s, 0 \leqslant y < s\}$ of s^2 integers. Since $s^2 > m$ the pigeonhole principle tells us that at least one pair of these integers are congruent modulo m, $ax_1 - y_1 \equiv ax_2 - y_2 \pmod{m}$, say, where perhaps $x_1 = x_2$ or $y_1 = y_2$ *but not both.*

Setting $x_0 = x_1 - x_2$ and $y_0 = y_1 - y_2$ we see easily that $ax_0 \equiv y_0 \pmod{m}$. Also, since $0 \leqslant x_1, x_2 \leqslant s - 1 \leqslant \sqrt{m}$, we have $-\sqrt{m} \leqslant x_0 \leqslant \sqrt{m}$. Likewise, $-\sqrt{m} \leqslant y_0 \leqslant \sqrt{m}$. Finally if y_1 were equal to y_2 we'd have $y_0 = 0$ and hence $ax_0 \equiv 0 \pmod{m}$. Since $(a, m) = 1$ we could deduce $x_0 \equiv 0 \pmod{m}$, i.e. $m | x_0$. But this implies, immediately, that $x_0 = 0$, that is $x_1 = x_2$. Likewise, but more easily, if $x_1 = x_2$ then $y_1 = y_2$. Consequently, since not both $x_1 = x_2$, $y_1 = y_2$ hold, neither can. That is, neither x_0 nor y_0 is 0, as claimed. □

* Theorem 8.4.5.
† Axel Thue, 19 February 1863 – 7 March 1922.

Exercises 4.1

1 Find complete sets of (pairwise incongruent) solutions—if any—to each of the following congruences: (i) $5x \equiv 6 \pmod 7$; (ii) $6x \equiv 7 \pmod 8$; (iii) $7x \equiv 8 \pmod 9$; (iv) $2x \equiv 0 \pmod 4$.

2 Find the number of (pairwise incongruent) solutions—if any—to each of the following congruences: (i) $777x \equiv 888 \pmod{999}$; (ii) $123x \equiv 456 \pmod{789}$; (iii) $4^2x \equiv 5^2 \pmod{6^2}$.

3 Find the general solution, if there is one, of each of the congruences: (i) $3x + 5y \equiv 7 \pmod 9$; (ii) $3x + 5y + 7z \equiv 9 \pmod{11}$.

4 (Bachet c1610) Show that the equation $ax + by = c$ has a solution x, y iff $(a, b)|c$. Show further that if x_0, y_0 is a solution then all solutions are given by $x_0 + nb/d, y_0 - na/d$ where $d = (a, b)$ and $0 \leqslant n \leqslant d - 1$.

5 Euler proved the existence of a solution of the linear equation $ax + by = c$ where $(a, b) = 1$, by considering the remainders r (with $0 \leqslant r < b$) when the b integers $c - ax (0 \leqslant x < b)$ are divided by b. Show that each integer d with $0 \leqslant d < b$ occurs once and once only as a remainder. In particular, for some x, $c - ax$ is divisible by b.

6 Show that if $(a, m) = 1$ then the congruence $ax \equiv b \pmod m$ has solution $x = a^{\phi(m)-1}b$.

7 (Brahmagupta, 7th C.) When eggs in a basket are removed 2, 3, 4, 5, 6 at a time there remain, respectively, 1, 2, 3, 4, 5 left over. What is the minimum possible number of eggs that were originally in the basket?

8 (Regiomontanus 1436–76) Find the least positive number with remainders 3, 11, 15 on division by 10, 13, 17 respectively.

9 Solve for x the simultaneous congruences:

(i) $x \equiv 11 \pmod{17}$ and $x \equiv 17 \pmod{11}$;
(ii) $x \equiv 11 \pmod{111}$ and $x \equiv 12 \pmod{345}$.

10 Solve each of the following sets of simultaneous congruences:

(i) $x \equiv 2 \pmod 3$, $2x \equiv 3 \pmod 5$ and $3x \equiv 4 \pmod 7$;
(ii) $3x \equiv 1 \pmod 5$, $5x \equiv 2 \pmod 7$, $7x \equiv 3 \pmod 9$ and $9x \equiv 4 \pmod{11}$.

11 (i) Find four consecutive integers which are divisible, respectively, by 2, 3, 5, 7.
(ii) Find three consecutive integers divisible by a square, a cube and a fourth power respectively (each of these powers being greater than 1).

12 Prove that the simultaneous congruences $x \equiv a \pmod m$, $x \equiv b \pmod n$ have a solution iff $(m, n)|a - b$. Show that any two solutions are congruent modulo $[m, n]$ (the least common multiple of m and n).

13 Solve, if possible, the simultaneous congruences:
(i) $x \equiv 47 \pmod{84}$, $x \equiv -11 \pmod{20}$; (ii) $3x \equiv 7 \pmod{10}$, $5x \equiv 9 \pmod{12}$.

14 (a) Show that the system of simultaneous linear congruences:

$$ax + by \equiv e \pmod{m}$$

$$cx + dy \equiv f \pmod{m}$$

has a solution if $(ad - bc, m) = 1$.
(b) Find the general solution, of the systems:

(i) $1x + 3y \equiv 5 \pmod{13}$, $7x + 9y \equiv 11 \pmod{13}$; (ii) $2x + 3y \equiv 4 \pmod{8}$, $5x + 6y \equiv 7 \pmod{8}$.

15 Does Thue's lemma necessarily hold if $(a, m) > 1$? (A proof or counter example is required.)

Computer problems 4.1

1 Write a program to solve $ax \equiv b \pmod{m}$ by trial and error (i.e. by systematically trying $x = 0, 1, 2, \ldots, m-1$) and compare its speed with that presented in the text.

2 Use Program 4.2 to solve the system of simultaneous congruences

(i) $11x \equiv 38 \pmod{45}$, $6x \equiv 46 \pmod{122}$;
(ii) $7x \equiv 47 \pmod{55}$, $13x \equiv 97 \pmod{128}$, $-17x \equiv 49 \pmod{73}$, $-16x \equiv 8 \pmod{237}$.

3 Modify Program 4.1 so that it checks whether or not a solution exists before proceeding to look for one.

4 Modify Program 4.2 so that it checks whether or not a solution exists before proceeding to look for one.

5 Write a program to solve the congruence $ax \equiv b \pmod{m}$ when m is composite by (i) finding the prime power factors p^α of m and then (ii) solving each $ax \equiv b \pmod{p^\alpha}$ and finally (iii) using Theorem 4.1.5.

6 Write a program to solve the system of congruences of Theorem 4.1.5 by a systematic search technique. Compare its performance with the program presented in the text.

7 Write a program to solve simultaneous congruences—as in Exercise 14 above.

4.2 Congruences of higher degree

Having dealt with linear congruences it is natural to ask what can be said about congruences of higher degree. That is, we ask: given a polynomial $f(x)$ with coefficients in $\mathbb{Z}$ and given an integer $m \geq 2$, how can we find those integers u, if any, for which $f(u) \equiv 0 \pmod m$? Since only the values $u = 0, 1, \ldots, m-1$ need to be tested the problem is a finite one which can be resolved by trial and error. But here we are looking for something more sophisticated which will be of practical value when m is large. We have, of course, already given some consideration to the problem of the *existence* of solutions. For example, we know that if $f(x) = x^2 + 1$ and m is a prime, then $f(x) \equiv 0 \pmod m$ has a solution if and only if either $m = 2$ or m is (a prime) of the form $4k+1$. Then again, for each integer $m \geqslant 2$, the equation $x^{\phi(m)} - 1 \equiv 0 \pmod m$ has exactly $\phi(m)$ (pairwise incongruent) solutions (Theorem 3.4.1).

It was Gauss who, having introduced the concept of congruence, made the first deep study of the problem posed above.

In looking at a congruence of the form $f(x) \equiv 0 \pmod m$ we can, as in Problem 4.1.5, reduce the problem to the case where m is a prime power. Indeed, let $m = p_1^{\alpha_1} p_2^{\alpha_2} \cdots p_r^{\alpha_r}$. If, for some i, $f(x) \equiv 0 \pmod{p_i^{\alpha_i}}$ has no solution, then surely neither can $f(x) \equiv 0 \pmod m$. On the other hand, suppose that for each i the congruence $f(x) \equiv 0 \pmod{p_i^{\alpha_i}}$ is solvable with (pairwise incongruent) solutions $u_i(1), u_i(2), \ldots, u_i(l_i)$. Now selecting, for each i, one such solution $u_i(t_i)$, say, the Chinese remainder theorem shows the existence of an integer u such that $u \equiv u_i(t_i) \pmod{p_i^{\alpha_i}}$ for each i. It then follows, for each i, that $f(u) \equiv f(u_i(t_i)) \equiv 0 \pmod{p_i^{\alpha_i}}$. Thus $f(u) \equiv (\bmod m)$ as required.

In fact this analysis shows more, namely

Theorem 4.2.1 Let $S(m)$ denote the number of solutions (pairwise incongruent modulo m) of the congruence $f(x) \equiv 0 \pmod m$. If $m = p_1^{\alpha_1} p_2^{\alpha_2} \cdots p_r^{\alpha_r}$ then $S(m) = S(p_1^{\alpha_1}) S(p_2^{\alpha_2}) \cdots S(p_r^{\alpha_r})$. □

Example 4.2.2 Solve, if possible, the congruence $x^2 + 18x - 23 \equiv 0 \pmod{200}$.

Solution Since $200 = 2^3 5^2$ we examine the given congruence modulo 8 and modulo 25. The solutions of $x^2 + 18x - 23 \equiv 0 \pmod 8$ are easily seen (by trial and error) to be $x \equiv 3$ and $x \equiv 7$: the solutions of $x^2 + 18x - 23 \equiv 0 \pmod{25}$ are (less easily!) seen to be $x \equiv 14$ and $x \equiv 18$. We therefore need a solution for each of the four possibilities: (i) $x \equiv 3 \pmod 8$ and $x \equiv 14 \pmod{25}$; (ii) $x \equiv 3 \pmod 8$ and $x \equiv 18 \pmod{25}$; (iii) $x \equiv 7 \pmod 8$ and $x \equiv 14 \pmod{25}$; (iv) $x \equiv 7 \pmod 8$ and $x \equiv 18 \pmod{25}$.

We now solve each of these cases using either Theorem 4.1.5 or proceeding naively. We'll use the formula given in Theorem 4.1.5; you can check the result using the direct method, as an exercise.

In the notation of the Chinese remainder theorem the data in this example yield: $M_1 = 200/8 = 25$, $M_2 = 200/25 = 8$. We can therefore take $c_1 = 1$ and $c_2 = 22$ and we find that

$$x = 1 \cdot 25b_1 + 22 \cdot 8b_2 \text{ where } b_1 = 3 \text{ or } 7 \text{ whilst } b_2 = 14 \text{ or } 18.$$

We therefore have

$$x = 25 \cdot 3 + 176 \cdot 14 = 2539 \quad \text{or} \quad x = 25 \cdot 3 + 176 \cdot 18 = 3243 \quad \text{or}$$

$$x = 25 \cdot 7 + 176 \cdot 14 = 2639 \quad \text{or} \quad x = 25 \cdot 7 + 176 \cdot 18 = 3343.$$

Thus the complete set of four (pairwise incongruent) solutions is given by $x \equiv 39$ or 43 or 139 or $143 \pmod{200}$.

In the above example the solutions of the congruences when taken modulo 8 and modulo 25 were found by inspection. What could we have done if the modulus had instead, been, say, 625 or maybe even 5^{17}? In fact we shall show that all the difficulties in solving congruences modulo some large prime power p^α lie at the seemingly easiest level—namely in that of solving $f(x) \equiv 0 \pmod p$. Indeed, suppose that all solutions of the congruence $f(x) \equiv 0 \pmod{p^\alpha}$ have been found, p being a prime, and let us try to find all solutions of the congruence $f(x) \equiv 0 \pmod{p^{\alpha+1}}$. Let the solutions (pairwise incongruent mod p^α) to the former be $u_1, u_2, \ldots, u_r$ and let v be any solution of the latter. Then $f(v) \equiv 0 \pmod{p^{\alpha+1}}$ and hence, trivially, $f(v) \equiv 0 \pmod{p^\alpha}$. We deduce immediately that $v \equiv u_j \pmod{p^\alpha}$, that is $v = u_j + tp^\alpha$ for some j and t. Since the u_j are known we only have to find t.

To do this we use *Taylor's* theorem* (the one from calculus but here employed on the rather easy (polynomial) function $f(x)$). Let $f(x)$ be a polynomial of degree n. Then

$$f(x+h) = f(x) + h\frac{f'(x)}{1!} + h^2\frac{f''(x)}{2!} + \cdots + h^n\frac{f^{(n)}(x)}{n!} \qquad (*)$$

$f^{(t)}(x)$ being the tth derivative of $f(x)$.

In our case $x = u_j$ and $h = tp^\alpha$. Further, if $f(x)$ has integer coefficients so does each polynomial $f^{(i)}(x)/i!$.

Hence each $f^{(i)}(u_j)/i!$ is an integer. Thus, noting that, if $\alpha \geqslant 1$, then $p^{\alpha+1}$ divides h^2 and all higher powers of h, we can rewrite $(*)$ as

$$0 \equiv f(v) \equiv f(u_j) + tp^\alpha f'(u_j) \qquad \pmod{p^{\alpha+1}} \qquad (**)$$

But $p^\alpha | f(u_j)$, so $(**)$ can be rewritten

$$f'(u_j)t \equiv \frac{-f(u_j)}{p^\alpha} \pmod p. \qquad (***)$$

The problem of finding solutions to $f(x) \equiv 0 \pmod{p^{\alpha+1}}$ has therefore been reduced to that of finding solutions to $f(x) \equiv 0 \pmod{p^\alpha}$ together with the solving of a few linear congruences modulo p.

So how many solutions are there to $f(x) \equiv 0 \pmod{p^{\alpha+1}}$? Theorem 4.1.1 gives the answer:

If $p \nmid f'(u_j)$, then $(***)$ defines t uniquely so that u_j gives rise to just one v.
If $p | f'(u_j)$ but $p \nmid f(u_j)/p^\alpha$ then u_j gives rise to no v at all.
If $p | f'(u_j)$ and $p | f(u_j)/p^\alpha$ then u_j gives rise to p distinct $v \pmod{p^{\alpha+1}}$.

The following example illustrates these points nicely.

Example 4.2.3 Find all the solutions of $f(x) = x^3 + 4x^2 + 5x + 2 \pmod{27}$.

* Brook Taylor, 18 August 1685 – 29 December 1731.

Solution By inspection $f(x) \equiv 0 \pmod 3$ iff $x \equiv 1$ or $2 \pmod 3$. Now $f'(x) = 3x^2+8x+5$. Therefore $f'(1)=16$, $f'(2)=33$. Consequently solutions v of $f(x) \equiv 0 \pmod 9$ are given by

$v = 1+t\cdot 3$, where $16t \equiv -f(1)/3 = -12/3 \pmod 3$, whence $t \equiv 2 \pmod 3$

and

$v = 2+t\cdot 3$, where $33t \equiv -f(2)/3 = -36/3 \pmod 3$, whence $t \equiv 0, 1, 2 \pmod 3$.

This means that

$$v = 1+(2+3s)\cdot 3 \quad \text{or}$$

$$v = 2+(3s)\cdot 3 \quad \text{or} \quad 2+(1+3s)\cdot 3 \quad \text{or} \quad 2+(2+3s)\cdot 3$$

that is $v \equiv 7$ or 2 or 5 or $8 \pmod 9$.

Now suppose that w is a solution, mod 27, of the given congruence. We know that $w = v+9t$ where $v = 7$, 2, 5 or 8.

By the above theory we find t by solving the four congruences:

$$208t = f'(7)t \equiv -f(7)/9 = -64 \pmod 3,$$

$$33t = f'(2)t \equiv -f(2)/9 = -4 \pmod 3,$$

$$120t = f'(5)t \equiv -f(5)/9 = -28 \pmod 3,$$

$$261t = f'(8)t \equiv -f(8)/9 = -90 \pmod 3.$$

Since $3|33$, $3|120$ and $3|261$ whilst $3 \nmid 208$ we see that $v=7$ leads to a unique value of w, namely $w=25$; $v=2$ and $v=5$ lead to no values of w and, finally, $v=8$ leads to three values of w, namely $w = 8+9\cdot 0$, $8+9\cdot 1$ and $8+9\cdot 2$. The four solutions of the given congruence are therefore, (mod 27), 25, 8, 17 and 26.

Since it is rather nice to draw a little picture showing how all these roots arise let us do just that!

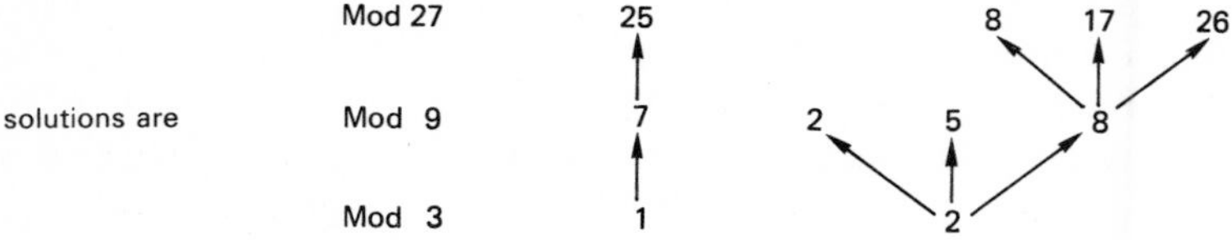

Isn't that pretty?

We can summarise this method for constructing solutions in the following algorithm. Since it uses programs previously described we leave readers to piece together the complete program themselves.

Algorithm

1 Perform the prime factorisation of $m = p_1^{\alpha_1} p_2^{\alpha_2} \cdots p_r^{\alpha_r}$. (See Program 1.5.)

2 For each prime factor p_i in turn:

(a) Solve the congruence $f(x) \equiv 0 (\bmod p_i)$ to obtain solution u_j, $j = 1$ to l. (See Program 4.1.)

(b) For each of these solutions (if there are any):

Generate the solutions, for successive values of c to

$$f(x) \equiv 0 (\bmod p_i^c)$$

until either no solution is obtained or $c = \alpha_1$. Note: These solutions are found by solving

$$f'(u_j)t \equiv -f(u_j)/(p_i^c)(\bmod p_i). \text{ (See Program 4.1.)}$$

3 If m is a prime power (i.e. $r = 1$) the solutions generated at step 2b are the solutions of the given equation. Otherwise solve the system of simultaneous linear congruences

$$\frac{m}{p_i^{\alpha_i}} x \equiv 1 \bmod (p_i^{\alpha_i}) \text{ where } m = p_1^{\alpha_1} p_2^{\alpha_2} \cdots p_r^{\alpha_r}$$

to produce values c_i.

Then the solution is $\sum_{i=1}^{r} c_i \left(\frac{m}{p_i^{\alpha_i}} \right) b_i(j)$, where the $b_i(j)$ are one set of solutions from step 2b.

Exercises 4.2

1 Prove the assertion made in the text that in checking for solutions of $f(x) \equiv 0 (\bmod m)$ one only needs values of x for which $0 \leqslant x \leqslant m - 1$.

2 Show that the equation $x^6 + 38x^4 - 43x^3 - 17x^2 + 8 = 0$ has no solution in $\mathbb{Z}$. [*Hint*: Show it has none modulo 3.]

3 Solve the congruences $x^2 + x + 4 \equiv 0 (\bmod 7)$; (ii) $x^2 + 2x + 4 \equiv (\bmod 7)$; (iii) $x^2 + 3x + 4 \equiv 0 (\bmod 7)$. [*Hint*: Since 7 is small use trial and error.]

4 Denote the number of solutions of $f(x) \equiv k (\bmod m)$ by $F(k)$. Prove that $\sum_{k=1}^{m} F(k) = m$.

5 Given $m = 2^2 3^3 5^5 7^7$, for which x $(0 \leqslant x < m)$ is $x^4 \equiv 0 (\bmod m)$? How many solutions (pairwise incongruent modulo m) does this congruence have?

6 Find the number of solutions to the equation $24x^3 + 218x^2 + 121x + 17 \equiv 0 (\bmod 15\,015)$. [*Hint*: $15\,015 = 3 \cdot 5 \cdot 7 \cdot 11 \cdot 13$.]

7 Show that the congruence $x^2 \equiv a (\bmod p)$ has at most two (pairwise incongruent) solutions if p is a prime. Show that if $p = 4k + 3$ then each solution is congruent to a power of a.

8 Solve, if possible, the congruences: (i) $x^2 \equiv 3 (\bmod 83)$ [*Hint*: $169 - 3$?]; (ii) $x^2 \equiv 5 (\bmod 19)$.

9 (a) Show that $x^2 \equiv 2 \pmod 4$ and $x^2 \equiv 3 \pmod 4$ are congruences with no solutions.
(b) Find all solutions of: (i) $x^2 \equiv 1 \pmod 4$; (ii) $x^2 \equiv 1 \pmod 8$.
(c) Find the number of solutions of $x^2 \equiv 1 \pmod{2^\alpha}$ for $\alpha \geqslant 4$. [*Hint*: Relate solutions modulo 2^α to solutions modulo $2^{\alpha-1}$.]

10 Discover the roots, if any, of $x^5+3x^2+1 \equiv 10 \pmod{11}$ and of $x^4+5x^2+6 \equiv 0 \pmod{11}$ by trial and error. [*Hint*: Modulo 11 we have $10 \equiv -1$, $9 \equiv -2$, etc.]

11 Find all x, if any, satisfying the congruences:
(i) $x^3+6x^2+2x+6 \equiv 0 \pmod 7$; (ii) $x^3-1 \equiv 0 \pmod{101}$;
(iii) $x^4-1 \equiv 0 \pmod{101}$; (iv) $x^3+1 \equiv 0 \pmod{101}$.
[*Hint*: $a^{100} \equiv 1 \pmod{101}$.]

12 Solve the congruences: (i) $x^3+6x^2+2x+6 \equiv 0 \pmod{35}$;
(ii) $x^2+1 \equiv 0 \pmod{65}$.

13 Solve the congruence $x^3+16x^2-6x+12 \equiv 0 \pmod{30}$.

14 Solve the congruences: (i) $x^3+2x^2+4x+8 \equiv 0 \pmod{125}$;
(ii) $x^3+3x^2+x+5 \equiv 0 \pmod{1125}$.

15 Show that if $a, b, c \in \mathbb{Z}$ and $a^3+b^3=c^3$ then $3 \mid abc$. [*Hint*: Try $a=3u\pm 1$, $b=3v\pm 1$; $c=3w\pm 1$ and work modulo 9.]

16 Find all solutions of the congruence $x^{p-2}+x^{p-3}+\cdots+x^2+x+1 \equiv 0 \pmod p$ where p is a prime.

17 Show that for p an odd prime and a an integer such that $(a, p)=1$ the congruence $x^2 \equiv a \pmod{p^c}$, has two or no solutions according as $x^2 \equiv a \pmod p$ has two or no solutions. (Cf. Exercise 9(b), (c).)

Computer problems 4.2

1 Write a program to solve the congruence $f(x) \equiv 0 \pmod m$ where $f(x)$ is a polynomial of degree n using the algorithm described in the text. Use it to solve the following problems:

(i) $2x^3+3x^2+4x+5 \equiv 0 \pmod{7^3}$;
(ii) $x^3+2x^2+x+2 \equiv 0 \pmod{5^3}$;
(iii) $6x^5+31x^4+2x^2+x+17 \equiv 0 \pmod{168}$.

It is instructive to produce a display, similar to that in the text, to illustrate how each solution has arisen.

2 Write a (much simpler) program to find solutions by brute force and compare its performance with that of Problem 1.

4.3 Quadratic congruences modulo a prime

Lest the reader be overcome with joy at seeing the above method of dealing with congruences involving general polynomials and general moduli let us bring him back down to earth by reminding him that everything depends on being able to solve the given congruence modulo each prime dividing the modulus. Surely there is no difficulty here? For prime modulus one just proceeds, as in the above example, by trial and error? Of course one may but here we meet the same snag mentioned earlier: what if the prime is rather large—say 4999*. Wouldn't it be a might galling to find, after performing 4998 calculations that a given equation $f(x) \equiv 0 (\text{mod } 4999)$ had no solutions after all? This raises the question: Can we tell *in advance* whether a congruence $f(x) \equiv 0 (\text{mod } p)$ has a solution or not? It was this kind of question to which Euler, Legendre and especially Gauss devoted much deep thought. Let us see what is involved in the case of *quadratic* congruences, the linear case, $ax \equiv b (\text{mod } p)$—when $p \nmid a$—having the explicit solution $x \equiv ba^{p-2} (\text{mod } p)$ (Exercise 4.1.6).

To avoid possible ambiguities in the precise interpretation of the symbolism $f(x) \equiv 0 (\text{mod } m)$ we shall introduce a new kind of congruence between polynomials in

Definition 4.3.1 Let $f(x) = a_n x^n + a_{n-1} x^{n-1} + \cdots + a_0$ and $g(x) = b_n x^n + b_{n-1} x^{n-1} + \cdots + b_0$ be polynomials with integer coefficients. We say that $f(x)$ and $g(x)$ are *identically congruent* and write $f(x) \equiv_p g(x) (\text{mod } m)$ if and only if $a_i \equiv b_i (\text{mod } m)$ for each i $(1 \leqslant i \leqslant n)$. Note that, for each $a \in \mathbb{Z}$, the congruence $f(x) \equiv_p g(x) (\text{mod } m)$ implies the congruence $f(a) \equiv g(a) (\text{mod } m)$. The converse, as you might suspect, is false: for example $a^3 + a + 1 \equiv 2a + 1 (\text{mod } 3)$ for all $a \in \mathbb{Z}$ and yet $x^3 + x + 1 \not\equiv_p 2x + 1 (\text{mod } 3)$.

Now suppose we are to solve the congruence $f(x) \equiv 0 (\text{mod } p)$ where $f(x) = ax^2 + bx + c$, p is a prime and $p \nmid a$. Then there exists an integer a^* such that $aa^* \equiv 1 (\text{mod } p)$. Consequently

$$ax^2 + bx + c \equiv_p a(x^2 + a^*bx + a^*c) (\text{mod } p).$$

Now if we wish to write $x^2 + a^*bx + a^*c \equiv_p (x+d)^2 + e (\text{mod } p)$ we shall need to take $2d \equiv a^*b (\text{mod } p)$, a congruence with solution $d = a^*b(p+1)/2$—at least if $p \neq 2$, a condition which, from now on, we assume. But then $x^2 + a^*bx + a^*c \equiv_p (x+d)^2 + (a^*c - d^2) (\text{mod } p)$. Now setting $y = x + d$ and $z = d^2 - a^*c$ we see that the problem of solving $f(x) \equiv 0 (\text{mod } p)$ is equivalent to solving $y^2 \equiv z (\text{mod } p)$.

To illustrate four different situations in which you might find yourselves we give

Examples 4.3.2 (i) Solve, if possible, $5x^2 + 13x + 16 \equiv 0 (\text{mod } 17)$.

* Of course if you insist on using your computer, we shall feel free to replace 4999 by a (much) larger prime!

Solution Since $5 \cdot 7 \equiv 1 \pmod{17}$ we can rewrite the given congruence as

$$5(x^2+91x+112) \equiv_p 5(x^2+6x+10) \pmod{17}$$

and concentrate on solving the congruence $x^2+6x+10 \equiv 0 \pmod{17}$. Completing the square we get $(x+3)^2 \equiv -1 \pmod{17}$.

From Theorem 3.5.4 we know that $\left\{\left(\frac{17-1}{2}\right)!\right\}^2 \equiv -1 \pmod{17}$.

Hence $x+3 \equiv \pm(8!) \pmod{17}$, these being the only solutions by Exercise 4.2.7. Consequently $x \equiv 1$ or $10 \pmod{17}$.

(ii) Solve, if possible, $x^2+34x+2789 \equiv 0 \pmod{8999}$.

Solution Since $(x+17)^2+50^2 \equiv 0 \pmod{8999}$ and since 8999 is a prime of the form $4k+3$ we conclude, from Exercise 3.5.15(ii), that this congruence has no solution.

(iii) Solve, if possible, $x^2+34x+2789 \equiv 0 \pmod{9001}$.

Solution Here we know two solutions exist [do we? why?] and yet it is not so obvious what they are!

(iv) Solve, if possible, $x^2 \equiv 2223 \pmod{3779}$.

Solution Has it got one?

For problems such as the last, Euler and Legendre determined an infallible and fairly quick method for determining whether or not a solution exists. It was left to Gauss finally to prove that their method was indeed correct—see Chapter 8.

Program 4.3 *Solves the quadratic congruence* $ax^2 + bx + c \equiv 0 \pmod{p}$ *where p is prime.*

```
 10 DIM a(2),b(2)
 20 INPUT A,B,C,N
 30 PRINT "The solutions are ";
 40 I=1
 50 IF A=1 GOTO 100
 60 R=I*A - INT(I*A/N)*N
 70   IF R=1 GOTO 100
 80   I=I+1
 90 GOTO 60
100 A1=I
110 D=(A1*B*(N+1)/2)
120 D=D-INT(D/N)*N
130 Z=D*D-A1*C
140 Z=Z-INT(Z/N)*N
150 CNT=0
160 R=Z - INT(Z/N)*N
170 IF R<0 R=R+N
180 FOR X=0 TO N-1
190   S=X*X - INT(X*X/N)*N
200   IF S<>R GOTO 250
210     CNT=CNT+1
220 REM for each solution we solve the linear congruence
230 REM  Y+D = X (mod N)
240     PRINT X-D-INT((X-D)/N)*N;
250 NEXT X
260 IF CNT=0 PRINT "NONE"
270 END
```

Is there an alternative, more efficient, method? As in the case of the linear congruence the answer is again 'yes' but we will have to wait until the end of Chapter 8.

Exercises 4.3

1 Let $f(x)=x^2-1$. Show that, modulo 8, $(x-1)(x+1) \equiv_p (x-3)(x+3)$. {This exhibits the fact that factorisation into irreducible factors amongst polynomials modulo 8 is not unique. You may care to think why $(x-3)(x+3) \equiv_p (3x-1)(3x+1)$ *doesn't* prove that factorisation isn't unique. [*Hint*: $3 \cdot 3 \equiv 1$.]}

2 Write the following congruences in the form $y^2 \equiv z \pmod p$ and solve each for x, if possible (by hand): (i) $5x^2+7 \equiv 0 \pmod{17}$; (ii) $10x^2+2x+1 \equiv 0 \pmod{23}$.

3 Solve by hand $x^2+7x+12 \equiv 0 \pmod{19}$. [*Hint*: $7 \equiv 26 \pmod{19}$.]

4 Solve (by hand) if possible, $x^2+7x-12 \equiv 0 \pmod{323}$. [*Hint*: 323 isn't prime.]

5 Solve, by hand, $x^2+8x+17 \equiv 0 \pmod{65}$. [*Hint*: Use Exercise 4.2.12(ii).]

Computer problems 4.3

1 Write a program to find solutions to quadratic congruences using only trial and error and compare its performance with that of Program 4.3.

2 Solve
(i) $x^2+122x-4697 \equiv 0 \pmod{9787}$;
(ii) $x^2+34x+2789 \equiv 0 \pmod{9001}$.

Joseph-Louis Lagrange *(25 January 1736 – 10 April 1813)*
Lagrange was born in Turin, the first child and only survivor into adulthood, to parents from wealthy backgrounds. Fortunately for mathematics, Lagrange's father lost all his money on bad speculations,

Lagrange himself admitting that if he had inherited wealth he would probably not have become a mathematician. In fact he was at first attracted to the classics but was converted to mathematics after reading a paper of Halley's. Such was his application that aged 17 he was appointed to teach mathematics at the Royal Military Academy in Turin. Here he began his researches which were to mark him out as the founder of the calculus of variations.

In 1766, when Euler left for St Petersburg, he suggested Lagrange as the only suitable replacement. A message was sent to Turin by Frederick the Great inviting 'the greatest mathematician in Europe' to the court of 'the greatest king in Europe'! Lagrange accepted and stayed 20 years.

Around this period, specifically between the years 1764 and 1788, Lagrange several times won the biennial prize offered by the French Académie des Sciences. In the period 1767–1771 he published papers of great importance in the theory of equations both numerical and algebraic. In the latter he showed that the formulae giving the solutions of general equations of degree n (such as $x=(-b\pm\sqrt{(b^2-4ac)})/2a$ in the case of $ax^2+bx+c=0$) can be obtained in a uniform way by reducing the given equation to a simpler one, at least in the cases $n=2$, 3 and 4. Unfortunately in the case $n=5$ the resulting 'simpler' equation to be solved first is of degree 6 so that a similar approach in this case fails. These researches led the way towards the algebraic theory of groups.

In this book Lagrange figures because of his many contributions to the theory of numbers, but his greatest work, completed around 1782—conceived when he was no more than 23 years old—is his *Méchanique Analytique* (1788), a work providing a unified treatment of mechanics and which Lagrange, modest to a fault, proudly proclaims 'contains no pictures'. Sir William Rowan Hamilton described it as 'a kind of scientific poem'.

In 1787, a year after the death of Frederick, Lagrange returned to Paris at the invitation of Louis XVI. Excessive work had dulled Lagrange's appetite for mathematics—indeed he had suffered bouts of depression whilst still in Berlin. During one such spell, when aged 56, he was rescued by the daughter of his friend, the astronomer Lemonnier. Although almost 40 years his junior she insisted upon marrying him. His interest in life and mathematics returned and in turn he was appointed professor at the Ecole Normale (1795) and, upon its closure, at the Ecole Polytechnique (1797).

Between 1797 and 1801 Lagrange wrote three books, two of which, although not particularly successful themselves, may be regarded as the starting point from which Cauchy, Riemann, Weierstrass and others developed the theory of functions.

4.4 Lagrange's theorem

We have just seen that the theory of polynomial congruences can have its more painful aspects. Are there any nice things we can discover without too much effort? One illustration of the answer (which is 'yes') is a result due to Lagrange.

In the theory of equations one of the better known principles, roughly stated, says: *No polynomial of degree n can have more than n roots.* The reader has, presumably, used this result in the case of polynomials with real coefficients where real roots have been sought. The star result in this area is the fundamental theorem of algebra first proved, after unsuccessful attempts by D'Alembert*, Euler and others, by Gauss in 1799. It states that: *Each polynomial of degree n with complex number coefficients has, counting multiple roots an appropriate number of times, exactly n complex roots.* [This result clearly implies that above for polynomials with real coefficients.]

We have already seen examples, (see Exercise 4.2.9(b)(ii)) where the same principle fails for polynomials considered 'modulo m' and one can manufacture unpleasant examples *ad nauseam.* Even linear congruences aren't exempt: the congruence $2x-2\equiv 0 \pmod 4$ of degree one has two solutions, namely $x\equiv 1$ and $x\equiv 3$. Has this unpleasant behaviour anything to do with the composite nature of the modulus in these nasty examples? This question scores a bull's-eye, as Lagrange showed in 1768.

Theorem 4.4.1 (*Lagrange's theorem*) Let p be a prime and let $f(x)= a_nx^n+a_{n-1}x^{n-1}+\cdots+a_0$, where $p\nmid a_n$. Then the congruence $f(x)\equiv 0 \pmod p$ has at most n distinct (integer) solutions α such that $-p/2<\alpha\leqslant p/2$. (Proof on p. 120.)

Lagrange demonstrated his assertion by giving the proof for the 'typical' case $n=3$. We shall prove it making use of Gauss's congruence notation, and we shall begin with a theorem analogous to one used in the proofs of the results on real and complex roots mentioned above.

Theorem 4.4.2 Let c_1 be a solution of the congruence $f(x)\equiv 0 \pmod m$ where $f(x)$ is as above. Then we may write $f(x)\equiv_{\mathrm{p}} (x-c_1)f_1(x) \pmod m$ where $f_1(x)$ is a polynomial with integer coefficients and of degree $n-1$ in x.

Proof Since $f(c_1)\equiv 0 \pmod m$ we have $f(x)\equiv_{\mathrm{p}} f(x)-f(c_1) \pmod m$. But $f(x)-f(c_1)=\sum_{i=1}^n a_i(x^i-c_1^i)$ [why can we start the summation at $i=1$ rather than at $i=0$?] $=(x-c_1)\{\sum_{i=1}^n a_i(\sum_{k=0}^{i-1} x^{i-1-k}c_1^k)\}=(x-c_1)f_1(x)$, say, where clearly $f_1(x)$ has the properties claimed for it. □

As an immediate corollary we obtain

Corollary 4.4.3 Let $c_1, c_2, \ldots, c_r$ be r pairwise incongruent solutions of the congruence $f(x)\equiv 0 \pmod p$ where p is a prime. Then

$$f(x)\equiv_{\mathrm{p}} (x-c_1)(x-c_2)\cdots(x-c_r)f_r(x) \pmod p,$$

where $f_r(x)$ is a polynomial with integer coefficients of degree $n-r$.

* Jean-le-Rond D'Alembert, 17 November 1717 - 29 October 1783.

Proof From Theorem 4.4.2 we have $f(x) \equiv_p (x-c_1)f_1(x) \pmod p$ for some polynomial $f_1(x)$. Now, since c_2 is also a solution of $f(x)\equiv 0 \pmod p$ we have $(c_2-c_1)f_1(c_2)\equiv f(c_2)\equiv 0 \pmod p$. Thus $p|(c_2-c_1)f_1(c_2)$. Since $p\nmid c_2-c_1$ [why not?] we are forced to conclude that $p|f_1(c_2)$, that is, $f_1(c_2)\equiv 0 \pmod p$. Using Theorem 4.4.2 again we infer that

$$f_1(x) \equiv_p (x-c_2)f_2(x) \pmod p,$$

where $f_2(x)$ is a suitable polynomial of degree $n-2$. Thus

$$f(x) \equiv_p (x-c_1)(x-c_2)f_2(x) \pmod p.$$

Continuing in this way—at step 3 we have $p|(c_3-c_1)(c_3-c_2)f_2(c_3)$, from which we deduce that $p|f_2(c_3)$—we obtain the desired result. □

Question
Where does this proof break down if we try to establish the corollary for non-prime modulus?

We can now give the

Proof of Theorem 4.1.1 Let us suppose that $f(x)\equiv 0 \pmod p$ has solutions $c_1, c_2, \ldots, c_n$ and d all in the range $-p/2$ to $p/2$. Then by Corollary 4.4.3 applied* to the first n of these solutions, we have

$$f(x) \equiv_p (x-c_1)(x-c_2)\cdots(x-c_n)f_n(x) \pmod p$$

where $f_n(x)$ is of degree $n-n$, i.e. 0. Thus $f_n(x)$ is a constant b, say, where $b\equiv a_n \pmod p$. Now, by assumption, $f(x)\equiv 0$ has a further solution d lying between $-p/2$ and $p/2$. We thus have

$$(d-c_1)(d-c_2)\cdots(d-c_n)b\equiv f(d)\equiv 0 \pmod p.$$

Now since p is prime we deduce, by Note 1.8.2(ii), that either $p|d-c_i$ for some i or $p|b$. But none of these is possible. For since $-p<d-c_i<p$, the first condition implies that $d-c_i=0$, i.e. $d=c_i$, whereas the second implies that $a_n\equiv b\equiv 0 \pmod p$ contrary to the assumption that $(a_n, p)=1$. Thus $f(x)\equiv 0 \pmod p$ can have no more distinct roots than its degree. □

The main use we shall make of Lagrange's theorem is in applying one of its corollaries (4.4.6 below) to investigations in the next chapter. To obtain this corollary we first need to extract another consequence of Corollary 4.4.3, namely

Corollary 4.4.4 Let p be a prime. Then

$$x^{p-1}-1 \equiv_p (x-1)(x-2)\cdots(x-(p-1)) \pmod p.$$

* *Why* can we apply Corollary 4.4.3?

Proof By FLT (Theorem 3.2.1), we know that

$$x^{p-1}-1\equiv 0(\text{mod } p) \text{ for } x=1,2,\ldots,p-1.$$

Thus, by Corollary 4.4.3,

$$x^{p-1}-1 \equiv_{\text{p}} (x-1)(x-2)\cdots(x-(p-1))\cdot f_{p-1}(x)(\text{mod } p)$$

where we must clearly take $f_{p-1}(x)\equiv 1(\text{mod } p)$. This does it. □

As an amusing digression, Corollary 4.4.4 provides us with another proof of Wilson's theorem (Theorem 3.5.1). What we have here is essentially Lagrange's proof of it. It is interesting to note that although Lagrange had proved Theorem 4.4.1 in 1768, yet even in 1770 Waring was still seeking a proof of Wilson's result.

Corollary 4.4.5 (Wilson's theorem)

Proof In Corollary 4.4.4 assume that p is an odd prime and put $x=0$. Then $-1\equiv(-1)(-2)\cdots(-(p-1))(\text{mod } p)$. Hence, immediately, noting that $p-1$ is even, we get $-1\equiv(p-1)!(\text{mod } p)$. If $p=2$ the result is trivial.

We finish this chapter on a more serious note by establishing the important corollary to be used in Theorem 5.2.7.

Corollary 4.4.6 Let p be a prime and let $d|p-1$. Then the congruence $x^d-1\equiv 0(\text{mod } p)$ has exactly d distinct solutions between $-p/2$ and $p/2$.

Proof Since $d|p-1$ we can factorise $x^{p-1}-1$ as $(x^d-1)g(x)$ where $g(x)$ is a polynomial of degree $p-1-d$. Now consider the congruences $x^d-1\equiv 0(\text{mod } p)$ and $g(x)\equiv 0(\text{mod } p)$. The first has, by Lagrange's theorem, at most d solutions whilst the second has, likewise, at most $p-1-d$. Now since p is a prime, each solution u, say, of $x^{p-1}-1\equiv 0(\text{mod } p)$ is a solution of either $x^d-1\equiv 0(\text{mod } p)$ or $g(x)\equiv 0(\text{mod } p)$. Thus if $x^d-1\equiv 0(\text{mod } p)$ had fewer than d solutions modulo p the congruence $x^{p-1}-1\equiv 0(\text{mod } p)$ would have less than $d+(p-1-d)$. But $x^{p-1}-1\equiv 0(\text{mod } p)$ has exactly $p-1$ solutions, namely $1,2,\ldots,p-1$. Consequently the congruence $x^d-1\equiv 0(\text{mod } p)$ must have exactly d solutions, as claimed. □

Exercises 4.4

1 Find an integer m and a polynomial $f(x)$ of degree 1 in x such that $f(x)\equiv 0(\text{mod } m)$ has 100 pairwise incongruent solutions modulo m.

2 Prove Corollary 4.4.4 as did Lagrange, as follows:

(i) Write $(x-1)(x-2)\cdots(x-p+1)=x^{p-1}-a_1x^{p-2}+\cdots+a_{p-1}$;
(ii) Deduce $x(x-1)(x-2)\cdots(x-p+1)=x^p-a_1x^{p-1}+\cdots+xa_{p-1}$;

(iii) In (ii) replace x by $x-1$ giving $\{(x-1)(x-2)\cdots\}(x-p) = (x-1)^p - a_1(x-1)^{p-1} + \cdots + (x-1)a_{p-1} = \{x^{p-1} - a_1x^{p-2} + \cdots + a_{p-1}\}(x-p)$;
(iv) Equating coefficients deduce $p|a_i (1 \leqslant i \leqslant p-2)$ and $a_{p-1} \equiv -1 \pmod p$.

3 Use Exercise 4.4.2 to deduce that $\sum 1 \leqslant i < j \leqslant p-1\ ij \equiv 0 \pmod p$ if $p \geqslant 5$. (The sum $\sum$ is $1\cdot 2 + 1\cdot 3 + \cdots + 1\cdot(p-1) + 2\cdot 3 + 2\cdot 4 + \cdots + (p-2)(p-1)$. Identify where in the proof you *need* to assume $p \geqslant 5$.

4 (a) Show that the congruence $f(x) \equiv 0 \pmod p$ of degree $m < p$ has m congruent solutions iff there exists $h(x)$ such that $x^p - x \equiv_p f(x)h(x) \pmod p$. (In brief: $f(x)|x^p - x \pmod p$.) (b) If $f(x) = 2x + 1$ and if $p = 5$, find $h(x)$.

5 Let $f(x)$ be a polynomial of degree n and let p be a prime. (i) Given that $f(x) \equiv 0 \pmod p$ has more than n pairwise incongruent solutions show that each coefficient of $f(x)$ is divisible by p. (ii) Show that if $a, a+1, a+2, \ldots, a+n$ are $n+1$ consecutive integers such that $p|f(t)$ for $a \leqslant t \leqslant a+n$, then each coefficient of $f(x)$ is a multiple of p. (iii) Show that the conclusion of (ii) may fail to hold if the word 'consecutive' is deleted.

6 Use Corollary 4.4.6 and the methods of Section 4.2 to show that if p is a prime and if $d|p-1$, then there are exactly d roots $\pmod{p^n}$ of the congruence $x^d = 1 \pmod{p^n}$ where $n \geqslant 1$.

7 (J. Wolstenholme 1862). Let $p > 3$ be a prime. Show that the numerator of $1 + \frac{1}{2} + \frac{1}{3} + \cdots + 1/(p-1)$ is a multiple of p^2. [*Hint*: Using the equality of Exercise 4.4.2(i) show that
(i) $a_{p-1} = (p-1)!$;
(ii) $(p-1)! = p^{p-1} - a_1p^{p-2} + \cdots + a_{p-2}p + a_{p-1}$;
(iii) deduce that $p^2|a_{p-2}$.]

5

Primitive roots

5.1 A converse for the FLT

Fermat's little theorem (FLT; Theorem 3.2.1) tells us that: If p is a prime then for each integer a coprime to p we have $a^{p-1} \equiv 1 (\text{mod } p)$. The converse of this theorem would read

> (CFLT): If n is an integer such that $a^{n-1} \equiv (\text{mod } n)$ for each integer a coprime to n, then n is a prime.

Earlier we noted an example (due to Sarrus, 1819) showing $2^{340} \equiv 1 (\text{mod } 341)$ where, of course, 341 is not a prime. However 341 does not spoil CFLT's chances of reaching theoremhood because, as is easily checked, $(3,341) = 1$ and $3^{340} \not\equiv 1 (\text{mod } 341)$. Unfortunately, in 1909 R. D. Carmichael finally sunk CFLT's candidacy by finding composite numbers n such that $a^{n-1} \equiv 1 (\text{mod } n)$ for all a coprime to n. (You may care to try and compute the smallest such here and now: see Section 5.4). Such composite numbers are called *Carmichael numbers*; they are quite rare.

However, the correct hypotheses to get the desired conclusion that 'n is prime' had essentially already been supplied by the Frenchman Edouard Lucas in 1891. We have:

Theorem 5.1.1 Let n be an integer and let $q_1, q_2, \ldots, q_s$ be the distinct primes dividing $n-1$. If for some integer a we have $a^{n-1} \equiv 1 (\text{mod } n)$ but $a^{(n-1)/q_i} \not\equiv 1 (\text{mod } n)$ for all i $(1 \leqslant i \leqslant s)$, then n is a prime. □ (Proof below)

It may appear that attempting to prove n is prime by this theorem is as futile as attempting to prove n prime by using the converse of Wilson's theorem (Theorem 3.5.3), especially as there is no obvious way of finding the required integer a. However, appearances are deceptive: Fermat's little theorem and this converse lie at the heart of all known (efficient) tests for primality.

We begin with

Proof of Theorem 5.1.1 Consider the set E of all positive integers e such that $a^e \equiv 1 (\text{mod } n)$, and let d be the smallest integer in E. Given any e in E write $e = md + r$ by the division algorithm so that $0 \leqslant r < d$. We then have $a^e = (a^d)^m a^r$, so that $1 \equiv 1^m a^r (\text{mod } n)$. Thus $a^r \equiv 1 (\text{mod } n)$. But, by choice of d, this is impossible unless $r = 0$. Thus $e = md$, which means that each e in E is a multiple of the least member d of E. In particular $d | n-1$. Now if $d < n-1$ then $d | (n-1)/q_i$ for at least one of the primes q_i, $\alpha d = (n-1)/q_i$, say. But then we should have $a^{(n-1)/q_i} \equiv (a^d)^\alpha \equiv 1^\alpha = 1 \pmod n$, contradicting our hypothesis. Consequently $d = n-1$.

It follows immediately that n is prime. For, from Euler's theorem (Theorem 3.4.1), namely that $a^{\phi(n)} \equiv 1 \pmod n$, we conclude that $\phi(n) = n-1$, an equality which implies that n is prime (Exercise 3.3.11). □

One snag the reader might have noticed: it might be quite tricky to factorise $n-1$(!). Nevertheless the test can be quite fast in those cases where $n-1$ has few distinct prime factors, several of which are small, for example when n is of the form 2^k+1—see Theorem 5.4.1 below.

By way of illustration we present three examples. The calculations can be performed using the techniques described in Chapter 3 although for numbers as large as these multiprecision calculations are necessary. (The primality of numbers of the size used here can be established more quickly using Program 1.1, for example, but they serve to make the point.)

Examples 5.1.2

(i) 1 000 001 is not prime since $2^{1\,000\,000} \equiv 606\,496 \pmod{1\,000\,001}$ (Use Theorem 3.2.1. Actually you should be able to think of a factor without resorting to a computer.)

(ii) 700 001 is such that $2^{700\,000} \equiv 1 \pmod{700\,001}$ so there is still a fair chance that 700 001 is prime. The prime factors of 700 000 are 2, 5 and 7. However $2^{350\,000} \equiv 1 \pmod{700\,001}$ so Theorem 5.1.1 is no help yet. If we use $a = 3$ we find $3^{700\,000} \equiv 1 \pmod{700\,001}$. Since $3^{350\,000} \equiv 700\,000 \not\equiv 1 \pmod{700\,001}$, $3^{140\,000} \equiv 425\,344 \not\equiv 1 \pmod{700\,001}$ and $3^{100\,000} \equiv 591\,336 \not\equiv 1 \pmod{700\,001}$ we can conclude the 700 001 is indeed prime.

(iii) Finally consider 900 001. 900 000 has prime factors 2, 3, 5 and we summarize the results in Table 5.1 which gives values of $a^{(n-1)/q} \pmod n$ where $n = 900\,001$ and q takes the values 1, 2, 3 and 5.

Table 5.1

a \ q	1	2	3	5
2	1	1	519 434	550 388
3	1	1	519 434	1
5	1	1	519 434	550 388
7	1	1	380 566	596 402
11	1	1	1	596 402
13	1	900 000	1	596 402
17	1	1	380 566	550 388
19	1	1	380 566	596 402
23	1	900 000	519 434	596 402

In this case it is not until we use the value 23 that we definitely establish that 900 001 is indeed prime. However if we use the result of Exercise 5.1.4 we only need to compute the values $2^{(n-1)/q} \pmod n$ for $q = 2, 3, 5$ and then, since only $2^{(n-1)/2} \equiv 1 (\text{mod } n)$, try $a^{(n-1)/2} (\text{mod } n)$ for $a = 3, 5, 7, 11$ and 13. That is, we only need the first row and the column headed '2' in the above table, before confirming that 900 001 is prime.

Incidentally, are you surprised by the numerous repetitions in the above table? Should you be?

Exercises 5.1

1 Show that $3^{340} \not\equiv 1 (\text{mod } 341)$—and deduce that 341 is not a prime!

2 Show (by hand) that $2^{n-1} \equiv 1 (\text{mod } n)$ if $n = 19 \cdot 73$, $3 \cdot 5 \cdot 43$ and $17 \cdot 257$ but that none of these is a Carmichael number. [*Hint*: Use Exercise 3.2.12.]

3 (Malo 1903) Let $N = 2^p - 1$ where p is a prime. Show that $2^{N-1} \equiv 1 (\text{mod } N)$. [*Hint*: $N - 1 = 2(2^{p-1} - 1) = 2pm$. Then $2^{N-1} = (2^p)^{2m} = (N+1)^{2m}$]

4 (Brillhart, Lehmer, Selfridge 1975) Prove the following stronger version of Theorem 5.1.1: Suppose $N - 1 = q_1^{\beta_1} q_2^{\beta_2} \cdots q_n^{\beta_n}$, the q_i being distinct primes. If for each q_i there exists a number a_i such that $a_i^{(N-1)/q_i} \not\equiv 1 (\text{mod } N)$ and $a_i^{N-1} \equiv 1 (\text{mod } N)$, then N is a prime. [*Hint*: For each i let d_i be the least positive integer such that $a_i^{d_i} \equiv 1 (\text{mod } N)$. Show that $d_i \mid N - 1$ and yet $d_i \nmid (N-1)/q_i$. Deduce that $q_i^{\beta_i} \mid d_i$ so that $q_i^{\beta_i} \mid \phi(N)$. Conclude that $N - 1 \mid \phi(N)$.]

Computer problems 5.1

1 Using Program 3.2 as a basis write a program to implement Theorem 5.1.1 for numbers your computer can cope with without resorting to multiprecision arithmetic.

2 Modify your program to make use of the result of Exercise 5.1.4.

3 Using the multiprecision algorithms given in Appendix I, together with the algorithms you have developed and tested in Computer Problems 1 and 2 above, write a multiprecision program and use it to search for prime numbers of the form $10^n + 1$ for n even, (n odd is easy to deal with by hand, [why?]) and for primes of the form $r10^n + 1$ where $r = 3, 7, 9$. (Do you find many primes if $r = 5$?)

5.2 Primitive roots of primes. Order of an element

The conditions forced on a and n by the hypotheses of Theorem 5.1.1, namely that n is prime ($n = p$, say), that $(a, p) = 1$ and that $p - 1$ is the least positive integer e for which $a^e \equiv 1 (\text{mod } p)$, are precisely the conditions that a be a *primitive root* of (or 'for' or 'modulo') p according to Definition 5.2.1 below. In fact we take the opportunity of hindsight to introduce a definition which extends the class of integers for which the concept of primitive root is defined beyond the set of primes.

Definition 5.2.1 (Introduced for primes by Euler, 1773) Let n be any integer $\geqslant 2$ and let a be an integer such that $(a, n) = 1$ (so that $a^{\phi(n)} \equiv 1 (\text{mod } n)$ by Euler's theorem). If there is no integer e such that $1 \leqslant e < \phi(n)$ and such that $a^e \equiv 1(\text{mod } n)$ then a is called a *primitive root* of (for, modulo) n.

Example 5.2.2 $\phi(22) = 10$ and $1^1 \equiv 3^5 \equiv 5^5 \equiv 7^{10} \equiv 9^5 \equiv 13^{10} \equiv 15^5 \equiv 17^{10} \equiv 19^{10} \equiv 21^2 \equiv 1(\text{mod } 22)$, where the powers used are taken as small as possible. We therefore see that 7, 13, 17 and 19 are primitive roots of 22.

One immediately runs straight into the problems: (i) Is there a good way of finding, for each n, a primitive root of n? and, at a more fundamental level, (ii) Does each n necessarily *have* a primitive root?

In relation to the second question the German mathematician J. H. Lambert asserted, in 1769, that each prime does indeed have a primitive root. Four years later Euler gave a (defective) proof of this which he then used to give yet another demonstration of Wilson's theorem! (see Exercise 5.2.15). In the end it was Legendre who first correctly proved that each prime has a primitive root—indeed $\phi(p-1)$ of them—and then Gauss (who else?) who determined, in 1801, exactly which integers have primitive roots (see Theorem 5.3.9).

Adrien-Marie Legendre *(18 September 1752–9 January 1833)*
Legendre, who was born in Paris, was educated there at the College Mazarin where he was taught by the Abbé Francoise-Joseph Marie, himself a noted mathematician. Early in life Legendre was sufficiently well off financially that he didn't need to work. Nevertheless he taught mathematics at the Ecole Militaire from 1775 to 1780. Whilst there he wrote an essay on ballistics which won the 1782 prize offered by the Berlin Academy. Two years later there appeared in print the famous Legendre polynomials, which help us to solve problems in hydrodynamics, electricity and magnetism.

Although Legendre appears in this book because of his contributions to number theory, that subject was not his only love. For example he also returned many times to the study of elliptic integrals, an area in which he was the only important worker for almost forty years. He presented these results in 1825/6 in a two-volume work *Fonctions Elliptiques*. In an earlier book *exercises de Calcul Integral* Legendre had studied integrals called by him 'Eulerian'—subsequently called the beta and gamma functions. Earlier still (1794) he had written a lower-level text, a substitute for Euclid's. It was to become the standard text for 100 years! Later editions included a proof of the irrationality of π^2 and hence of π itself, a result obtained earlier by Lambert.

Several of Legendre's number-theoretic results are included in this text. One in particular, the law of quadratic reciprocity (see Chapter 8) brought him into conflict with Gauss. Each claimed priority for its demonstration, Gauss on the grounds that all previous proofs were incomplete, Legendre on the grounds that he had shown in detail how it was to be done. (More ill-will followed when, on the first publication by Legendre of the method of least squares, Gauss asserted that he'd been using the method privately for some time.)

Although Legendre was an energetic worker, Kline [31] ranks him behind Lagrange and Laplace as not matching their profundity nor originality. Indeed he was not one of the original 48 scholars elected to the French National Institute. He was, nevertheless, a member of many committees being, in particular, one of those responsible for the introduction of the metric system.

In one respect, the so-called 'human interest' angle, Legendre's life matched that of Lagrange, namely that in 1792* at the age of 40 he married a girl 22 years his junior. His financial security having been lost, Legendre reports that his young wife helped him put his affairs in order and also brought a tranquillity to his life which greatly aided him in his work.

---

* The same year as Lagrange, 16 years his senior, married a girl one third of his age.

The concept of primitive root is one of the most fundamental in number theory. We shall see how it offers the real explanation as to why, for some primes, the decimal expansion of $1/p$ has repeating length $p-1$ (for example $1/7 = 0.142857\ 142857\ 14\ldots$) whilst, for others, the repeating length is a proper divisor of $p-1$ (for example $1/11 = 0.09\ 09\ 09\ 0\ldots$). In a different direction the concept can be used to give an easy proof (Exercise 5.2.13(b)) of a very important criterion due to Euler. (It must be admitted that Euler established this criterion by different means—and earlier than 1769—see Lemma 8.3.1(iii).) At a different level of sophistication the idea of primitive root was vital for Gauss's construction, by straight edge and compass, of a regular 17-gon—the first 'new' constructible polygon for 2000 years. (Unfortunately we haven't the space to go into the details here. See, for example, [18].) In more modern times primitive roots have proved to be important in constructing primality tests and in generating sequences of pseudo-random numbers ([6] and [7]), whilst a slight generalisation which we shall introduce when investigating Carmichael numbers had an often quoted application, in the 1930s, to the more efficient splicing of underwater telephone cables! (see [I] and [19]). Finally, Schroeder's lovely book [4] reports applications to the improvement of concern hall acoustics!

To prove the existence of primitive roots for each prime *p*, it helps to make

Definition 5.2.3 (Gauss 1801) Let a, n be positive integers such that $(a, n) = 1$ The *order* of a modulo n* is the smallest positive integer e such that $a^e \equiv 1 (\text{mod } n)$. We denote it by $\text{ord}_n\, a$.

Example 5.2.4 In Example 5.2.2, 1 has order 1; 21 has order 2; 3, 5, 9 and 15 have order 5 whilst 7, 13, 17 and 19 have order 10—all modulo 22.

Note 5.2.5 By Theorem 3.4.1, e can never exceed $\phi(n)$. Indeed we always have $e|\phi(n)$ (see Exercise 5.2.6). This observation can lead to slight shortcuts in finding orders.

* e is also called the *exponent* to which a belongs modulo n.

Example 5.2.6 The order of 2 modulo 39 is a divisor of $\phi(39)=\phi(3)\cdot\phi(13)=2\cdot 12=24$. Now, modulo 39 we have, $2^2\equiv 4$, $2^4\equiv 16$, $2^8\equiv 256\equiv 22$, $2^{12}\equiv 22\cdot 16\equiv 352\equiv 1$. Thus the order of 2 divides 12 (Exercise 5.2.6 again). Since the order of 2 is clearly not 4 let us try 6 (6 being the other number which is one prime 'step' down from 12). Clearly $2^6\not\equiv 1 \pmod{39}$; this establishes that 2 has order exactly 12 modulo 39.

Let us now prove Legendre's theorem.

Theorem 5.2.7 Let p be an odd prime. Then there exist $\phi(p-1)$ primitive roots of p.

Proof Let us denote the number of solutions of the congruence $x^{p-1}-1\equiv 0 \pmod p$ which have order exactly e by $\psi(e)$. We claim that $\psi(e)=\phi(e)$. Certainly this equality holds for $e=1$ and $e=2$ (Exercise 5.2.4).

Observe that if a is an element of order exactly e then, by Note 5.2.5, $e\mid p-1$. That is, we can restrict attention to divisors of $p-1$. Thus let d be any such divisor and suppose the equality $\psi(\delta)=\phi(\delta)$ has already been proved for all smaller divisors of $p-1$. By Corollary 4.4.6 the congruence $x^d-1\equiv 0 \pmod p$ has d solutions. Furthermore each of its solutions is a solution (with order dividing d) of $x^{p-1}-1\equiv 0 \pmod p$—and vice versa: each solution of $x^{p-1}-1\equiv 0 \pmod p$ with order dividing d is (trivially!) a solution of $x^d-1\equiv 0 \pmod p$. Hence we can say that $d=\sum_{\delta\mid d}\psi(\delta)$. By hypothesis we know that $\psi(\delta)=\phi(\delta)$ whenever $\delta\mid d$ and $\delta<d$. Hence we may rewrite the above summation as $d=\sum_{\delta\mid d}\psi(\delta)=\sum_{\delta\mid d}\phi(\delta)-\phi(d)+\psi(d)$. But, by Theorem 3.3.12, we know that, for each positive integer t, $t=\sum_{\tau\mid t}\phi(\tau)$. Consequently $d=d-\phi(d)+\psi(d)$, that is $\psi(d)=\phi(d)$, as claimed.

The theorem then follows immediately; taking $e=p-1$ we obtain $\psi(p-1)=\phi(p-1)$, as required. □

Example 5.2.8 If $p=11$ then, mod p, $1^1\equiv 2^{10}\equiv 3^5\equiv 4^5\equiv 5^5\equiv 6^{10}\equiv 7^{10}\equiv 8^{10}\equiv 9^5\equiv 10^2$. (Recall that the orders can only be 1, 2, 5 or 10.) As a consequence 2, 6, 7 and 8 are the $\phi(10)=4$ primitive roots of 11.

Although the above result indicates there is no scarcity of primitive roots for any given prime p, the task of identifying them (efficiently) can be quite a problem. Gauss said 'Their distribution is a great mystery' and Euler '. . . knew no rule for finding one'. Of course one can always resort to trial-and-error methods, and for small primes this is probably the best means of attack. The divising of an efficient, explicit method for producing primitive roots is one of the most important unsolved problems in number theory.

Program 5.1 finds the primitive roots of any given number n by searching over all possible candidates. For each number (coprime to n) that is not a primitive root its order is displayed.

Program 5.1 *Finds the primitive roots (if any) of any given integer N*

```
 10 REM Determine the value of Eulers φ using program 3.4 (stored in P)

500 FOR a= 2 TO N-1
510 REM check whether a is coprime to N
520    a1=N
530    b1=a
540    r=a1 - INT (a1/b1)*b1
550      a1=b1
560      b1=r
570    IF r<> 0 GOTO 540
580    IF a1<>1 GOTO 700
590 REM Compute succesive powers of a (mod n)
600      a1=a
610      e=1
620      e=e+1
630      a1=a1*a
640      a1=a1 - INT(a1/N)*N
650      IF a1=1 AND e<P GOTO 690
660      IF e < P GOTO 620
670      PRINT "primitive root";a,e
680    GOTO 700
690    PRINT a;" has order ";e
700 NEXT a
```

One immediate improvement that can be made to this program is to stop the search when e reaches $\phi(N)/2$. Why?

Gauss offered some thoughts on how one might produce primitive roots more efficiently than by mere trial-and-error methods. The following example shows the kind of ideas he had in mind—ideas which C. G. J. Jacobi* used in his *Canon Arithmeticus* (1839) to help him find primitive roots for primes p between 200 and 1000.

Example 5.2.9 Find a primitive root for 47.

Solution Let's begin by trying 2. Since $2^{\phi(47)} \equiv 1 (\text{mod } 47)$ and since $\phi(47) = 46$ we know that the order of 2 modulo 47 is 1 or 2 or 23 or 46. Which? Clearly it isn't 1, nor 2. Working modulo 47 we have $2^1 = 2$, $2^2 = 4$, $2^4 = 16$, $2^8 = 256 \equiv 21$, $2^{16} \equiv 441 \equiv 18$. Hence $2^{23} = 2^{16+4+2+1} \equiv (18 \cdot 2) \cdot (16 \cdot 4) \equiv (-11) \cdot 17 \equiv -187 \equiv 1$. Thus 2 has order 23 and is not a primitive root of 47. But not to despair! Note that (-1) has order 2, modulo 47, and that $(23, 2) = 1$. According to Exercise 5.2.10—though you can also see it directly—this means that $(-1) \cdot 2$ has order 23.2, that is 46. Thus -2 ($\equiv 45$) is a primitive root of 47.

* See p. 197.

What about the others (all $\phi(46)=22$ of them)? How can we find them? The answer is 'pretty easily'—by means of

Theorem 5.2.10 Let g be a primitive root of p. Then g^α is also a primitive root if and only if $(\alpha, p-1)=1$.

Proof Suppose g^α is a primitive root and that $d=(\alpha, p-1)>1$. Indeed let $\alpha=kd$ and $p-1=ld$. then $(g^\alpha)^l=g^{kdl}=(g^{p-1})^k\equiv 1^k=1(\text{mod } p)$. Thus g^α has order $l<p-1$—which contradicts the assumption that g^α is a primitive root. Therefore $d=1$.

Conversely, if $(\alpha, p-1)=1$ we may write $u\alpha+v(p-1)=1$ for suitable $u, v \in \mathbb{Z}$. If g^α is not a primitive root then $(g^\alpha)^w\equiv 1(\text{mod } p)$ for some $w<p-1$. But then $g^w=g^{u\alpha w+v(p-1)w}=(g^{\alpha w})^u\cdot(g^{p-1})^{vw}\equiv 1(\text{mod } p)$ which contradicts the fact that g is a primitive root. □

Example 5.2.11 The primitive roots of 47 are given by evaluating $(-2)^i$ where $(i, 46)=1$ and $1\leqslant i\leqslant 46$.

We shall leave you to find all these primitive roots, in particular the 'smallest' of them (in the range from 2 to 46). In fact Computer Problem 5.2.1 asks you to find the smallest primitive root for each of the primes less than 200. You should also be in for a surprise towards the end of you calculations!

Note 5.2.12 Used the other way round, Theorem 5.2.10 has applications to the generation of pseudo-random numbers. Without going into details, what one requires, given an (invariably rather large) prime p, is a primitive root which is neither too small nor too large, within the range $1\leqslant x\leqslant p-1$ (see [7]). On those occasions when a small primitive root almost leaps at you out of the paper you can use Theorem 5.2.10 to find primitive roots of a somewhat larger size by taking powers of this small one.

Exercises 5.2

1 Find, by hand, all primitive roots of n for each n such that $2\leqslant n\leqslant 14$. Does any pattern emerge? If not move to Problem 5.2.2 below.

2 Find two primitive roots for n when n is: (i) 13; (ii) 17; (iii) 19; (iv) 27. In each case express each of these two roots as a power (mod n) of the other.

3 Show that 2 is not a primitive root of $F_n=2^{2^n}+1$ if $n>1$. (3 is—if F_n is prime. We'll prove this important fact later—Theorem 8.5.5.)

4 Show that if p is a prime then $x^2\equiv 1(\text{mod } p)$ iff $x\equiv\pm 1(\text{mod } p)$. Conclude that if r is a primitive root for p then $r^{(p-1)/2}\equiv -1(\text{mod } p)$. Deduce: (i) if r and s are primitive roots of p then rs is not; (ii) if r' is such that $r\cdot r'\equiv 1(\text{mod } p)$, then r' is a primitive root iff r is.

5 Show that if r is a primitive root of p where p is of the form $4k+1$, then $-r$ is also a primitive root. Show by example that this conclusion is false if p is of the form $4k+3$.

6 Show that if $a^t \equiv 1 \pmod{m}$ then $\text{ord}_m a | t$. [*Hint*: Use the division algorithm as in Theorem 5.1.1.] Deduce, in particular, that $\text{ord}_m a | \phi(m)$.

7 Show that if $\text{ord}_m a = e$ then $\text{ord}_m a^u = e/(e, u)$. Deduce that if a is a primitive root of m then a^u is a primitive root of m iff $(\phi(m), u) = 1$.

8 Use Exercise 7 to find all primitive roots of 14, 17, 19, 23, 27, 29, and 31.

9 Show that if there exists an integer a with order $m-1$ modulo m then m is a prime.

10 Prove that if $\text{ord}_m a = \alpha$ and $\text{ord}_m b = \beta$ and if $(\alpha, \beta) = 1$ then $\text{ord}_m ab = \alpha\beta$. What can you say about $\text{ord}_m ab$ if $(\alpha, \beta) > 1$?

11 Suppose $(a, m) = 1$. Show that $a^i \equiv a^j \pmod{m}$ iff $i \equiv j \pmod{\text{ord}_m a}$.

12 Prove that if a has order n modulo m then $a, a^2, a^3, \ldots, a^n$ are pairwise incongruent modulo m. Deduce that if m has a primitive root g then $1, g, g^2, \ldots, g^{\phi(m)-1}$ forms a r.r.s modulo m (see Definition 3.3.4).

13 (a) Let $(a, p) = 1$ where p is an odd prime. Prove that $a^{(p-1)/2} \equiv 1$ or $-1 \pmod{n}$.
(b) Prove that $x^2 \equiv a \pmod{p}$ has a solution iff $a^{(p-1)/2} \equiv 1 \pmod{p}$. (Cf. Lemma 8.3.1(iii) and its proof.)
(c) Generalise (b) as follows: Assume that m has a primitive root and that $(a, m) = 1$. Show that $x^k \equiv a \pmod{m}$ has a solution iff $a^{\phi(m)/d} \equiv 1 \pmod{m}$ where $d = (\phi(m), k)$. [*Hint*: Assume $a = g^s$, g being a primitive root. Show that $d | s$ so that $ky \equiv s \pmod{\phi(m)}$ for some y. Then $g^{ky} \equiv g^s \pmod{m}$.]

14 Find all positive integers of order 6 modulo 43 and then modulo 49. [*Hint*: First show that 3 is a primitive root of each.]

15 Use the fact that the prime p has a primitive root g to prove Wilson's Theorem. [*Hint*: If $1 \leq a \leq p-1$ then, by Exercise 12, $a \equiv g^u \pmod{p}$ for some unique u such that $1 \leq u \leq p-1$. Then $(p-1)! \equiv g^{1+2+\cdots+p-1} \pmod{p}$.]

16 (Lionnet 1842) If p is an odd prime and if $0 < m < p-1$, then $p | 1^m + 2^m + \cdots + (p-1)^m$. (cf. Exercise 3.2.8.)

17 Conclude from Exercises 7 and 12 that, *if* m has a primitive root, *then* it has $\phi(\phi(m))$ of them. How many primitive roots has the number 30? [Careful!]

18 Use Exercise 7 to give Gauss's proof of the existence of primitive roots for primes as follows. For each $d | p-1$ let $\psi(d)$ be as in the text. If $\psi(d) \neq 0$ let a be an integer of order d. Then a^u also has order d iff $(d, u) = 1$. There are $\phi(d)$ such u for which $1 \leq u \leq d$.

19 Find the number of primitive roots of (i) 101; (ii) 4999. Find all primes which have no more than 10 primitive roots.

20 Use Exercise 6 to show that if an odd prime p divides a number of the form $a^4 + 1$ then p must be of the form $8k+1$. Deduce, by considering a number of the form $(2p_1p_2 \cdots p_r)^4+1$ that there are infinitely many primes of the form $8k+1$.

21 Show that if $a^2+a+1\equiv 0 \pmod p$ then $(a+1)^3 \equiv -1 \pmod p$. Deduce that if in addition $a \not\equiv 1 \pmod p$ then $a+1$ has order 6 modulo p. Use this to prove that each prime divisor other than 3 of the (odd) integer b^2+b+1 is of the form $6k+1$. Prove that there are infinitely many primes of the form $6k+1$. [*Hint*: To prove the second statement you should check $(a+1)^2 \not\equiv 1 \pmod p$.]

22 Use Exercise 7 to prove that if $p(\neq 3)$ is prime then the product of the primitive roots (less than p) is congruent to 1 modulo p. [*Hint*: Use Exercise 3.3.15.] Gauss showed [17] that their sum is congruent to 0 or $(-1)^n$ modulo p according as $p-1$ is divisible by the square of some prime or is a product of n distinct primes. Can you do it?

23 Given that m has a primitive root show that $\prod_{t=1,(t,m)=1}^{m} t \equiv -1 \pmod m$. (This sharpens Exercise 3.3.25(b). It is known as Gauss's generalisation of Wilson's theorem.

Computer problems 5.2

1 Produce a table of the smallest primitive roots of all primes <100. Use this information to make a conjecture. Test it on the primes up to 200.

2 Determine which integers less than 500 have primitive roots. Can you make a conjecture? Does each integer n possessing a primitive root necessarily possess one, r, say, such that $0<r<n$ and r is prime?

3 Produce a list of all primes <500 which have 10 as a primitive root.

4 Use Theorem 5.2.10 to write a program to find all the primitive roots of an integer. Find the first primitive root by (i) trial and error and (ii) by the methods outlined in Example 5.2.9. Compare the performance of these programs with the trial-and-error method of Program 5.1.

5.3 Gauss's theorem

Let us now answer the second (fundamental) question raised earlier. (See p. 126.) Following Gauss we investigate primitive roots for composite integers.

First some examples to light the way:

Examples 5.3.1

(a) 8 has no primitive root. For $\phi(8)=4$ and yet $1^1 \equiv 3^2 \equiv 5^2 \equiv 7^2 \equiv 1 \pmod 8$.

(b) 15 has no primitive root. For $\phi(15)=8$ and yet $1^1 \equiv 2^4 \equiv 4^2 \equiv 7^4 \equiv 8^4 \equiv 11^2 \equiv 13^4 \equiv 14^2 \equiv 1 \pmod{15}$.

(c) 27 has a primitive root. For example 2 is such.

This looks pretty chaotic! Some cubes have primitive roots, others don't; some numbers with two prime factors (e.g. 22) have primitive roots others don't. Can we bring some order to this chaos?

First we look at odd prime powers.

Theorem 5.3.2 Let p be an odd prime and let r be a primitive root of p. Then either r or $r+p$ is a primitive root of p^2.

Proof Let r have order $n \bmod p^2$ so that $r^n \equiv 1 (\bmod p^2)$. It follows that $r^n \equiv 1 (\bmod p)$. From these two congruences we deduce (i) $n | \phi(p^2) = p(p-1)$ (Note 5.2.5) and (ii) $p-1 | n$ (Exercise 5.2.6). Consequently $n = p-1$ or $n = p(p-1)$. We see that if $n = p(p-1) = \phi(p^2)$, then r is a primitive root for p^2. So suppose $n = p-1$. Put $s = r+p$. Since $s \equiv r (\bmod p)$ we see that s is also a primitive root of p. The order of s, modulo p^2, is, as for r, either $p-1$ or $p(p-1)$. We prove it *isn't* $p-1$.

Now

$$\begin{aligned} s^{p-1} &= (r+p)^{p-1} = r^{p-1} + (p-1)r^{p-2}p \\ &\quad + \frac{(p-1)(p-2)}{2!} r^{p-3}p^2 + \cdots + p^{p-1} \\ &\equiv r^{p-1} - pr^{p-2} (\bmod p^2) \equiv 1 - pr^{p-2} (\bmod p^2). \end{aligned}$$

Consequently, if $s^{p-1} \equiv 1 (\bmod p^2)$ we should have $0 \equiv -pr^{p-2} (\bmod p^2)$, that is, $p^2 | pr^{p-2}$. But this would imply that $p | r^{p-2}$, which is impossible since $(r, p) = 1$. It follows that s is a primitive root of p^2 as asserted. □

Example 5.3.3 It is easy to check that 2 is a primitive root of 11. Consequently 2 (or 13) is a primitive root of 121. (You might care to check which. Can both be?)

Given the apparently necessary alternatives in Theorem 5.3.2 the following result is remarkable! It was noted by C. G. J Jacobi in 1839.

Theorem 5.3.4 Let p be an odd prime and let r be a primitive root of p^2. Then r is a primitive root of p^k for each $k \geq 2$.

Proof (by induction on k) With r as given the case of $k = 2$ is immediate. Note that $\phi(p^k) = p^{k-1}(p-1)$. The proof will therefore be complete* if we can show that

$$\text{for each } k\colon r^{p^{k-2}(p-1)} \not\equiv 1 (\bmod p^k). \qquad (*)$$

So suppose (*) holds for each k such that $2 \leq k \leq l$ and let us prove (*) for $k = l+1$.

* Why? What about the cases $r^{p^{k-1}d} \not\equiv 1 (\bmod p^k)$ where d is a divisor of $p-1$?

From Euler's result we know that $r^{\phi(p^{l-1})} \equiv 1 \pmod{p^{l-1}}$, that is:

$$\text{for some } a \in \mathbb{Z},\ r^{\phi(p^{l-1})} = 1 + ap^{l-1}. \qquad (**)$$

In fact $p \nmid a$. For if it did we should have $r^{p^{l-2}(p-1)} \equiv 1 \pmod{p^l}$, contradicting the assumption that $(*)$ holds for $k = l$. Raising each side of $(**)$ to the pth power we obtain

$$r^{p^{l-1}(p-1)} = (1 + ap^{l-1})^p \equiv 1 + pap^{l-1} \pmod{p^{l+1}}.$$

Since $p \nmid a$ it follows that $r^{p^{l-1}(p-1)} \not\equiv 1 \pmod{p^{l+1}}$. Thus $(*)$ holds for $k = l+1$ and the proof is complete. □

Note 5.3.5 The fact that a primitive root of p^2 is also a primitive root of p^k for each $k \geqslant 2$ makes one ask, especially in the light of Example 5.3.3: Is it true that each primitive root of p is also a primitive root of p^2? In fact the answer is 'no' as E. Desmarest observed from a table he constructed around 1852. His example is of the smallest prime p such that 10 is a primitive root modulo p but not modulo p^2. You might like to marvel at it once you've found it! Actually it is not difficult to find smaller examples even if one is not prepared to accept the somewhat 'unsporting' examples (such as 7, which is a primitive root modulo 5 but not modulo 25), in which the number (7) is greater than the modulus (5). Computer Problem 5.3.2 invites you to find some of the more sporting primes.

An argument like that for odd primes p also clears up the case of $p = 2$.

Theorem 5.3.6 Let $n = 2^k$. For $k = 1$ and 2, n has a primitive root. For $k \geqslant 3$, n has no primitive root.

Proof 1 and 3 are easily seen to be primitive roots of 2 and 4 respectively. If a is a primitive root of 2^k then a is odd. Suppose that $k \geqslant 3$. We claim that $a^{2^{k-2}} \equiv 1 \pmod{2^k}$ whereas $\phi(2^k) = 2^{k-1}$ (Example 3.3.2(v)). This claim (you've already proved it (?) as Exercise 3.1.8) is easily proved by induction. For $k = 3$, Example 5.3.1(a) suffices. So suppose that, for $3 \leqslant k \leqslant l$, we have $a^{2^{l-2}} = 1 + b2^l$ for some $b \in \mathbb{Z}$. Squaring each side we get

$$a^{2^{l-1}} = (1 + b2^l)^2 = 1 + 2b \cdot 2^l + b^2 \cdot 2^{2l} \equiv 1 \pmod{2^{l+1}}.$$

Thus our claim holds for $k = l+1$. Induction does the rest. □

Examples 5.2.2 and 5.3.1(b) show that 22 (=2.11) has primitive roots whereas 15 (=3.5) has not. What distinguishes these cases? We have

Theorem 5.3.7 Let $u, v \in \mathbb{Z}$ be such that $(u, v) = 1$ and $u, v > 2$. Then uv has no primitive root.

Proof Assume that a is a primitive root of uv. Then $(a, uv) = 1$ and, consequently, $(a, u) = (a, v) = 1$. It follows that $a^{\phi(u)} \equiv 1 \pmod{u}$ and

$a^{\phi(v)} \equiv 1 (\bmod v)$. Since $u, v > 2$, $\phi(u)$, $\phi(v)$ are both even. (Use Theorem 3.3.10.) It follows that

$$a^{\phi(u) \cdot \phi(v)/2} \equiv 1 (\bmod u) \qquad \text{whilst} \qquad a^{\phi(v) \cdot \phi(u)/2} \equiv 1 (\bmod v).$$

But $(u, v) = 1$. Hence by Exercise 1.5.13(v), we can infer that $a^{\phi(u)\phi(v)/2} \equiv 1 (\bmod uv)$. Since $\phi(uv) = \phi(u)\phi(v)$ (Theorem 3.3.7) we see that uv cannot have a primitive root after all. □

Theorem 5.3.7 covers all integers n having (i) at least two distinct odd prime factors or (ii) a factor 2^α where $\alpha \geq 2$ (as well as an odd prime factor). Consequently the only integers whose status is still unclear are those of the form $2p^k$, where p is an odd prime and $k \geq 1$. We tidy up this case with

Theorem 5.3.8 Let p be an odd prime and $k \geq 1$. Then $2p^k$ has a primitive root.

Proof Let r be a primitive root of p^k. If r is even replace r by the odd primitive root $r + p^k$ of p^k. As a result we may assume, WLOG, that r is odd.

Now $r^{\phi(p^k)} \equiv 1 (\bmod p^k)$ and, since r is odd, $r^{\phi(p^k)} \equiv 1 (\bmod 2)$. It follows that $r^{\phi(p^k)} \equiv 1 (\bmod 2p^k)$. Now suppose that $r^u \equiv 1 (\bmod 2p^k)$ where $u | \phi(2p^k)$. Since $\phi(2p^k) = \phi(2) \cdot \phi(p^k) = \phi(p^k)$, we know that $u | \phi(p^k)$. But from $r^u \equiv 1 (\bmod 2p^k)$ we may infer that $r^u \equiv 1 (\bmod p^k)$, from which we deduce that $\phi(p^k) = u$—since r is a primitive root of p^k. All this implies that $u = \phi(2p^k)$—so that r is a primitive root of $2p^k$ as required. □

We summarise Theorems 5.3.2, 5.3.4, 5.3.6, 5.3.7 and 5.3.8 in

Theorem 5.3.9 (Gauss 1801) Let $n > 1$ be an integer. Then n has a primitive root if and only if $n = 2$, 4, p^k or $2p^k$, p being an odd prime. □

Note 5.3.10 Although the powers 2^k $(k \geq 3)$ don't possess primitive roots, it is important for later in this chapter to note that they 'only just fail' to do so. Indeed Exercise 5.3.6 asks you to show that, for each $k \geq 3$, 3 has order 2^{k-2} modulo 2^k. That is, 3 has order not $\phi(2^k)$ but rather $\frac{1}{2}\phi(2^k)$, modulo 2^k.

Exercises 5.3

1 Which of the following have primitive roots? 12, 18, 42, 52, 222. What is the smallest integer of the form $4k + 2$ which has no primitive root? (Cf. Exercise 5.2.17.)

2 Find, where possible, primitive roots for: 35, 121, 169, 242, 289, 625, 686, 1331 and 7^{100000}. Find a primitive root of 1331 which lies between 500 and 600.

3 If r is a primitive root of p^n, is it a primitive root of $p^i (1 \leq i \leq n)$?

4 Confirm that 7 is a primitive root of 5 but not of 25.

5 Let p be an odd prime. Show that p^k and $2p^k$ have the same *number* of primitive roots but that a primitive root r of p^k is *simultaneously* a primitive root of $2p^k$ iff r is odd.

6 Show that for $k \geq 3$ the integer 3 has order $2^{k-2}(=\phi(2^k)/2)$ modulo 2^k. Deduce that for $k \geq 3$ the integers $\{(-1)^u 3^v \colon u = 0, 1 \text{ and } 0 \leq v \leq 2^{k-2}-1\}$ form a reduced residue system modulo 2^k.

7 Let p be a prime and let $n \geq 1$ and a be integers with $(a, p) = 1$. Show that $x^n \equiv a \pmod p$ has either no solution or $(n, p-1)$ of them.

8 Show that if $a = 3$ or 9 and $p = 11$ then $a^{p-1} \equiv 1 \pmod{p^2}$. Why is neither of these the 'smallest' example referred to in Note 5.3.5?

Computer problems 5.3

1 Find the smallest prime p such that 10 is a primitive root of p but not p^2. (It's one of the 'fascinating' numbers mentioned in Chapter 1.)

2 More generally find the primitive roots α of p $(0 < \alpha < p)$ which are not primitive roots p^2 for $p < 500$.

5.4 Some simple primality tests. Pseudoprimes. Carmichael numbers

We saw earlier (Chapter 3) how Fermat *should* have discovered that his sixth number, $F_5 = 2^{32}+1$, is composite by applying ... his own Little Theorem. Indeed he could have used his theorem in another way. For, suppose that $(a, n) = 1$ and yet $a^{n-1} \not\equiv 1 \pmod n$. Then, of course, n cannot be a prime! In particular if we put $n = F_5 = 4\,294\,967\,297$ and consider $3^{n-1} = 3^{2^{32}}$ we find*, after 32 squarings $(3, 3^2, 3^4, 3^8, \ldots, 3^{2^{32}})$ working modulo n, that $3^{2^{32}} \not\equiv 1 \pmod{4\,294\,967\,297}$. Hence F_5 is not prime.

How did we think to use the number 3 here? Well, the number 2 is soon found to be useless in this context. For, since $2^{2^5} \equiv -1 \pmod{F_5}$ we have $2^{2^6} \equiv 1$ from which $2^{2^{32}} \equiv 1 \pmod{F_5}$ follows trivially—so it neither confirms F_5 is prime nor suggests that it might be composite.

In fact, not only is the number 3 useful for confirming the compositeness of F_5, it also lies at the heart of a test, used in practice, for checking the primeness or otherwise of the next few larger Fermat numbers. (Have a look at [J]†, for example. It's interesting both for its contents and for the style in which it is written, being slightly more expansive than would be 'allowed' in today's research papers.) The test is

Theorem 5.4.1 (Pepin 1877) For $n \in \mathbb{Z}^+$ the Fermat number $F_n = 2^{2^n}+1$ is prime if and only if $3^{2^\alpha} \equiv -1 \pmod{F_n}$, where $\alpha = 2^n - 1$.

* You should check this yourself with a bit of multiprecision arithmetic.
† More recent efforts can be found in the *Mathematics of Computation* journal. See, for example, Vol. 15, 1961, p. 420. We leave you the pleasure of finding others.

Proof One way round the proof is straightforward. (To prove the other part we shall have to wait until Chapter 8.)

So suppose now that $3^{2^\alpha} \equiv -1 (\text{mod } F_n)$. Squaring up $3^{F_n-1} = 3^{2^{\alpha+1}} \equiv 1 (\text{mod } F_n)$. Now 2 is the only prime dividing $F_n - 1$ and $(F_n - 1)/2 = 2^\alpha$. Hence $3^{(F_n-1)/2} \equiv -1 \not\equiv 1 (\text{mod } F_n)$. Thus, by Theorem 5.1.1, F_n is prime.

Conversely: suppose that F_n is a prime. Then F_n has primitive roots. Let r be one of them. By Exercise 5.2.4 we see that $r^{(F_n-1)/2} \equiv -1 (\text{mod } F_n)$. Thus our task is to show that 3 is a primitive root of F_n (for each prime F_n). This we shall do with the aid of Euler's criterion and the Euler-Legendre-Gauss law of quadratic reciprocity, in Chapter 8 (Theorem 8.5.5). □

In 1877 Lucas asserted that he could test the primality of $F_6 = 2^{2^6} + 1$ in about 30 hours (using a special test he had devised—see Theorem 9.6.1 for a similar test he devised for dealing with the primeness of Mersenne numbers).

If we restrict ourselves to numbers which are no larger than this, Theorem 5.1.1 is very helpful despite the existence of nasty examples such as 341 which, as we have seen, does not reveal its compositeness—at least when using the 'base' 2. Let us investigate this phenomenon by introducing

Definition 5.4.2 An odd composite number n for which $a^{n-1} \equiv 1 (\text{mod } n)$ is called an *a-pseudoprime* (briefly *a-psp*).

Examples 5.4.3 341 is the smallest 2-psp, 91 is a 3-psp (is it the smallest?) and 561 is an a-psp for each a for which $(a, 561) = 1$. As such it is called a *Carmichael number*, such numbers being the subject of investigation made by R. D. Carmichael in 1909 (see [K]).

Given any odd integer n less than, say, 10^{10}, we can test it quickly for primeness by evaluating $2^{n-1} (\text{mod } n)$. If the result is not congruent to 1 modulo n, then n is composite by the FLT. If, on the other hand, $2^{n-1} \equiv 1$, then n is 'quite likely' to be prime, though we cannot be *sure* until we examine a table of 2-psps $\leqslant 10^{10}$. If our n is in the list then it is composite; if not then it is prime. In fact the 2-psps are spread pretty thinly. Amongst the integers up to 10^{10} only 14 884 are 2-psps, whereas 455 052 512 are primes! ([7])

Of course we can also check our n for a-pseudoprimeness for $a = 3$, 5, 7 etc.: only 1770 composite integers $< 25 \cdot 10^9$ try to fool us into thinking they primes by being a-psps for *each* of $a = 2$, 3, 5 and 7 ([20]).

It would be very nice if we could find an integer a for which all a-psps could be determined (and stored). Unfortunately this can't be expected, as the following result of Cipolla (1903) shows.

Theorem 5.4.4 For each integer $a > 1$ there exist infinitely many a-psps.

Proof Let p be any one of the infinitely many odd primes such that $p \nmid a(a^2-1)$. Set

$$m = \frac{a^p-1}{a-1}\frac{a^p+1}{a+1}$$

so that m is a composite integer. It follows that

$$(a^2-1)(m-1) = a^{2p} - a^2 = a(a^{p-1}-1)(a^p+a).$$

Since a and a^p are both odd or both even we know that $2|a^p+a$. Also $p|a^{p-1}-1$ and $a^2-1|a^{p-1}-1$ (since $2|p-1$). Now $p \nmid a^2-1$ (by choice!) and so $p(a^2-1)|a^{p-1}-1$. This implies that $2p(a^2-1)|(a^2-1)(m-1)$, so that $2p|m-1$. Writing $m = 1+2up$ and working modulo m we get

$$a^{m-1} = a^{2up} =^* \{1+m(a^2-1)\}^u \equiv 1^u = 1.$$

Since different values of p lead to different values of m, we have the desired result. □

Example 5.4.5 Taking $a=2$, $p=5$ we note that $5 \nmid 2\cdot 3$.

Hence $m = \dfrac{2^5-1}{2-1}\cdot\dfrac{2^5+1}{2+1}$ is a 2-psp. (This should raise a question or two in your minds!)

We saw above that applying further a-psp tests for various a to a given (composite) integer appears to reduce its chances of fooling us into thinking that it is a prime. Perhaps the number of integers n satisfying $a^{n-1} \equiv 1 (\text{mod } n)$ for *all* a coprime to n is finite? That is, we ask: is the set of all Carmichael numbers finite? No one knows! Nevertheless, Carmichael numbers can be characterised—in terms of their prime factors. To prove this we use Note 5.3.10 to sharpen Euler's theorem. Given m, we wish to identify the least positive integer L† such that $a^L \equiv 1 (\text{mod } m)$ for all a for which $(a, m) = 1$. The reasoning behind the following definition should be clear.

Definition 5.4.6 The function $\lambda : \mathbb{Z} \to \mathbb{Z}$ is defined by: $\lambda(1) = 1$; $\lambda(p^\alpha) = \phi(p^\alpha) = p^{\alpha-1}(p-1)$ if p is an odd prime; $\lambda(2^\alpha) = \phi(2^\alpha)$ if $\alpha = 1$ or 2; $\lambda(2^\alpha) = \frac{1}{2}\phi(2^\alpha)$ if $\alpha \geqslant 3$. Finally if

$$m = 2^\alpha p_1^{\alpha_1} \cdots p_t^{\alpha_t}, \lambda(m) = \text{lcm}\{\lambda(2^\alpha), \lambda(p_1^{\alpha_1}), \ldots, \lambda(p_t^{\alpha_t})\},$$

the p_i being, of course, distinct odd primes.

We can then prove

Theorem 5.4.7 Let $m = 2^{\alpha_0} p_1^{\alpha_1} \ldots p_t^{\alpha_t}$ be an integer greater than 1. Then, for each a such that $(a, m) = 1$, we have $a^{\lambda(m)} \equiv 1 (\text{mod } m)$. Furthermore for each

* Why?

† The so called *universal exponent* modulo m.

m, there exists an integer a for which $\lambda(m)$ is the smallest such (positive) exponent.

Proof Since, for each prime p_i including $p_0 = 2$ we have $a^{\lambda(p_i^{\alpha_i})} \equiv 1 (\text{mod } p_i^{\alpha_i})$, it is immediate that $a^{\lambda(m)} \equiv 1 (\text{mod } p_i^{\alpha_i})$ and hence that $a^{\lambda(m)} \equiv 1 (\text{mod } m)$, by the coprimeness of the $p_i^{\alpha_i}$. To exhibit an a for which $\lambda(m)$ is the least such power choose a so that $a \equiv 3 (\text{mod } 2^{\alpha_0})$, $a \equiv r_1 (\text{mod } p_1^{\alpha_1}), \ldots, a \equiv r_t (\text{mod } p_t^{\alpha_t})$ the r_i being primitive roots of the corresponding $p_i^{\alpha_i}$. Such an a exists by Theorem 4.1.5. Finally, if L is the least positive integer such that $a^L \equiv 1 (\text{mod } m)$ we conclude that $a^L \equiv 1 (\text{mod } p_i^{\alpha_i})$ for each i, whence, by choice of a, $\lambda(p_i^{\alpha_i}) | L$. Consequently $\lambda(m) | L$. Since $L | \lambda(m)$, by minimality of L, the theorem is proved. □

And now for half of the promised characterisation! The other half is in Exercise 5.4.6.

Theorem 5.4.8 Let $C > 2$ be a Carmichael number. Then $C = p_1 p_2 \cdots p_r$ where $r \geq 3$ and where the pairwise distinct primes p_i are such that $p_i - 1 | C - 1$ for each i.

Proof Since C is Carmichael we have $b^{C-1} \equiv 1 (\text{mod } C)$ for each b such that $(b, C) = 1$. Now, by Theorem 5.4.7 there exists an integer a such that $(a, C) = 1$ and a has order $\lambda(C)$ modulo C. But then $\lambda(C) | C - 1$ (Exercise 5.2.6). Also, since $C > 2$, we have $\lambda(C)$ is even [why?]. Hence $C - 1$ itself is even so that C is odd.

Suppose that $C = p_1^{\alpha_1} p_2^{\alpha_2} \cdots p_r^{\alpha_r}$, where $\alpha_i \geq 2$ for some i. Then $\lambda(p_i^{\alpha_i}) = \phi(p_i^{\alpha_i}) = p_i^{\alpha_i - 1}(p_i - 1) | \lambda(C)$ whilst $\lambda(C) | C - 1$. This implies that $p_i | C - 1$—which is blatantly false since $p_i | C$. Hence C is a product of distinct odd primes. We also observe that $p_i - 1 = \lambda(p_i) | \lambda(C) | C - 1$, as claimed.

Finally, $r \geq 2$ (since C is composite!) If $C = pq$ with, say, $p > q$ we should have $p - 1 | C - 1 = pq - 1 = (p-1)q + q - 1$, from which we could derive the impossibility $p - 1 | q - 1$. Hence C has at least three prime factors. □

Note 5.4.9 In his 1909 paper, Carmichael identified four Carmichael numbers, namely $3 \cdot 11 \cdot 17$ $(= 561)$, $5 \cdot 13 \cdot 17$ $(= 1105)$, $7 \cdot 13 \cdot 31$ $(= 2821)$ and $7 \cdot 31 \cdot 73$ $(= 15\,841)$ by inspection. The following argument shows how such numbers can be found.

Theorem 5.4.10 561 is the only Carmichael number of the form $3pq$, p and q being primes.

Proof Let $C = 3pq$ be a Carmichael number where (by Theorem 5.4.8) 3, p, q must be distinct odd primes. By Theorem 5.4.8, $p - 1$ and $q - 1$ divide $3pq - 1$. It follows that $p - 1 | 3q(p-1) + 3q - 1$ and hence that $p - 1 | 3q - 1$. Likewise $q - 1 | 3p - 1$. Clearly we may suppose that $3 < p < q$. Let $(p-1)u = 3q - 1$ and

$(q-1)v=3p-1$. Then

$$(p-1)uv=3(q-1)v+2v=3(3p-1)+2v=9p-9+6+2v.$$

Therefore $p-1|6+2v$ and, consequently,

$$(p-1)(q-1)|6(q-1)+2v(q-1)=6q-6+6p-2=6p+6q-8.$$

Now it is easy to see that this equality will limit the possible choices of p and q since $(p-1)(q-1)$ is a quadratic in p and q whereas $6p+6q-8$ is linear. For example if $p \geqslant 13$, then $q \geqslant 17$ and one soon sees that then $(p-1)(q-1) > 6p+6q-8$. So we try the various pairs (p, q), beginning with $p=5$ and $q-1|3 \cdot 5-1=14$. Hence $q-1=1, 2, 7$ or 14—none of which yields a suitable value for q (recall $q>p$). The case $p=7$ can be dismissed immediately [why?]. For $p=11$ we have $q \geqslant 13$ and $q|3 \cdot 11-1=32$. Thus $q=17$ is the only possibility. Checking these values we find $3pq-1$ is divisible by $3-1$, $p-1$ and $q-1$. This shows that $C=3pq=3 \cdot 11 \cdot 17=561$ is a Carmichael number, and by the above discussion that it is the only one. □

The concept of a-pseudoprime can be tightened so as to yield a test, of practical and theoretical value, which permits even fewer composites to fool us into thinking they are primes. Indeed let n be a prime and a a positive integer such that $(a, n)=1$ and suppose that $n-1=2^\alpha t$, where t is odd. Setting $n_i=(n-1)/2^i (0 \leqslant i \leqslant \alpha)$ we see, since $a^{n-1} \equiv 1 \pmod n$, that either $a^{n_1} \equiv 1$ or $a^{n_1} \equiv -1 \pmod n$. (See Exercise 5.2.4.) In the former case we can likewise deduce that $a^{n_2} \equiv 1$ or $a^{n_2} \equiv -1 \pmod n$. Continuing in this way indicates that each prime satisfies the conditions placed on n in

Definition 5.4.11 Let n be a composite positive integer with $n-1=2^\alpha t$, t being odd. Suppose $(a, n)=1$ and that either (i) for some i $(0<i \leqslant \alpha)$, $a^{n_i} \equiv -1 \pmod n$ or (ii) $a^{n_\alpha} \equiv 1 \pmod n$. Then a is called a *strong a-pseudoprime* (*strong a-psp*).

It is immediate from this definition that each *strong* a-psp is necessarily an a-psp. One advantage of using strong psps is their greater rarity; the smallest of the strong 2-psps is greater than 2000 and there is no number less than $3 \cdot 10^9$ which is a strong a-psp for each $a=2, 3, 5$ *and* 7. Furthermore one can prove the following:

Theorem 5.4.12 Let n be an odd composite integer. Then n is a strong a-psp for no more than one quarter of the integers a for which $1 \leqslant a \leqslant n-1$.

Proof See [7] □

This result tells us that if n is a given composite integer and if we randomly pick k distinct integers a with $1 \leqslant a \leqslant n-1$, then the chance that the compositeness of n will not have been revealed to us after putting it through k tests for strong a-pseudoprimeness is less than $(1/4)^k$ which, for $k=50$, is approximately $1/10^{30}$.

Testing whether numbers are a-psps using a computer can be achieved by using Program 3.2 to compute $a^{n-1} \pmod n$. To search for such values we can either test each odd integer n for primeness using Program 1.1, or check whether it is on a stored list of primes, and then compute $a^{n-1} \pmod n$ only for composite n.

Testing whether a given integer is a strong a-pseudoprime requires only a small alteration and can be done using the following algorithm

Algorithm

```
1.  set m = n-1
2.  set m = INT(m)
3   calculate b such that b ≡ a^m (mod n) using the algorithm of program 3.2
4   set m=m/2
5.  IF b=-1 and m = INT(m) (i.e. m is even) GOTO step 2
6.  IF b=1 and m is not even then n is a strong a-psp
```

Exercises 5.4

1 Show that, for $n \geqslant 1$, $(2^{2^n}+1, 3)=1$. Show that Theorem 5.4.1 can be rewritten: F_n is prime iff 3 is a primitive root for F_n.

2 Use Pepin's test to check, by hand, that 257 ($=F_3$) is prime.

3 Show that 1105, 1729,* 1905 are 2-psps.

4 Show that each F_n is a prime or a 2-psp. Show that if p is prime then $M_p = 2^p - 1$ is a prime or a 2-psp. (Cf. Exercise 5.1.3.)

5 Let p and q be distinct odd primes such that $2^{pq-1} \equiv 1 \pmod{pq}$. Show that $2^{q-1} \equiv 1 \pmod p$ and $2^{p-1} \equiv 1 \pmod q$. (Cf. Exercise 3.2.12.) Assuming that $p<q$ show that for $p=3, 5, 7$ no corresponding q can be found. For $p=11$ show that 2 is a primitive root so that $q-1$ must be a multiple of $p-1$ ($=10$) whilst $q \mid 2^{10}-1$. Find the three smallest 2-psps of the form pq.

6 Prove the converse of Theorem 5.4.8. That is, exchange the words 'let' and 'then', then the order of the two sentences and finally prove the resulting assertion.

7 Show that $(6t+1)(12t+1)(18t+1)$ is a Carmichael number—if each factor is a prime. [This result is intriguing since there are known to be infinitely many triples of primes in arithmetic progression ([5], p. 12) and yet the infinitude of the set of Carmichael numbers is not known.]

8 Show that 1729* is a Carmichael number. [*Hint*: Use Exercise 7.]

* 1729!

9 Show that there can only be a finite number of Carmichael numbers of the form pqr where p, q, r are distinct primes and p is fixed. Does your argument hold for numbers of the form $pqrs$ or for those of the form pqr with p not necessarily fixed?

10 Show that 341 is a 2-psp but not a strong 2-psp.

11 Show that 2047 is a strong 2-psp and hence a 2-psp.

12 Is 91 is a strong 3-psp? [Exercise 3.1.11 shows it is a 3-psp.]

13 (Cf. Exercise 5.1.3) Show that if n is composite and if $2^{n-1} \equiv 1 \pmod{n}$, so that n is a 2-psp, then setting $N = 2^n - 1$ we have $2^{N-1} \equiv 1 \pmod{N}$. Deduce that there are infinitely many strong 2-psps.

Computer problems 5.4

1 Write a program to find a-psps. Use it to find all the a-psps less than 2000 for $a = 2, 3, 4, 6, 9$. Should you expect any relationship between the smallest a-psps where $a = 2, 3$ and 6?

2 Confirm that 161 038 is a 2-psp. (It is the least even one.)

3 Find all the Carmichael numbers less than 2000.

4 Find all Carmichael numbers of the form $5pq$ where $5, p, q$ are distinct primes.

5 Show that (i) 1 373 653 is a strong pseudoprime to bases 2 and 3 simultaneously; (ii) 25 326 001 is a strong pseudoprime to bases 2, 3 and 5 simultaneously. (iii) 3 215 031 751 is a strong pseudoprime to bases 2, 3, 5 and 7 simultaneously. These numbers are, respectively, the smallest numbers of their kinds.

6 *Miller's test* (see [7] and [20]) for primality of numbers less than $25 \cdot 10^9$ is based on the observation what within this range 3 215 031 751 is the only strong psp with respect to 2, 3, 5 and 7 simultaneously. Using this fact write a program which checks for primeness any given number less than $25 \cdot 10^9$.

7 Theorem 5.4.12 forms the basis of *Rabin's probabilistic test* (see [6] and [7]) for primality. Write a program which selects several values of a at random and checks whether the integer n is a strong psp with respect to each of these values. An integer which is strong psp for *all* the values of a chosen has a very high probability of being a prime.

5.5 Special repeating decimals

We shall round off this chapter by considering what might appear to be a rather more light-hearted topic, namely the repeating blocks in the decimal expansions of the rational numbers $1/p$, p being a prime $\neq 2, \neq 5$.

The infinite decimal $d = a \cdot a_1a_2 \ldots a_k \ldots$ is said to be *periodic* if there exist positive integers m, n such that for each $s \geqslant m$ we have $a_s = a_{s+n}$. The least such n is called the *periodic length* of d. We include amongst decimals of periodic length 1 those like $5/8 = 0.62500\ldots$ which are often said to have *finite* decimal expansion.

Examples 5.5.1 In decimal form

$\frac{1}{7} = 0.142857\ 142857\ 14\ldots,\ \frac{1}{11} = 0.09\ 09\ 09\ 0\ldots\ \frac{1}{13} = 0.076923\ 076923\ 07\ldots$ etc.,

expansions which are denoted more briefly by $0.\overline{142857}$, $0.\overline{09}$, $0.\overline{076923}$, the bars indicating the repeating blocks (of lengths 6, 2 and 6 respectively).

Can we inject some order here too? Indeed we can! Note that, for example, $10^6/7 - 1/7 = 142857$—an integer. Likewise $10^2/11 - 1/11$ and $10^6/13 - 1/13$ are integers. Put another way, $10^6 \equiv 1 \pmod 7$, $10^2 \equiv 1 \pmod{11}$ and $10^6 \equiv 1 \pmod{13}$ with 6, 2 and 6 being the orders of 10 modulo 7, 11 and 13 respectively. Note, as the young Gauss did (c. 1795) that $6|7-1$, $2|11-1$ and $6|13-1$. From these and similar observations Gauss rediscovered Fermat's Little Theorem for himself. (Unknown to Gauss, Lambert (1769) had already gone in the other direction using FLT to show that the periodic length of $1/p$ $(p \neq 2, 5)$ is always a divisor of $p-1$.)

Note that the assertion that there are infinitely many primes p for which $1/p$ has periodic length $p-1$ is equivalent to the statement that 10 is a primitive root of infinitely many primes. This is part of Artin's* famous conjecture of 1927 that: *To each integer $a \neq -1$ which is not a square, there correspond infinitely many primes p for which a is a primitive root.* (For recent progress see D. R. Heath-Brown's paper in the Quarterly Journal of Mathematics Vol 37, 1986).

Finding the decimal expansion of $1/p$ involves repeated calculations of the form $10r_i = m_ip + r_{i+1}$ where $r_1 = 1$, $m_i \in \mathbb{Z}$ and $1 \leqslant r_i \leqslant p-1$ for each i. The following program is based on the obvious fact that on the first occasion when a remainder r_{i+1} appears for the second time then the periodic part of p has been determined.

Program 5.2 *Finds the periodic decimal representation of 1/p working to base 10.*

```
  5 DIM Q(100)
 10 INPUT "Enter the value of the integer p",P
 20 Q(1)=1
 30 I=1
 40 I=I+1
 50    c=INT(10*Q(I-1)/P)
 60    Q(I)=10*Q(I-1)-c*P
 70    PRINT c;
 80    J=I
 90    J=J-1
100       IF Q(J)=Q(I) GOTO 130
110       IF J=1 GOTO 40
120    GOTO 90
130 PRINT
140 PRINT " period = ",I-J
```

* Emil Artin, 3 March 1898 - 20 December 1962.

Exercises 5.5

1 Show that the decimal representation of the real number α is periodic iff α is a rational number (Lambert 1758). Show that for each positive integer n the periodic length of $1/n$ is at most n. (Leibniz 1677.)

2 Find the rational numbers represented by: (i) $0.\overline{296}$ (Euler's 'Algebra') (ii) $0.\overline{181942}$; (iii) $0.\overline{4321321211}$; (iv) $0.\overline{0123456789}$; (v) $0.\overline{012345679}$. [To write (v) as a fraction in lowest terms it helps if you first *multiply* (v) by 9.]

3 Does the repeating block of the decimal expansion of $1/p$ (p being prime $p \neq 2, p \neq 5$) necessarily start immediately after the decimal point? Explain why it does—or find a counterexample.

4 For which primes p does the decimal representation of $1/p$ have periodic length (a) 2; (b) 3; (c) 4?

5 Show that for each $n \in \mathbb{Z}^+$ there exists at most a finite number of primes for which $1/p$ has periodic length n.

6 Leibniz asserted (1677) that the periodic length of $1/n$ for $(n, 10) = 1$ is a divisor of n. Prove him wrong! [*Hint*: $n = 21$.] Find the periodic length of $\frac{1}{7}$, $\frac{1}{17}$ and $\frac{1}{119}$.

7 (Lambert 1769) Let g be an odd integer. Show that if $1/g$ has period $g-1$ then g is prime. Show that if $1/g$ has period m where $m \nmid g-1$, then g is composite.

8 (Thibault 1843) Prove that if, for $i = 1, 2$, m_i is the length of $1/d_i$, then $d_1 | d_2 \Rightarrow m_1 | m_2$.

9 Show that, for primes $p \neq 2$, $p \neq 5$, $1/p$ and $1/p^2$ have the same length iff $10^{p-1} \equiv 1 \pmod{p^2}$.

10 Explain why the restrictions in Artin's conjecture that $a \neq -1$ and a is not a square are necessary.

Computer problems 5.5

1 Calculate the length of (and print out) repeating decimals for $1/p$. $(7 \leqslant p \leqslant 3001.)$ What percentage have periodic length $p-1$?

2 Dickson ([1], Vol I, p. 159) reports John Wallis* (1676) as asserting that the periodic length of $1/mn$ is the lcm of those for $1/m$ and $1/n$. Find a counterexample to this assertion.

* John Wallis, 3 December 1616 – 8 November 1703.

3 Modify Program 5.2 to determine the periodic decimal representation of any rational number $n = q/p$. What features occur which do not arise in the case of $1/p$? Note that the stopping rule needs careful consideration in this case and it may be necessary to store successive c or Q values in an array to check for the period.

4 Making a further change to Program 5.2, explore the patterns of decimal representations when working to a base other than 10 for the arithmetic.

6

Diophantine equations and Fermat's last theorem

6.1 Introduction

In order to lead naturally into one of the deepest (and most beautiful) theorems of elementary number theory—the law of quadratic reciprocity (Chapter 8)—it is appropriate first to return to Fermat and consider, in this chapter and the next, two types of problems, intimately related, which engaged Fermat's attention fairly early in his mathematical career. The first comes under the heading of *Diophantine equations*, the second is much concerned with the representability of integers as sums of integer squares. Both types made appearances in letters he wrote in 1636. But, first, a little scene setting.

Diophantine equations are named after Diophantus who lived in Alexandria around 250 A.D. The only personal details we have of him come in the form of an epigram written most probably (according to [21], p. 3) by a personal friend whose interest was aroused by Diophantus' type of mathematics. The epigram states that: 'Diophantus' boyhood lasted 1/6th of his life; his beard grew after 1/12th more; after 1/7th more he married and his son was born 5 years later. The son lived to half his father's age and the father died 4 years after his son.' These (amazingly convenient) facts imply that, if Diophantus was x years old when he died, then

$$x = x/6 + x/12 + x/7 + 5 + x/2 + 4.$$

We deduce that Diophantus died aged . . . how old?

The works on which Diophantus' fame rests are (i) *The Arithmetica*—of which six books from the (proposed?) original thirteen survive and (ii) a tract on polygonal numbers (see Chapter 7)—a part of which survives. In addition the Arithmetica contains references to a (lost) book of 'Porisms'*.

The first book of Diophantus deals with determinate equations, several being of the above kind. Later books deal with indeterminate equations, examples of which are:

(i) (Book 2, problem 8) To divide a square into a sum of two squares (i.e. solve $z^2 = x^2 + y^2$).

* Thought to have been a collection of properties of numbers—for example that each difference of two (rational) cubes is expressible as a sum of two such—which could be quoted without proof in the *Arithmetica.*

Solution [If] Given square number is 16 [then] $16 = 256/25 + 144/25$.

(ii) (Book 3, problem 12) To find three numbers such that the product of any two added to the third gives a square (i.e. find x, y, z, u, v, w such that $xy + z = u^2$, $yz + x = v^2$, $zx + y = w^2$).

Solution The numbers are $1, 7, 9$.

Diophantus showed his working but was content with one solution even when there were infinitely many and was happy to accept rational number solutions. Nowadays the subject of Diophantine equations investigates solutions of (systems of) equations in several unknowns and, in general, requires the solutions to be integers. This insistence on integral solutions can turn an easy Diophantine problem into an extremely difficult one. For example, it is easy enough to find rational solutions x, y of the equation $x^2 - 61y^2 = 1$ (Exercise 11.6.1) but rather difficult to solve the equation in integers. (Recall Problem 0.1.1 and see Chapter 11.)

Exercise 6.1

1 Fill in the details below to obtain Diophantus's solutions to problems (i) and (ii) above and then with Xylander*, the first to make a translation (1575) of Diophantus into Latin, admit to being 'overwhelmed by Diophantus's method and reasoning'.

(i) Given 16, let x^2 and $16 - x^2$ be the desired (rational) squares. Taking m to be any non-zero integer, suppose $16 - x^2$ to be the square of $4 - mx$. Solve for x in terms of m (discarding the choice $x = 0$). (Do you see the purpose of the 4 in the term $4 - mx$?) What value of m gives Diophantus' solution?
(ii) Take $u^2 = (n+3)^2$ and choose $z = 9$. Then $xy = n^2 + 6n$. Take $x = n$ and $y = n + 6$. Deduce that $10n + 54$ and $10n + 6$ are both squares so that $48 = X^2 - Y^2$ is a difference of two squares. There are infinitely many (rational) solutions for X and Y. One such yields $x = 1$, $y = 7$, $z = 9$. (Cf. Computer problem 6.1.1.) What is the result of starting with $u^2 = (n+1)^2$, $z = 1$?

Computer problems 6.1

1 Can you find positive *primes* x, y, z satisfying the conditions of Exercise 6.1.1(ii)? [It is possible to save yourself a lot of (computing) time by first making observations about the forms x, y, z must necessarily take. One answer to the problem suggested the following, which is weaker than either Goldbach's conjecture or the problem of the infinitude of primes of the form $2p + 1$ where p is a prime and may therefore be easier to resolve: Do there exist infinitely

* The Greek pseudonym of Heidelberg professor Wilhelm Holzmann.

many pairs of primes p, q such that $p+q+1$ is also a prime? Write a program to find such primes.]

2 Diophantus (Problem 1, Book 3) determines, in approximately half a dozen lines of working, three integers x, y, z such that $x+y$, $y+z$, $z+x$ and $x+y+z$ are all squares. He finds 41, 80, 320 is a solution. Is it the least solution with x, y, z distinct positive integers?

6.2 Pythagorean triples

The simplest indeterminate equations to deal with are of the form $ax+by=c$, where a, b, c are integers and (integer) values of x and y satisfying the equation are sought. As we have, essentially, already discussed such equations (see Section 4.1) let us move up to degree two and continue our story with the most celebrated of all Diophantine equations: $x^2+y^2=z^2$. Solutions of this problem were known to the Babylonians of 2000 B.C.—and not only 'small' solutions such as (3, 4, 5), (5, 12, 13), (8, 15, 17), . . . but even some 'big' ones, for example (4961, 6480, 8161)! How many do *you* know? We've listed four. Are there* any more? How many? If you can't yet answer these questions you are in for two pleasant surprises very soon!

The reader who has studied elementary geometry will recognise the equation from a different context—that of Pythagoras'† theorem. This theorem, which must have been known to the Bablyonians—even if they hadn't a proof—says: *If a right-angled triangle has hypotenuse of length c and perpendicular 'legs' of lengths a and b, then* $a^2+b^2=c^2$—that is, looking at Fig. 6.1, the area of the

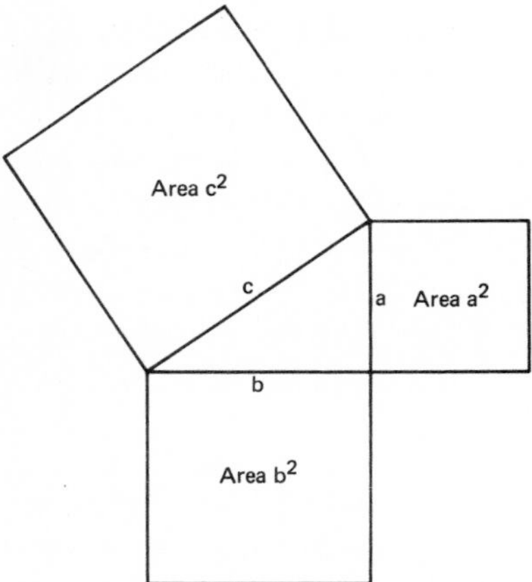

Fig. 6.1

* To avoid trivialities we assume that none of x, y, z is zero. Then there is no harm in assuming that x, y, z are all positive.
† Pythagoras, c560–480 B.C.

largest square is equal to the sum of the areas of the two smaller squares. Because of this association with Pythagoras' theorem we make

Definition 6.2.1 Let u, v, w be three positive integers such that $u^2+v^2=w^2$. The triple (u, v, w) is called a *Pythagorean triple.*

The following theorem, showing how to obtain infinitely many triples, provides the first of the pleasant surprises promised above.

Theorem 6.2.2 Let a, b, s be positive integers $a>b$. Then the integers $u=s(a^2-b^2)$, $v=s(2ab)$, $w=s(a^2+b^2)$ form a Pythagorean triple.

Proof Trivial! □ (Try it!)

Note 6.2.3 Euclid was aware that these values of u, v, w formed a Pythagorean triple. According to Proclus (5th century A.D.) the Pythagoreans knew of the solution $(2n+1, 2n^2+2n, 2n^2+2n+1)$ and, earlier still, the numbers known to the Babylonians must surely have been produced by some formula or method rather than just guessed at.

Much more amazing—and the second surprise—is the following converse theorem, essentially known to Diophantus, which says that Theorem 6.2.2 shows you *all possible triples*!

Theorem 6.2.4 Let u, v, w (all positive) be a Pythagorean triple. Then there exist positive integers a, b, s such that $u=s(a^2-b^2)$, $v=s(2ab)$, $w=s(a^2+b^2)$—or the same with the formulae for u and v interchanged.

Proof Let u, v, w satisfy $x^2+y^2=z^2$ and suppose first that $(u, v)=d$. Then $d^2|u^2$, $d^2|v^2$ and hence $d^2|u^2+v^2$, i.e. $d^2|w^2$. Consequently $d|w$ (cf. Exercise 1.4.6). Then, clearly, $d|(u, w)$ and $d|(v, w)$. The symmetry of the situation then shows that $d=(u, v)=(v, w)=(w, u)$. Thus, if we write s for d we see that $u=sk$, $v=sl$, $w=sm$ for (positive) integers k, l, m such that $(k, l)=(l, m)=(m, k)=1$. Also, from $(sk)^2+(sl)^2=(sm)^2$ we deduce that $k^2+l^2=m^2$. Such a solution (k, l, m), with k, l, m having no common factor greater than 1, is called a *primitive* solution of the equation $x^2+y^2=z^2$.

By primitivity no two of k, l, m can be even. Nor can k, l both be odd. [If so we'd have $m^2=k^2+l^2\equiv 1+1=2 \pmod 4$ which is impossible for a square by Exercise 4.2.9(a).] Thus one of k, l is even, the other odd—and then m, too, is odd.

Suppose, WLOG, that l is even, $l=2t$, say, and k is odd. The equality $l^2=m^2-k^2$ leads to

$$t^2=\frac{m+k}{2}\cdot\frac{m-k}{2}.$$

Now $m+k$ and $m-k$ are both even [why?] and so $(m+k)/2$ and $(m-k)/2$ are both integers. Further

$$\left(\frac{m+k}{2}, \frac{m-k}{2}\right) = 1;$$

for any common divisor would divide their sum m and their difference k and hence (m, k), which is 1. Thus $(m+k)/2$ and $(m-k)/2$ are (positive) coprime integers whose product is a square. Hence each is a square (Exercise 1.5.6); $(m+k)/2 = a^2$, $(m-k)/2 = b^2$, say, where we might as well assume $a, b > 0$. But then adding and subtracting yields $m = a^2 + b^2$, $k = a^2 - b^2$. Thus, since $l = 2t = 2ab$ [why?], we have $u = s(a^2 - b^2)$, $v = s(2ab)$ and $w = s(a^2 + b^2)$ as claimed. □

Using Theorems 6.2.2 and 6.2.4, taking $s = 1$, we can compute primitive Pythagorean triples. However, to ensure that each occurs once and once only we also need to adopt the restriction $0 < b < a$. This, of course, is not enough to guarantee that each triple is primitive. To achieve this we must also insist that $(a, b) = 1$ and that a and b are not both odd [why not?]. We claim that these necessary conditions on a and b are also sufficient to produce distinct primitive triples. Naturally enough the proof of this fact is left . . . to you!

These ideas are incorporated into Program 6.1.

PROGRAM 6.1 *Program to produce a list of primitive Pythagorean triples*

```
 10 FOR A=2 TO 10
 20   FOR B=1 TO A-1
 30   REM Check that one of a and b is even and the other odd
 40     IF (B/2=INT(B/2)) AND (A/2=INT(A/2)) GOTO 140
 50     IF (B/2<>INT(B/2)) AND (A/2<>INT(A/2)) GOTO 140
 60     REM Check that a and b are coprime
 70     X=A: Y=B
 80     R=X - INT(X/Y)*Y
 90       X=Y
100       Y=R
110     IF R<>0 GOTO 80
120     IF X<>1 GOTO 140
130     PRINT A, B, 2*A*B, A*A-B*B, A*A+B*B
140   NEXT B
150 NEXT A
```

As you will see this program does not produce the list of triples in order of increasing u or v or w. However, Program 6.2 does, giving a list of primitive Pythagorean triples in increasing order of the even side. We make use of the fact that each triple contains a number which is a multiple of 4 (see Exercise 6.2.5). We then search over the values of a and b which produce this multiple of four. How many primitive triples will there be for each multiple of four? (see Exercise 6.2.6).

Program 6.2 *Program to produce Pythagorean triples in increasing magnitude of the even side between two limits*

```
 10 INPUT "Enter the values of lower and upper ",l,u
 20 f=INT((l-1)/4)*4
 30 f=f+4
 40 h=f/2
 50 T=INT(SQR(h))
 60 FOR B=T TO 1 STEP -1
 70    A=h/B
 80    IF h<>INT(A)*INT(B) GOTO 180
 90    IF (B/2=INT(B/2)) AND (A/2=INT(A/2)) GOTO 180
100    IF (B/2<>INT(B/2)) AND (A/2<>INT(A/2)) GOTO 180
110    X=A:Y=B
120    R=X - INT(X/Y)*Y
130      X=Y
140      Y=R
150    IF R<>0 GOTO 120
160    IF X<>1 GOTO 180
170    PRINT A,B,2*A*B,A*A-B*B,A*A+B*B
180 NEXT B
190 IF f<INT(u/4)*4 GOTO 30
```

Exercises 6.2

1 Show that if $x^2+y^2=z^2$ and $(x, y, z)=1$ then $(x, y)=(y, z)=(z, x)=1$.

2 Show that not all x, y, z in a Pythagorean triple can be primes. Show that if two are primes then these must be the largest and the smallest of x, y, z.

3 Show that, given any integer $n \geqslant 3$, there is a Pythagorean triple with one of x, y, z equal to n.

4 Show that if $(x, x+1, z)$ is a Pythagorean triple then so is $(X, X+1, Z)$ where $X=2z+3x+1$, $Z=3z+4x+2$.

5 Show that if (x, y, z) is a Pythagorean triple then at least one of x, y is a multiple of 3, at least one of x, y is a multiple of 4 and at least one of x, y, z is a multiple of 5.

6 Show that each multiple of four has 2^r primitive Pythagorean triples associated with it where r is the number of distinct odd prime factors of the multiple of four.

7 Find all Pythagorean triples (x, y, z) such that x, y, z are in arithmetic progression. [*Hint*: $\alpha-d, \alpha, \alpha+d$.]

8 Show that there is no isosceles right-angled triangle with integral sides. Show, however, that, given any positive angle β no matter how small, there exists a right-angled triangle with integer sides and angles $\pi/4+\alpha$ and $\pi/4-\alpha$ where $0<\alpha<\beta$. [*Hint*: Show there is a Pythagorean triple (x, y, z) with x/z and y/z as near to $1/\sqrt{2}$ as one wishes.]

9 Find the general solutions of the equations: (i) $x^2+2y^2=z^2$; [*Hint*: If $(x, y)=(y, z)=(z, x)=1$, then x, z are odd, y is even. Put $z-x=2u$ and $z+x=2v$.]
(ii) $x^2+py=z^2$ where p is an odd prime.

10 Show that the equation $x^2+y^2=z^3$ has infinitely many solutions. [*Hint*: $x=a(a^2-3b^2)$, $y=b(b^2-3a^2)$.]

11 Diophantus, Book 6, Problem 1, asks for a right-angled triangle such that the hypotenuse minus each of the 'legs' is a cube. He offers the solution 40, 96, 104. Use Theorem 6.2.4 to obtain a formula which will generate infinitely many such triangles. Does your formula generate them all? Is Diophantus's the smallest with integer sides?

12 Prove, as Bachet did (1621), that the rational number A is the area of some right-angled triangle iff $(2A)^2+B^4$ can be made into a perfect (rational) square by appropriate choice of rational B. [*Hint*: Take $2A/B$ and B as the legs of the triangle.]

13 Solve completely in positive integers: (i) $n^x+n^y=n^z$; (ii) $x!+y!=z!$.

14 Solve completely, in integers, the equation: $1/x^2+1/y^2=1/z^2$ where $(x, y, z)=1$. [*Hint*: $x=2uv(u^2+v^2)$, $y=u^4-v^4$, $z=2uv(u^2-v^2)$ certainly works.]

Computer problems 6.2

1 Using the result that in each primitive Pythagorean triple (x, y, z), z is of the form $4k+1$, write a program to list the primitive Pythagorean triples in increasing magnitude of z.

2 Produce a table of the 50 smallest primitive Pythagorean triples ordered according to the size of the hypotenuse. Also display the values of $|x-y|$. Noting that $|x-y|=|(a-b)^2-2b^2|$ and $z=a^2+b^2$, can you make some conjectures? (See, in due course, Sections 8.4 and 7.1.)

3 Modify Program 6.2 so as to produce for each fixed even value of x the various primitive Pythagorean triples in order of increasing magnitude of y.

4 Write a program to list (primitive) Pythagorean triples (x, y, z) with $y=x+1$ for $z<3000$. Does the formula derived in Exercise 6.2.4 produce all such triples?

5 Write programs to produce lists of Pythagorean triples with $z=y+1$ and $z=y+2$. What happens in the case of $z=y+3$? Is there a theorem here?

6 Write a program to search for integer values x, y, z such that $x+y+z+x^2$, $x+y+z+x^2+y^2$ and $x+y+z+x^2+y^2+z^2$ are all squares. (Fibonacci was challenged to find a rational solution. He did! Do your findings lead to a theorem?)

7 Produce a list of Pythagorean triples that contain two primes. (Cf. Exercise 6.2.2.) Can you make any conjectures concerning such triples and can you prove them? Can a Pythagorean triple be primitive if none of its three numbers is prime?

8 Let r, s, t be integers each greater than 1. Theorem 6.3.1 will show that there is no right-angled triangle with sides r^2, s^2, t^2. Show that there *are* right-angled triangles with sides r^2-1, s^2-1, t^2-1. [It appears to be an open question as to whether there are infinitely many such triples.]

6.3 Fermat's last theorem

Theorem 6.2.2 shows that the equation $x^2+y^2=z^2$ has infinitely many solutions, even infinitely many primitive ones. But as soon as one raises the powers in this equation to 3 and beyond very curious things seem to happen. Fermat, given to making assertions about numbers but not accompanying them with proofs wrote, in his copy of Bachet's translation of the *Arithmetica*, '... it is impossible to separate a cube into two cubes, or a biquadrate into two biquadrates, or, in general, any power beyond the second into two powers of like degree. I have discovered a truly remarkable proof of this which this margin is too small to contain'. In symbols this reads:

Fermat's last theorem* (FC) *Let n be any integer greater than* 2. *Then the equation $x^n+y^n=z^n$ has no solution in positive integers.*

Actually, Fermat supplied a proof for this for the case $n=4$. Since we already have the tools to do the job we can give a proof now. (The proof for the case $n=3$ lies somewhat deeper and must wait until Chapter 9.) Fermat's proof for the case $n=4$ is obtained as a consequence of his proving '... not without much labour...' the following result† relating to a problem posed by Bachet in his translation, namely: The area of a right-angled triangle, the sides of which are rational in length, cannot itself be the square of a rational number. (This statement is easily seen to be equivalent to the one obtained by replacing 'rational' by 'integral'.) Fermat's proof is interesting since it illustrates what Fermat believed to be one of his major contributions, the method of proof 'by descent'—a method he expected would permit '... wonderful progress in number theory'.

Let us illustrate Fermat's method by investigating a slightly different Diophantine equation from which Fermat's conjecture for $n=4$ can be deduced. We prove

Theorem 6.3.1 The equation $x^4+y^4=z^2$ has no solution in non-zero integers.

* So called because it is the last of Fermat's proofless assertions which still awaits verification. It is more accurately, and quite often, called *Fermat's conjecture.* We shall call it that so we can use the abbreviation FC—and avoid (a second) use of the symbolism FLT.
† Leibniz also left a proof dating from 1678.

Proof Assume that $u^4+v^4=w^2$, u, v, w being (non-zero) integers which we may, by the usual argument, suppose to be coprime in pairs. Since $(u^2)^2+(v^2)^2=w^2$ Theorem 6.2.4 tells us that $u^2=a^2-b^2$, $v^2=2ab$, $w=a^2+b^2$—or the same with the roles of u and v reversed—where $(a, b)=1$ [since $(u, v)=1$]. In particular a and b cannot both be even. Nor can they both be odd [why not?]. In fact a must be odd and b must be even (or else $u^2\equiv 0-1 \pmod 4$) which is impossible). Thus from $b^2+u^2=a^2$ we must have $b=2mn$, $a=m^2+n^2$ for suitable $m, n\in\mathbb{Z}$. Note that $(m, n)=1$ [why?]. From $v^2=a(2b)$ we deduce that a and $2b$ are both squares [why?]. Since $2b=4mn$ we deduce that mn and then m and n themselves are all squares [why?]. Set $m=\alpha^2$, $n=\beta^2$ and $a=\gamma^2$. We then have $\alpha^4+\beta^4=m^2+n^2=a=\gamma^2$—a perfect square.

We now apply Fermat's 'method of descent'. Having assumed a solution (u, v, w) of the equation $x^4+y^4=z^2$ we have obtained a 'smaller' one, namely α, β, γ. Repeating the above procedure leads, argues Fermat, to an infinite sequence of solutions with smaller and smaller (positive) values for, say, z^2. Since no infinite decreasing sequence of positive integers can exist, the proof is complete. □

Note 6.3.2 Clearly the method of descent is, then, nothing other than a different way of expressing the WO principle.

The proof of the FC in the case $n=4$ is now immediate.

Corollary 6.3.3 The equation $x^4+y^4=z^4$ has no solutions for which $xyz\neq 0$.

Proof If u, v, w were a solution then u, v, w^2 would be a solution of $x^4+y^4=z^2$ which, by Theorem 6.3.1, is impossible. □

This corollary 'reduces' the proving of the FC to the case where n is prime. For we have

Theorem 6.3.4 To prove the FC for each $n\geqslant 3$ it remains only (!) to prove it for each odd prime.

Proof Let $n=kp$ be a composite number, p being a prime factor of n. Suppose that u, v, w is a solution of the equation $x^n+y^n=z^n$. Then u^k, v^k, w^k is a solution of the equation $x^p+y^p=z^p$. Thus, if we know that the FC is true for all odd prime exponents p, then it will also be valid for each n as described here—except in the case where n has no odd prime factor, that is where n is a power of 2. But in this case n is a multiple of 4 (since $n>2$), and to prove the FC in this case we can appeal to Corollary 6.3.3. □

Exercises 6.3

1 Show that $x^4+y^4=z^4$ has no solution in (non-zero) rational numbers.

2 From the assertion that there is no right-angled triangle with integer sides and area a square, deduce that $x^4-y^4=z^4$ has no solution in (non-zero) integers. [*Hint*: Consider a triangle with sides x^4-y^4, $2x^2y^2$, x^4+y^4.]

3 Prove that $x^4-y^4=z^2$ where $(x, y)=1$ has only the solutions (i) $x^2=y^2=1$, (ii) $x^2=z^2=1$. [*Hint*: Suppose u, v, w is a (positive) solution with $uvw\neq 0$ and u as small as possible. Show u is odd. Show that if v is odd, then

$$(uv)^2=(a^2+b^2)(a^2-b^2)=a^4-b^4$$

is a 'smaller' solution. Show that if v is even, then $u^2=a^2+b^2$, $v^2=2ab$, where $a=2c^2$, $b=d^2$ with d odd and $(c, d)=1$. Complete the proof by 'descent'.]

4 (i) Find all integer solutions of $x^2+y^2=z^4$. (ii) Show that $x^2+y^4=z^2$ has infinitely many primitive solutions (i.e. with $xyz\neq 0$ and $(x, y)=1$.)

5 Show that $x^4+4y^4=z^4$ has no solution in non-zero integers.

6 Show that (i) $x^4-y^4=2z^2$ has no solution in non-zero integers and that (ii) the only primitive 'positive' solutions of $x^4+y^4=2z^2$ are given by $x^2=y^2=1$. [*Hint*: (i) Factorise x^4-y^4. (ii) Look at $z^4-(xy)^4$.]

7 Show that there exist no non-zero integers x, y, z, t such that $x^2+y^2=z^2$ and $y^2+z^2=t^2$ simultaneously.

8 Let p be a prime. Show that if $x^{p-1}+y^{p-1}=z^{p-1}$ then $p|xyz$ and that if $x^p+y^p=z^p$ then $p|x+y-z$.

9 Show that if $x^n+y^n=z^n$ has no solution in positive integers then it has no solution in non-zero integers.

10 (Grunert 1856) Assuming that $a^n+b^n=c^n$, show that $a>n$ and $b>n$. [*Hint*: Set $c=a+u$ and use the binomial theorem to get $b^n>na^{n-1}u$.]

11 (de Jonquières* 1883) If $a^n+b^n=c^n$ and $n>1$ then the greater of a, b is composite. [*Hint*: Suppose $a<b$. Set $c=a+k$. Show that $1<k<b$ and look at $b^n=(a+k)^n-a^n$.]

12 V. A. Lebesgue (1840) showed that if $x^n+y^n=z^n$ is impossible in integers then so is $x^{2n}+y^{2n}=z^2$. Prove this! [*Hint*: From $x^n=u^2-v^2$, $y^n=2uv$ deduce $u+v=\alpha^n$, $u-v=\beta^n$ and $u=2^{n-1}\gamma^n$, $v=\delta^n$ (or vice versa). Look at $\alpha^n\pm\beta^n$.]

13 (Talbot 1857) Show that if n is odd and if p is a prime then $a^n+b^n=p^n$ is impossible. [*Hint*: Show $p<a+b<2p$. Hence $p\nmid a+b$.]

14 If $x, y, z>0$ if $x^l+y^l=z^l$ and if $m>l$ then $x^m+y^m\neq z^m$ (Nemeth 1909).

6.4 History of the FC

One can't be sure of the date on which Fermat first asserted the FC. It was in 1636 that he proposed to Sainte-Croix that the latter should find two cubes

* Ernest Jean Philippe Fauque de Jonquières, 3 July 1820 – 12 August 1901.

whose sum is a cube and a (rational) right triangle whose area is a (rational) square or, equivalently two fourth powers whose difference is a square—proposals he repeated to Frenicle in 1640 and others later. With this and Diophantus' problem 8 above in mind the passage to the formulation of the FC itself is immediate. Since Fermat gave us the proof of the FC only in the case of $n=4$ it was left to others to supply proofs where they could. As we've seen we may concentrate on the case of odd prime exponent p. Fermat repeatedly offered the case $p=3$ to other mathematicians but no proof was forthcoming until Euler produced one which was essentially correct (but incomplete) in 1770. (Gauss too produced a proof—see Chapter 9—which was published posthumously.) The case $p=5$ was dealt with in the 1820s, independently, by Dirichlet and Legendre. The case $p=7$ was established by Lamé in 1839 but clearly something deeper was needed if *all* remaining cases were to be covered. In 1847 Lamé thought he'd found it. At a meeting of the Paris Academy he revealed his methods. Taking $x^p+y^p=z^p$, factorise the left-hand side as $(x+y)(x+\zeta y)\cdots(x+\zeta^{p-1}y)$ where ζ is a primitive pth root of 1. Writing $\zeta^{p-1}=-1-\zeta-\cdots-\zeta^{p-2}$ (Exercise 6.4.1) each factor is of the form $a_0+a_1\zeta+\cdots+a_{p-2}\zeta^{p-2}$ where the $a_i\in\mathbb{Z}$. So we consider the set $\mathbb{Z}[\zeta]=\{a_0+a_1\zeta+\cdots+a_{p-2}\zeta^{p-2}: a_i\in\mathbb{Z}\}$. The sum of two members of $\mathbb{Z}[\zeta]$ is again in $\mathbb{Z}[\zeta]$; so too is their product if one uses the above expression for ζ^{p-1} repeatedly. Thus the set $\mathbb{Z}[\zeta]$ constitutes what algebraists call a *ring*. In this ring, Lamé argued, each pair of the factors $x+y, x+\zeta y, \ldots, x+\zeta^{p-1}y$ has no common divisor 'larger' than 1 and their product is an nth power. It then follows, he continued, that each factor is essentially an nth power—just as it would be in $\mathbb{Z}$. From this Lamé was able to 'prove' the FC. In so doing he secured the plaudits of several mathematicians, one of whom suggested he become the recipient of a collection for making 'the greatest mathematical discovery of the century'.

The reader who has looked at Exercise 1.4.1 may have detected a potentially cavernous gap in Lamé's argument. It is the assumption that in $\mathbb{Z}[\zeta]$ each element can be factorised into a product of unfactorisable (i.e. 'prime') elements of $\mathbb{Z}[\zeta]$ in an essentially unique way. Factorisation into primes exists all right; it's the uniqueness which is not so clear. Intuition isn't helped by the fact that factorisation *is* unique for each prime <23; it's only at $p=23$ that things begin to go wrong. (And, in fact, stay wrong: in 1971 K. Uchida proved that for each $p\geqslant 23$ the analogue in $\mathbb{Z}[\zeta]$ of the fundamental theorem of arithmetic (see Theorems 1.4.1 and 9.4.1) fails.

According to [22], though contrary to popular belief, Kummer* already knew of this problem for $p=23$ as early as 1843. His remedy was to introduce extra 'ideal' prime divisors—somewhat along the lines of Exercise 1.4.1—in order to restore uniqueness of factorisation. He was then able to determine conditions, expressible in terms of the so called *Bernoulli numbers*, which enabled him to show that the FC was true for all prime powers <100 except

* Ernst Eduard Kummer, 29 January 1810 - 14 May 1893.

37, 59 and 67—the first three examples of 'irregular' primes. Although Kummer thought he'd proved the FC for infinitely many primes it is still not known if the regular primes are infinite in number. (Curiously there are infinitely many irregular ones.)

Even before the age of the computer, indeed by 1908, L. E. Dickson had, by taking into account conditions known to hold if a solution to the FC is to exist, established the FC for all primes p (in the case where $p \nmid xyz$) up to 7000. More necessary criteria for solubility followed. In 1909 A. Wieferich showed that if the FC holds for $n=p$ with $p \nmid xyz$, then $2^{p-1} \equiv 1 (\mathrm{mod}\ p^2)$, the first such prime being 1093. (See Problem 3.2.2.) In 1910 D. Miriamoff provided a similar necessary condition: $3^{p-1} \equiv 1 (\mathrm{mod}\ p^2)$.

The advent of the computer age has, of course aided calculations along these lines and progress and interest continue to be made and maintained (now helped not at all by the generous gesture of P. Wolfskehl who, in 1908, offered a prize of 100 000 marks—which inflation subsequently reduced to zero—for the first complete proof of the FC). At present the FC is known to be valid (whether $p|xyz$ or not) for all integers n possessing a prime factor less than 125 000(!)—see [L].

In view of Wolfskehl's generosity it is appropriate that the most recent major advance on the FC front was made by a young German mathematician G. Faltings. His proof—for which he was awarded the 1986 Fields Medal, the 'Nobel Prize' of mathematics—of a 60-year-old conjecture of Mordell, when specialised to the FC, shows that: If, for some n, the equation $x^n + y^n = z^n$ has a solution in non-zero integers, then it has at most finitely many solutions for that value of n. The magnitude of this advance should be clear!

Exercises 6.4

1 Let p be an odd prime and ζ a pth root of 1—other than 1 itself. Show that

(i) $x^p + y^p = (x+y)(x+\zeta y) \cdots (x+\zeta^{p-1}y)$.
(ii) $\zeta^{p-1} = -1-\zeta-\cdots-\zeta^{p-2}$.
(iii) For $p=5$ write $(3+2\zeta+\zeta^4)(1+2\zeta+3\zeta^2)$ in the form $a+b\zeta+c\zeta^2+d\zeta^3$ with $a, b, c\ d \in \mathbb{Z}$.

2 The Bernoulli numbers, B_n, introduced by Jacob Bernoulli* in connection with finding the formula for sums $1^n + 2^n + \cdots + r^n$ for $n = 1, 2, 3, \ldots$, can be defined by

$$\frac{e^x - 1}{x} \sum_{n=0}^{\infty} B_n \frac{x^n}{n!} = 1.$$

Deduce that for $t \geqslant 1$,

$$\frac{B_t}{t!1!} + \frac{B_{t-1}}{(t-1)!2!} + \cdots + \frac{B_1}{1!t!} + \frac{B_0}{0!(t+1)!} = 0.$$

* Jacob Bernoulli, 27 December 1654 - 16 August 1705.

Evaluate $B_t = n_t/d_t$ for $1 \leqslant t \leqslant 12$. Kummer showed that the prime p is regular—and hence the FC holds for p—if $p \nmid n_{2s}$ for $s = 1, 2, \ldots, (p-3)/2$. Deduce that the FC holds for $p = 5, 7, 11, 13$.

Computer problems 6.4

1 Find the next prime p, after 1093, for which p^2 divides $2^{p-1} - 1$.

2 Write a program to calculate Bernoulli numbers as a fraction. Hence confirm Kummer's assertion that 37 is the only irregular prime less than 40.

Sophie Germain *(1 April 1776 – 27 June 1831)*
Born in Paris, Sophie Germain's early education was gained at home. When only just in her teens she learned from her father's extensive library how Archimedes had been murdered by the Romans. She resolved to follow the great man and study mathematics, beginning by reading Newton and Euler.

Aged 18 she obtained some of Lagrange's lecture notes and she wrote to him using the pseudonym M. Le Blanc. Lagrange was so amazed at what he received that he sought a meeting with this 'student' only to discover that 'he' was a young lady!

She then set about writing to other prominent mathematicians, in particular to Legendre who included many of her number theoretic results in his 'Theorie des Nombres'. She also wrote to Gauss, again using the pseudonym M. Le Blanc. He too was impressed with the mathematics and was incredulous when he discovered it had been written by 'a person of the sex which, according to our prejudices, must encounter infinitely many more difficulties than men to familiarise [itself] with these thorny researches' that she must have 'quite extraordinary talents and superior genius'. (This may sound very condescending nowadays but, given the time it was said, Gauss was being almost indecently 'forward'.) Gauss obviously felt warmly towards Mlle Germain and her mathematics; he ends a letter to her with 'Brunswick, 30th April, 1807, my birthday'.

Sophie Germain's contribution to this book lies in Theorem 6.5.1, but her interests were not restricted to pure mathematics. She also contributed to the theories of acoustics and elasticity. Indeed in 1816 she was awarded the grand prize of the Académie des Sciences for a paper on the vibration of curved elastic surfaces.

Having never met Gauss, Sophie Germain died just before she was to receive, from the University of Göttingen, the award, of a doctorate recommended by Gauss himself.

6.5 Sophie Germain's theorem

In view of the apparent difficulty of establishing the FC in individual cases of small prime exponent such as 5 and 7, general theorems of the kind obtained by Kummer and others become all the more intriguing. How does one prove such theorems which deal with many exponents all at once? Kummer's theory is much too involved to reproduce here but, if you are prepared to accept slightly less, we can show you how the FC—or at least a part of it—was established around 1805 by the French mathematician Sophie Germain, for all prime exponents less than 100. The theorem leading to this is:

Theorem 6.5.1 Let n be an odd prime. Suppose that there exists an odd prime p such that:

(i) each solution of the equation $X^n + Y^n + Z^n \equiv 0 \pmod p$ has $p|XYZ$.
(ii) the equation $T^n \equiv n \pmod p$ has no integer solution.

Then, for each solution of the equation $x^n + y^n + z^n = 0$, we have $n|xyz$. □
(Proof below.)

Notes 6.5.2
(i) The equivalence of the statements that $x^n + y^n = z^n$ and $x^n + y^n + z^n = 0$ have no solutions in non-zero integers is immediate (see Exercise 6.5.1).
(ii) The FC is usually split into two cases. That considered here—where we assert that even if $x^n + y^n + z^n = 0$ has solutions, it certainly has none with $n \nmid xyz$—is called Case I.

Proof of Theorem 6.5.1 As usual we assume that the equation $x^n + y^n + z^n = 0$ has a solution u, v, w, where $uvw \neq 0$ and u, v, w are pairwise coprime and we now assume further that none of u, v, w is a multiple of the prime n. First note that

$$-w^n = u^n + v^n = (u+v)(u^{n-1} - u^{n-2}v + \cdots + v^{n-1}).$$

We claim that the bracketed terms are coprime. For, if q were a common prime divisor, we should have $u \equiv -v \pmod q$ so that, from the second bracket, $nv^{n-1} \equiv 0 \pmod q$. From this we deduce that $q|n$ or $q|v$. The first condition implies $q = n$, from which $n|w$, contradicting the assumption that $n \nmid uvw$. The second condition $q|v$ (together with $q|u+v$) implies that $(u, v) > 1$, contradicting the choice of u, v (and w).

It follows that the bracketed terms, being coprime, are each nth powers. Let us put

$$u+v=a^n, \quad u^{n-1}-u^{n-2}v+\cdots+v^{n-1}=A^n, \qquad \text{so that } w=-aA. \tag{α}$$

By a symmetrical argument we can clearly also assume that

$$v+w=b^n, \quad v^{n-1}-v^{n-2}w+\cdots+w^{n-1}=B^n, \qquad \text{so that } u=-bB \tag{β}$$

$$w+u=c^n, \quad w^{n-1}-w^{n-2}u+\cdots+u^{n-1}=C^n, \qquad \text{so that } v=-cC. \tag{γ}$$

Now let p be the prime whose existence is supposed by hypothesis (i) and consider the congruence $u^n+v^n+w^n \equiv 0 \pmod p$. By hypothesis (i) at least one of u, v, w is a multiple of p. WLOG suppose $p|u$. Then $a^n+c^n+(-b)^n = 2u \equiv 0 \pmod p$. Using hypothesis (i) again we infer that $p|abc$. Now if $p|a$ then $p|u+v$ and hence $p|u$ and $p|v$, thus contradicting $(u, v)=1$. Similarly $p|c$ leads to a contradiction. Hence $p|b$. Consequently $w \equiv -v \pmod p$. Equations (α) and (β) then show that $A^n \equiv v^{n-1} \pmod p$ – since $p|u$—and $B^n \equiv nv^{n-1} \pmod p$—since $v \equiv -w$. We deduce immediately that $B^n \equiv nA^n \pmod p$.

Now $p \nmid A$ (why not?). Consequently there exists an integer D such that $DA \equiv 1 \pmod p$. It follows that $(DB)^n \equiv n \pmod p$, contradicting hypothesis (ii) of the theorem. The theorem is therefore proved. □

Note 6.5.3 Here is a theorem which warms the heart! The result is non-trivial and yet the hypotheses are exactly what is needed to prove it. In particular the *coup de grace* in the final sentence of the proof is almost thrilling. Of course the big question is: Are the hypotheses easily usable? As implied by earlier comments the anwser is 'Yes'. No wonder Gauss was impressed!

Exercises 6.5

1 Prove the assertion of 6.5.2(i).

2 Show that if both n and $2n+1$ are odd primes, then the equation $x^n+y^n+z^n=0$ has no solutions in integers other than those for which $n|xyz$. Find all primes less than 100 for which $2n+1$ is also a prime.

3 Show that if $n=7$ then $p=29$ satisfies the hypotheses of Sophie Germain's theorem. [*Hint*: If $X=x^7$, then $X^4 \equiv 1 \pmod{29}$. This implies that $X \equiv 1$ or -1 or that $29|X^2+1$. Deduce that for, $x \in \mathbb{Z}$, $x^7 \equiv 0, 1, -1, 12$ or -12.]

4 For the next three primes after 7 for which Exercise 2 is no help, find primes p to satisfy the hypotheses of Theorem 6.5.1.

Computer problem 6.5

1 (Cf. Exercise 6.5.2.) Find primes p such that $2p+1$ is also prime. Explore the percentage of primes of this form over various intervals of length 500.

6.6 Cadenza

The very statement of the FC gives rise to a whole industry of problems easily manufactured by anyone whose interest in the (hidden) relations between integers is unbounded. (Of course the *answers* are often that bit more difficult to manufacture!) For example, if $x^3+y^3=z^3$ is insoluble in non-zero integers, what about equations of the form $x^3+y^3=z^3+t^3$ or $x^3+y^3+z^3=t^3$, where positive integer solutions are required in each case? We've already offered a simple program which will apparently generate solutions to the former equation *ad nauseam.* But can we expect infinitely many? Frenicle provided several solutions in 1657. Euler went one better. He exhibited a formula which will generate all the rational solutions. He also produced a formula to generate infinitely many solutions of the equation $x^4+y^4=z^4+t^4$, though in an article in 1929 G. H. Hardy was not sure if this formula gave the smallest solution. On the equation $x^4+y^4+z^4=t^4$ Euler pronounced there was no (non-trivial) solution and that for a sum of non-zero nth powers to equal an nth power at least n summands would be needed. This latter assertion was shown to be false in 1966 when Lander and Parkin exhibited four 5th powers whose sum is a 5th power. We leave you the pleasure of finding this solution. (The sum is less than 150^5.) And very recently Euler's specific assertion about 4th powers has been contradicted*.

More problems suggested by the FC (if you've not already thought up a hundred for yourself!) are considered in Section 7.3.

Exercises 6.6

1 Check Euler's formulae, namely:

$$x=a^7+a^5b^2-2a^3b^4+3a^2b^5+ab^6$$
$$y=a^6b-3a^5b^2-2a^4b^3+a^2b^5+b^7$$
$$z=a^7+a^5b^2-2a^3b^4-3a^2b^5+ab^6$$
$$t=a^6b+3a^5b^2-2a^4b^3+a^2b^5+b^7$$

yield solutions to the equation $x^4+y^4=z^4+t^4$.

* On $A^4+B^4+C^4=D^4$ by Noam D. Elkies. To appear in *Mathematics of Computation.*

Do these formulae generate infinitely many solutions?

2 Show that

$$x = 9ta^4$$

$$y = 3ta(1 - 3a^3)$$

$$z = t(1 - 9a^3)$$

gives infinitely many rational solutions of the equation $x^3 + y^3 + z^3 = t^3$ but that $3^3 + 4^3 + 5^3 = 6^3$ (known in 1591) isn't one of them.

3 Use Exercise 2 to show that there are infinitely many *positive integer* solutions to $x^3 + y^3 = z^3 + t^3$. Does our example $9^3 + 10^3 = 1^3 + 12^3$ arise from these formulae?

Computer problem 6.6

1 Are there in Exercise 6.6.1 values of *a*, *b* which yield the smallest non-zero solution to $x^4 + y^4 = z^4 + t^4$, which you found in Computer problem 0.1.2?

7
Sums of squares

7.1 Sums of two squares

The second type of problem which attracted Fermat's attention from 1636 onwards was, as we have already indicated, that of representing integers as sums of squares. Again the motivation comes from Diophantus. First, in Book 6, Problem 14, it is asserted that 15 is not a sum of two (rational) squares. Then Problem 9 of Book 5 asks for rationals a, b such that $a+b=1$ and that $a+c$ and $b+c$ both be squares, conditions which imply that $2c+1$ is a sum of two squares. Finally, Problem 19 of Book 3 seeks numbers x_1, x_2, x_3, x_4 such that each of the eight numbers $t \pm x_i$, where $t=(x_1+x_2+x_3+x_4)^2$ and $i=1, 2, 3, 4$, should be a square. Diophantus shows that this can be achieved if we can find four different right-angled triangles with integer sides and with the same hypotenuse. This in turn is equivalent to finding a square which can be expressed as a sum of two squares in four different ways. Commenting on this, Fermat claimed, amongst other things, that: *Every prime of the form* $4k+1$ *is the hypotenuse of a right-angled triangle in exactly one way*—a result he would have noticed from tables of the kind you were asked to provide in Computer Problem 6.2.2 and one which he communicated to Mersenne on 25 December 1640. In letters of 1654 and 1658 he stated that he had irrefutable proof of this and, in 1659, that his method was that of 'descent'.

Of course it was Euler (1747) who supplied a proof for all to see. Let's see how he did it.

First we shall need a result which was known to Diophantus.

Lemma 7.1.1 Let a, b, c, d be real numbers. Then

$$(a^2+b^2)(c^2+d^2)=(ac \pm bd)^2+(ad \mp bc)^2. \quad \square$$

The equality is easily checked. In 1770 Euler proved it by considering the complex numbers $\alpha=a+ib$ and $\beta=c+id$ and using the well-known expression $|\alpha\beta|=|\alpha||\beta|$ for the modulus of a product (see Note 9.2.3).

We shall break Euler's proof of part of Fermat's claim into easily digestible bits.

(i) *If* $m=a^2+b^2=pl$ *where* $p=c^2+d^2$ *is a prime, then* l *is a sum of two squares.*

Proof Since $(bc+ad)(bc-ad)=c^2(a^2+b^2)-a^2(c^2+d^2)$ is divisible by p, at least one of $bc+ad$, $bc-ad$ must be. Suppose WLOG that $bc+ad=pt$. Set

$b = tc + x$, $a = td + y$. Then $cx + dy = 0$. But $(c, d) = 1$ [why?]. Hence $cw = y$ and $-dw = x$ for some $w \in \mathbb{Z}$ [why?]. It follows that

$$pl = m = a^2 + b^2 = t^2(c^2 + d^2) + 2t(cx + dy) + (x^2 + y^2)$$
$$= (c^2 + d^2)(t^2 + w^2).$$

Consequently $l = m/p = (t^2 + w^2)$—as claimed. □

(ii) *Let $m = a^2 + b^2 = nk$. If k is not a sum of two squares then n has a (prime) factor which is not a sum of two squares.*

Proof Write $n = p_1 p_2 \cdots p_r$ as a product of primes. Using part (i) successively on the numbers m/p_1, $m/p_1p_2, \ldots, m/p_1p_2 \cdots p_r = k$, we see that if each p_i is a sum of two squares then so too is each quotient listed, k included. This contradiction shows that at least one of the p_i is not a sum of two squares. □

(iii) *Let $m = a^2 + b^2$ where $(a, b) = 1$. Then each factor u of m is a sum of two squares.*

Proof Write $a = \rho u + \alpha$, $b = \sigma u + \beta$ where $-u/2 \leqslant \alpha, \beta \leqslant u/2$. Then

$$u | a^2 + b^2 = (\rho u + \alpha)^2 + (\sigma u + \beta)^2,$$

from which it follows that $u | \alpha^2 + \beta^2 \leqslant u^2/2$. Hence $\alpha^2 + \beta^2 = uv$, where $v \leqslant u/2$. Let $\delta = (\alpha, \beta) \geqslant 1$. Then $(\delta, u) = 1$—since $(a, b) = 1$. We deduce that $M = (\alpha/\delta)^2 + (\beta/\delta)^2 = uz$ where $z = (v/\delta^2)$ is an integer. But then $z \leqslant v \leqslant u/2$, too. Now if u were not the sum of two squares then, by part (ii), z would have a factor U, say, which is not a sum of two squares. We would then have started on a path of infinite descent passing from u (a divisor of a sum of two coprime squares but not itself a sum of two squares) to another smaller such number namely U—a divisor of a sum, namely M, of two coprime squares. □

We can now complete the proof of Fermat's claim as did Lagrange in 1775.

Theorem 7.1.2 Let p be a prime of the form $4k + 1$. Then p is a sum of two squares.

Proof By FLT, $(x^{2k} - 1)(x^{2k} + 1) = x^{p-1} - 1 \equiv 0 \pmod p$. This congruence has solutions $1, 2, \ldots, p - 1$ of which, by Corollary 4.4.6, exactly $2k$ must be roots of $x^{2k} + 1$ (the other $2k$ being roots of $x^{2k} - 1$) modulo p. Thus, for some a, $1 \leqslant a \leqslant p - 1$ we have $(a^k)^2 + 1 \equiv 0 \pmod p$, *i.e.* $p | 1 + (a^k)^2$. Thus, by (iii) above, p is a sum of two squares. □

Notes 7.1.3

(i) Our use of Lagrange's theorem (1768) in the above should have left you asking how Euler proved more than 20 years earlier that $x^{2k} + 1$ had any root

(modulo p) at all. His ingenious method is indicated in the footnote to Exercise 8.3.5.
(ii) And what about Fermat's claim of uniqueness? We shall give a rather splendid proof later (Theorem 9.4.2) using the so-called Gaussian integers. For a direct proof see Exercise 7.1.7.

Having seen which *primes* can be represented as a sum of two squares, we return to Diophantus' Problem 9, which requires $2c+1$ to be expressible as a sum of two squares. Just which *integers* are so expressible?

Since $2=1^2+1^2$(!), Theorem 7.1.2 and Lemma 7.1.1 show immediately that each integer of the form $2^\alpha p_1 p_2 \dots p_r s$, where the p_i are primes of the form $4k+1$ and s is any perfect square, is representable as a sum of two squares. For example, since $37=6^2+1^2$ and $89=8^2+5^2$, we see that

$$161\,357=7^2\cdot 37\cdot 89=7^2\cdot(6\cdot 8\pm 1\cdot 5)^2+7^2\cdot(6\cdot 5\mp 1\cdot 8)^2,$$

that is

$$161\,357=(7\cdot 53)^2+(7\cdot 22)^2=(7\cdot 43)^2+(7\cdot 38)^2.$$

(Note that, for ease of stating theorems, we accept each square, s^2, as a sum of the squares s^2 and 0^2.)

In fact Diophantus knew that not all integers are so representable—those of the form $4k+3$ for example. (Exercise 7.1.8 generalises this.) Xylander further claimed it is enough to ask that c (above) be twice a prime, a claim refuted by Bachet by citing $c=10$, even though he couldn't prove that $2c+1=21$ is not a sum of two (rational) squares (see Exercise 7.1.13). In fact Fermat gave the correct result as had A. Girard, unknown to Fermat, a little earlier. The full story is:

Theorem 7.1.4 The integer N is expressible* as a sum of two squares iff when N is divided by its greatest square factor s, say, then N/s is divisible by no prime of the form $4k+3$.

Proof We have just indicated the 'if' part. For the 'only if' part suppose $N=a^2+b^2$ and let $d=(a,b)$. Then $N=d^2(u^2+v^2)$ where $a=du$ and $b=dv$. Write $M=N/d^2=u^2+v^2$ where $(u,v)=1$. By Exercise 7.1.8 no prime of the form $4k+3$ can divide M. This completes the proof. □

Note 7.1.5 This theorem allows us to say more: N is expressible as the sum of two *rational* squares iff it has the form indicated (see Exercise 7.1.13).

The central point in this proof—that no primes of the form $4k+3$ can divide a sum of coprime squares is also central in proving certain results about Bachet's equation $y^2=x^3+k$.

* Fermat also indicated in how many different ways N could be so expressed (see Exercise 9.4.8).

Louis Joel Mordell *(28 January 1888 – 12 March 1972)*
Mordell was born in Philadelphia of Lithuanian parents who had emigrated to the USA earlier in the decade. He reveals in his *Reminiscences*..., [M], that, at the age of 14, he came across some old algebra books on the 5–10 cent shelf of a second-hand bookstore. Noting that many of the exercises were from examination papers set by the University of Cambridge, he resolved to try to obtain a place there.

On being accepted by St John's College he telegrammed his father with the single word 'Hurrah'—all he could afford to send!

After graduating, Mordell stayed at Cambridge and began researching in number theory. No doctorates were on offer in Britain at the time but Mordell won the second Smith prize with an essay on the solutions of the equation $y^2 = x^3 + k$—now sometimes called the Mordell equation.

After moves to Birkbeck College (1913) and Manchester College of Technology (1920), Mordell was elected to a professorship at the University of Manchester in 1923. The following year he was elected a Fellow of the Royal Society.

Mordell's non-mathematical interests included climbing and swimming. He tells, in [M], that many at Manchester regarded him very highly—not for his F.R.S. but because he could dive off the 5 metre board! He also played bridge and was, apparently, 'the world's worst good player'.

Mordell's method of dealing with the ubiquitous tele(phone)-sales person is widely known but worth repeating. Answering the phone on one occasion in the USA, Mordell was told—on giving the correct reply to a question put to him that he had 'just won $45 worth of dancing lessons'. He then asked the sales-girl the name of the first President of the USA. On receiving the correct response Mordell announced, 'Congratulations, you have just won them back again!'

Theorem 7.1.6 (L. J. Mordell) The equation $y^2 + 4a^2 = x^3 + (4b-1)^3$, where a has no prime factor $\equiv 3 \pmod 4$, has no solution in the integers.

Proof Since we have $y^2 \equiv x^3 - 1 \pmod 4$ it is easy to check (since $y^2 \equiv 2, 3 \pmod 4$ is impossible) that $x \equiv 1 \pmod 4$. But then $x^2 - x(4b-1) + (4b-1)^2$—a factor of $x^3 + (4b-1)^3$—is both positive and congruent to 3 mod 4.

It therefore has a prime factor q of the form $4k+3$ which divides y^2+4a^2. Thus $q|y$ and $q|4a^2$, an impossibility, which proves the theorem. □

Searching with a computer to find numbers which cannot be expressed as the sum of two squares can be attempted in several ways. Given an integer N Program 7.1 will express it as the sum of two squares—provided a solution exists.

Program 7.1 *Expresses a given integer N (≥4) as the sum of two squares (if possible)*

```
 10 INPUT N
 20 I=-1
 30 I=I+1
 40    A=SQR(N-I*I)
 50    IF A=INT(A) GOTO 90
 60 IF I<=A GOTO 30
 70 PRINT "No solution found"
 80 STOP
 90 PRINT ;N;" = ";I;"^2 + ";A;"^2"
100 END
```

However, if we want to find all the integers, less than some given integer N, which are expressible as a sum of two squares a better method—illustrated in Program 7.2—is to create an array of size N in which initially all places have been assigned the value zero. Then for $0 \leqslant a \leqslant b \leqslant \sqrt{N}$ set $S(a^2+b^2)=1$ for values of $a^2+b^2 \leqslant N$. Clearly there is still some unnecessary calculation but the total number of operations is less, and hence the process is more efficient, than using the method in Program 7.1 successively for each $n \leqslant N$.

Program 7.2 *Finds all the integers less than some given integer N that can be expressed as the sum of two squares*

```
  5 INPUT N
 10 DIM S(N)
 20 FOR I= 1 TO N
 30    S(I)=0
 40 NEXT I
 50 FOR A=0 TO SQR(N)
 60    A2=A*A
 70    FOR B= A TO SQR(N)
 80       V=A2+B*B
 90       IF V<=N S(V)=1
100    NEXT B
110 NEXT A
120 FOR I=1 TO N
130    IF S(I)=1 PRINT ;I;"  ";
140 NEXT I
```

Exercises 7.1

1 Write 41, 97 and 3977 as sums of two squares. [*Hint*: For 3977 use Lemma 7.1.1]

2 Write 1105 ($=5\cdot 13\cdot 17$) as a sum of squares in as many ways as possible.

3 Find the least integer expressible as a sum of two squares in two (essentially) different ways. (That is, find n such that $n=a^2+b^2=c^2+d^2$ where $0<a<c\leqslant d<b$.)

4 Find a *square* N^2 which can be expressed as a sum of two squares in four different ways (excluding N^2+0^2). Hence determine four triangles as required by Diophantus.

5 Show that the positive integer n can be represented as a *difference* of two squares iff $n\neq 4k+2$.

6 Prove that each odd prime divisor q of a number of the form x^2+3y^2, where $(x, y)=1$, is of the form u^2+3v^2—as follows:

(i) $(a^2+3b^2)(c^2+3d^2)=(ac-3bd)^2+3(ad+bc)^2$;
(ii) $(bc+ad)(bc-ad)=b^2(c^2+3d^2)-d^2(a^2+3b^2)$;
(iii) if $m=a^2+3b^2=pl$, where $p=c^2+3d^2$ is prime, then l is of the form e^2+3f^2;
(iv) If $2|a^2+3b^2$ then $4|a^2+3b^2$ and

$$\tfrac{1}{4}(a^2+3b^2)=(a/2)^2+3(b/2)^2 \qquad \text{or} \qquad \left(\frac{a\mp 3b}{4}\right)^2+3\left(\frac{a\pm b}{4}\right)^2$$

(v) If $a^2+3b^2=nk$ is odd and k is not of the form e^2+3f^2, then n has a prime factor not of the form g^2+3h^2.
(vi) Use the condition $(x, y)=1$.

7 Let $p=a^2+b^2$ be a prime of the form $4k+1$. Prove the uniqueness of a and b (>0) as follows. From $p=a^2+b^2=c^2+d^2$ with $a, b, c, d>0$ deduce (i) that $a^2d^2-b^2c^2=p(d^2-b^2)$; (ii) that $p|ad-bc$ or $p|ad+bc$; if $p|ad+bc$ then

$$p^2=(a^2+b^2)(c^2+d^2)=(ad+bc)^2+(ac-bd)^2,$$

whence $p^2=(ad+bc)^2$ and $ac=bd$.

(*Note*: $p|ad-bc$ likewise implies $ad-bc=0$ since $ac+bd=0$ is impossible). Since $(a, b)=1$, $a|d$ and $b|c$ in $\mathbb{Z}$. Now look at $p=a^2+b^2=c^2+d^2$.

8 (Fermat 1640: proved by Euler 1742) Let p be an odd prime and suppose that $p|a^2+b^2$ where $(a, b)=1$. Show that p is of the form $4k+1$. [*Hint*: use $a^2\equiv -b^2 \pmod p$ and $a^{p-1}\equiv b^{p-1}\equiv 1 \pmod p$.]

9 Prove, as Fermat asked Frenicle to do, that no odd prime of the form x^2+2 can divide a number of the form a^2-2. [*Hint*: $a^2+x^2=(a^2-2)+(x^2+2)$.]

10 Show that there are instances of three successive integers each of which is a sum of two non-zero squares but no instance of four such integers. [*Hint*: $2n^2(n+1)^2$ is the first of these.]

11 Which of 715 and 12 005, if either, is a sum of two squares?

12 What is the smallest non-square integer which is a sum of two squares and is divisible by 111?

13 Fermat claimed (1638) that 'No integer of the form $4k+3$ is a sum of two *rational* squares.' (Diophantus and Bachet claimed the same about the numbers 15 and 21 respectively.) Prove that the integer n is expressible as a sum of two rational squares iff it is expressible as a sum of two integral squares.

14 Show that if $u, v \in \mathbb{Z}^+$, if u is not a sum of two squares and if $(u, v)=1$, then uv is not a sum of two squares. Show, by example, that the conclusion may be false if the hypothesis $(u, v)=1$ is omitted.

15 Use Exercise 8 above to show (Mordell, 1913) that if $a, b \in \mathbb{Z}$ and if $2a+1$ has no prime factor of the form $4k+3$, then the equation $y^2+(2a+1)^2=x^3+(4b+2)^3$ is insoluble in $\mathbb{Z}$. Deduce (Gerono 1877) that $y^2=x^3-17$ (i.e. $y^2+25=x^3+8$) cannot be solved in $\mathbb{Z}$. Deduce, likewise, (V. A. Lebesgue 1869), that $y^2=x^3+7$ has no solution in $\mathbb{Z}$.

16 Show that (i) $y^2=x^3+11$ and (ii) $y^2=x^3+23$ have no solutions in integers. [*Hint*: Add (i) 16; (ii) 4 to each side.]

Computer problems 7.1

1 Produce a list of the integers less than 1000 that can be expressed as the sum of two squares. Confirm the results of Theorems 7.1.2 and 7.1.4 in this range.

2 Use Lemma 7.1.1 to write a program to determine all the ways, if any, that a given number can be represented as the sum of two squares. Compare its performance with the appropriate modifications of the programs given in the text.

3 If $d|n=a^2+b^2$, where $(a, b)=1$, is it true that $d=u^2+v^2$ implies $(u, v)=1$? Legendre (1798) said 'yes'—prove him wrong.

4 Let $S_2(n)$ be the number of formally distinct ways in which n can be expressed as the sum of two squares. Thus, for example, we can represent 5 as $(\pm 1)^2+(\pm 2)^2=(\pm 2)^2+(\pm 1)^2$ in eight formally different ways. Adapt the programs suggested above to determine $S_2(n)$ for each $n \leqslant 1000$.

Explore what happens to $(1/t)\sum_{n=0}^{t} S_2(n)$ as $t \to \infty$. (See Section 10.4.)

5 Use Theorem 7.1.6 and Exercise 7.1.15 to find values of $k \leqslant 1000$ such that $y^2=x^3+k$ has no solution.

7.2 Sums of more than two squares

Since not all integers are expressible as sums of *two* squares it seems appropriate to ask which are expressible as sums of *three* squares. Again Diophantus poses a problem which requires this information and notes that each integer of the form $8k+7$ is not so expressible. Is this the whole story? Nearly, but not quite. And, once again, we can offer necessary and sufficient conditions. The result is

Theorem 7.2.1 (Legendre 1798) The integer N is expressible as a sum of three squares iff N is not of the form $4^\alpha(8k+7)$.

Note 7.2.2 Once again we permit any of the squares to be zero—otherwise the statements of this and subsequent theorems become a little unwieldy.

Proof This time the 'if' part of the theorem is rather hard so we offer a proof only of the 'only if' part.

So suppose N is a sum of three squares: $N=a^2+b^2+c^2$, say. Then certainly N cannot be of the form $8k+7$. For N would then be odd and hence just one or all three of a, b, c would be odd. Since the square of each even (respectively odd) integer is congruent to 0 or 4 (respectively 1) modulo 8 we see that (the odd integer) $a^2+b^2+c^2$ is congruent, modulo 8, to any one of $1, 3$ or 5 but not to 7.

Now suppose that $\alpha>0$ and that $4^\alpha(8k+7)=a^2+b^2+c^2=N$. Then $0\equiv a^2+b^2+c^2 \pmod 4$. But a^2, b^2, c^2 are each congruent to 0 or 1 modulo 4. Consequently the congruence $0\equiv N \pmod 4$ implies that each of a, b, c is even. Thus $4^\alpha(8k+7)=a^2+b^2+c^2$ leads to

$$4^{\alpha-1}(8k+7)=(a/2)^2+(b/2)^2+(c/2)^2,$$

a sum of three *integral* squares. This does it [why?]. □

Notes 7.2.3

(i) The first proof of the hard part of the theorem was given by Legendre in 1798. A proof can be found in, for example, [24] and [25]. The present formulation of it appears to be due to Cauchy; for an alternative way of writing it see Exercise 7.2.5.

(ii) As with Theorem 7.1.4 above, Theorem 7.2.1 can be used to extend itself to rational squares (Exercise 7.2.4).

At this point the most obvious question is probably: Is it worth pressing on to find out exactly which integers are (or are not!) expressible as sums of four, five, six, ... squares? The answer is a definite 'Yes' for we have the following splendid theorem.

Theorem 7.2.4 Every non-negative integer is expressible as a sum of four integer* squares. □ (Proof below.)

* Euler had previously shown that each non-negative integer is a sum of 4 rational squares—see Exercises 7.2.4. and 7.2.7.

Notes 7.2.5
(i) As distinct from the cases of two and three squares, Diophantus expresses no restriction on which integers might be sums of four squares. Accordingly several authors, including Fermat, have attributed Diophantus with at least empirical knowledge of Theorem 7.2.4.
(ii) In 1621 Bachet checked it for all integers ≤ 325—and said he would 'welcome a proof'. Fermat later claimed to have a proof which he subsequently stated was 'by descent'.
(iii) As above, we allow one or more of the squares to be 0. The theorem was first proved by Lagrange in 1770. He acknowledged his debt to Euler's earlier efforts—in return Euler found a very polished proof of the theorem, the one we give below!

One of Euler's achievements was the discovery of the four-squares analogue of Lemma 7.1.1, thus reducing the problem to that of showing the theorem to be true for the (positive) primes.

Lemma 7.2.6 (Euler 1748) For all $x_1, x_2, x_3, x_4, y_1, y_2, y_3, y_4 \in \mathbb{Z}$ we have:

$$\begin{aligned}(x_1^2+x_2^2+x_3^2+x_4^2)(y_1^2+y_2^2+y_3^2+y_4^2) &= (x_1y_1+x_2y_2+x_3y_3+x_4y_4)^2\\ &\quad+(x_1y_2-x_2y_1-x_3y_4+x_4y_3)^2\\ &\quad+(x_1y_3+x_2y_4-x_3y_1-x_4y_2)^2\\ &\quad+(x_1y_4-x_2y_3+x_3y_2-x_4y_1)^2. \quad \square\end{aligned}$$

To show that each prime p is a sum of four squares we begin by showing that, at least, some multiple of p is so expressible. Indeed we can go one better!

Theorem 7.2.7 (Euler 1751) Let p be an odd prime. Then there exist integers x and y and an integer m such that $0<m<p$ and $mp=x^2+y^2+1$.

Proof Let S be the set of all squares x^2 where $0 \leq x \leq (p-1)/2$. Since with x_1^2 and x_2^2 in S the congruence $x_1^2 \equiv x_2^2 \pmod p$ implies $x_1 = x_2$ [why?], S contains $(p-1)/2+1$ incongruent integers modulo p.

Similarly, the set T of $(p-1)/2+1$ integers $-1-y^2$, where $0 \leq y \leq (p-1)/2$ comprises numbers which are pairwise incongruent modulo p.

Since each complete residue system modulo p has exactly p members, we deduce that there must exist x^2 in S and $-1-y^2$ in T such that $x^2 \equiv -1-y^2 \pmod p$. That is, $x^2+y^2+1=mp$ for some $m \in \mathbb{Z}$. Finally, since $0 \leq x, y \leq (p-1)/2$ we have

$$0<x^2+y^2+1<(p/2)^2+(p/2)^2+1=p^2/2+1<p^2.$$

It follows that $m<p$. $\square$

We can now give Euler's proof of Lagrange's (four squares) theorem.

Proof Lemma 7.2.6 and the equality $2=1^2+1^2+0^2+0^2$ show that we only need prove the theorem for odd primes. Let p be such a prime. By Theorem 7.2.7 some multiple of p is a sum of three, and hence four, squares. Let kp be the least multiple of p which is expressible as a sum of four squares $kp=a^2+b^2+c^2+d^2$, say. By Theorem 7.2.7 we know that $k<p$. We should like to show $k=1$ so let us suppose it is not.

Now, if k is even, then of a, b, c, d (i) all are even or (ii) all are odd or (iii) two are even and two are odd. In case (iii) suppose WLOG that a, b are even. Then in all three cases

$$k/2\cdot p=\left(\frac{a+b}{2}\right)^2+\left(\frac{a-b}{2}\right)^2+\left(\frac{c+d}{2}\right)^2+\left(\frac{c-d}{2}\right)^2$$

contradicting the choice of k. Hence k is odd.

Not all of a, b, c, d are divisible by k—or else $k|p$, which would be contrary to $1<k<p$. We now find integers A, B, C, D all lying between $-k/2$ and $k/2$ such that $a\equiv A, b\equiv B, c\equiv C, d\equiv D \pmod k$. (This is possible—see Exercise 0.3.3) Furthermore at least one of A, B, C, D is non-zero [why?]. Hence

$$0<A^2+B^2+C^2+D^2<4\cdot(k/2)^2=k^2.$$

On the other hand setting $S=A^2+B^2+C^2+D^2$ and $s=a^2+b^2+c^2+d^2$, we have $S\equiv s\equiv 0 \pmod k$.

So suppose that $S=mk$ where, necessarily, $m<k$ [why?]. We look at

$$k^2mp=kp\cdot mk=s\cdot S=X^2+Y^2+Z^2+T^2 \qquad (*)$$

where X, Y, Z, T correspond to the four summands on the right of the equality in Lemma 7.2.6. Consequently

$$X=aA+bB+cC+dD\equiv aa+bb+cc+dd\equiv 0 \pmod k,$$

$$Y=aB-bA-cD+dC\equiv ab-ba-cd+dc\equiv 0 \pmod k$$

and likewise $Z\equiv T\equiv 0 \pmod k$. Consequently $X=kx$, $Y=ky$, $Z=kz$, $T=kt$ for suitable $x, y, z, t\in\mathbb{Z}$. But then $(*)$ shows that $mp=x^2+y^2+z^2+t^2$, contradicting the (minimal) choice of k. Hence k must be equal to 1—as wanted. □

There are many questions which spring immediately to mind

(i) If you insist that we use only *non-zero* squares, then not every non-negative integer is the sum of four squares—for example $0, 1, 2, 3, 5, 6, \ldots$ aren't. Is there a largest integer not so expressible? What if we allow five squares? (See Computer problems 7.2.3 and 7.2.6.)

(ii) Remembering the case of sums of two squares we ask: is each prime uniquely representable as a sum of four squares?

(iii) (Cf. Theorem 7.2.7) Are there infinitely many primes of the form x^2+y^2+1?

Exercises 7.2

1 Beguelin (1773) asserted that if the odd number n of the form $4k+1$ is a sum of three non-zero squares, then n must be composite. (Find a counter-example.) Using the identity $a^2+b^2=((2a-b)/3)^2+((2b-a)/3)^2+((2a+2b)/3)^2$ (Aubry 1911) show that each prime of the form $12k+5$ and greater than 17 is a sum of three distinct squares. [*Hint*: if $p=12k+5=a^2+b^2$, then $(ab,3)=1$ [why?]. So we can assume $a+b\equiv 0 \pmod 3$ [why?]. Hence the summands are integers. They are distinct if $p>17$.]

2 (i) Find integers u and v each expressible as a sum of three non-zero squares whose product uv requires four non-zero squares.
(ii) Show that if a, b are two integers which cannot be represented as a sum of three or fewer squares then their product can be.

3 Show that each positive integer n is expressible in the form $\pm x^2 \pm y^2 \pm z^2$ (indeed $x^2+y^2\pm z^2$) for suitable $x, y, z \in \mathbb{Z}$. [*Hint*: Given n, select x so that $n-x^2$ is positive and odd. Then use Exercise 7.1.5.] Show (Euler) that not *every* integer is expressible in the form $\pm x^2 \pm y^2$ with $x, y \in \mathbb{Z}$. [Try 6.]

4 (Fermat 1638) Show that a positive integer is expressible as a sum of three *integer* squares iff it is expressible as a sum of three *rational* squares.

5 Show that Theorem 7.2.1 is equivalent to the assertion that the positive integer n is a sum of three squares iff n is not of the form $t^2(8k+7)$.

6 Show that the equation $x^2-15y^2+z^2=7$ has no solution in $\mathbb{Z}$. [*Hint*: Work modulo 8.]

7 By 1751 Euler had shown that each positive rational number is expressible as a sum of four rational squares. Show that this is a consequence of Theorem 7.2.4. Explain why, conversely, Theorem 7.2.4 doesn't follow immediately from this result of Euler.

8 (Euler 1749) Show that each sum s of four *odd* squares can be written as a sum of four *even* squares. [*Hint*: $(2p+1)^2/2+(2q+1)^2/2=(p+q+1)^2+(p-q)^2$. Hence

$$\begin{aligned} s/2 &= (a+b+1)^2+(a-b)^2+(c+d+1)^2+(c-d)^2 \\ &= (2m+1)^2+(2n+1)^2+4u^2+4v^2. \end{aligned}$$

Now find $s/4$ using $2u^2+2v^2=(u+v)^2+(u-v)^2$.]

9 Prove that every positive odd integer can be expressed in the form (i) $x^2+y^2+2z^2$ and also in the form (ii) $x^2+y^2+z^2+(z+1)^2$ [*Hints*: (i) Write $4n+2=x^2+y^2+z^2$ with even z and then $2n+1$ as

$$\left(\frac{x+y}{2}\right)^2+\left(\frac{x-y}{2}\right)^2+2(z/2)^2;$$

(ii) write $4n+1=x^2+y^2+z^2$ with z odd. Then use $(z^2+1)/2=((z+1)/2)^2+((z-1)/2)^2$.]

10 Prove that every positive integer is a sum $x^2+y^2+kz^2$, where $k=1$ or 2.

11 Let a, b be coprime to the prime p. Show that the congruence $x^2+ay^2+b \equiv 0 \pmod p$ has a solution.

12 Write 169 as a sum of two, of three, of four and of five non-zero squares.

Computer problems 7.2

1 Write a program to list positive integers which can be represented as the sum of three squares. Modify the program to determine the number $S_3(n)$ of such representations for each n and examine what happens to the average $(1/N)\sum_{n=0}^{N} S_3(n)$ number of representations as $N \to \infty$. What searching method is the most efficient way of tackling this problem?

2 Consider representations of integers in the binary quadratic form a^2+Ab^2. What primes are so represented for different values of A?

3 Find the integers <1000 that *cannot* be expressed as the sum of four non-zero squares. Does this give you any ideas for determining whether or not there exist only finitely many such integers?

4 Write a program to explore whether or not each $4k+1$ prime can be uniquely expressed as the sum of four squares. (Cf. Exercise 7.1.7.) What happens in the case of $4k+3$, $8k+1$, $8k+3$, $8k+5$ and $8k+7$ primes?

5 Let $L(n)$ be the least integer *not* expressible as a sum $x^2+y^2+z^2+t^2$, where $0 \leq x, y, z, t \leq n$. Is it true if $m<n$ then $L(m)<L(n)$?

6 Find the least integer N expressible as a square and as a sum of two, of three, of four, of five non-zero squares. Hence find all positive integers not expressible as the sum of five non-zero squares.

7 Von Sterneck (1903) claimed that $3k^3$ is not the sum of 3 cubes unless all are equal. Fleck (1906) stated this was not true. Can you confirm this?

8 Investigate whether or not each integer, from some point onwards, is a sum of at most eight squares of *odd* integers.

7.3 Diverging developments—and a little history

Polygonal numbers

Theorem 7.2.4 was only part of what Fermat asserted in a letter to Mersenne in 1638. To describe the rest we need a (pictorial) definition. Using Fig. 7.1

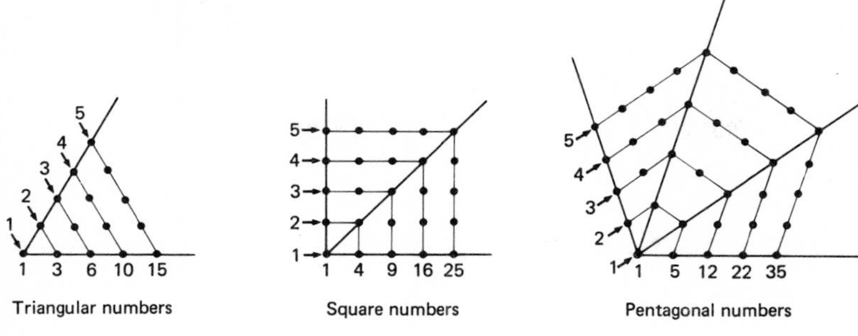

Fig. 7.1

and taking the cumulative numbers of dots associated with the (arrowed) paths 1, 2, 3, 4, . . . we have

Definition 7.3.1

The *triangular numbers* are 1, 3, 6, 10, 15, . . .
The *square numbers* are 1, 4, 9, 16, 25, . . .
The *pentagonal numbers* are 1, 5, 12, 22, 35, . . . etc.

The numbers defined in this way are the *polygonal numbers.* Theon of Smyrna and Nichomachus (c.100 A.D.) and Diophantus (c.250 A.D.) wrote about them in books but the concept goes back to the Pythagoreans. However, their observations (see Exercises 7.3.1–7.3.4) were simple as compared with the following deep assertion made by Fermat in the letter mentioned above.

Theorem 7.3.2 Each positive integer is a sum of (at most) 3 triangular, (at most) 4 square, (at most) 5 pentagonal, . . . , (at most) n n-gonal numbers. □

The first demonstration of this was given by Cauchy (1813/5)—the proof showing that all but four of the numbers can be taken to be 0 or 1.

Waring's problem

A second rather obvious question which arises from the four-squares theorem is: If four squares will suffice to represent every non-negative integer, how many cubes, fourth powers, fifth powers, . . . etc. are needed? In his book of 1770 Waring asserted that:

To each integer $k \geqslant 2$ there exists a positive integer $g(k)$ such that every non-negative integer N can be expressed as a sum $u_1^k + u_2^k + \cdots + u_{g(k)}^k$ of $g(k)$ non-negative kth powers.

Note that for each k there are two problems:

(a) prove $g(k)$ exists and
(b) find its minimum value.

We've just seen that $g(2)=4$. Waring asserted that $g(3)=9$ and $g(4)=19$. These are in fact correct assertions though the latter has only been verified fully within the last couple of years ([N]). ($g(4)\geqslant 19$ by Exercise 0.1.4.)

To demonstrate one of the early efforts (Liouville* c.1850), let us show

Theorem 7.3.3 $g(4)\leqslant 50$.

Proof Let n be any non-negative integer. Then $n=6m+r$, where m is non-negative and $0\leqslant r\leqslant 5$. By Theorem 7.2.4 we may write $m=x_1^2+x_2^2+x_3^2+x_4^2$ so that $n=6x_1^2+6x_2^2+6x_3^2+6x_4^2+r$. We now use the fact that each x_i can be expressed as a sum of four squares along with the identity:

$$\begin{aligned}6(a^2+b^2+c^2+d^2)^2 &= (a+b)^4+(a-b)^4+(c+d)^4+(c-d)^4\\ &\quad +(a+c)^4+(a-c)^4+(b+d)^4+(b-d)^4\\ &\quad +(a+d)^4+(a-d)^4+(b+c)^4+(b-c)^4\end{aligned}$$

—a sum of 12 fourth powers—to deduce that n can be expressed using no more than $12+12+12+12+5=53$ fourth powers. 53? Oh dear! We promised 50. In fact we can fiddle 53 down to 50 by writing each integer n in the form $n=6m+r$ where m is non-negative and $r=0$ or 1 or 2 or 81 or 16 or 17(!)—at least if n is 81 or greater [why can we?]. Then, since each of 0, 1, 2, 81, 16 and 17 can be expressed using no more than 2 fourth powers, we can clearly reduce our 53 down to 50 (q.e.d.?) Well, not quite! We still have to check that all integers less than 81 are sums of no more than 50 fourth powers! (Before rushing to your computer do note that there isn't *too* much difficulty in representing the first 50 integers!) □

In 1896, E. Maillet proved that $g(5)\leqslant 192$; in 1908 he proved $g(8)$ exists but gave no value. (Exercise 7.3.16 helps you obtain an upper bound for $g(6)$). 1909 saw Wieferich prove $g(5)\leqslant 59$ and $g(7)\leqslant 3806$ but the giant leap was due to Hilbert. He proved, at last, Waring's assertion: For each k the number $g(k)$ does exist! For a proof see [O].

It is not difficult to find lower bounds for the $g(k)$. Indeed J. A. Euler (Leonhard's son) stated (c.1772) that: in order to express every positive integer as a sum of $g(k)$ non-negative kth powers we must have $g(k)\geqslant [(3/2)^k]+2^k-2=t(k)$, say. The proof is quite easy. See Exercise 7.3.15.

What is very curious is that this easily obtained lower bound gives the correct value of $g(k)$ for almost every value of k. In particular it is known that $g(k)=t(k)$ for all k from some point onward and in any case for all k such that $6\leqslant k\leqslant 200\,000$. Weiferich proved $g(3)=t(3)=9$ in 1909 and Chen proved $g(5)=t(5)$ in 1964.

Program 0.4 will find the larger, N, of the two numbers which actually *need* 9 cubes. (The above formula gives the smaller). Thus all integers greater than

* Joseph Liouville, 24 March 1809 - 8 September 1882.

this N require no more than 8 cubes and from some point onwards* 7 always suffice [O]. Thus, if we denote by $G(k)$ the smallest integer r such that every sufficiently large integer is a sum of at most r kth powers, then $G(3) \leqslant 7$. In fact $G(2)=4$ (because of all the $4^{\alpha}(8k+7)$) and $G(4)=16$ are the only two values of $G(k)$ that are known exactly. So there is still lots to be done.

Exercises 7.3

1 Show that the triangular numbers are precisely those of the form $n(n+1)/2$, n being a positive integer, whilst the pentagonal numbers are those of the form $n(3n-1)/2$.

2 (Nichomachus c.100 A.D.) Prove (i) that the sum of two consecutive triangular numbers is a perfect square: (ii) that the $(r-1)$th triangular number added to the rth square number produces the rth pentagonal number. [*Hint*: Try fitting triangles or a triangle and a square together to obtain, respectively, a square and a (not necessarily regular) pentagon.]

3 (Plutarch c.100 A.D.) Show that 8 times a triangular number is always 1 less than a perfect square.

4 (Aryabhatta c.500 A.D.) Prove that the sum of the first n triangular numbers is $n(n+1)(n+2)/6$. (It is the number of cannonballs which can be stacked in a triangular based pyramid of n layers!) [*Hint*: Sum them in pairs and use Exercise 2(i).]

5 Find four numbers which are both triangular and square. Do you think there are infinitely many—or not? (See Exercise 11.6.7.)

6 Barlow (1811) said there are no integers, other than 1, which are simultaneously triangular and pentagonal. In fact there are infinitely many. [Determine how determined a person you are (!) by seeing if you can beat Barlow and find the smallest of them *without* resorting to your computer.]

7 Define the concept of hexagonal number and find a formula giving the nth one.

8 Show that no triangular (respectively pentagonal; hexagonal) number can end in a 2, 4, 7 or 9 (respectively 3, 4, 8 or 9; 2, 4, 7 or 9).

9 Demonstrate what Euler noted namely, that proving that each positive integer is a sum of at most three triangular numbers is equivalent to proving that each number of the form $8k+3$ is a sum of three squares.

10 Fermat (1646) asked Brouncker and Wallis to show that no triangular number other than 1 is a fourth power. Can *you* prove it? [*Hint*: (i) Either $s^8-r^4=(s^4-1)^2$] (Nor can a triangular number $(\neq 1)$ be a cube—see [1], Vol. 2, p. 17.)

* Probably 8042.

11 Euler (1773) noted that not every positive rational is a sum of three 'rational triangular' numbers; i.e. numbers of the form $n(n+1)/2$ where n is rational. Indeed $\frac{1}{2}$ is not so expressible. [*Hint*: $4+3 \neq (2a+1)^2+(2b+1)^2+(2c+1)^2$]

12 Use the congruence $n^3 \equiv n \pmod 6$ and the identity $(t+1)^3+(t-1)^3-2t^3=6t$ to prove that each integer is the sum of at most five (positive or negative) cubes. (Oltramore 1894. In fact it is conjectured that four cubes will always suffice.)

13 Show that no integers of the form $9k+4$, $9k+5$ are expressible as a sum of at most three cubes. [*Hint*: For $a \in \mathbb{Z}$, $a^3 \equiv 0, 1$ or $8 \pmod 9$]

14 Show that $g(4) \leqslant 45$ as follows. Write $n=6p+r$ $(r=0, 1, 2, 3, 4, 5)$. If $p=8h+j$ $(j=1, 2, 3, 5, 6)$ then p is a sum of three squares and hence a sum of at most $3 \cdot 12+5$ fourth powers. If $p=8h$ or $8h+4$ write $p=(p-27)+27$. If $p=8h+7$ write $p=(p-14)+14$ (Lucas 1878).

15 (J. A. Euler 1772) Prove that $g(k) \geqslant 2^k+[3^k/2^k]-2$. [*Hint*: Express $n(k)=2^k[3^k/2^k]-1$ as a sum of kth powers. Note $n<3^k$.] For $2 \leqslant k \leqslant 8$ find the minimum value of $g(k)$ and of $n(k)$.

16 (Kempner 1912) Using the identity

$$120(a^2+b^2+c^2+d^2)^3 = \textstyle\sum_8 (a \pm b \pm c \pm d)^6 + 8\sum_{12} (a \pm b)^6 + \sum_4 (2a)^6,$$

where $\sum_i$ indicates i summands, show that each integer $120m^3$ is a sum of 108 sixth powers. Thus each integer $120M+r$, where $0 \leqslant r \leqslant 119$, is a sum of at most $108g(3)+119$ sixth powers.

17 (André 1871) Show that each even positive integer is a sum of a (positive) cube and three squares. Prove the same for the odd (positive) integers or find the least odd positive integer which is not so expressible.

Computer problems 7.3

1 Write a program to generate m-gonal numbers.

2 55 and 66 are triangular numbers with all digits equal. Can you find any more?

3 Find more integers that are both triangular and square.

4 Use Program 0.4 to explore the percentage of integers which are not expressible as a sum of k fourth powers for various k less than 19.

5 Consider a similar problem for rth powers for various r.

8
Quadratic reciprocity

8.1 Introduction

In the last chapter we noted Fermat's (1638) claim concerning polygonal numbers. In 1654 he repeated this claim in a letter to Pascal* adding that 'to arrive at this it is necessary to prove' [amongst other things]

(i) *Each prime of the form* $4k+1$ *is also of the form* x^2+y^2; (*Theorem* 7.1.2);
(ii) *Each prime of the form* $3k+1$ *is also of the form* x^2+3y^2; (*Exercise* 8.3.5);
(iii) *Each prime of the form* $8k+1$ *or* $8k+3$ *is also of the form* x^2+2y^2; (*Execise* 8.4.4).

We have also seen how, by looking at Pythagorean triangles, one is led, naturally, as were Fermat and Frenicle, to considering numbers expressible in the forms x^2-2y^2 and $2x^2-y^2$. (See Computer problem 6.2.2.)

In October 1729 Euler, at the suggestion of Daniel Bernoulli†, wrote to Christian Goldbach in Moscow communicating to him some results on the gamma function. In December of that year‡ Goldbach replied, finishing his letter with the question 'Is Fermat's observation known to you that all the numbers $2^{2^n}+1$ are primes?' Following more encouragement from Goldbach, Euler began reading Fermat's work, noted Fermat's statements on sums of squares and eventually set about trying to prove them. In 1742 he sent Goldbach a proof of Theorem 7.1.2 as well as offering him experimental evidence concerning the prime divisors of numbers of the form x^2-2y^2, x^2-3y^2 and x^2-5y^2. Weil ([26], p. 207) reports that by 1744 Euler had amassed numerical evidence on the prime divisors of numbers of the form x^2+Dy^2 for 34 different values of D.

Computer problem 8.1

1 Goldbach stated that if $p=4k+1$ is prime and if $d|k(d>0)$, then $p=u^2+dv^2$ for suitable $u, v\in\mathbb{Z}$. Follow Euler by proving Goldbach wrong!

8.2 The law of quadratic reciprocity

Let us begin with a fairly simple observation regarding the representation of primes in the form x^2+Dy^2 (remembering that Euler hadn't the advantage of the congruence notation that we are about to employ).

* Blaise Pascal, 19 June 1623 - 19 August 1662.
† Daniel Bernoulli, 8 February 1700 - 17 March 1787.
‡ 1729! Weil [26] identifies this letter as the one which awakened Euler's interest in Fermat's work and led to the rebirth of modern number theory. Now aged over 250 it is thriving!

Suppose that p is a prime and that $p|u^2+Dv^2$, u and v being coprime integers and D being an integer $\neq 0, -1$. [Why do we make these restrictions on D?] Then it is easy to check that $(p, v)=1$. Consequently, as Euler knew, there exists w such that $p|wv-1$, i.e. $wv \equiv 1 \pmod p$. From $-Dv^2 \equiv u^2 \pmod p$ we can then deduce that $-D \equiv (wu)^2 \pmod p$. Thus, in terms of the following definition, Euler wanted to know for which primes p is $-D$ a *quadratic residue* mod p.

Definition 8.2.1 Let $n \geqslant 2$ be an integer and let a be an integer such that $(a, n)=1$. If there exists an integer z such that $z^2 \equiv a \pmod n$, then a is called a *quadratic residue* (*q.r.*)* mod(ulo) *n*. If no such z exists then a is a *quadratic non-residue* (*q.n.r.*)* mod(ulo) *n*.

Notes 8.2.2

(i) It was Euler who coined the terms *residue* and *non-residue*.

(ii) We shall most often consider the case of $n=p$, a prime.

(iii) Since, for $a \equiv b \pmod n$, a is a q.r. (q.n.r.) according as b is a q.r. (q.n.r.) modulo n, we shall, in general, restrict attention to those a for which $1 \leqslant a \leqslant n-1$ (and $(a, n)=1$).

Example 8.2.3 Since, mod 13, we have $1^2 \equiv 12^2 \equiv 1$, $2^2 \equiv 11^2 \equiv 4$, $3^2 \equiv 10^2 \equiv 9$, $4^2 \equiv 9^2 \equiv 3$, $5^2 \equiv 8^2 \equiv 12$ and $6^2 \equiv 7^2 \equiv 10$ we see that 1, 3, 4, 9, 10, 12 are the q.r.s. whilst 2, 5, 6, 7, 8, 11 are the q.n.r.s. Notice that there are six of each. This is no accident (see Exercise 8.2.2).

Leonhard Euler *(15 April 1707 - 18 September 1783)*
Euler, the greatest mathematician of the 18th century, was born in Basel, the son of a preacher. The father's wish was that his son should follow in his footsteps but, on entering the University of Basel in 1720, Euler met Johann Bernoulli and learned much mathematics from him. Nevertheless he emerged with a Master of Philosophy degree and joined the department of Theology. Fortunately for mathematics, Euler's abilities in theology, Greek and Hebrew were less pronounced than in

* Plurals; q.r.s and q.n.r.s.

mathematics, although a strong religious conviction remained with him all his life.

At 18 Euler produced his first research paper. Aged 19 he won a prize from the French Academy of Sciences for a paper on the masting of ships. A dozen more prizes followed from the same source in the period 1738 to 1772.

In 1726 Euler was invited to join the Academy of Sciences in St Petersburg—nominally to study physiology! At an age (19) when Johann Bernoulli addressed him as a 'most gifted and learned man of science' he accepted. As it turned out, he was able to get on with mathematics and, in 1733, when Daniel Bernoulli (Johann's son) returned to Basel, Euler succeeded him.

Euler's output, range and energy were phenomenal. In the index of [31] his mathematical contributions appear under the headings: algebra, differential and integral calculus, calculus of variations, functions of a complex variable, coordinate and differential geometry, differential equations, infinite series, philosophy of science, special functions, trigonometric series, theory of numbers.

In 1740, having recently lost the sight of one eye, things became less agreeable in St Petersburg and Frederick the Great persuaded Euler to join the scientific community in Berlin. Euler was to stay for 25 years. Still his energy was incredible. Maintaining ties with St Petersburg, his duties in Berlin included supervising the observatory, the botanic gardens and the publication of maps and calendars. He also advised on financial matters including lotteries and pensions. In addition he was required to work on canal improvements and to translate a military book into German. (Naturally enough(!) he added appendices which were several times the length of the original.)

During his stay in Berlin, Euler published hundreds of papers and several books on a wide range of topics. One of these, 'Letters to a German princess', describing lessons he had given to Frederick's niece, went to nearly 40 editions in 9 languages.

By 1763 Frederick and Euler were on cooler terms. In 1766 he returned to St Petersburg. By 1771 he had become totally blind. Did this slow the output? Of course not! In 1772 he produced—with the help of three assistants—an 800-page book on lunar motion; in 1776 appeared 50 research papers totalling 1000 pages. As might be obvious, Euler had a prodigious memory: it is said he knew Virgil's *Aeneid* by heart.

Presumably all this work left Euler no time for other activities! On the contrary. He fathered thirteen children and enjoyed playing with them whilst simultaneously contemplating his mathematics.

At tea-time on 18 September 1783, whilst playing with his grandchildren, he suffered a brain haemorrhage and announced 'I am dying'. This final assertion was proved correct the very same day.

One outcome of Euler's deliberations was a result which was to become known as the *law of quadratic reciprocity* (Theorem 8.2.7 below). Euler was near to it in 1742, yet in a paper of 1772 (published 1783, the year of his death) he could still only offer a challenge to 'whoever likes to indulge' to 'enquire in to [its] demonstration, since it cannot be doubted that from this the theory of numbers will receive great additions'.

Euler's assertion was: *Let p be some prime number, let only the odd squares* $1, 9, 25, \ldots, (p-2)^2$ *be divided by* $4p$ *and let the residues be noted—which will all be of the form* $4k+1$*—of which any may be denoted by R and the other numbers of the form* $4k+1$*, which do not appear amongst the residues be denoted by some letter N. Then*

For primes of the form	*we shall have*	
$4kp+R$	p is a residue;	$-p$ is a residue
$4kp-R$	p is a residue;	$-p$ is a non-residue
$4kp+N$	p is a non-residue;	$-p$ is a non-residue
$4kp-N$	p is a non-residue;	$-p$ is a residue.

Let's see what this means by way of an example.

Example 8.2.4 For which primes is 11 a quadratic residue?

Solution Taking the odd squares up to $9^2 \bmod 44$ we find residues $1, 9, 25, 5(\equiv 49)$, and $37(\equiv 81)$. Consequently, Euler's claim is that 11 is a quadratic residue of primes of the forms $44k \pm R$ where $R = 1, 5, 9, 25$ or 37.

In order to state the law in a compact, elegant and symmetrical form Legendre introduced the symbol now named after him.

Definition 8.2.5 Let p be an odd prime and let $(a, p) = 1$.

The *Legendre symbol* (a/p) is defined by:

$$(a/p) = \begin{cases} 1 & \text{if } a \text{ is a q.r. mod } p \\ -1 & \text{if } a \text{ is a q.n.r. mod } p. \end{cases}$$

Examples 8.2.6

(i) Example 8.2.3 above shows that

$$(1/13) = (4/13) = (9/13) = (3/13) = (12/13) = (10/13) = 1$$

whereas

$$(2/13) = (5/13) = (6/13) = (7/13) = (8/13) = (11/13) = -1.$$

(ii) 3779 is prime and, in fact, $(2223/3779) = -1$. That is, there is no integer z such that $z^2 \equiv 2223 \pmod{3779}$.

How do we prove this provocative assertion? Well we could just use trial and error, ploughing through all possible values of z from 1 to 3778. In fact with the aid of Theorem 8.2.7 (and Lemma 8.3.1(i), (iv)) below you can check (ii) almost as quickly as your computer could do it naively even if you've already entered the program! (We haven't experimented with this claim; perhaps we can persuade you to!)

So here's the big theorem: Gauss called it 'fundamental', Kummer called it and its generalisations 'the most important subject in number theory'.

Theorem 8.2.7 (*The law of quadratic reciprocity: LQR*) Let p and q be distinct odd primes. Then

(I) $(p/q)(q/p)=(-1)^{(p-1)(q-1)/4}$;
(II) $(-1/p)=(-1)^{(p-1)/2}$;
(III) $(2/p)=(-1)^{(p^2-1)/8}$. □ (Proof in Section 8.5.)

Notes 8.2.8
(i) (I) is Legendre's 'Loi de réciprocité'—the 'dual' nature of (I) suggesting the 'reciprocity'; (II) and (III) are termed the 'supplementary laws'.
(ii) Probably the most amazing aspect of the LQR is the assertion, in (I), that the problems (A): Has $x^2 \equiv p \pmod q$ got a solution? and (B) Has $x^2 \equiv q \pmod p$ got a solution? are one and the same. Once you know the answer to one you also know the answer to the other! There certainly seems no obvious reason why this should be so—but the LQR says that it is.
(iii) Part (II) says that (for p odd) $x^2 \equiv -1 \pmod p$ iff $(p-1)/2$ is even—i.e. $p=4k+1$. This is the content of Theorems 3.5.4 and 3.5.6.
(iv) The equivalence of the LQR to Euler's statement is not very difficult to establish. We leave it for the reader to play with.

Legendre attempted a proof of the LQR basing it on a theorem of his giving conditions under which the equation $ax^2+by^2+cz^2=0$ with non-zero coefficients a, b, c has a solution other than $x=y=z=0$. Unfortunately this attempt relied upon (a special case of) another result he was sure of but couldn't confirm, namely Theorem 2.2.2 whose proof didn't appear until 50 years later. Not knowing of the work of Euler and Legendre, Gauss rediscovered the LQR, most probably after extensive calculations, at the age of . . . 18(!). It then took him a whole year 'of strenuous effort' before he found a proof. 'It tortured me' he confessed. Gauss eventually offered seven proofs! This was not an attempt at overkill but rather an attempt to discover a proof which would generalise from the quadratic case to higher powers. See [P] and [27].

Exercises 8.2

1 Find, by hand, the quadratic residues modulo n for each n with $10 \leqslant n \leqslant 20$. List how many there are in each case. Have you enough evidence to make a conjecture or two? If not, move to Computer Problem 8.2.1.

2 Let p be an odd prime. Show that a is a quadratic residue modulo p iff $a \equiv k^2 \pmod p$ for some k such that $1 \leqslant k \leqslant (p-1)/2$. Deduce that exactly half of the integers x such that $1 \leqslant x \leqslant p-1$ are quadratic residues modulo p, the other half being non-residues.

3 Determine all eleven quadratic non-residues modulo 23 by the above means. Is $(7/23)=1$ or -1?

4 For which primes is 13 a quadratic residue?

5 Use Exercise 2 to prove that for $(a, p)=1$ we have

$$(a/p)+(2a/p)+\cdots+((p-1)a/p)=0.$$

6 Let $(a, p)=(b, p)=1$. Show that ab is a quadratic residue modulo p iff either (i) a, b are both residues or (ii) a, b are both non-residues—modulo p. [*Hint*: If b is a non-residue and $a_1, \ldots, a_{(p-1)/2}$ are the residues then the ba_i are all the distinct non-residues.]

7 Let p be an odd prime and let r be a primitive root of p. Obtain the result of Exercise 2 by showing that a is a quadratic residue iff $a \equiv r^k \pmod p$ where k is even.

8 It is of interest to know how the quadratic residues modulo p are distributed in the range $1 \leqslant x \leqslant p-1$. Show that for $p \geqslant 7$ there exist integers a, b such that $a, a+1$ are both residues and $b, b+1$ are both non-residues. [*Hint*: If 2, 5 are both non-residues then 10 is a residue modulo p.]

9 Show that the product of the quadratic residues of p is

$$r^{(p^2-1)/4} \equiv (-1)^{(p+1)/2} \pmod p$$

and that of the non-residues

$$r^{(p-1)^2/4} \equiv (-1)^{(p-1)/2} \pmod p,$$

r being a primitive root of p.

10 We know that no quadratic residue can be a primitive root of the prime p. Show that, unless p is a Fermat prime, then p also has a quadratic non-residue which is not a primitive root. [*Hint*: $(p-1)/2-\phi(p-1)>0$ unless $p=2^{2^n}+1$.]

11 Let p be an odd prime. Show that r is a q.r. modulo p iff r is a q.r. modulo p^n for each positive integer n.

Computer problems 8.2

1 By searching through the set of possible values compute a list of quadratic residues mod p where p is a prime. For each $p<10\,000$ confirm that there is at least one prime quadratic non-residue q such that $1<q \leqslant 19$. (Noticed by Landry 1854.) Modify the program to determine the number of quadratic residues mod N (where N is prime or non-prime).

2 We have already shown that -1 is a q.r. of primes of the form $4k+1$ (Theorem 3.5.4). Obtain experimental evidence as to which primes have d as a q.r. where d takes the values $2, -2, 3$, etc.

3 Are quadratic residues distributed at random? You could approach this problem by writing programs to gather evidence as follows (in each case comparing your observations with what should be the case if the distribution were random):

(i) Count the number of quadratic residues in the ranges from 1 to $(p-1)/2$ and from $(p-1)/2+1$ to $p-1$;
(ii) count the number of triples of (that is, three consecutive) quadratic residues;
(iii) given that $0<\alpha<\beta<1$, is it true that for large p half the numbers between αp and βp are q.r. whilst the others are q.n.r.?

4 Write a program to determine the sum of the q.r.s. mod N and the sum of the q.n.r.s. Do you see any pattern in the results?

5 Given an integer $n>2$ solve the equation $x^2 \equiv p(\bmod n)$ for various primes p. Do you draw any conclusion? Can you prove it?

8.3 Euler's criterion

We first gather together the easy results needed to check Example 8.2.6(ii).

Lemma 8.3.1 Let p be an odd prime and let a, b be integers such that $(a, p)=(b, p)=1$. Then

(i) If $a \equiv b(\bmod p)$, then $(a/p)=(b/p)$,
(ii) $(a^2/p)=1$,
(iii) $a^{(p-1)/2} \equiv (a/p)(\bmod p)$. In words: $a^{(p-1)/2} \equiv 1$ or $-1(\bmod p)$, so that a is a q.r. iff $a^{(p-1)/2} \equiv 1(\bmod p)$,
(iv) $(ab/p)=(a/p)(b/p)$.

Proof Parts (i) and (ii) are left to the reader. Part (iii) is known as *Euler's criterion.* The proof as usually given uses the concept of primitive root (cf. Exercise 5.2.13), which was not even a glint in Lambert's eye when Euler proved his criterion (c.1755). So, how did Euler proceed? In fact he established the more general result:

Let $p=mn+1$ be prime and let $(a, p)=1$. Then $a^m \equiv 1(\bmod p)$ iff $a \equiv b^n(\bmod p)$ for some b.

First, if $a \equiv b^n(\bmod p)$ then $a^m \equiv b^{mn}(\bmod p)$. But the latter is congruent to 1 by FLT.

Second, suppose that $a^m \equiv 1(\bmod p)$. Since $x^{mn} \equiv 1(\bmod p)$ for *all* x coprime to p, we see that, for all such x, $p \mid x^{mn}-a^m=(x^n-a) \cdot f(x)$, where

$$f(x)=(x^{(m-1)n}+ax^{(m-2)n}+\cdots+a^{m-1}).$$

Now, says Euler, there exists a value t, say, of x $(0 \leq x<p)$ such that $p \nmid f(t)$. For otherwise $p \mid f(x)$ for all x $(0 \leq x<p)$. But then setting $(Df)(x)=$

$f(x+1)-f(x)$ we find* that, for each $k \geqslant 1$,

$$(D^k f)(x) = f(x+k) - \binom{k}{1} f(x+k-1)$$
$$+ \binom{k}{2} f(x+k-2) - \cdots \pm f(x).$$

Hence, if $p \mid f(x)$ for all x, $0 \leqslant x < p$, then, in particular, $p \mid (D^{(m-1)n} f)(1)$. But $(D^{(m-1)n} f)(x) = ((m-1)n)!$ for all x. Consequently, $p \mid ((m-1)n)!$, a clear contradiction since $(m-1)n < p$. Thus for some integer t we must have $p \mid t^n - a$, in other words, $a \equiv t^n \pmod{p}$.

Part (iii) now follows immediately. For if $a^{(p-1)/2} \equiv 1 \pmod{p}$ then $a \equiv t^2 \pmod{p}$ for some t, that is, $(a/p) = 1$. On the other hand, Exercise 5.2.13 tells us that if $a^{(p-1)/2} \not\equiv 1 \pmod{p}$, then $a^{(p-1)/2} \equiv -1 \pmod{p}$. In this case FLT tells us that a cannot be a q.r. mod p, i.e. $(a/p) = -1$. This does it.

Part (iv) is much quicker (and quite pretty!). From (iii) we have $(ab/p) \equiv (ab)^{(p-1)/2} = a^{(p-1)/2} \cdot b^{(p-1)/2} \equiv (a/p)(b/p) \pmod{p}$. Now (ab/p) and $(a/p)(b/p)$ are each equal to 1 or -1. Thus their difference is -2 or 0 or 2. But $p \geqslant 3$. Hence $(ab/p) - (a/p)(b/p) = 0$, as claimed. □

Notes 8.3.2

(i) The proof of (iii) here was given not only out of historical interest but also to help you see how to tackle Exercise 8.3.5.

(ii) In words, (iv) asserts that the *product of a residue and a non-residue is a non-residue whereas the product of two residues or of two non-residues is a residue*—a fact which permits a more sophisticated proof that the numbers of residues and non-residues of the (odd) prime p are equal (see Exercise 8.2.2).

(iii) Euler's criterion is useful as a theoretical tool as Lemma 8.3.1(iv)—and so Note 8.3.2(ii)—indicates. It is of much less use as a computational tool except, perhaps, for small values of p (see Exercises 8.3.2 and 8.3.3 and Computer problem 8.3.1).

Returning to Example 8.2.6 we have:

$$\begin{aligned}(2223/3779) &= (3^2 \cdot 13 \cdot 19/3779)\\ &= (3^2/3779) \cdot (13/3779) \cdot (19/3779)\\ &= 1 \cdot (3779/13) \cdot -(3779/19)\end{aligned}$$

(since 13 is of the form $4k+1$ whereas 19 and 3379 are both of the form $4k+3$). Now $(3779/13) = (9/13) = (3^2/13) = 1$, whilst

$$\begin{aligned}(3779/19) &= (-2/19) = (-1/19)(2/19)\\ &= (-1)^{(19-1)/2}(-1)^{(19^2-1)/8} = (-1)^9(-1)^{18\cdot 20/8}\\ &= (-1)^9(-1)^{9\cdot 5} = 1.\end{aligned}$$

* $(D^m f)(x)$—as the notation suggests—is just the mth derivative of $f(x)$—as you can easily prove by induction.

Consequently $(2223/3779)=1\cdot 1\cdot(-1)$, showing that $z^2\equiv 2223(\text{mod } 3379)$ has no solution, as we said.

Exercises 8.3

1 Suppose that $b^2\equiv a(\text{mod } p)$. Show that b and $p-b$ are the only solutions (up to congruence modulo p) of the equation $x^2\equiv a(\text{mod } p)$. Use the congruence $b(p-b)\equiv -a(\text{mod } p)$ to deduce Euler's criterion from Wilson's theorem. [*Hint*: Show that if α is *not* a q.r. modulo p, then the integers c_i with $1\leqslant c_i\leqslant p-1$ can be paired off so that $c_ic_j\equiv a(\text{mod } p)$ with $c_i\neq c_j$. If α is a q.r. with $\beta^2\equiv\alpha(\text{mod } p)$, where $1\leqslant\beta\leqslant p-1$, pair off β with $p-\beta$ and pair the *other* c_i, with $1\leqslant c_i\leqslant p-1$, as above. Multiply the pairs together and then use Wilson.]

2 Use Euler's criterion to evaluate $(7/23)$. [Cf. Exercises 8.3.6 and 8.4.2.]

3 Let p be an odd prime and a an integer such that $(a, p)=1$ and $(a/p)=1$. Show that $(-a/p)=1$ or -1 according as $p\equiv 1$ or 3 modulo 4. Use Euler's criterion to determine whether or not 5 is a quadratic residue modulo 97. Is $(92/97)$ equal to 1 or -1? [There must be an easier way? Yes—use the LQR!]

4 Use Euler's criterion to show that $x^4\equiv -1(\text{mod } p)$ has a solution iff $p\equiv 1(\text{mod } 8)$. (From this one can prove that there are infinitely many primes of the form $8k+1$ (Exercise 5.2.20).)

5 Prove—as Euler did—that each prime p of the form $6n+1$ is also of the form x^2+3y^2.

(i) For $1\leqslant a\leqslant p-1$, $p|a^{6n}-1=(a^{2n}-1)(a^{4n}+a^{2n}+1)$.
(ii) There exists a, $1<a<p$, such that $p\nmid a^{2n}-1$. [*Hint*: Use Theorem 4.4.1 or, as in Lemma 8.3.1(iii), that $2n$th differences* in $f(x)=x^{2n}-1$ are all $(2n)!$]
(iii) If a is even, then $b=p-a$ is odd.
(iv) $b^{4n}+b^{2n}+1=((b^{2n}-1)/2)^2+3((b^{2n}+1)/2)^2$.

This proves that p *divides* some number of the form x^2+3y^2 where $(x, y)=1$. (It is then *equal* to such a number by Exercise 7.1.6—see also Exercise 9.5.14.)

6 Use the LQR to check if 7 is a quadratic residue modulo 23. (Cf. Exercises 8.3.2 and 8.4.2.)

7 Use the LQR to evaluate $(133/577)$, $(123/4567)$ and $(209/409)$.

8 Use the LQR to determine whether or not $x^2\equiv 1000(\text{mod } 1987)$ is soluble. (1987 is a prime.)

9 Show that 3 is a quadratic non-residue of each Mersenne prime $M_n=2^n-1$ which is greater than 3.

* Likewise, using $2n$th differences shows that, if $p=4n+1$ is a prime, then there exists a such that $1<a<p$ and $p\nmid a^{2n}-1$. Since $p|b^{4n}-1$ for all b coprime to p, we deduce that $p|(a^n)^2+1$ for all such a. (See Notes 3.5.5 and 7.1.3.)

10 Use the LQR to determine whether or not $x^2 \equiv 56 \pmod{10\,403}$ has a solution. ($10\,403 = 101 \cdot 103$)

11 Let p be an odd prime and let $f(x) = ax^2 + bx + c$, where $(a, p) = 1$. Define $d = d(f)$ to be $b^2 - 4ac$. Show that solutions of the congruence $f(x) \equiv 0 \pmod{p}$ may be obtained from $y^2 \equiv d \pmod{p}$ where $y = 2ax + b$. (Cf. Section 4.3.) Deduce that $f(x) \equiv 0 \pmod{p}$ has 0, 1 or 2 (distinct) roots iff $(d/p) = -1$, $d \equiv 0 \pmod{p}$ or $(d/p) = 1$ respectively. Why does this analysis not apply in the case of $p = 2$?

12 Is either of the congruences (i) $5x^2 + 16x + 12 \equiv 0$; (ii) $5x^2 + 16x + 13 \equiv 0$ soluble modulo 23?

13 (a) Use the LQR to determine the primes p for which -5 is a quadratic residue.
(b) Use part (a) to determine whether or not the following numbers are primes: (i) $1909 = 17^2 + 5 \cdot 18^2$; (ii) $2009 = 27^2 + 5 \cdot 16^2$; (iii) $5669 = 57^2 + 5 \cdot 22^2$. [*Hint*: If p is a prime dividing 1909, then $p < 44$ and $(-5/p) = 1$.]
(c) Use part (a) to prove the existence of infinitely many primes of the form $5k + 4$.

14 Use the LQR to determine those primes for which 15 is a quadratic residue.

15 Show that (part I of) the LQR can be written, as Gauss himself did: $(p/q) = ((-1)^{(q-1)/2} q/p)$.

16 Use Dirichlet's theorem (2.2.2) to show that if p is a prime of the form $4k + 1$, then there exists a prime of the form $4t + 3$ such that $(p/q) = -1$. (It was his inability to prove this result which stopped Legendre from being the first to prove the LQR.)

Computer problem 8.3

1 Write a program which uses Euler's criterion to determine whether or not a given integer a is a q.r. modulo p and hence evaluate the Legendre symbol (a/p). Compare the performance of this method with the direct search method suggested earlier (Problem 8.2.1).

8.4 Gauss's lemma and applications

We now begin the proof of the LQR. Two of Gauss's proofs were built round the following result, also due to him.

Theorem 8.4.1 (*Gauss's lemma*) Let p be an odd prime and let $(a, p) = 1$. Let $S = \{a, 2a, 3a, \ldots, ((p-1)/2)a\}$ and let the remainders of these integers, on division by p, be denoted by $\alpha_1, \alpha_2, \ldots, \alpha_\mu, \beta_1, \beta_2, \ldots, \beta_\nu$, where $0 \leq \alpha_i < p/2$ and $p/2 < \beta_i < p$. Then $(a/p) = (-1)^\nu$.

Proof Since $p \nmid a$ none of the numbers in S is congruent to 0 modulo p, nor are any two congruent to each other. It follows that the α_i are pairwise distinct as are the β_i. Now consider the set of $(p-1)/2$ integers $\alpha_1, \alpha_2, \ldots, \alpha_\mu$, $p-\beta_1, p-\beta_2, \ldots, p-\beta_\nu$, all of which lie strictly between 0 and $p/2$. We claim that these integers are pairwise distinct and are, consequently, the integers $1, 2, \ldots, (p-1)/2$ in some order. From the above remarks we need only check that $\alpha_r = p - \beta_s$ is impossible for $1 \leqslant r \leqslant \mu$ and $1 \leqslant s \leqslant \nu$. To do this, note that the congruences $\alpha_r \equiv ua(\text{mod } p)$ and $\beta_s \equiv va(\text{mod } p)$ imply that

$$\alpha_r + \beta_s \equiv (u+v)a \not\equiv 0(\text{mod } p),$$

since (i) $p \nmid a$ and (ii) $p \nmid u+v$, the latter because

$$0 < u+v \leqslant (p-1)/2 + (p-1)/2 = p-1.$$

Thus, modulo p,

$$\alpha_1 \cdot \alpha_2 \cdots \alpha_\mu \cdot (-\beta_1) \cdot (-\beta_2) \cdots (-\beta_\nu) \equiv 1 \cdot 2 \cdots (p-1)/2 = \left(\frac{p-1}{2}\right)! \tag{$*$}$$

whereas

$$\alpha_1 \cdot \alpha_2 \cdots \alpha_\mu \cdot \beta_1 \cdot \beta_2 \cdots \beta_\nu \equiv 1a \cdot 2a \cdots \left(\frac{p-1}{2}\right)a = a^{(p-1)/2}\left(\frac{p-1}{2}\right)! \tag{$**$}$$

Putting $(*)$ and $(**)$ together we find

$$a^{(p-1)/2}\left(\frac{p-1}{2}\right)! \equiv (-1)^\nu \left(\frac{p-1}{2}\right)!(\text{mod } p)$$

from which $a^{(p-1)/2} \equiv (-1)^\nu (\text{mod } p)$—since $p \nmid ((p-1)/2)!$

Now, using Euler's criterion, we obtain $(a/p) \equiv a^{(p-1)/2} \equiv (-1)^\nu (\text{mod } p)$. Since each of (a/p) and $(-1)^\nu$ has value 1 or -1 we infer immediately that $(a/p) = (-1)^\nu$, as required. □

Example 8.4.2 With $a = 10$ and $p = 23$ we have

$$S = \{10, 20, 30, 40, 50, 60, 70, 80, 90, 100, 110\}$$

having remainders, modulo 23,

$$R = \{10, 20, 7, 17, 4, 14, 1, 11, 21, 8, 18\}.$$

Since 5 of these lie between 23/2 and 23 we conclude that $(10/23) = (-1)^5 = -1$ and that 10 is not a q.r. mod 23.

Gauss's lemma, like Euler's criterion, is mainly of theoretical use except for smallish values of p, as above. It is however also useful for large values of p provided a is 'controllable'. For example, it can be used to prove (III) of Theorem 8.2.7.

Theorem 8.4.3

$$(2/p)=\begin{cases} 1 & \text{if } p=8k+1 \text{ or } 8k+7\\ -1 & \text{if } p=8k+3 \text{ or } 8k+5.\end{cases}$$

Proof By Gauss's lemma $(2/p)=(-1)^\nu$ where ν is the number of integers in $S=\left\{1\cdot 2, 2\cdot 2, \dots, \left(\frac{p-1}{2}\right)\cdot 2\right\}$ which, on division by p, leave remainders greater than $p/2$. In this particular case this simply means all those members of S which are greater than $p/2$. Clearly, for $1\leqslant k\leqslant(p-1)/2$ we have $p/2<2k(<p)$ when and only when $p/4<k$.

The number of such k is therefore $\nu=(p-1)/2-[p/4]$ where, as usual, $[x]$ denotes the greatest integer not exceeding the real number x. We evaluate ν most easily by taking four cases:

(i) If $p=8k+1$ then $\nu=4k-[2k+\frac{1}{4}]=4k-2k=2k$.
Hence $(-1)^\nu=1$.
(ii) If $p=8k+3$ then $\nu=4k+1-[2k+\frac{3}{4}]=4k+1-2k=2k+1$.
Hence $(-1)^\nu=-1$.
(iii) If $p=8k+5$ then $\nu=4k+2-[2k+\frac{5}{4}]=4k+2-(2k+1)=2k+1$.
Hence $(-1)^\nu=-1$.
(iv) If $p=8k+7$ then $\nu=4k+3-[2k+\frac{7}{4}]=4k+3-(2k+1)=2k+2$.
Hence $(-1)^\nu=1$.

Thus $(2/p)=1$ iff $p=8k+1$ or $8k+7$.

Then to get part (III) of Theorem 8.2.7 one only needs note that: If $p=8k+1$ or $8k+7$ then $(p^2-1)/8$ is even and so $(-1)^{(p^2-1)/8}=(-1)^\nu=1$, whilst if $p=8k+3$ or $8k+5$ then $(p^2-1)/8$ is odd and so $(-1)^{(p^2-1)/8}=(-1)^\nu=-1$. □

An immediate consequence of this theorem (first proved fully by Lagrange in 1775) is a result promised in Chapter 3 (and known to Frenicle by 1647).

Corollary 8.4.4 Each odd prime divisor p of a number of the form x^2-2y^2 where $(x, y)=1$ is itself of the form $8k+1$ or $8k-1$.

Proof Since $p|x^2-2y^2$ the condition $(x, y)=1$ implies that $p\nmid y$ and hence that $(p, y)=1$. Thus, from $x^2\equiv 2y^2(\text{mod } p)$ we deduce $(vx)^2\equiv 2(\text{mod } p)$ where $vy\equiv 1(\text{mod } p)$. Consequently $(2/p)=1$ which implies that $p=8k+1$ or $8k+7$, as claimed. □

A nice converse is

Theorem 8.4.5 Let $p=8k+1$ be a prime. Then $p=x^2-2y^2$—in infinitely many ways—using suitable $x, y\in\mathbb{Z}$.

Proof Since $(2/p)=1$ we see that $z^2 \equiv 2 \pmod p$ for some $z \in \mathbb{Z}$ such that $(z, p)=1$. By Thue's result (Lemma 4.1.7) there exist $u, v \in \mathbb{Z}$ such that $zv \equiv u \pmod p$ with* $0<|u|<\sqrt{p}$ and $0<|v|<\sqrt{p}$. It follows that $2v^2 \equiv z^2v^2 \equiv u^2 \pmod p$, that is $p|u^2-2v^2$. Further $-2p<u^2-2v^2<p$. Since $u^2-2v^2=0$ is impossible we infer that $-p=u^2-2v^2=-(u+2v)^2+2(u+v)^2$ so that p is of the form x^2-2y^2 as asserted. (For the infinitude of representations see Exercise 8.4.5.) □

We can also use Theorem 8.4.3 to establish a result whose proof defeated us earlier (see Exercise 1.3.6).

Theorem 8.4.6 There are infinitely many primes of the form $8k+7$.

Proof Assume, as usual, that there are only finitely many and that $p_1, p_2, \ldots, p_t$ is a list of them all. Put $N=(p_1p_2\cdots p_t)^2-2$ and let q be any (odd) prime *divisor of* N. Then $2 \equiv (p_1p_2\cdots p_t)^2 \pmod q$, that is, 2 is a q.r. mod q. Thus q is of one of the forms $8k+1$, $8k+7$. But not every prime divisor of N can be of the form $8k+1$—if so, so too would be their product, namely N whereas N is of the form $8k+7$ [why?]. Thus at least one of the (odd) prime divisors of N is one of the p_i. One deduces that $p_i|2$—a contradiction. □

Another interesting application is

Theorem 8.4.7 The numbers $M_q=2^q-1$ are composite for $q=11, 23, 83, 131, 179, \ldots$.

Note 8.4.8 Each q is a prime so there is no chance of revealing M_q to be composite by writing $2^q-1=(2^r-1)s$ for some $r|q$.

Proof Euler's criterion tells us that $2^{(p-1)/2} \equiv (2/p) \pmod p$. Now if p is of the form $8k+1$ or $8k+7$, then $(2/p)=1$. For such p, $p|2^{(p-1)/2}-1$. Of course, if $p=8k+1$, then $(p-1)/2=4k$ is not prime. But, for $p=8k+7$, $(p-1)/2=4k+3$, which can be prime for certain primes p. Examples where both $8k+7$ and $4k+3$ are primes include the values $k=2, 5, 20, 32, 44, \ldots$. □

(We leave you to find other such k. It is not known whether there are infinitely many or not.)

And another application, time to to primitive roots.

Theorem 8.4.9 Suppose that $p=4k+1$ and $q=2p+1$ are both primes. Then 2 is a primitive root of q.

* Lemma 4.1.7 says $0<|u|, |v| \leqslant \sqrt{p}$. Why can we replace $\leqslant$ by $<$ here?

Proof By Euler's criterion $2^p = 2^{(q-1)/2} \equiv (2/q) \pmod q$. Since $q = 8k+3$, Theorem 8.4.3 lets us deduce that $2^p \equiv -1 \pmod q$. Since the order of 2 modulo q is a divisor of $\phi(q) = q-1 = 2p$, the order of 2 is 1, 2, p or $2p$. Now, modulo q, $2^1 \not\equiv 1, 2^2 \not\equiv 1$ (since $k>0$) and $2^p \not\equiv 1$ as we have just noted. Hence 2 is a primitive root for q. □

Finally, the following program uses Gauss's lemma to determine the Legendre symbol (a/p).

Program 8.1 *Calculation of the Legendre Symbol using Gauss's Lemma*

```
10 INPUT A,P
20 V = 0
30 E = 0
40 FOR I = 1 TO (P-1)/2
50    V = V + A
60    R = V - INT(V/P)*P
70    IF R > P/2 THEN E = E + 1
80 NEXT I
90 L = -1
100 IF E/2 = INT(E/2) L = 1
110 PRINT "The Legendre symbol (";A;"/";P") has value ";L
```

Exercises 8.4

1 Use Gauss's lemma to determine (3/13), (7/17), (9/19) and (13/23).

2 Use Gauss's lemma to determine whether or not 7 is a quadratic residue modulo 23. (Cf. Exercises 8.3.2 and 8.3.6. Which method of solution was easiest?)

3 Let p be a prime. Use Gauss's lemma to show that $(-2/p) = 1$ iff p is of the form $8k+1$ or $8k+3$.

4 (i) Show that if $p = 8k+1$ or $8k+3$ is a prime, then p is *uniquely* expressible in the form x^2+2y^2. [*Hint*: Here $(-2/p) = 1$. Proceed as in Theorem 8.4.5 and Exercise 7.1.7.]
(ii) Show, likewise, that each prime of the form $6k+1$ is expressible uniquely in the form x^2+3y^2. (Cf. Exercise 8.3.5 and Exercise 7.1.7.) [*Hint*: Here $(-3/p) = 1$. Also $u^2+3v^2 = 2p$ implies $2|p$—impossible!]

5 Prove that each prime p of the form $8k \pm 1$ is expressible in the form x^2-2y^2—in infinitely many ways. [*Hint*: For existence copy Theorem 8.4.5. To prove infinitely many solutions define $a_1 = b_1 = 1$ and $a_{n+1} = a_n + b_n$, $b_{n+1} = 2a_n + b_n$. Prove $b_n^2 - 2a_n^2 = (-1)^n$. Finally use $(u^2-2v^2)(a^2-2b^2) = (ua+2vb)^2 - 2(va+ub)^2$.]

6 Show that there are infinitely many primes of the form $8k+r$ where $r = 3, 5$ respectively. [*Hint*: Consider the numbers: $(p_1 p_2 \cdots p_t)^2+2$, and $4(p_1 \cdots p_t)^2+1$ respectively.]

7 (i) Prove that if p is a prime of the form $4k+3$ such that $2p+1$ is also a prime, then $2^{p-1}M_p$ is not perfect.
(ii) Prove that the 1481 digit number M_{4919} is composite. [How do we know that it has exactly 1481 digits?] [*Hint*: Yes, 4919 *is* prime!]

8 Show that:

(i) If p and $q=4p+1$ are both primes, then 2 is a primitive root of q;
(ii) if p and $q=2p+1$ are odd primes, then $(-1)^{(p-1)/2}2$ is a primitive root of q;
(iii) if p and $2p+1$ are odd primes, then -4 is a primitive root of q.

Computer problem 8.4

1 Compare the computation times for calculating the Legendre symbol using Program 8.1 and the methods of Problems 8.2.1 and 8.3.1.

8.5 Proof of the LQR—more applications

We now progress to a proof of the LQR by, first of all, re-examining Gauss's lemma. We retain the notation introduced there.

Lemma 8.5.1 Let p be an odd prime and let $(a, p)=1$ where a is odd. Then

$$(a/p)=(-1)^T, \text{ where } T=\sum_{k=1}^{(p-1)/2}[ka/p].$$

Proof Let $s=\{a, 2a, \dots, ((p-1)/2)a\}$, as before. Once again divide each of the ka by p. We have $ka=m_k p+r_k$ where $0\leqslant r_k<p$.

It follows that $m_k=[ka/p]$ and hence that

$$\sum_{k=1}^{(p-1)/2} ka=\sum_{k=1}^{(p-1)/2}[ka/p]\cdot p+\sum_{i=1}^{\mu}\alpha_i+\sum_{j=1}^{\nu}\beta_j. \tag{1}$$

Since the α_i and the $p-\beta_i$ are just the integers $1, 2, \dots, (p-1)/2$ in some order we have

$$\sum_{k=1}^{(p-1)/2} k=\sum_{i=1}^{\mu}\alpha_i+\sum_{j=1}^{\nu}(p-\beta_j)=\nu p+\sum_{k=1}^{\mu}\alpha_i-\sum_{j=1}^{\nu}\beta_j. \tag{2}$$

Subtracting (2) from (1) gives:

$$(a-1)\sum_{k=1}^{(p-1)/2} k=p\cdot T-p\nu+2\sum_{j=1}^{\nu}\beta_j. \tag{3}$$

Since a and p are both odd (3) yields the congruence, modulo 2,

$$0\equiv T-\nu \pmod 2).$$

Hence, immediately, $(a/p)=(-1)^{\nu}=(-1)^{T}$—since each of the two indices is even or each is odd. □

We can now complete the proof of the LQR using a method due to a student of Gauss—Ferdinand Eisenstein*—whom Gauss regarded as one of the three greatest of mathematicians.

By Lemma 8.5.1 we have $(p/q)(q/p)=(-1)^{E}$, where

$$E=\sum_{c=1}^{(q-1)/2}[cp/q]+\sum_{d=1}^{(p-1)/2}[dq/p].$$

So, clearly, what we need is:

Lemma 8.5.2 Let p, q be distinct odd primes. Then $E\equiv(p-1)(q-1)/4$ (mod 2). [In fact we shall prove equality.]

Proof Draw† in the x-y plane, the rectangle R with vertices at the points $(0,0)$, $(0,q/2)$, $(p/2,0)$, $(p/2,q/2)$. Inside this rectangle there clearly lie $(p-1)/2\cdot(q-1)/2$ (so called 'lattice') points whose coordinates are integers. The diagonal line D from $(0,0)$ to $(p/2,q/2)$ has equation $y=qx/p$. Since $(p,q)=1$ no lattice points lie on D (since $b=qa/p$ is impossible in integers a, b unless $p|a$ and $q|b$.)

Let A denote the region of R above the line D and B the region below it. Adding the number of lattice points inside A to those inside B will yield (since no lattice points lie on D) the sum $(p-1)/2\cdot(q-1)/2$.

Now, in B, the number of lattice points which lie directly above $(d,0)$ is clearly $[qd/p]$. Thus the total number of lattice points in B is $\sum_{d=1}^{(p-1)/2}[qd/p]$. Likewise, the total number in A is (count parallel to the y-axis—or use 'symmetry') $\sum_{c=1}^{(q-1)/2}[pc/q]$.

Consequently

$$(p-1)/2\cdot(q-1)/2=\sum_{c=1}^{(q-1)/2}[pc/q]+\sum_{d=1}^{(p-1)/2}[qd/p],$$

as required. □

The LQR is thus proved. But we take the opportunity to restate it as:

Theorem 8.5.3 Let p, q be distinct odd primes. Then $(p/q)=(q/p)$—except when $p\equiv q\equiv 3 \pmod 4$, in which case $(p/q)=-(q/p)$. □

In solving Diophantine equations the LQR might be expected to arise whenever a squared term is present as, for example, in Bachet's equation $y^2=x^3+k$. As we saw in Section 7.1 certain cases of Bachet's equation can be

* Ferdinand Gottfried Max Eisenstein, 16 April 1823 - 11 October 1852.

† Draw you own picture. It will get you more involved in the proof.

dealt with using fairly straightforward congruence arguments. Others, as we shall see later (Theorem 9.5.1), require knowledge of the arithmetic of certain special number systems. Yet others make use of quadratic reciprocity as we now show. The restrictions placed on the quantities appearing in the theorem below may look involved but they mostly arise quite naturally when one tries to ensure that the given equation has few or, as here, no solutions. In fact the following is a very special case of a much more general result of L. J. Mordell (1913).

Theorem 8.5.4 Let $y^2-3b^2=x^3-a^3$ and suppose that (i) $a\equiv 1(\text{mod } 4)$; (ii) $b\equiv \pm 2(\text{mod } 6)$; (iii) b has no prime factor of the form $12k\pm 5$. Then the given equation has no integer solutions.

Proof Working modulo 4 we find, using (ii) and (i), $y^2\equiv x^3-1$. It is then immediate that $x\not\equiv 0, 2, 3(\text{mod } 4)$, that is, $x\equiv 1(\text{mod } 4)$. Further $x\not\equiv a-1(\text{mod } 3)$; for $y^2\equiv(a-1)-a=-1(\text{mod } 3)$, which is impossible, would follow. If $x\equiv a(\text{mod } 3)$ we could deduce $y^2\equiv 3(\text{mod } 9)$ which is also impossible. We are thus forced to accept that $x\equiv a+1(\text{mod } 3)$. It then follows that $f=x^2+ax+a^2$ (which is a factor of x^3-a^3—hence the reason for the special form of the given equation) is congruent to $1(\text{mod } 3)$ as well as to $3(\text{mod } 4)$, facts which show it to be congruent to $7(\text{mod } 12)$. But this means that f must have a prime factor p, say, of the form $12k\pm 5$ [why?]. However, Exercise 8.5.1 then shows that $(3/p)=-1$ so that p cannot divide y^2-3b^2, a contradiction. □

We leave to you the pleasure of finding other values of $k=3b^2-a^3$ for which $y^2=x^3+k$ has no integral solution.

We conclude this section by tidying up Theorem 5.4.1 as promised (see also Exercise 5.4.1). We require

Theorem 8.5.5 Let F_n be the nth Fermat number. If F_n is prime and if $n\geqslant 1$, then 3 is a primitive root for F_n.

Proof $F_n=2^{2^n}+1=2^{2m}+1=4^m+1$ for suitable m. Thus $F_n\equiv 1(\text{mod } 4)$ whilst $F_n\equiv 1+1=2(\text{mod } 3)$. Hence $(3/F_n)=(F_n/3)$ [why?] $=(2/3)=-1$. Euler's criterion tells us immediately that $3^{(F_n-1)/2}\equiv -1(\text{mod } F)$ as required. □

In the case of F_5 the above test requires we find $3^{2^{31}}$ mod F_5. In fact $3^{2^{31}}\equiv 10\,324\,303\not\equiv -1(\text{mod } 4\,294\,967\,297)$ so that F_5 isn't prime. This calculation is hardly any shorter than that given in Chapter 5. What we have gained is what we there took for granted, namely that use of the number 3 will always disclose the prime/composite status of each F_n. As we have already reported in Section 5.4, this test has been used to establish the compositeness of several larger Fermat numbers.

Exercises 8.5

1 Let p be a prime >3. Show that

$$(3/p)=\begin{cases} 1 & \text{if } p\equiv \pm 1 \pmod{12} \\ -1 & \text{if } p\equiv \pm 5 \pmod{12} \end{cases}$$

and that

$$(-3/p)=\begin{cases} 1 & \text{if } p\equiv 1 \pmod 6 \\ -1 & \text{if } p\equiv -1 \pmod 6. \end{cases}$$

2 Show that there are infinitely many primes of the form $6k+1$. [*Hint*: Consider $(2p_1p_2\cdots p_t)^2+3$ and use $(-3/p)$ as in Exercise 1.]

3 Let $y^2-2b^2=x^3-a^3$ where (i) $a\equiv 2$ or $4 \pmod 8$; (ii) b is odd and has no prime factors of the form $8k\pm 3$. Then the given equation has no integer solution. [*Hint*: Show that $x\equiv 0, 1, 2 \pmod 4$ lead to impossibilities. If $x\equiv 3 \pmod 4$ then $x\equiv -1$ or $3 \pmod 8$. If $x\equiv -1 \pmod 8$ then $x-a\equiv -3$ or $3 \pmod 8$. Now use Corollary 8.4.4. If $x\equiv 3 \pmod 8$ then $x^2+ax+a^2\equiv \pm 3 \pmod 8$.]

4 Show that if 341 *were* a prime, then $(2/341)$ would be equal to -1 (by LQR III) from which Euler's criterion would yield $2^{170}\equiv -1 \pmod{341}$. Since this is false—prove it directly—we see that 341 can't be a prime! [An odd composite number which *does* fool us, via Euler's criterion, into thinking it is a prime is called an *Euler pseudoprime.*] Thus 341 is a (Fermat) 2-psp (see Definition 5.4.2) but not an Euler 2-psp. Prove that each Euler a-psp is a Fermat a-psp.

5 Show that if $2^{2^n}\equiv -1 \pmod p$ then 2 has order 2^{n+1} *exactly* modulo p. Earlier we showed that if $p|F_n=2^{2^n}+1$ then $p=2^{n+1}k+1$ and so, for $n\geqslant 2$, p is of the form $8t+1$. Show this implies that $2^{(p-1)/2}\equiv 1 \pmod p$ and hence that $2^{n+1}|(p-1)/2$. Deduce (Lucas 1877) that $p=2^{n+2}l+1$ for some l. Show that with this information Euler would only have had to have tried, unsuccessfully, *one* potential divisor of F_5 before finding 641.

6 Prove Pepin's full result (1877)—namely: For $n>1$, F_n is prime iff $k^{(F_n-1)/2}\equiv -1 \pmod{F_n}$ where k is any q.n.r. of F_n. (Cf. Theorem 5.4.1.)

Computer problems 8.5

1 Write a program to test the first few Fermat numbers for primeness using Pepin's result with $k=3$.

2 Use Theorem 8.5.4 and Exercise 8.5.3 to find some values of k, $0\leqslant k\leqslant 1000$, such that $y^2=x^3+k$ has no solution. Compare these results with those obtained in Problem 7.1.5. Can you be sure you have obtained all k $(0\leqslant k\leqslant 1000)$ satisfying these restrictions?

Carl Gustav Jacob Jacobi *(10 December 1804 – 18 February 1851)*
Jacobi was born in Potsdam, the son of a banker. After being educated at home by an uncle, he entered the Gymnasium at Potsdam in 1816. Here he excelled in Latin, Greek and History. His mathematical knowledge he enhanced by reading Euler's work on analysis. He also tried to solve the problem—subsequently shown insoluble by Abel and Galois—of exhibiting a formula for the roots of the general equation of degree 5.

Entering the University of Berlin, he eventually decided to concentrate solely on mathematics, pursuing his studies independently of the lecture courses. He obtained his doctorate in 1825.

Jacobi proved to be not only an excellent researcher but also a splendid teacher, impressing all his listeners by his clarity and enthusiasm. However, as promotion prospects at Berlin were bleak, Jacobi accepted advice to move to the University of Königsberg where he joined, amongst others, Friedrich Bessel. Accordingly Jacobi soon took an interest in problems of applied mathematics.

In almost 20 years at Königsberg Jacobi's enthusiasm never dimmed. He would lecture his students on his most recent work on elliptic functions. He also introduced the idea of holding research seminars. In 1829 he collected together his results on elliptic functions in a work which was to earn him a wide and fine reputation.

In 1843 Jacobi became seriously ill with diabetes. Via the efforts of Dirichlet and von Humboldt he was granted financial support to enable him to travel to Italy where his health began to improve. Returning to Berlin the following year his health again deteriorated. In 1851 he first contracted influenza and then, on the point of recovery, caught smallpox. Within a week he was dead.

Jacobi's talent was widespread, taking in differential equations, dynamics, celestial mechanics, fluid dynamics, hyperelliptic integrals and functions. His name is perhaps most familiar to the reader via the Jacobian, a determinant with functions as entries, which appears, amongst other places, when changes of variable are made in multiple integrals.

Jacobi's contributions to number theory were extensive. In 1827 he stated the law of cubic reciprocity—a feat which impressed Gauss.

Subsequently he applied his favourite theory—of elliptic functions—to the theory of numbers obtaining, in particular, the Fermat–Lagrange four-square theorem (Theorem 7.2.4). Furthermore Jacobi's theory could tell how many distinct ways each number can be represented.

Jacobi also stood up for number theory in his general pronouncements. For example he once asserted that 'God ever arithmetises'. On another occasion he clashed with Fourier's belief that the only valuable mathematics was that which is applied to practical problems, replying that 'Problems of number theory are just as important as problems from the real world. The honour of the human spirit is at stake'.

8.6 The Jacobi symbol

In Exercise 8.5.4 we evaluated $(2/341)$ according to the rules of the LQR as if 341 were a prime and got the result $(2/341)=(-1)^{(341^2-1)/8}=-1$ which is 'correct' since 2 is a q.n.r. modulo 341 ($2^{170}\equiv -1(\text{mod } 341)$). Can one usefully extend the definition of the Legendre symbol (a/n) to include the case where n is any odd positive integer? The answer is 'Yes—but not naively'—at least if one wishes the LQR to extend too. Exercises 8.6.2 and 8.6.3 below show that if one wishes to preserve the LQR for such symbols then one must forfeit the interpretation that $(P/Q)=1$ iff P is a quadratic residue modulo Q. This is not any great loss. Indeed, by defining (P/Q) naively as in Exercise 8.6.2, we lose the LQR for such symbols and are left with what is then no more than a usefully brief notation.

The appropriate definition is

Definition 8.6.1 Let P, Q be integers with P, Q odd, $Q\geqslant 3$ and $(P, Q)=1$. If $Q=q_1q_2\cdots q_r$, the q_i being primes (not necessarily distinct) we define the *Jacobi symbol* (P/Q) by $(P/Q)=(P/q_1)(P/q_2)\cdots(P/q_r)$ where each (P/q_i) is the usual Legendre symbol.

Notes 8.6.2

(i) If q is an odd prime the Jacobi symbol (P/q) and the Legendre symbol (P/q) coincide.

(ii) Exercises 8.6.4 and 8.6.5 show that Definition 8.6.1 is just the right one if our main aim is to preserve the LQR.

In adopting Definition 8.6.1 we lose the knowledge that $(P/Q)=1$ iff P is a quadratic residue modulo Q (Exercise 8.6.3 indicates the problem). Despite this Jacobi's symbol *can* be used to determine more rapidly *and with certainty* whether or not an integer is a quadratic residue modulo a *prime.*

Example 8.6.3* (See Exercises 8.3.7—and read Exercise 8.6.3 first so as to be more impressed with the following conclusions.)

$$\left(\frac{209}{409}\right)=\left(\frac{409}{209}\right)=\left(\frac{200}{11\cdot 19}\right)=\left(\frac{2}{11}\right)\left(\frac{10^2}{11}\right)\left(\frac{2}{19}\right)\left(\frac{10^2}{19}\right)$$
$$=(-1)^{(11^2-1)/8}\cdot 1\cdot(-1)^{(19^2-1)/8}\cdot 1=1.$$

Hence 209 is a q.r. for the prime 409.

Note how the length of the calculation has been reduced by use of the Jacobi symbol. Your solution to Exercise 8.3.7 should have read something like

$$\left(\frac{209}{409}\right)=\left(\frac{11}{409}\right)\left(\frac{19}{409}\right)=\left(\frac{409}{11}\right)\left(\frac{409}{19}\right)=\left(\frac{2}{11}\right)\left(\frac{10}{19}\right)$$
$$=(-1)^{(11^2-1)/8}\left(\frac{2}{19}\right)\left(\frac{5}{19}\right)$$
$$=(-1)(-1)^{(19^2-1)/8}\left(\frac{19}{5}\right)$$
$$=(-1)(-1)\left(\frac{2^2}{5}\right)=1.$$

Exercises 8.6

1 Evaluate (21/55), (17/217), (269/889).

2 For integers P, Q with Q odd, $Q\geqslant 3$ and $(P, Q)=1$ define

$$(P/Q)=\begin{cases}1 & \text{if } P \text{ is a q.r. mod } Q\\ -1 & \text{if } P \text{ is a q.n.r. mod } Q.\end{cases}$$

With *this* definition and taking $P=5$ and $Q=9$ show that part I of Theorem 8.2.7 fails, that $(-1/Q)\neq 1$ and that $(2/Q)\neq 1$.

3 Prove, *using Definition 8.6.1*, that if $(P/Q)=-1$ then P is not a quadratic residue of Q. Give an example to show that the converse is false.

4 Using Definition 8.6.1 prove that: if Q, Q' are odd integers $\geqslant 3$ and if P, P' are integers such that $(PP', QQ')=1$ then

(i) If $P\equiv P'(\text{mod } Q)$ then $(P/Q)=(P'/Q)$;
(ii) $(P^2/Q)=(P/Q^2)=1$;
(iii) (a) $(P/Q)(P'/Q)=(PP'/Q)$; (b) $(P/Q)(P/Q')=(P/QQ')$;
(iv) Show that $P^{(Q-1)/2}\equiv(P/Q)(\text{mod } Q)$ may fail.

* In the rest of this chapter we shall sometimes use $(\frac{x}{y})$ instead of (x/y) just for convenience.

5 Given that P, Q are odd integers with $P, Q \geqslant 3$ and $(P, Q)=1$ prove the LQR:

(i) $(-1/Q)=(-1)^{(Q-1)/2}$;
(ii) $(2/Q)=(-1)^{(Q^2-1)/8}$;
(iii) $(P/Q)(Q/P)=(-1)^{(P-1)(Q-1)/4}$. [*Hint*: Show that, if a, b are odd, then

$$(a-1)/2+(b-1)/2 \equiv (ab-1)/2 \pmod 2$$

and

$$(a^2-1)/2+(b^2-1)/2 \equiv (a^2b^2-1)/2 \pmod 2).]$$

8.7 Programming points

To compute the Jacobi symbol efficiently we can use a modified version of the division algorithm. If a and b are relatively prime and $a>b>0$ then we can proceed as follows. Let $U_0=a$ and $U_1=b$. Then using the division algorithm we can write

$$U_0 = U_1 q_1 + R_0.$$

Before proceeding to the next step of the division algorithm we remove from R_0 the powers of 2 by writing $R_0=2^{P_1}U_2$. We then apply the division algorithm to U_1 and U_2 to get

$$U_1 = U_2 q_2 + R_1.$$

We proceed in this way until $U_n=1$ for some n. Thus at the $(k-1)$st step we have

$$U_{k-2} = U_{k-1} q_{k-1} + 2^{P_{k-1}} U_k.$$

We can express the Jacobi symbol $\left(\frac{U_{k-2}}{U_{k-1}}\right)$ in terms of $\left(\frac{U_{k-1}}{U_k}\right)$ as follows:

$$\begin{aligned}
\left(\frac{U_{k-2}}{U_{k-1}}\right) &= \left(\frac{R_{k-2}}{U_{k-1}}\right) && \text{by Exercise 8.6.4(i)} \\
&= \left(\frac{2^{P_{k-1}}U_k}{U_{k-1}}\right) = \left(\frac{2}{U_{k-1}}\right)^{P_{k-1}} \left(\frac{U_k}{U_{k-1}}\right) && \text{by Exercise 8.6.4(iii)} \\
&= (-1)^{P_{k-1}(U_{k-1}^2-1)/8} \left(\frac{U_k}{U_{k-1}}\right) && \text{by Exercise 8.6.5(ii)} \\
&= (-1)^{P_{k-1}(U_{k-1}^2-1)/8} (-1)^{(U_{k-1}-1)(U_k-1)/4} \left(\frac{U_{k-1}}{U_k}\right).
\end{aligned}$$

Using this result we can calculate $(\frac{a}{b}) = (-1)^T$ where

$$T = \sum_{i=2}^{n} P_{i-1}(U_{i-1}^2 - 1)/8 + \sum_{i=2}^{n} (U_{i-1} - 1)(U_i - 1)/4.$$

The following program uses this algorithm to calculate the Jacobi symbol.

Program 8.2 *Evaluation of the Jacobi Symbol*

```
 10 INPUT A,B
 20 PRINT "Jacobi symbol (";A;"/";B;") = ";
 30 P = 0
 40 R = A - INT(A/B)*B
 50    S = 0
 60    R = R/2
 70       IF R<>INT(R) GOTO 100
 80       S = S + 1
 90    GOTO 60
100    R = R * 2
110    P = P + S * (B*B-1)/8 + (B-1)*(R-1)/4
120    IF R = 1 GOTO 160
130       A = B
140       B = R
150 GOTO 40
160 J=-1
150 IF P/2 = INT(P/2) J=1
160 PRINT;J
```

If $b > a$ we simply use

$$\left(\frac{a}{b}\right) = (-1)^{(a-1)(b-1)/4}\left(\frac{b}{a}\right)$$

and apply the algorithm with b and a switched. This is achieved by adding to the previous program the lines

```
16 IF b>a GOTO 20
17 p = (a-1)*(b-1)/4
18 t=a
19 a=b : b=t
```

Computer problems 8.7

1 The definition of Euler pseudoprime is given in Exercise 8.5.4. Using Programs 3.2 and 8.2 write a program to check whether a number is an Euler pseudoprime to base *b*.

2 Modify your program to find the smallest Euler psp to bases 2, 3, 5 etc.

3 It can be shown [7] that the probability of an odd composite number n being an Euler b-psp to any base $b < n$ is $< \frac{1}{2}$. Therefore if we check whether a number is an Euler psp to k bases $b_1, b_2, \ldots, b_k$ chosen at random, the probability of its not being prime is $< (\frac{1}{2})^k$. This is known as the *Solovay–Strassen probabilistic primality test.* Write a program to perform this test.

9
The Gaussian integers

9.1 Introduction

In Book 6, Problem 17, Diophantus asks us to find a right-angled triangle such that its area, A, added to its hypotenuse, h, gives a square whilst its perimeter, p, is a cube. To solve this problem, Diophantus takes 2 and A as the (perpendicular) legs of the triangle and tries $h+A=16$, whence $h+A+2=18$—'which is not a cube'. Thus we must 'find some square (for $h+A$) which, when increased by 2, becomes a cube'. Noting that $5^2+2=3^3$ we try $h+A=25$. Since $h^2=A^2+2^2$ (by Pythagoras) we deduce that $A=621/50$. Bachet, who took the opportunity to insert questions of his own into his translation of *The Arithmetica*, noted that we can easily find other rational y for which y^2+2 is a (rational) cube (Exercise 9.1.1). But Fermat wrote, in his copy of Bachet's translation, that $y=5$, $x=3$ is the only positive solution, *in integers*, of the equation $y^2+2=x^3$ and that he could prove it.

Euler who, as we have seen, spent a fair amount of time trying to prove Fermat's assertions, remarked in his *Algebra* (Art. 188, Chapter 12 of Part II) that $ay^2+cz^2=(y\sqrt{a}+z\sqrt{-c})(y\sqrt{a}-z\sqrt{-c})$ and that 'to reduce ay^2+cz^2 to a cube we may suppose that $y\sqrt{a}+z\sqrt{-c}=(p\sqrt{a}+q\sqrt{-c})^3$' for suitable integers p and q. From this, on multiplying out the cube and equating the coefficients of $\sqrt{a}$ and $\sqrt{-c}$ we get $y=ap^3-3cpq^2$ and $z=3ap^2q-cq^3$. In particular, given the equation $y^2+2=x^3$ we take $a=1$, $c=2$, $z=\pm1$, whence $q(3p^2-2q^2)=\pm1$. Thus* $q=\pm1$ and so $3p^2-2q^2=3p^2-2=\pm1$. Since $3p^2=2-1$ is impossible, we must have $3p^2=2+1=3$. Consequently $p=\pm1$ so that

$$y=(\pm1)[1\cdot(\pm1)^2-3\cdot2(\pm1)^2]=\pm5.$$

Hence $x^3=y^2+2=27$ so that $x=3$. Euler concludes that no (integral) square except 25 has the desired property. He then goes on to show that this method fails to show up the solution $y=4$ of the equation $2y^2-5=x^3$ and lays the blame at the door of the minus sign and the existence (as we'll see later) of the infinitely many solutions of the so-called Pell equation $x^2-10y^2=1$. However H. Delannoy (1898) showed that, even with the plus sign, Euler's proof is incomplete since, in the case of the equation $y^2+47=x^3$, Euler's method yields only the solution $x=63$, $y=\pm500$, but misses a smaller one. (Find it!)

* Recall that q is an integer.

Exercises 9.1

1 Show that if $y^2+d=x^3$ has x_0, y_0 as one (rational) solution then others arise as follows. Set $x_1=x_0-X$ and $y_1=y_0-Y$ where X, Y are to be chosen. Then

$$y_1^2+d=x_1^3 \Leftrightarrow -2y_0Y+Y^2=-3x_0^2X+3x_0X^2-X^3. \qquad (*)$$

Choose Y so that $2y_0Y=3x_0^2X$ and now find X by solving the final cubic in $(*)$ for X. Can you think of two snags which would prevent us from saying that $y^2+d=x^3$ has infinitely many rational solutions?

2 (Euler) Show that $y^2-1=x^3$ has no integer solutions other than those corresponding to $x=0, -1, 2$. Euler claimed $y^2+1=x^3$ could be treated similarly. Try it! If you fail see Exercise 9.4.6.

3 Show that the only solution to $y^2+47=x^3$ given by Euler's method is $x=63$, $y=\pm 500$.

4 Using the same approach find a solution to $y^2+11=x^3$.

Computer problem 9.1

1 Search for other solutions to the equations $y^2+47=x^3$ and $y^2+11=x^3$ of Exercises 9.1.3 and 9.1.4.

Carl Friedrich Gauss *(30 April 1777 – 23 February 1855)*
Gauss was born in Brunswick, Germany, into a poor family. His father, Gerhard, who at various times was a gardener, general labourer and merchant's assistant was honest but rough mannered. Gauss's mental abilities seem to have derived from his mother's side, for she, though not fully literate, was intelligent whilst, in the words of Gauss himself, her brother was 'a born genius'.

Gauss's remarkable career started early. It is said that, aged 3, he corrected an arithmetic slip his father made in a wages list and that when aged 10 (some say 8) he wrote down in a moment the answer to the problem, set in class: Find the sum of the integers from 1 to 100. (Presumably he saw that the answer just *had* to be 50×101.)

Various sources claim that before he was aged 20 he had, amongst other things, rediscovered—and given the first proof of—the law of quadratic reciprocity, discovered the double periodicity of elliptic functions, proved that each positive integer is a sum of three triangular numbers, formulated the principle of least squares, conjectured the prime number theorem (which took a further 100 years to be proved) and shown the constructibility, by compass and straight-edge, of a regular 17-gon—the first 'new' such n-gon for 2000 years. And, as if this were not enough, his doctoral thesis contained the first acceptable proof of the fundamental theorem of algebra, a result whose proof had defeated such giants as Euler and Lagrange.

Gauss's abilities were not restricted to mathematics. Indeed it was only his discoveries relating to the 17-gon which persuaded him to take up mathematics rather than to devote himself to philology! On the other hand, whilst he did fundamental work in probability, geodesy, mechanics, optics, actuarial science and electromagnetism—including the manufacture, in 1833, in a (rare) joint collaboration (with Wilhelm Weber) of the first operating electric telegraph—the higher arithmetic (that is, the theory of numbers) was closest to his heart. He said that mathematics is the Queen of science and that number theory is the Queen of mathematics.

In 1801 his name became famous with the general public when he located the position of the newly found (and subsequently lost!) planet Ceres, all this being based on complicated calculations with meagre evidence (and where the best astronomers had failed). But 1801 is best remembered as the year of publication of the *Disquisitiones Arithmeticae*, a text which was begun in 1795 and which, according to Lagrange, 'has raised you, at once, to the rank of the first mathematicians.'

In 1807 Gauss was asked to follow Euler to St Petersburg. Instead he accepted the post of Director of the Göttingen observatory, a position which allowed him much time for uninterrupted research.

Gauss was, like Euler, a prodigious calculator; one piece of research began by his calculating the decimal representations of all fractions $1/n$ for $1 \leqslant n \leqslant 1000$. Unlike Euler he restricted the amount of his research he made public. Before publication he would leave no stone unturned in taking his research to its conclusion and, much to the annoyance of most other mathematicians, also obliterate any description of how his ideas had been generated. He stuck to his motto 'Few, but ripe'. His success in solving problems where others failed he modestly ascribed, as did Newton, to 'always thinking about them'.

Unfortunately Gauss took his motto too far. In his unpublished notes it was discovered, after his death, that Gauss had considered non-Euclidean geometry before Lobatchevsky, quaternions before Hamilton, elliptic functions before Abel and Jacobi as well much of Cauchy's complex variable theory.

Gauss did not seem to relish travel. Indeed in the last 27 years of his life he slept away from his observatory only once. The Prince of Mathematicians, as his contempories called him, died there peacefully in his 78th year.

9.2 Divisibility in the Gaussian integers

The proper approach to factorisation problems of the above kind was indicated by Gauss whilst extending the LQR to one of biquadratic reciprocity (i.e. concerning $x^4 \equiv q(\text{mod } p)$). We shall not discuss these extensions here (see [P] and [27]) but we shall make good use of the ideas introduced by Gauss to help him solve his problem. We begin with

Definition 9.2.1 A complex number of the form $a+ib$ $(=a+b\sqrt{-1})$ where $a, b \in \mathbb{Z}$ is called a *Gaussian integer.* The set of all Gaussian integers will be denoted by $\mathbb{Z}[i]$ (or $\mathbb{Z}[\sqrt{-1}]$).

We shall need to compare Gaussian integers for 'size'. This is achieved by making

Definition 9.2.2 The *norm* $N(\lambda)$ of the complex number $\lambda = \mu + i\nu$, where $\mu, \nu \in \mathbb{R}$ is the real number $N(\lambda) = \mu^2 + \nu^2$.

Notes 9.2.3
(i) $N(\lambda) = (\mu + i\nu)(\mu - i\nu) = \lambda\bar{\lambda} = |\lambda|^2$ where $|\lambda|$ is the (usual) modulus of λ.
(ii) For complex numbers λ, ρ we have $|\lambda\rho| = |\lambda||\rho|$. Equivalently $N(\lambda\rho) = N(\lambda)N(\rho)$.
(iii) If $\lambda \in \mathbb{Z}[i]$ then $N(\lambda)$ is a non-negative *integer.*

Using Definition 9.2.2 we can establish, for $\mathbb{Z}[i]$, an analogue of the division algorithm for $\mathbb{Z}$(Section 0.3). First we need (cf. Definitions 1.1.1 and 1.5.1).

Definition 9.2.4
(i) Let $\alpha, \beta \in \mathbb{Z}[i]$. We say that α *divides* β (in $\mathbb{Z}[i]$) and write $\alpha|\beta$ iff there exists $\gamma \in \mathbb{Z}[i]$ such that $\alpha\gamma = \beta$.
(ii) Let $\delta \in \mathbb{Z}[i]$. Suppose that $\delta|\alpha$ and $\delta|\beta$. Then δ is a *greatest common divisor* (gcd) of α and β iff, whenever $\kappa \in \mathbb{Z}[i]$ is such that $\kappa|\alpha$ and $\kappa|\beta$, then $\kappa|\delta$.

We shall give examples shortly. But before that we obtain the analogue just referred to due to Gauss (1832).

Theorem 9.2.5 (*The division algorithm for* $\mathbb{Z}[i]$.) Let $\alpha, \beta \in \mathbb{Z}[i]$ be such that $\beta \neq 0$. Then there exist Gaussian integers m and r such that $\alpha = m\beta + r$ where $0 \leqslant N(r) < N(\beta)$.

Proof We set $\alpha = a + ib$, $\beta = c + id$. Then

$$\alpha/\beta = \frac{(a+ib)(c-id)}{c^2+d^2} = u + iv,$$

where $u, v \in \mathbb{Q}$. We now choose $U, V \in \mathbb{Z}$ such that $|u-U| \leqslant \frac{1}{2}$ and $|v-V| \leqslant \frac{1}{2}$ by choosing U to be the nearest integer to u (or either of the two nearest if u is midway between two integers) and likewise for V and v. We then write

$$\alpha = \beta\{U + \mathrm{i}V\} + \beta\{(u-U) + \mathrm{i}(v-V)\}.$$

Setting $m = U + \mathrm{i}V$ and $r = \beta\{(u-U) + i(v-V)\}$ we see that $m \in \mathbb{Z}[\mathrm{i}]$ and claim that $N(r) < N(\beta)$. This claim is easy to prove. For, $N(r) = N(\beta)N\{(u-U) + \mathrm{i}(v-V)\}$, by Note 9.2.3(ii). Then, by Definition 9.2.2,

$$N\{(u-U)+\mathrm{i}(v-V)\} = (u-U)^2 + (v-V)^2 \leqslant (\tfrac{1}{2})^2 + (\tfrac{1}{2})^2 = \tfrac{1}{2} < 1.$$

Hence $N(r) < N(\beta)$, as asserted. Note, too, that $r = \alpha - m\beta$ certainly belongs to $\mathbb{Z}[\mathrm{i}]$—since α, m and β all do. □

This result immediately suggests the following extension.

Theorem 9.2.6 (*The Euclidean algorithm for* $\mathbb{Z}[\mathrm{i}]$) Let $\alpha, \beta \in \mathbb{Z}[i]$, not both being zero. Then α, β have a gcd δ, say, which is expressible in the form $s\alpha + t\beta$ where $s, t \in \mathbb{Z}[\mathrm{i}]$. Furthermore, if δ and δ_1 are any two gcds of α and β then $\delta_1 = \delta$ or $-\delta$ or $\mathrm{i}\delta$ or $-\mathrm{i}\delta$.

Proof The proof parallels that for $\mathbb{Z}$ (as given in Section 1.6) the sequence $|b| = r_1 > r_2 > \cdots (\geqslant 0)$ used there being replaced by the sequence $N(\beta) = N(r_1) > N(r_2) > \cdots (\geqslant 0)$ here. If, at step (t), we reach $r_{t-1} = m_t r_t + r_{t+1}$ where $N(r_{t+1}) = 0$ we deduce immediately that $r_{t+1} = 0$ so that (just as in $\mathbb{Z}$) r_t—the 'last' remainder with non-zero norm—is a gcd of α and β.

Copying Theorem 1.6.2 we see how we can express r_t in terms of r_{t-1} and r_{t-2}, finishing up, as there, with r_t being expressed as a linear combination, with coefficients in $\mathbb{Z}[\mathrm{i}]$, of α and β.

To show that any two gcds differ by multiplication by 1, −1, i or −i note that, if δ and δ_1 are two gcds of α and β then, by Definition 9.2.4(ii), $\delta|\delta_1$ and $\delta_1|\delta$. That is, there exist ε and ε_1 in $\mathbb{Z}[\mathrm{i}]$ such that $\varepsilon\delta = \delta_1$ and $\varepsilon_1\delta_1 = \delta$. It follows that $\varepsilon\varepsilon_1 = 1$ in $\mathbb{Z}[\mathrm{i}]$. Clearly 1, −1, i, −i are solutions to this equality. That they are the only solutions is the content of Exercise 9.2.9. □

An example should* help convince any doubters.

Example 9.2.7 Find the gcds of $\alpha = 71 + 25\mathrm{i}$ and $\beta = 15 + 9\mathrm{i}$ and write each in the form $s\alpha + t\beta$ where $s, t \in \mathbb{Z}[\mathrm{i}]$.

Solution

$$\text{(a)}\quad \frac{71+25\mathrm{i}}{15+9\mathrm{i}} = \frac{(71+25\mathrm{i})(15-9\mathrm{i})}{15^2+9^2} = \frac{1290-264\mathrm{i}}{306} = (4-\mathrm{i}) + \frac{66+42\mathrm{i}}{306}$$

* Indeed it should *not*! Confirmation of a general assertion in a single instance is no substitute for a proof which covers all possible cases.

Step (i) $71+25i=(4-i)(15+9i)+(2+4i)$

(b) $$\frac{15+9i}{2+4i}=\frac{(15+9i)(2-4i)}{2^2+4^2}=\frac{66-42i}{20}=(3-2i)+\frac{(6-2i)}{20}$$

Step (ii) $15+9i=(3-2i)(2+4i)+(1+i)$

(c) $$\frac{2+4i}{1+i}=\frac{(2+4i)(1-i)}{1^2+1^2}=\frac{6+2i}{2}=(3+i)+\frac{0+0i}{2}$$

Step (iii) $2+4i=(3+i)(1+i)+(0+0i)$.

As we have now reached a zero remainder we deduce that the previous remainder, namely $1+i$, is a gcd of $71+25i$ and $15+9i$. The other three are then $-(1+i)$, $i(1+i)$, $-i(1+i)$, that is, $-1-i$, $-1+i$, $1-i$.

Climbing back through steps (ii) and (i) we find:

$$\begin{aligned}1+i&=15+9i-(3-2i)(2+4i)\\&=15+9i-(3-2i)\{71+25i-(4-i)(15+9i)\}\\&=(11-11i)(15+9i)+(2i-3)(71+25i).\end{aligned} \qquad (*)$$

We have thus written one of the gcds of $71+25i$ and $15+9i$ as asserted by the theorem with $s=2i-3$ and $t=11-11i$. The other three are easily obtained.

Note 9.2.8 It is less clear here than in $\mathbb{Z}$ which, if any, of the four gcds is any more special than the others. (In $\mathbb{Z}$ the positive member of the pair d, $-d$ stands out). Accordingly we just don't make any choice here between the four but rather give equal status to each.

Theorem 9.2.6 is the vital ingredient required to prove the analogue (Theorem 9.4.1 below) for $\mathbb{Z}[i]$ of Theorem 1.4.1 (the fundamental theorem of arithmetic for $\mathbb{Z}$. See also the second proof in Section 1.8.). To state it clearly we need the following formal definition:

Definition 9.2.9

(i) Let $u\in\mathbb{Z}[i]$ be such that $u|1$ in $\mathbb{Z}[i]$. Then u is a *unit* of $\mathbb{Z}[i]$.

(ii) Let $\alpha,\beta\in\mathbb{Z}[i]$ be such that $\alpha=u\beta$ where u is a unit. Then α and β are *associates* (in $\mathbb{Z}[i]$).

(iii) (Cf. Definition 1.1.4.) Let $\pi\in\mathbb{Z}[i]$ be such that $\pi\neq 0$ and $\pi\neq$ unit. Then π is a *prime* in $\mathbb{Z}[i]$ if and only if: From an equality $\pi=\gamma\delta$ ($\gamma,\delta\in\mathbb{Z}[i]$) we are forced to deduce that one of γ, δ is a unit u, say, whilst the other is $v\pi$ where $uv=1$. That is, one factor of π is a unit and the other an associate of π.

Examples 9.2.10

(i) In the proof of Theorem 9.2.6 we observed that $1, -1, i, -i$ are units of $\mathbb{Z}[i]$ whilst Exercise 9.2.9 asks you to show there are no more.

(ii) $3+2i$ is a prime in $\mathbb{Z}[i]$. For, if $3+2i=\gamma\delta$ with $\gamma, \delta \in \mathbb{Z}[i]$, we have $N(\gamma)N(\delta)=N(3+2i)=3^2+2^2=13$. Since $N(\gamma)$, $N(\delta)$ are non-negative integers we have $N(\gamma)=1$ (or $N(\delta)=1$), from which it follows that $\gamma=1$ or -1 or i or $-i$ (or $\delta=1$ or -1 or i or $-i$).
(iii) 5 is not a prime in $\mathbb{Z}[i]$—since $5=(2+i)(2-i)$ with neither factor a unit. On the other hand 11 is a prime in $\mathbb{Z}[i]$.
(iv) $6+43i$ is not a prime. Indeed $6+43i=(2+i)(3+2i)(5+2i)$. How did we find this? Note that $N(6+43i)=6^2+43^2=1885=5\cdot 13\cdot 29$. Now the '5' can only arise as a norm of one of the integers $w(\pm 2\pm i)$ where $w=1$ or i. Likewise 13 and 29 can only arise from integers $w(\pm 3\pm 2i)$ and $w(\pm 5\pm 2i)$ respectively. Trying out these possibilities soon reveals the factorisation given.

(An obvious question arises. Will this method *invariably* produce the (correct?) factorisation? We leave you to ponder this.)

The property, noted in Theorem 1.8.1(i), satisfied by the primes in $\mathbb{Z}$, is also available here. Indeed the proof of Theorem 1.8.1(i) can be taken over almost word for word. (It might be instructive for you to compare Theorems 1.8.1(i) and 9.2.11 and their proofs side by side to see where they differ.)

Theorem 9.2.11 Let π be a prime in $\mathbb{Z}[i]$ and let $\alpha, \beta \in \mathbb{Z}[i]$ be such that $\pi|\alpha\beta$ (in $\mathbb{Z}[i]$). Then $\pi|\alpha$ or $\pi|\beta$ (in $\mathbb{Z}[i]$).

Proof Let α, β, π be as given. If $\pi|\alpha$ there is nothing left to prove. So suppose that $\pi\nmid\alpha$. Now the only divisors of π are ± 1, $\pm i$, $\pm\pi$, $\pm i\pi$, and, of these, only ± 1, $\pm i$ also divide α (since $\pi\nmid\alpha$). The four gcds of π and α are therefore 1, -1, i, $-i$. From Theorem 9.2.6 we deduce the existence of $s, t \in \mathbb{Z}[i]$ such that $s\alpha+t\pi=1$. It follows that $s\alpha\beta+t\pi\beta=\beta$. But $\pi|\alpha\beta$ (given) and $\pi|t\pi\beta$ (clearly!). Hence $\pi|s\alpha\beta+t\pi\beta$, i.e. $\pi|\beta$—as required. □

Exercises 9.2

1 Show that, if $\alpha|\beta$ in $\mathbb{Z}[i]$ then $N(\alpha)|N(\beta)$ in $\mathbb{Z}$.

2 In $\mathbb{Z}[i]$ does $2+3i|5+i$? Does $13+7i|114-23i$?

3 Let $\alpha=-4+i$, $\beta=5+3i$. Find $m, r \in \mathbb{Z}[i]$ such that $\alpha=m\beta+r$ with $0\leq N(r)<N(\beta)$. Are these m, r uniquely determined by α and β?

4 Must one always choose m as in the text, that is with $|U-u|\leq\frac{1}{2}$, $|V-v|\leq\frac{1}{2}$ in order to ensure that $\alpha=m\beta+r$ with $0\leq N(r)<N(\beta)$?

5 Find the gcds of the pairs of Gaussian integers in Exercises 2 and 3 and of the pair $11+21i$, $7+9i$. For this last pair write the gcd as in (*) of Example 9.2.7.

6 If $x, y \in \mathbb{Z}$ and if $(x, y)=1$ in $\mathbb{Z}$, is it necessarily true that x and y have no common divisors in $\mathbb{Z}[i]$ other than 1, -1, i, $-i$?

7 Show, in $\mathbb{Z}[i]$, that if π is a prime and u a unit, then $u\pi$ is a prime.

8 Is 2, or any of its associates, a square in $\mathbb{Z}[i]$? A cube in $\mathbb{Z}[i]$? Show that -4 is a fourth power in $\mathbb{Z}[i]$.

9 Show that if u is a unit in $\mathbb{Z}[i]$, then $N(u)=1$. Deduce that the only units in $\mathbb{Z}[i]$ are 1, -1, i and $-$i.

10 Show that if $N(\alpha)$ is a prime in $\mathbb{Z}$, then α is a prime in $\mathbb{Z}[i]$. Give an example to show that the converse is false. Deduce that there are infinitely many primes in $\mathbb{Z}[i]$.

11 Prove the existence of a gcd for each pair α, β (not both zero) of elements of $\mathbb{Z}[i]$ as follows. (Cf. Exercise 1.6.3) Let $S=\{m\alpha+n\beta: m, n\in\mathbb{Z}[i]\}$. Let $\omega\neq 0$ be an element of S whose norm is as small as possible. Now let $\zeta\in S$. Write $\zeta=k\omega+l$ using the division algorithm. Show $l=0$. Deduce that $S\subset W$ where W is the set $\{t\omega: t\in\mathbb{Z}[i]\}$. Show also that $W\subset S$. Since $\alpha, \beta\in S$, ω is common divisor of α and β. Finally show that each common divisor of α and β divides each element of S, in particular ω.

12 Given the prime $\pi\in\mathbb{Z}[i]$, show that there is exactly one prime p in $\mathbb{Z}$ such that $\pi|p$ in $\mathbb{Z}[i]$. [*Hint*: If $\pi=a+ib$, then $\pi|a^2+b^2=p_1p_2\cdots p_r$ in $\mathbb{Z}[i]$. Hence $\pi|p_i$ for some i. If $\pi|p$ and $\pi|q$, then $\pi|1$.]

9.3 Computer manipulation of Gaussian integers

The proofs of Theorems 9.2.5 and 9.2.6 are constructive and outline algorithms which allow us to apply the division algorithm and compute the gcd in $\mathbb{Z}[i]$. Program 9.1 computes the quotient and remainder in $\mathbb{Z}[i]$ using the method outlined in the proof of Theorem 9.2.5.

Program 9.1 *The Division Algorithm in $\mathbb{Z}[i]$*

```
10 DIM a(2),b(2),m(2),r(2)
20 INPUT "enter the components of the first Gaussian integer ",a(1),a(2)
30 INPUT "enter the components of the second Gaussian integer ",b(1),b(2)
40 c=b(1)^2+b(2)^2
50 u=(a(1)*b(1)+a(2)*b(2))/c
60 v=(a(2)*b(1)-a(1)*b(2))/c
70 m(1)=INT(u+0.5)
80 m(2)=INT(v+0.5)
90 r(1)=a(1)-m(1)*b(1)+m(2)*b(2)
100 r(2)=a(2)-m(1)*b(2)-m(2)*b(1)
110 PRINT "quotient is ";m(1);" + ";m(2);"i"
120 PRINT ;" and remainder is ";r(1);" + ";r(2)"i"
```

This forms the basis of Program 9.2 which computes the gcd of α and β in $\mathbb{Z}[i]$ using Euclid's algorithm. The division algorithm is applied iteratively until $N(r)=0$.

Program 9.2 *Computation of the GCD in $\mathbb{Z}[i]$*

```
 10 DIM a(2),b(2),m(2),r(2)
 20 INPUT "enter the components of the first Gaussian integer ",a(1),a(2)
 30 INPUT "enter the components of the second Gaussian integer ",b(1),b(2)
 40 c=b(1)^2+b(2)^2
 50 REM calculate r=a-bm
 60    u=(a(1)*b(1)+a(2)*b(2))/c
 70    v=(a(2)*b(1)-a(1)*b(2))/c
 80    m(1)=INT(u+0.5)
 90    m(2)=INT(v+0.5)
100    r(1)=a(1)-m(1)*b(1)+m(2)*b(2)
110    r(2)=a(2)-m(1)*b(2)-m(2)*b(1)
120    a(1)=b(1)
130    a(2)=b(2)
140    b(1)=r(1)
150    b(2)=r(2)
160    c=r(1)^2+r(2)^2
170 IF c<>0 GOTO 60
180 PRINT "A gcd is ";a(1);" + ";a(2);"i"
```

To compute the coefficients c and $d \in \mathbb{Z}[i]$ such that the gcd $(a, b) = ca + db$ we can use the same technique as in Program 1.8 for computing the corresponding linear combination in $\mathbb{Z}$.

Program 9.3 *Computation in $\mathbb{Z}[i]$ of a linear combination expressing the GCD in terms of the original numbers*

```
 10 DIM a(3,2),b(3,2),m(2),r(3,2)
 20 INPUT "Enter the first number ",a(3,1),a(3,2)
 30 INPUT "Enter the second number ",b(3,1),b(3,2)
 40 a(1,1)=1:a(1,2)=0
 50 a(2,1)=0:a(2,2)=0
 60 b(1,1)=0:b(1,2)=0
 70 b(2,1)=1:b(2,2)=0
 80 c=b(3,1)^2+b(3,2)^2
 90    u=(a(3,1)*b(3,1)+a(3,2)*b(3,2))/c
100    v=(a(3,2)*b(3,1)-a(3,1)*b(3,2))/c
110    m(1)=INT(u+0.5)
120    m(2)=INT(v+0.5)
130    FOR i=1 TO 3
140      r(i,1)=a(i,1)-m(1)*b(i,1)+m(2)*b(i,2)
150      r(i,2)=a(i,2)-m(1)*b(i,2)-m(2)*b(i,1)
160      a(i,1)=b(i,1)
170      a(i,2)=b(i,2)
180      b(i,1)=r(i,1)
190      b(i,2)=r(i,2)
200    NEXT i
210    c=r(3,1)^2+r(3,2)^2
220 IF c<>0 GOTO 90
230 PRINT "The coefficient of the first number is ";a(1,1);" + ";a(1,2);"i"
240 PRINT "The coefficient of the second number is ";a(2,1);" + ";a(2,2);"i"
250 PRINT "The GCD is ";a(3,1);" + ";a(3,2);"i"
```

To obtain a factorisation of the Gaussian integer α on a computer we can proceed in several ways. Program 9.4 uses a trial search technique over all Gaussian integers $\beta = b_1 + ib_2$ such that $N(\beta) < N(\alpha)$. A factor is found if the remainder in the division algorithm is zero. Once a factor is found the quotient becomes the new α and the search proceeds for the next factor. The process only stops once the quotient at any stage is a unit Gaussian integer.

Program 9.4 *Factorization of a Gaussian Integer by trial division*

```
 10 DIM a(2),b(2),m(2),r(2)
 20 INPUT "Enter the coefficients of the Gaussian Integer",a(1),a(2)
 30 c=a(1)^2+a(2)^2
 40 croot=SQR(c)
 50 FOR i=1 TO INT(croot)
 60   FOR j=0 TO INT(croot)
 70     c1=i^2+j^2
 80     IF c1>c OR c1=1 GOTO 200
 90 REM Try the four possible factors generated by the values i and j
100       k=1
110       b(1)=i:b(2)=j
120       IF k=2 THEN b(1)=-i
130       IF k=3 THEN b(2)=-j
140       IF k=4 THEN b(1)=i
150       u=(a(1)*b(1)+a(2)*b(2))/c1
160       v=(a(2)*b(1)-a(1)*b(2))/c1
170       IF (u=INT(u)) AND (v=INT(v)) GOTO 220
180         k=k+1
190         IF k<5 GOTO 120
200   NEXT j
210 NEXT i
220 PRINT b(1);" + ";b(2);"i"
230 c=u^2+v^2
240 IF c=1 PRINT u;" + ";v;"i": STOP
250 a(1)=u:a(2)=v
260 GOTO 40
```

The discussion of Example 9.2.10(iv) suggests an alternative approach. An algorithm based on this would be along the following lines.

1 Factorise $N(\alpha)$ [use Program 1.5].
If $N(\alpha)$ is prime then α is prime in $\mathbb{Z}[i]$ (see Exercise 9.2.10).

2 For each prime factor of the form $4k+1$ express it as the sum of two squares [see Program 7.1]. Trial division by all Gaussian integers formed from this representation should determine one factor of α.

3 Each prime factor p_i of the form $4k+3$ must have even exponent (Theorem 7.1.4). In this case $\pm p_i$, $\pm ip_i$ are the only possible factors in $\mathbb{Z}[i]$ since a $4k+3$ prime cannot be expressed as the sum of two squares.

We leave the reader to construct the program using this algorithm and compare its performance with Program 9.4.

Computer problems 9.3

1 Modify Program 9.4 to display all possible factorisations of a given Gaussian integer.

2 If your computer has a graphics capability, plot the Gaussian primes on an Argand diagram.

3 Write a program that uses only primes in $\mathbb{Z}[\mathrm{i}]$ to factorise $\alpha \in \mathbb{Z}[\mathrm{i}]$ by trial division.

9.4 The fundamental theorem

We are now in a position to prove

Theorem 9.4.1 (*The fundamental theorem of arithmetic for* $\mathbb{Z}[\mathrm{i}]$) Let a ($\neq 0$, $\neq \pm 1$, $\neq \pm \mathrm{i}$) be an element of $\mathbb{Z}[\mathrm{i}]$. Then a is expressible as a product $a = \pi_1 \pi_2 \cdots \pi_r$ of primes in $\mathbb{Z}[\mathrm{i}]$. Further, if $a = \rho_1 \rho_2 \cdots \rho_s$, where the ρ_i are primes in $\mathbb{Z}[\mathrm{i}]$, then (i) $s = r$ and (ii) the π_i and the ρ_j can be paired off so that $\pi_i = u(i, j)\rho_j$ where each $u(i, j)$ is a unit in $\mathbb{Z}[\mathrm{i}]$.

Proof (Sketch: Cf. Theorem 1.3.2 and the informal proof of Theorem 1.4.1 on pp. 43, 44)

(i) (*Existence of the product*) If $N(a)$ is prime in $\mathbb{Z}$, then a itself is a prime element of $\mathbb{Z}[\mathrm{i}]$—by the argument given in Example 9.2.10(ii). In particular, if $N(a) = 2$, then a is expressible as a 'product' with $r = 1$. Now suppose that there is at least one element of $\mathbb{Z}[\mathrm{i}]$ *not* expressible as claimed and of these choose one b, say, with norm $N(b)$ as small as possible. Now b is not itself a prime [why not ?] and so we may write $b = \gamma\delta$, where neither γ nor δ is a unit. But then $N(\gamma) \neq 1$ and $N(\delta) \neq 1$ and, consequently, $N(\gamma) < N(b)$ and $N(\delta) < N(b)$. By choice of b we infer that γ and δ *are* expressible as products of primes—and hence so is b. Thus there are no 'nasty' elements like b. In other words, each a in $\mathbb{Z}[\mathrm{i}]$ *is* expressible as claimed.

(ii) (*Essential uniqueness of the product*) Suppose $a = \pi_1 \pi_2 \cdots \pi_r = \rho_1 \rho_2 \cdots \rho_s$, the π_i, ρ_j being primes in $\mathbb{Z}[\mathrm{i}]$. Then $\pi_1 | a$ and so $\pi_1 | \rho_1 \rho_2 \cdots \rho_s$. By Theorem 9.2.11 we deduce that $\pi_1 | \rho_1$ or $\pi_1 | \rho_2 \rho_3 \cdots \rho_s$. In the former case $\pi_1 = \pm 1$, $\pm \mathrm{i}$, $\pm \rho_1$ or $\pm \mathrm{i}\rho_1$—since ρ_1 is a prime—and, indeed, $\pi_1 = \pm \rho_1$ or $\pm \mathrm{i}\rho_1$ since π_1 is a prime. In the latter case we infer that $\pi_1 | \rho_2$ or $\pi_1 | \rho_3 \cdots \rho_s$, from which $\pi_1 = \pm \rho_2$ or $\pm \mathrm{i}\rho_2$ or $\pi_1 | \rho_3(\rho_4 \cdots \rho_s)$. Continuing in this way we find, eventually, that, for some k, $(1 \leqslant k \leqslant s)$, we have $\pi_1 = \pm \rho_k$ or $\pm \mathrm{i}\rho_k$.

We now rewrite the equality $\pi_1 \pi_2 \cdots \pi_r = \rho_1 \cdots \rho_k \cdots \rho_s$ as

$$u(1, k)\rho_k \pi_2 \cdots \pi_r = \rho_1 \cdots \rho_k \cdots \rho_s,$$

where $u(1, k)$ is one of the units $1, -1, \mathrm{i}, -\mathrm{i}$. Cancelling ρ_k yields $u(1, k)\pi_2 \cdots \pi_r = \rho_1 \cdots \hat{\rho}_k \cdots \rho_s$, the 'hat' indicating that ρ_k is missing from the product. Now apply the same argument to π_2 and the equality $u(1, k)\pi_2 \cdots \pi_r = \rho_1 \cdots \hat{\rho}_k \cdots \rho_s$. Clearly $\pi_2 | \rho_1 \rho_2 \cdots \hat{\rho}_k \cdots \rho_s$ and so $u(2, l)\pi_2 = \rho_l$ for some l $(1 \leqslant l \leqslant s, l \neq k)$ where $u(2, l)$ is a unit. Continuing in this way we pair off the π_i with the ρ_j and then cancel corresponding pairs of πs and ρs from the original equality. It is then clear that $r<s$ and $s<r$ are both impossible—for in each case one would end up with a product of primes (namely the ρs or the πs respectively) being a product of units and hence itself a unit. Thus $r=s$ follows and, on the cancellation of π_{r-1} (with ρ_m, say), we are left with $u(l,k)u(2,l)\cdots u(r-1,m)\pi_r=\rho_t$ (for some t, $1\leqslant t\leqslant s=r$). □

In order to consolidate these ideas we give a swift proof of Theorem 7.1.2 and Exercise 7.1.7.

Theorem 9.4.2 Let p be a prime, in $\mathbb{Z}$, of the form $4k+1$. Then there exist integers u and v such that $p=u^2+v^2$. Furthermore u and v are essentially unique.

Proof As before (see Theorem 3.5.4) we note that, with $x=((p-1)/2)!$, we have $p|1+x^2$ in $\mathbb{Z}$. Thinking of this division as being in $\mathbb{Z}[\mathrm{i}]$, we may write $p|(1+\mathrm{i}x)(1-\mathrm{i}x)$. Now p is not a prime in $\mathbb{Z}[\mathrm{i}]$—since that would imply that $p|1+\mathrm{i}x$ or $p|1-\mathrm{i}x$ in $\mathbb{Z}[\mathrm{i}]$—both of which are impossible since $1/p\pm \mathrm{i}x/p$ do not belong to $\mathbb{Z}[\mathrm{i}]$. Consequently we may write $p=(u+\mathrm{i}v)(a+\mathrm{i}b)$—a product of non-units in $\mathbb{Z}[\mathrm{i}]$.

Taking norms yields $p^2=(u^2+v^2)(a^2+b^2)$. Since neither u^2+v^2 nor a^2+b^2 is equal to 1 [why not?] we are forced to conclude that $u^2+v^2=a^2+b^2=p$, a sum of two squares, as required.

As for uniqueness: suppose $p=c^2+d^2=e^2+f^2$ with $c, d, e, f\in\mathbb{Z}$. Then, in $\mathbb{Z}[\mathrm{i}]$, we have $(c+\mathrm{i}d)(c-\mathrm{i}d)=(e+\mathrm{i}f)(e-\mathrm{i}f)$.

Now each factor has prime norm—namely $c^2+d^2=e^2+f^2=p$ and hence each factor is prime in $\mathbb{Z}[\mathrm{i}]$. From Theorem 9.4.1 we immediately deduce that

$$\begin{aligned} c+\mathrm{i}d = \quad & e+\mathrm{i}f \text{ or } -1(e+\mathrm{i}f) \text{ or } \mathrm{i}(e+\mathrm{i}f) \text{ or } -\mathrm{i}(e+\mathrm{i}f)\\ \text{or } & e-\mathrm{i}f \text{ or } -1(e-\mathrm{i}f) \text{ or } \mathrm{i}(e-\mathrm{i}f) \text{ or } -\mathrm{i}(e-\mathrm{i}f)\,! \end{aligned}$$

and hence that the pair of integers (c, d) is one of the pairs

$$\begin{aligned} & (e,f) \text{ or } (-e,-f) \text{ or } (-f,e) \text{ or } (f,-e)\\ \text{or } & (e,-f) \text{ or } (-e,f) \text{ or } (f,e) \text{ or } (-f,-e). \end{aligned}$$

This establishes the (essential) uniqueness of u and v. □

Exercises 9.4

1 Let $\alpha, \beta, \gamma\in\mathbb{Z}[\mathrm{i}]$ be such that $\alpha\beta=\gamma^2$ and $(\alpha,\beta)=1$. Is it true that α and β are both necessarily squares? What if $\alpha\beta=\gamma^3$? Are α, β each necessarily cubes?

2 Factorise into primes in $\mathbb{Z}[\mathrm{i}]$: 10, 11, 11i, 12 and 27+96i. [*Hint*: $27^2+96^2=3^2\cdot 5\cdot 13\cdot 17$.]

3 Exactly which primes in $\mathbb{Z}$ remain prime in $\mathbb{Z}[\mathrm{i}]$?

4 Show that if $p=\pi_1\pi_2$, where p is an odd prime in $\mathbb{Z}$, then π_1 and π_2 are not associates in $\mathbb{Z}[\mathrm{i}]$.

5 Suppose $u^2+v^2=w^2$ with $u, v, w \in \mathbb{Z}$, $(u, v)=(v, w)=(w, u)=1$ and $uvw \neq 0$. Write $w^2=(u+\mathrm{i}v)(u-\mathrm{i}v)$. Show that $u+\mathrm{i}v$ and $u-\mathrm{i}v$ have gcd equal to 1. Deduce that $u+\mathrm{i}v=\alpha(a+\mathrm{i}b)^2$ where $a, b \in \mathbb{Z}$ and α is a unit. Hence re-prove Theorem 6.2.4.

6 Find all the solutions in integers of the equation $y^2+1=x^3$. [*Hint*: Show y can't be odd—work mod 8. Write $(y-\mathrm{i})(y+\mathrm{i})=x^3$ in $\mathbb{Z}[\mathrm{i}]$. Show that if $d=(y-\mathrm{i}, y+\mathrm{i})$, then $d=u$ or $u(1+\mathrm{i})$ or $2u$, where u is a unit in $\mathbb{Z}[\mathrm{i}]$, and deduce that $d=u$ is the only possibility. Conclude that $y-\mathrm{i}$ and $y+\mathrm{i}$ are cubes, $y+\mathrm{i}=(a+\mathrm{i}b)^3$ say, where $a, b \in \mathbb{Z}$.]

7 Solve completely the equation $y^2+4=x^3$ in $\mathbb{Z}$. (The solution was sent to Frenicle by Fermat.) [*Hint*: If x is odd write $(y-2\mathrm{i})(y+2\mathrm{i})=x^3$. Prove $(y-2\mathrm{i}, y+2\mathrm{i})=1$ and deduce that $y+2\mathrm{i}=(a+\mathrm{i}b)^3$. If x is even, then y is even. Set $x=2u$, $y=2v$ so that

$$\left(\frac{v-1}{2}\right)^2+\left(\frac{v+1}{2}\right)^2=u^3.$$

Now apply the same technique to this equality.]

8 Find the number $S_2(n)$ of representations of $n=u^2+v^2$ as a sum of two squares as follows:

Write $n=2^\alpha\cdot\prod p_j^{r_j}\prod q_k^{s_k}$ in $\mathbb{Z}$ where $p_j(q_k)$ are primes of the form $4k+1$ $(4k+3)$.

Write $n=\mathrm{i}^\alpha(1-\mathrm{i})^{2\alpha}\prod\{(a_j+\mathrm{i}b_j)(a_j-\mathrm{i}b_j)\}^{r_j}\prod q_k^{s_k}$ in $\mathbb{Z}[\mathrm{i}]$, where $a_j>0$, $b_j>0$. Each divisor of n in $\mathbb{Z}[\mathrm{i}]$ is of the form

$$x+\mathrm{i}y=\mathrm{i}^\gamma(1-\mathrm{i})^\beta\prod(a_j+\mathrm{i}b_j)^{\rho_j}(a_j-\mathrm{i}b_j)^{\tau_j}\prod q_k^{\sigma_k}.$$

Then

$$x-\mathrm{i}y=(-\mathrm{i})^\gamma(1+\mathrm{i})^\beta\prod(a_j-\mathrm{i}b_j)^{\rho_j}(a_j+\mathrm{i}b_j)^{\tau_j}\prod q_k^{\sigma_k}.$$

Thus $x^2+y^2=2^\beta\prod(a_j^2+b_j^2)^{\rho_j+\tau_j}\prod q_k^{2\sigma_k}=n$ provided $\beta=\alpha$, $\rho_j+\tau_j=r_j$, $2\sigma_k=s_k$. (Note that each s_k must be even for a representation to exist. See Theorem 7.1.4.) Deduce that $S_2(n)=4\prod(r_j+1)$

9.5 Generalisation: Two problems of Fermat

We now indicate how similar techniques can establish, rigorously, Fermat's claim regarding the integral solutions of the equation $y^2+2=x^3$.

Let d be any integer other than a perfect square. We denote the sets $\{a+b\sqrt{d};\ a, b \in \mathbb{Z}\}$ and $\{a+b\sqrt{d}:\ a, b \in \mathbb{Q}\}$ by $\mathbb{Z}[\sqrt{d}]$ and $\mathbb{Q}[\sqrt{d}]$ respectively. For $\alpha=r+s\sqrt{d} \in \mathbb{Q}[\sqrt{d}]$ we define the *norm* $N(\alpha)$ of α to be the quantity $|r^2-ds^2|$. (Note that the modulus sign, introduced to keep norms from being negative, is unnecessary if $d<0$.) It is easily checked that for $\alpha, \beta \in \mathbb{Q}[\sqrt{d}]$, $N(\alpha\beta)=N(\alpha)N(\beta)$. Using definitions and proofs which correspond word for word with those of Definitions 9.2.4 and 9.2.9 and Theorems 9.2.5, 9.2.6, 9.2.11 and 9.4.1, we can prove the fundamental theorem of arithmetic for the sets $\mathbb{Z}[\sqrt{-2}]$, $\mathbb{Z}[\sqrt{2}]$ and $\mathbb{Z}[\sqrt{3}]$. Noting that the only units in $\mathbb{Z}[\sqrt{-2}]$ are 1 and -1 (Exercise 9.5.1(b)) we are ready to prove

Theorem 9.5.1 The only integral solutions of the equation $y^2+2=x^3$ are $(x, y)=(3, 5)$ and $(3, -5)$.

Proof We first rewrite the equation as $(y+\sqrt{-2})(y-\sqrt{-2})=x^3$. We shall prove that the two factors on the left-hand side have (in $\mathbb{Z}[\sqrt{-2}]$) no common divisors other than 1 and -1 and will then deduce, legally, that each of these factors is a cube of some element in $\mathbb{Z}[\sqrt{-2}]$, so that Euler's conclusion, given in Section 9.1 is valid.

So assume that π is a prime element in $\mathbb{Z}[\sqrt{-2}]$ which divides (in $\mathbb{Z}[\sqrt{-2}]$) each of $y+\sqrt{-2}$ and $y-\sqrt{-2}$. Then π divides $(y+\sqrt{-2})-(y-\sqrt{-2})=2\sqrt{-2}=-(\sqrt{-2})^3$. It follows that $\pi|\sqrt{-2}$; $\pi v=\sqrt{-2}$, say. This implies that $N(\pi)N(v)=N(\sqrt{-2})$ in $\mathbb{Z}$. Since $N(\pi)\neq 1$ and $N(\sqrt{-2})=2$ we deduce that $N(\pi)=2$ and $N(v)=1$. Thus $v=\pm 1$ and $\pi=\pm\sqrt{-2}$. Consequently $\sqrt{-2}|y+\sqrt{-2}$, implying that $\sqrt{-2}|y$ (still in $\mathbb{Z}[\sqrt{-2}]$). It follows that $N(\sqrt{-2})|N(y)$, that is, $2|y^2$ in $\mathbb{Z}$. Hence y is even and y^2 is a multiple of 4. This implies that x^3 $(=y^2+2)$ is even and therefore a multiple of 8. But since $y^2\equiv 0 \pmod 4$ we see that $y^2+2\not\equiv 0 \pmod 4$ and hence, certainly, $y^2+2\not\equiv 0 \pmod 8$. This contradiction shows that there can be no prime divisor common to $y+\sqrt{-2}$ and $y-\sqrt{-2}$. Uniqueness of factorisation in $\mathbb{Z}[\sqrt{-2}]$ now implies (cf. Exercises 9.4.1 and 9.5.4), that each of $y+\sqrt{-2}$ and $y-\sqrt{-2}$ is a cube* in $\mathbb{Z}[\sqrt{-2}]$, as claimed.

Euler's argument then finishes the proof. □

The above wording that 'we can prove the fundamental theorem of arithmetic for the sets $\mathbb{Z}[\sqrt{-2}]$, $\mathbb{Z}[\sqrt{2}]$ and $\mathbb{Z}[\sqrt{3}]$' implicitly suggests that the same approach cannot establish the fundamental theorem for, say, $\mathbb{Z}[\sqrt{-3}]$. The first sign of trouble arises on trying to establish the analogue of Theorem 9.2.5. Applying the same techniques to $\mathbb{Z}[\sqrt{-3}]$ one finds that, with $\alpha=a+b\sqrt{-3}$ and $\beta=c+d\sqrt{-3}$, one has $\alpha/\beta=u+v\sqrt{-3}$ where $u, v\in\mathbb{Q}$. Choosing $U, V\in\mathbb{Z}$ such that $|u-U|\leq\frac{1}{2}$ and $|v-V|\leq\frac{1}{2}$ and writing $\alpha=\beta\{U+\mathrm{i}V\}+r$, where $r=\beta\{(u-U)+(v-V)\sqrt{-3}\}$, we find

$$N(r)=N(\beta)\{(u-U)^2+3(v-V)^2\}\leq N(\beta)\{(\tfrac{1}{2})^2+3(\tfrac{1}{2})^2\}=N(\beta).$$

That is, $N(r)$ *may not be strictly less than* $N(\beta)$.

This failure of the division algorithm for $\mathbb{Z}[\sqrt{-3}]$ does not of itself imply failure of the fundamental theorem. Maybe it is accessible by a different route? Sadly one is doomed to disappointment!—as the following example shows.

* In fact each of $y\pm\sqrt{-2}$ is of the form uc^3, where u is a unit in $\mathbb{Z}[\sqrt{-2}]$. But since $1=1^3$ and $-1=(-1)^3$ we can rewrite uc^3 as $(uc)^3$—a cube!

Example 9.5.2 Consider, in $\mathbb{Z}[\sqrt{-3}]$, the number 4 $(=4+0\sqrt{-3})$. Now $4=(2+0\sqrt{-3})(2-0\sqrt{-3})=(1+\sqrt{-3})(1-\sqrt{-3})$. We claim that each of these factors is a prime in $\mathbb{Z}[\sqrt{-3}]$.

For if, say, $1+\sqrt{-3}=(a+b\sqrt{-3})(c+d\sqrt{-3})$ we should have, on taking norms, that $4=(a^2+3b^2)(c^2+3d^2)$ in $\mathbb{Z}$. Since neither $a^2+3b^2=2$ nor $c^2+3d^2=2$ is possible for integers a, b, c, d, we see that one of a^2+3b^2, c^2+3d^2 is 1, the other being 4. (Why can't we have -1 and -4?) But, if $a^2+3b^2=1$ then $a=\pm 1$ and $b=0$. Consequently $a+b\sqrt{-3}$ is 1 or -1, that is, it is a unit of $\mathbb{Z}[\sqrt{-3}]$. This proves that $1+\sqrt{-3}$ is a prime in $\mathbb{Z}[\sqrt{-3}]$. The primeness of the factors $1-\sqrt{-3}$ and 2 is proved likewise. Now, if the fundamental theorem did hold we should be able to infer from the two representations of 4 that $2=\pm(1+\sqrt{-3})$ or $2=\pm(1-\sqrt{-3})$, both of which are silly. Thus the fundamental theorem must fail in $\mathbb{Z}[\sqrt{-3}]$.

Curiously enough, the very desirable property of uniqueness of factorisation can be regained by extending $\mathbb{Z}[\sqrt{-3}]$ to the slightly larger set $E=\{(a+b\sqrt{-3})/2\colon a, b\in\mathbb{Z}$ and a, b are both even or both odd$\}$ (This is reminiscent of Exercise 1.4.1 where, when the set H of Hilbert numbers with its lack of unique factorisation is replaced by the set of all positive odd integers, uniqueness of factorisation is restored.) Exercise 9.5.5 shows that E is nothing other than the set $\{a+b\zeta\colon a, b\in\mathbb{Z}\}$ where $\zeta=(-1+\mathrm{i}\sqrt{3})/2$ is one of the complex cube roots of unity. Thus E is, for the case $p=3$, the same set with which Lamé had hoped to prove the FC (see Section 6.4). In fact, for $p=3$, Lamé's programme *can* be carried through as, following Gauss, we shall now show.

Working with E in its $\mathbb{Z}[\zeta]$ form we first note that

$$N(a+b\zeta)=N(a-b/2+\mathrm{i}b\sqrt{3}/2)=a^2-ab+b^2=(a+b\zeta)(a+b\zeta^2),$$

since $0=\zeta^3-1=(\zeta-1)(\zeta^2+\zeta+1)$, so that $\zeta^2+\zeta=-1$. Of course, the equality $N(\alpha\beta)=N(\alpha)N(\beta)$ above immediately implies that here

$$N\{(a+b\zeta)(c+d\zeta)\}=N(a+b\zeta)N(c+d\zeta).$$

We claim that for E, as distinct from $\mathbb{Z}[\sqrt{-3}]$, there is a division algorithm in which the norm function N behaves properly. That is, we have

Theorem 9.5.3 (*The division algorithm in E*) Let $\alpha=a+b\zeta$, $\beta=c+d\zeta\in E$ with $\beta\neq 0$. Then there exist $m, r\in E$ such that $\alpha=m\beta+r$, where $0\leqslant N(r)<N(\beta)$.

Proof

$$\frac{\alpha}{\beta}=\frac{a+b\zeta}{c+d\zeta}=\frac{(a+b\zeta)(c+d\zeta^2)}{(c+d\zeta)(c+d\zeta^2)}=u+v\zeta,$$

where $u, v\in\mathbb{Q}$ and where $(c+d\zeta)(c+d\zeta^2)=c^2-cd+d^2\in\mathbb{Z}$.

We now choose $U, V\in\mathbb{Z}$ such that (again!) $|u-U|\leqslant\frac{1}{2}$ and $|v-V|\leqslant\frac{1}{2}$. Then $\alpha=\beta\{U+V\zeta\}+r$, where $r=\beta\{(u-U)+(v-V)\zeta\}$. It follows that

$$\begin{aligned}N(r)&=N(\beta)N\{(u-U)+(v-V)\zeta\}\\&=N(\beta)\{(u-U)^2-(u-U)(v-V)+(v-V)^2\}.\end{aligned}$$

Now the second term has absolute value not exceeding

$$(u-U)^2+|u-U|\cdot|v-V|+(v-V)^2\leqslant(\tfrac{1}{2})^2+(\tfrac{1}{2})^2+(\tfrac{1}{2})^2<1.$$

Consequently $N(r)<N(\beta)$ as required. □

It is this result which allows the Euclidean algorithm to function in E which, in turn, allows us to prove that each pair α, β of non-zero numbers from E has a gcd expressible in the form $s\alpha+t\beta$ with s and t in E. This then permits the proof for E of the analogue of Theorem 9.2.11 and hence the fundamental theorem of arithmetic for E in the manner we have seen above for $\mathbb{Z}[i]$.

From this follows Gauss's proof of the FC in the case $n=3$. The method used is 'descent'.

Theorem 9.5.4 The equation $x^3+y^3+z^3=0$ has no solution in non-zero elements of

$$\mathbb{Z}[\zeta]=\mathbb{Z}\left[\frac{-1+\sqrt{-3}}{2}\right].$$

In particular it has no solution in non-zero integers.

Proof Suppose that $\alpha, \beta, \gamma\in\mathbb{Z}[\zeta]$ *do* satisfy $x^3+y^3+z^3=0$ and that $\alpha\beta\gamma\neq 0$. We may suppose that α, β, γ have no common prime factor in $\mathbb{Z}[\zeta]$—otherwise cancel it and start afresh. We may therefore assume that $(\alpha,\beta)=(\beta,\gamma)=(\gamma,\alpha)=1$ in $\mathbb{Z}[\zeta]$ [why?]. Set $a=\beta+\gamma$, $b=\gamma+\alpha$, $c=\alpha+\beta$. Then

$$(a+b+c)^3-24abc=(b+c-a)^3+(c+a-b)^3+(a+b-c)^3=0.$$

Setting $\pi=1-\zeta$ we get $N(\pi)=3$. Hence π is a prime in $\mathbb{Z}[\zeta]$. Now

$$-\zeta^2\pi^2=-\zeta^2(1-\zeta)^2=-\zeta^2(1-2\zeta+\zeta^2)=3.$$

Hence $\pi|3$ in $\mathbb{Z}[\zeta]$ and so $\pi|24abc=(a+b+c)^3$. Consequently $\pi^3|(a+b+c)^3=24abc$, whence $\pi|abc$. [For if $\pi^3|24$, then $\pi^3|24-3^3=-3=\pi^2\zeta^2$ so that $\pi|\zeta^2$, a contradiction since ζ is a unit in $\mathbb{Z}[\zeta]$.] If $\pi|a$ then

$$\pi|a^3=(\beta+\gamma)^3=\beta^3+\gamma^3+3\beta^2\gamma+3\beta\gamma^2.$$

Since $\pi|3$ we have $\pi|\beta^3+\gamma^3=-\alpha^3$. Hence $\pi|\alpha$ so that $\pi\nmid\beta$ and $\pi\nmid\gamma$.

Now it can be shown (Exercise 9.5.15) that there are e and f belonging to $\mathbb{Z}$ such that* $\beta\zeta^e\equiv 1$ or $-1 \pmod 3$ and $\gamma\zeta^f\equiv 1$ or $-1\pmod 3$ in $\mathbb{Z}[\zeta]$. Since $(\beta\zeta^e)^3=\beta^3$ and $(\gamma\zeta^f)^3=\gamma^3$, we may assume that the β and γ given at the outset satisfy $\beta\equiv 1$ or -1 and $\gamma\equiv 1$ or -1. However, we cannot have $\beta\equiv 1$ *and* $\gamma\equiv 1$. For, if so, we would have $\beta^3+\gamma^3\equiv 1+1\pmod 3$ in $\mathbb{Z}[\zeta]$. Since $\pi|\alpha$ we have $\pi|\alpha^3$ and since $\pi|3$ we should have $\pi|\alpha^3+\beta^3+\gamma^3-2=0-2=-2$, from which $\pi|-2+3=1$, a contradiction. The congruences $\beta\equiv\gamma\equiv -1$ lead to a similar contradiction. Thus WLOG we may suppose that $\beta\equiv 1$ and that $\gamma\equiv -1$, that is $\beta=1+3\lambda$, $\gamma=-1+3\mu$, where $\lambda, \mu\in\mathbb{Z}[\zeta]$.

* As you might expect, we write $\alpha\equiv\beta\pmod\gamma$ (in $\mathbb{Z}[\zeta]$) to mean $\gamma|\alpha-\beta$ (in $\mathbb{Z}[\zeta]$).

It follows that $\beta^3+\gamma^3=(1+3\lambda)^3+(-1+3\mu)^3$ is a multiple of 3^2 and hence of π^4 in $\mathbb{Z}[\zeta]$. Set

$$A=\frac{\beta+\gamma\zeta}{\pi}, \qquad B=\frac{\beta\zeta+\gamma}{\pi}, \qquad C=\frac{(\beta+\gamma)\zeta^2}{\pi}.$$

[Do $A, B, C\in\mathbb{Z}[\zeta]$?]

Then $A+B+C=0$ whilst $ABC=(\beta^3+\gamma^3)/\pi^3=(-\alpha/\pi)^3$. Recalling that $\pi^3|\beta^3+\gamma^3$, we see that $\pi|ABC$ and hence $\pi^3|ABC$.

Next $\beta=-\zeta A+\zeta^2 B$ and $\gamma=\zeta^2 A-\zeta B$ so that $(A, B)=1$ in $\mathbb{Z}[\zeta]$. [Otherwise we would have $(\beta, \gamma)\neq 1$ in $\mathbb{Z}[\zeta]$.] Thus from $A+B+C=0$ we find $(B, C)=(C, A)=1$ in $\mathbb{Z}[\zeta]$.

From $(A, B)=(B, C)=(C, A)=1$ and $\pi^3|ABC=(-\alpha/\pi)^3$ we deduce that (i), except for the possible presence of units, A, B, C are all cubes in $\mathbb{Z}[\zeta]$ (cf. Exercise 9.5.4) and (ii) π divides exactly one of A, B, C—let us suppose C. Set $A=u_1\phi^3$, $B=u_2\chi^3$, $C=u_3\psi^3$, where u_1, u_2, u_3 are units in $\mathbb{Z}[\zeta]$. From $A+B+C=0$ we get, on multiplying through by u_1^{-1}, $\phi^3+u_4\chi^3+u_5\psi^3=0$, where u_4, u_5 are units. Since $\pi^3|C$ we have $\phi^3+u_4\chi^3\equiv 0(\text{mod }\pi^3)$. Since $\pi\nmid\phi$ and $\pi\nmid\chi$ we may write $\phi^3\equiv\pm 1(\text{mod }\pi^3)$ and $\chi^3\equiv\pm 1(\text{mod }\pi^3)$. [For, each element ν, say, of $\mathbb{Z}[\zeta]$ is of the form $z_1+z_2\zeta$ and hence of the form $z_3+z_4\pi$ where $z_1, z_2, z_3, z_4\in\mathbb{Z}$. From $\pi\nmid z_3+z_4\pi$ we deduce that $\pi\nmid z_3$. Since $\pi|3$ we see that z_3 is not a multiple of 3, in $\mathbb{Z}$. Hence $z_3\equiv 1$ or $z_3\equiv -1(\text{mod }3)$ in $\mathbb{Z}$. It follows that z_3, and hence ν, is congruent to 1 or $-1(\text{mod }\pi)$ in $\mathbb{Z}[\zeta]$. From $\nu=\pm 1+\sigma\pi$ $(\sigma\in\mathbb{Z}[\zeta])$, we find that

$$\nu^3=\pm 1+3\sigma\pi\pm 3\sigma^2\pi^2+\sigma^3\pi^3\equiv\pm 1(\text{mod }\pi^3)$$

as required.] We deduce that, mod π^3, $0\equiv\phi^3+u_4\chi^3\equiv\pm 1\pm u_4$. But, by Exercise 9.5.5, $u_4=\pm 1$, $\pm\zeta$ or $\pm\zeta^2$. The congruence $\pm 1\pm u_4\equiv 0(\text{mod }\pi^3)$ shows that $u_4=1$ or $u_4=-1$ are the only possibilities. Since $u_4=u_1^{-1}u_2$ we find that $u_2=\pm u_1$. But $u_1u_2u_3$ is a unit and a cube. Hence $u_1u_2u_3=\pm 1$ whence $u_3=\pm 1/u_1u_2=\pm 1/u_1^2=\pm u_1$. Thus the equalities $A+B+C=0$ and $ABC=(-\alpha/\pi)^3$ yield the equations $\phi^3+(\pm\chi)^3+(\pm\psi)^3=0$ and $(\phi\chi\psi)^3=(\pm\alpha/\pi)^3$.

Finally note that if the total number of πs (or associates of π) occurring in the decomposition of $\alpha\beta\gamma$ into a product of primes is n then, since they all occur in α, their total number in $\phi\chi\psi$ is $n-1$. Repeating the above process a further $n-1$ times we arrive at a solution to $x^3+y^3+z^3=0$ in which no πs are present. But this is a contradiction of the remarks of the opening paragraph of this proof, a contradiction which completes the proof. □

The programs in Section 9.4 can be easily modified to handle numbers in $\mathbb{Z}[\sqrt{d}]$ and $\mathbb{Z}[\zeta]$. We present without further comment just two of the modified programs to indicate the changes, which are highlighted in italics.

Program 9.5 *The division algorithm in $\mathbb{Z}[\sqrt{D}]$ (for suitable D)*

```
 10 DIM a(2),b(2),m(2),r(2)
 20 INPUT "enter the first number ",a(1),a(2)
 30 INPUT "enter the second number ",b(1),b(2)
 40 INPUT " enter the value of D ",D
 50 c=b(1)^2-D*b(2)^2
 60 u=(a(1)*b(1)-D*a(2)*b(2))/c
 70 v=(a(2)*b(1)-a(1)*b(2))/c
 80 m(1)=INT(u+0.5)
 90 m(2)=INT(v+0.5)
100 r(1)=a(1)-m(1)*b(1)-D*m(2)*b(2)
110 r(2)=a(2)-m(1)*b(2)-m(2)*b(1)
120 PRINT "The quotient is ";m(1);" + ";m(2);"root(";D;")"
130 PRINT "The remainder is ";r(1);" + ";r(2);"root(";D;")"
140 c1=ABS(r(1)^2-D*r(2)^2)
150 IF c1=ABS(c) PRINT "failed - Norm r = ";c1," is >= to Norm a = ";ABS(c)
```

Program 9.6 *Factorization by trial division in $\mathbb{Z}[\xi]$*

```
 10 DIM a(2),b(2),m(2),r(2)
 20 INPUT a(1),a(2)
 30 c=a(1)^2+a(2)^2-a(1)*a(2)
 40 croot=SQR(c)
 50 FOR i=1 TO INT(croot)
 60   FOR j=0 TO INT(croot)
 70     k=1
 80     b(1)=i:b(2)=j
 90       IF k=2 THEN b(1)=-i
100       IF k=3 THEN b(2)=-j
110       IF k=4 THEN b(1)=i
120       c1=b(1)^2+b(2)^2-b(1)*b(2)
130       IF c1>c OR c1=1 GOTO 230
140       u=(a(1)*b(1)+a(2)*b(2)-a(1)*b(2))/c1
150       v=(a(2)*b(1)-a(1)*b(2))/c1
160       IF (u=INT(u)) AND (v=INT(v)) GOTO 210
170       k=k+1
180     IF k<5 GOTO 90
190   NEXT j
200 NEXT i
205 REM z represents zeta
210 PRINT b(1);" + ";b(2);"z"
220 c=u^2+v^2-u*v
230 IF c=1 PRINT u;" + ";v;"z": STOP
240 a(1)=u:a(2)=v
250 GOTO 40
```

Exercises 9.5

1 (a) Show that if, in $\mathbb{Z}[\sqrt{d}]$, $a+b\sqrt{d}\,|\,r+s\sqrt{d}$, then $a-b\sqrt{d}\,|\,r-s\sqrt{d}$.
(b) Show that $a+b\sqrt{d}$ is a unit in $\mathbb{Z}[\sqrt{d}]$ iff $a^2-db^2=\pm 1$. Hence show that for $d<0$ the only units in $\mathbb{Z}[\sqrt{d}]$ are 1 and -1.
(c) Show that, for each $n\in\mathbb{Z}$, $\pm(\sqrt{2}-1)^n$ is a unit in $\mathbb{Z}[\sqrt{2}]$. Are there any more (apart from 1 and -1)? What about units in $\mathbb{Z}[\sqrt{13}]$? (You'll find the answer in Chapter 11.)

2 Show that the analogues of Theorems 9.2.5, 9.2.6 and 9.2.11 hold for the systems $\mathbb{Z}[\sqrt{d}]$ for $d=-2$, 2 and 3. [*Hint*: Work in $\mathbb{Z}[\sqrt{d}]$ without specifying the value of d but checking that what you write is, at each stage, equally acceptable for $d=-2$, 2 and 3. Don't work out each case separately in full.]

3 Show that the fundamental theorem of arithmetic (cf. Theorem 9.4.1) holds for $\mathbb{Z}[\sqrt{-2}]$, $\mathbb{Z}[\sqrt{2}]$ and $\mathbb{Z}[\sqrt{3}]$. [*Hint*: Same as for the previous exercise.]

4 Let $\alpha, \beta, \gamma \in \mathbb{Z}[\sqrt{3}]$ be such that $\alpha\beta = \gamma^3$ where α, β have 1 as a gcd. Show that $\alpha = ua^3$, $\beta = vb^3$ where $a, b \in \mathbb{Z}[\sqrt{3}]$, u and v being units in $\mathbb{Z}[\sqrt{3}]$.

5 Show that E, that is the set $\{(a+b\sqrt{-3})/2\colon a, b \in \mathbb{Z}, a \equiv b \pmod 2\}$, is identical to the set $\{c+d\zeta\colon c, d \in \mathbb{Z}\}$ where $\zeta = (-1+\sqrt{-3})/2$. Find the units in E. (There are six.)

6 Let $d \in \mathbb{Z}$, $d \neq 0, 1$. Show that each non-zero non-unit element of $\mathbb{Z}[\sqrt{d}]$ is expressible as a product of primes of $\mathbb{Z}[\sqrt{d}]$. Prove that $\mathbb{Z}[\sqrt{d}]$ has infinitely many primes.

7 Let $\alpha = 10+69\sqrt{-2}$, $\beta = 10+18\sqrt{-2}$ in $\mathbb{Z}[\sqrt{-2}]$. Find an m and an r in $\mathbb{Z}[\sqrt{-2}]$ such that $\alpha = m\beta + r$ where $0 \leqslant N(r) < N(\beta)$. Go on to find the gcd of α and β in $\mathbb{Z}[\sqrt{-2}]$.

8 Show that 3 is not a prime in $\mathbb{Z}[\sqrt{-3}]$. Is it a prime in $\mathbb{Z}[\sqrt{5}]$ or in $\mathbb{Z}[\sqrt{-5}]$?

9 Show that $(5+\sqrt{2})(2-\sqrt{2}) = (11-7\sqrt{2})(2+\sqrt{2})$ with all factors prime in $\mathbb{Z}[\sqrt{2}]$. Doesn't this contradict the statement of the Exercise 3?

10 Show, in $\mathbb{Z}[\sqrt{-7}]$, that 8 is expressible as a product of two and also of three primes. (Consequently, out of the window goes the plausible 'Theorem' that 'Even if the prime factorisation isn't unique, at least the number of prime factors in each decomposition of an element into primes is unique.')

11 Find five values of d for which $\mathbb{Z}[\sqrt{d}]$ does not have uniqueness of factorisation—that is it does not satisfy the analogue of Theorem 9.4.1.

12 Show that $\mathbb{Z}[\sqrt{5}]$ does not satisfy the analogue of Theorem 9.4.1 but that $\mathbb{Z}(\sqrt{5}) = \{(a+b\sqrt{5})/2\colon a, b \in \mathbb{Z}$ and $a \equiv b \pmod 2\}$, which contains $\mathbb{Z}[\sqrt{5}]$, does.

13 Let d be such that $\mathbb{Z}[\sqrt{d}]$ has unique factorisation. Let p be a prime in $\mathbb{Z}$. Then p is a product of no more than two primes in $\mathbb{Z}[\sqrt{d}]$. Show that if p is odd and if $(p, d)=1$ in $\mathbb{Z}$, then p is a product of exactly two primes iff $(d/p)=1$. [*Hint*: $(d/p)=1 \Leftrightarrow p \mid (x-\sqrt{d})(x+\sqrt{d})$ for suitable $x \in \mathbb{Z}$.]

14 Let p be an odd prime in $\mathbb{Z}$ such that $p \mid a^2+3b^2$ in $\mathbb{Z}$, where $(a, b)=1$. Then $p \mid (a-\sqrt{-3}b)(a+\sqrt{-3}b)$ in E. Deduce (i) p cannot be prime in E; (ii) $4p$ and hence p is of the form $u^2+3v^2 (u, v \in \mathbb{Z})$. [*Hint*: The formulae of Exercise 7.1.6(iv) might help again.]

15 Show that there exist integers e, f as in the proof of Theorem 9.5.4 as follows. Let $\beta = x+y\zeta \in \mathbb{Z}[\zeta]$. Then $\beta = u+v\pi$ where $u, v \in \mathbb{Z}$. Since $\pi \nmid \beta$

in $\mathbb{Z}[\zeta]$ we see that $3 \nmid u$ in $\mathbb{Z}$. Hence $u \equiv 1$ or $-1 \pmod 3$. Suppose $\beta \equiv 1 + v\pi \pmod 3$ in $\mathbb{Z}[\zeta]$ (the other case being similar). Since $3 \mid \pi^2$,

$$\begin{aligned}\beta\zeta^e &\equiv (1+v\pi)(1-\pi)^e \equiv (1+v\pi)(1-e\pi)\\ &\equiv 1+(v-e)\pi \pmod{\pi} \text{ in } \mathbb{Z}[\zeta].\end{aligned}$$

Taking $e = v$ does the trick. (Any problem if v is negative?)

Computer problems 9.5

1 Modify Program 9.4 to factorise integers in $\mathbb{Z}[\sqrt{d}]$ and use it to examine the behaviour of the primes in $\mathbb{Z}$ when considered as elements of $\mathbb{Z}[\sqrt{-2}]$.

2 Using Program 9.6 as a basis, explore the behaviour of the $\mathbb{Z}$ primes when considered as elements of $\mathbb{Z}[\zeta]$. Use the resulting prime factors to construct a picture in the Argand diagram of the primes in $\mathbb{Z}[\zeta]$.

9.6 Lucas's test

We end this chapter by obtaining a test, first proposed by Edouard Lucas in 1876, which, in theory if not always in practice, can determine whether or not a given Mersenne number M_p, p being any odd prime, is itself prime or composite. A curious feature here is that when M_p *is* composite no (non-trivial) factor is revealed!

Lucas's various statements of his results and, even more so, his proofs, were far from clear and it was left to others to tidy up and complete his efforts. Lucas originally employed certain divisibility properties of the Fibonacci numbers (see, for example, Exercise 0.5.2(viii)). As is often the case in mathematics, later workers have found different proofs once the pioneering work has been done. The proof we give here was found by A. E. Western in 1932 ([Q]). It makes use of the properties of the numbers $\mathbb{Z}[\sqrt{3}] = \{a + b\sqrt{3}\colon a, b \in \mathbb{Z}\}$ which, as we've seen (Exercise 9.5.3), is a number system in which the fundamental theorem of arithmetic holds. That is, factorisation into products of primes is (essentially) unique.

We prove Lucas's theorem before stating it so as not to burden you with too much preliminary notation. Note that if, in $\mathbb{Z}[\sqrt{3}]$, u, v and w are elements such that $w \mid u - v$, we shall write $u \equiv v \pmod w$—just as we have done in $\mathbb{Z}$ and in Section 9.5. So here we go . . .

(A) Let $N = M_p = 2^p - 1$ $(p \geqslant 3)$ be a Mersenne number and suppose that N is prime. Trivially, $N \equiv -1 \pmod 8$ and, since p is odd, $N \equiv 1 \pmod 3$, congruences which lead easily to $N \equiv 7 \pmod{12}$.

Put $\mu = 1 + \sqrt{3}$ and $\nu = 1 - \sqrt{3}$. Then, in $\mathbb{Z}[\sqrt{3}]$, we have, by the binomial theorem,

$$(1+\sqrt{3})^N \equiv 1^N + (\sqrt{3})^N = 1 + \sqrt{3}.(3)^{(N-1)/2} \pmod N.$$

(Recall N is prime in $\mathbb{Z}$ so that all the 'middle' coefficients in the binomial expansion are multiples of N in $\mathbb{Z}$ and hence in $\mathbb{Z}[\sqrt{3}]$.)

Next, by Lemma 8.3.1(iii), we have $3^{(N-1)/2} \equiv (3/N) \equiv -((12k+7)/3) \equiv -1 \pmod N$. Hence $\mu^N = (1+\sqrt{3})^N \equiv 1-\sqrt{3} = \nu \pmod N$. Now $\mu\nu = -2$. We therefore have

$$(\mu\nu)^{(N-1)/2} = (-2)^{(N-1)/2} \equiv (-2/N) \equiv -1 \pmod N$$

by Exercise 8.4.3—since N is of the form $8k+7$. Consequently

$$\mu^N(-1) \equiv \nu(\mu\nu)^{(N-1)/2} \pmod N \tag{I}$$

But $\mu = \sigma\nu$, where $\sigma = -2-\sqrt{3}$ is a unit in $\mathbb{Z}[\sqrt{3}]$. We may therefore rewrite (I) as

$$\sigma^N\nu^N(-1) \equiv \nu(\sigma\nu^2)^{(N-1)/2} \pmod N.$$

Since N is a prime in $\mathbb{Z}[\sqrt{3}]$ (Exercise 9.6.1) and $N \nmid \nu$ in $\mathbb{Z}[\sqrt{3}]$ and since σ is a unit, the previous congruence reduces to $\sigma^{(N+1)/2} \equiv -1 \pmod N$, that is,

$$\sigma^{2^{p-1}} \equiv -1 \pmod N. \tag{II}$$

If we now define the sequence $\{r_i\}$ by

$$r_i = \sigma^{2^{i-1}} + \tau^{2^{i-1}} \qquad \text{where } \tau = -2+\sqrt{3}, \tag{III}$$

we find $r_1 = -4$ and, for $i \geq 2$, $r_i = r_{i-1}^2 - 2$, and we obtain the sequence -4, 14, 194, 37 634, ...

From (II) and (III) we deduce immediately that

$$r_{p-1}^2 = r_p + 2 \equiv (-1-1)+2 \equiv 0 \pmod N.$$

At this point we end the first part of the argument.

(B) We now assume that $N = M_p = 2^p - 1$ is composite. We shall suppose that $r_{p-1} \equiv 0 \pmod N$ and aim to get a contradiction to this congruence.

Since N is of the form $12k+7$ at least one of its prime divisors (in $\mathbb{Z}$), q, say, must be of the form $12k+5$ or $12k+7$—and hence remain a prime when considered as a member of $\mathbb{Z}[\sqrt{3}]$. From our assumption on r_{p-1} we see that:

(i) $r_p = r_{p-1}^2 - 2 \equiv -2 \pmod N$ and
(ii) $0 \equiv r_{p-1} = \sigma^{2^{p-2}} + \tau^{2^{p-2}} \pmod N$.

From (ii) we deduce $\sigma^{2^{p-1}} \equiv \tau^{2^{p-1}} \pmod N$, so that

$$-2 \equiv r_p \equiv \sigma^{2^{p-1}} + \tau^{2^{p-1}} \equiv 2\sigma^{2^{p-1}}.$$

Hence $\sigma^{2^{p-1}} \equiv -1 \pmod N$, from which it follows that $\sigma^{2^{p-1}} \equiv -1 \pmod q$ and $\sigma^{2^p} \equiv 1 \pmod q$.

Now each prime factor q of $N = 2^p - 1$ is of the form $8k \pm 1$ (Theorems 3.2.6 and 3.2.7). Suppose first that $q \equiv 7 \pmod{12}$—so that $q \equiv -1 \pmod 8$ (why?). Then $(\mu\nu)^{(q-1)/2} = (-2)^{(q-1)/2} \equiv (-2/q) \equiv -1 \pmod q$, so that, as in part (A),

(i) $\mu^q \equiv \nu(\text{mod } q)$ and (ii) $\sigma^{(q+1)/2} \equiv -1(\text{mod } q)$. Now (ii) implies that $\sigma^{q+1} \equiv 1(\text{mod } q)$. From this and the congruence $\sigma^{2^p} \equiv 1(\text{mod } q)$ above we conclude that $\sigma^d \equiv 1(\text{mod } q)$, where $d = (q+1, 2^p) = 2^e$ for some $e \leqslant p$. But if $e < p$ we have the contradictory congruences $\sigma^{2^e} \equiv 1$ and $\sigma^{2^{p-1}} \equiv -1(\text{mod } q)$. Consequently $2^p | q+1$, that is, $q = 2^p k - 1$. But since $q|N$ this implies $k = 1$ and $q = N$.

Finally, if $q \equiv 5(\text{mod } 12)$—so that $q \equiv 1(\text{mod } 8)$—a similar argument shows that $q+1 \equiv 0(\text{mod } 2^{p+1})$—an impossibility since $q+1$ is of the form $2(6k+3)$.

This concludes the proof of the

Theorem 9.6.1 Let $N = M_p = 2^p - 1$ where p is any odd prime. Let $\{r_i\}$ be the sequence defined by $r_1 = 4$, $r_i = r_{i-1}^2 - 2$. Then N is prime iff $r_{p-1} \equiv 0(\text{mod } N)$. □

Exercises 9.6

1 Show that, if s is a prime (in $\mathbb{Z}$) of the form $12k+5$ or $12k+7$, then s remains prime in $\mathbb{Z}[\sqrt{3}]$. [*Hint*: If $s = (a+b\sqrt{3})(c+d\sqrt{3})$ where neither factor is a unit, then $s^2 = (a^2-3b^2)(c^2-3d^2)$. Then each of a^2-3b^2, c^2-3d^2 is equal to $\pm p$. Thus $(b, p) = 1$ and 3 is a q.r. mod p. Now use Exercise 8.5.1.)

2 Prove that the primes in $\mathbb{Z}[\sqrt{3}]$ are (i) $\sqrt{3}-1$ (ii) $\sqrt{3}$, (iii) all the primes of the form $12k \pm 5$ in $\mathbb{Z}$, (iv) all the numbers of the form $a + b\sqrt{3}$, where $|a^2 - 3b^2|$ is a prime of the form $12k \pm 1$, (v) all associates of primes of types (i), (ii), (iii), (iv). [*Hint*: If $a+b\sqrt{3}$ is a prime in $\mathbb{Z}[\sqrt{3}]$, then so is $a - b\sqrt{3}$. Their product is in $\mathbb{Z}$. Factorise it in $\mathbb{Z}$, if you can.]

3 Use Theorem 9.6.1 to check, by hand, that $M_7 = 127$ is a prime! [*Hint*: *Don't* calculate all the r_i $(1 \leqslant i \leqslant 7)$ *before* working mod 127.]

4 Prove, by hand, by Lucas's method, that $2^{13} - 1$ is prime. (Now marvel that Lucas showed, by hand, that $M_{127} = 2^{127} - 1$ is prime!)

Computer problem 9.6

1 Check M_{31} is prime by using Lucas's test.

10
Arithmetic functions

10.1 Introduction

In earlier chapters we have met various functions f whose domain of definition—that is, the set of all those x for which $f(x)$ is defined—is the set $\mathbb{Z}^+$ of all positive integers. One of the most important was Euler's ϕ function (Definition 3.3.1), another the function σ (Exercises 2.6) and another the function $\mathscr{F}$ defined by $\mathscr{F}(n) = u_n$, the nth term of the Fibonacci sequence. Sometimes interest extends to functions whose natural domain of definition is the real numbers, for example the function $f(x) = x^2 + x + 41$ whose ability to generate prime values for integer values of x is as we saw in Problem 2.2.1 astonishing. (At other times the tables are reversed: in Chapter 2 we found it convenient to define $\pi(x)$ to be the number of primes less than or equal to x for all positive reals x not just for integral values.) Accordingly we make

Definition 10.1.1 A function f whose domain of definition is $\mathbb{Z}^+$ (or, possibly, $\mathbb{N}$) is called an *arithmetic function* (or a *number-theoretic function*).

Examples 10.1.2

(i) Let $\tau : \mathbb{Z}^+ \to \mathbb{Z}^+$ be the function defined by: $\tau(n)$ is the number of distinct positive divisors of n. Thus $\tau(1) = 1$; $\tau(\text{prime}) = 2$; $\tau(1729) = 8$; $\tau(1728) = 28$.

(ii) Let $\omega : \mathbb{Z}^+ \to \mathbb{N}$ be the function defined by: $\omega(n)$ is the number of distinct positive *prime* divisors of n. Thus $\omega(2) = \omega(4) = \omega(8) = 1$; $\omega(1729) = 3$; $\omega(1728) = 2$.

(iii) Let $\Omega : \mathbb{Z}^+ \to \mathbb{N}$ be the function defined by: $\Omega(n)$ is the number of positive primes, counting each according to its power, dividing n. Thus $\Omega(2^n) = n$; $\Omega(12) = 3$; $\Omega(1729) = 3$; $\Omega(1728) = 9$.

(iv) Let $\Lambda : \mathbb{Z}^+ \to \mathbb{R}$ be the function defined by:

$$\Lambda(n) = \begin{cases} \log p & \text{if } n = p^k,\ p \text{ prime},\ k \geqslant 1 \\ 0 & \text{otherwise} \end{cases}$$

(v) Let $\sigma^* : \mathbb{Z}^+ \to \mathbb{Z}^+$ be the function defined by: $\sigma^*(n)$ is the sum of the *odd* positive divisors of n. Thus $\sigma^*(2) = 1$; $\sigma^*(1729) = 2240$; $\sigma^*(1728) = 40$.

(vi) Let $\sigma_j : \mathbb{Z}^+ \to \mathbb{Z}^+$ be the function defined by: $\sigma_j(n)$ is the sum of the jth powers of the positive divisors of n. Thus $\sigma_3(4) = 73$; $\sigma_4(18) = 112\,931$.

(vii) Let $S_2 : \mathbb{Z}^+ \to \mathbb{N}$ be the function defined by: $S_2(n)$ is the number of formally distinct ways of representing n as a sum of two squares. Thus $S_2(5) = 8$ since $5 = (\pm 1)^2 + (\pm 2)^2 = (\pm 2)^2 + (\pm 1)^2$ whilst $S_2(3) = S_2(105) = 0$ [why?].

There are many reasons to study such functions. One is that they can often reveal rather subtle properties of the integers. For example, the 'perfection' of 28 seems a little deeper than the more obvious 'cubicness' of its neighbour 27. Again, the function $\pi(x)$ is a natural one to look at, but the function Λ above might be expected to tell us more since, of the sums $\pi(x)=\sum_{p\leqslant x} 1$ and $\psi(x)=\sum_{p^\alpha\leqslant x}\log p=\sum_{n\leqslant x}\Lambda(n)$, the latter not only registers the primes but treats each one differently. (And, indeed, $\psi(x)$ plays an important role in proofs of the prime number theorem—see for example [11].) A final reason is necessity: for encryption purposes it is useful to know how many prime factors a large number of, say, 100 digits might be expected to have. (The answer is quite surprising! See problems 1.4.3 and 10.1.6 and Exercise 10.4.8.)

Earlier we saw how the apparently chaotic behaviour of the ϕ function can, in one sense*, be brought to some order by providing a simple formula (Theorem 3.3.10) for evaluating $\phi(n)$ for each $n\in\mathbb{Z}^+$. Let's do the same with the functions τ and σ.

First we have

Theorem 10.1.3 If $n=p_1^{\alpha_1}p_2^{\alpha_2}\cdots p_r^{\alpha_r}$ is the prime factorisation of n, then $\tau(n)=(\alpha_1+1)(\alpha_2+1)\cdots(\alpha_r+1)$.

Proof The proof rests upon the simple fact that each divisor of n is of the form $p_1^{\beta_1}p_2^{\beta_2}\cdots p_r^{\beta_r}$ where, for each i ($1\leqslant i\leqslant r$), we have $0\leqslant\beta_i\leqslant\alpha_i$ (Exercise 1.4.5). □

Example 10.1.4 $1440=2^5\cdot 3^2\cdot 5$ has $(5+1)(2+1)(1+1)=36$ distinct positive divisors.

Problem What is the smallest (positive) integer with exactly 15 distinct† divisors? (In 1657 Van Schooten asked for and found the least positive integer with 16 distinct† divisors. You might care to do the same.)

Solution Since $15=3\cdot 5$ the required integer is of the form p^2q^4 for distinct p, q—or p^{14} for a single prime p. In each case the least such integers are, fairly clearly, $2^4\cdot 3^2=144$ and 2^{14}. Of course 144 is the smaller of these.

The determination of $\sigma(n)$ is equally easy. We have

Theorem 10.1.5 If $n=p_1^{\alpha_1}p_2^{\alpha_2}\cdots p_r^{\alpha_r}$ is the prime factorisation of n, then

$$\sigma(n)=\frac{p_1^{\alpha_1+1}-1}{p_1-1}\cdot\frac{p_2^{\alpha_2+1}-1}{p_2-1}\cdots\frac{p_r^{\alpha_r+1}-1}{p_r-1}.$$

* For other senses see Problem 10.1.6 and Section 10.4.
† Positive, of course.

Proof Consider the product

$$P(n) = (1 + p_1 + \cdots + p_1^{\alpha_1})(1 + p_2 + \cdots p_2^{\alpha_2}) \cdots (1 + p_r + \cdots + p_r^{\alpha_r}).$$

It is easy to see that each positive divisor of n occurs exactly once amongst the $\tau(n)$ terms contained in the full expansion of this product. It follows immediately that $\sigma(n) = P(n)$. Finally, since

$$1 + p_1 + \cdots + p_i^{\alpha_i} = \frac{p_i^{\alpha_i+1} - 1}{p_i - 1},$$

we can tidy up the above expression for $P(n)$ to obtain the formula given in the theorem. □

Examples 10.1.6

(i) $\sigma(220) = \sigma(2^2 \cdot 5 \cdot 11) = \frac{8-1}{1} \cdot \frac{25-1}{4} \cdot \frac{121-1}{10} = 7 \cdot 6 \cdot 12 = 504.$

(ii) $\sigma(284) = \sigma(2^2 \cdot 71) = \frac{8-1}{1} \cdot \frac{71^2-1}{70} = 7 \cdot 72 = 504.$

This confirms that 220 and 284 form an amicable pair. (See Exercises 2.6.)

Problem Find the least n such (i) $\sigma(n) = 500$.

Solution Since 500 is divisible by no primes other than 2 and 5 it is not difficult to check that for very few primes is $(p^{\alpha+1} - 1)/(p-1)$ a factor of 500. Indeed a quick check by hand appears to show that $n = 499$ is the only possible value for n.

Theorems 10.1.3 and 10.1.5 allow us very simply to compute $\tau(n)$ and $\sigma(n)$ once we have the prime factorisation of n. This is available from Program 1.5 the r distinct primes being stored in array G and their powers in array M. Using this information we can compute $\tau(n)$ as follows.

Program 10.1 *Calculation of τ(n) and σ(n)*

τ(n) is computed by adding

```
T = 1
FOR I = 1 TO R
T = T * (M(I) + 1)
NEXT I
```

While σ(n) is computed using

```
S = 1
FOR I = 1 TO R
S = S * (G(I)^(M(I)+1) - 1)/(G(I) - 1)
NEXT I
```

Program 1.5 also computes the value of $\omega(n)$—it is the value of the variable K—whilst $\Omega(n)$ is the sum of the values in the array M.

Exercises 10.1

1 Find: (i) $\sigma(60)$; (ii) $\tau(60)$; (iii) $\omega(60)$; (iv) $\Omega(60)$; (v) $\Lambda(60)$; (vi) $\sigma^*(60)$; (vii) $\sigma_2(60)$; (viii) $S_2(60)$; (ix) $\sigma(2^5 3^4 7 \cdot 13^2)$; (x) $\tau(2^{3^3} 17^{17} 101^9)$; (xi) $\omega(3^3 5^5 7^7)$; (xii) $\Omega(3^3 5^5 7^7)$; (xiii) $\sigma^*(1990)$.

2 Show (Cardan* 1537) that if $n = p_1 p_2 \cdots p_r$, the p_i being distinct primes, then the number of divisors of n excluding n itself is $1+2+2^2+\cdots+2^{r-1}$.

3 Show that $n \leqslant \sigma(n) \leqslant n^2$ and that if $\sigma(n)$ is odd then n is a square or the double of a square.

4 Show (Waring 1770) that $\tau(n)$ is odd iff n is a square and that $\tau(n) \leqslant 2\sqrt{n}$. [*Hint*: Pair off divisors k and n/k.]

5 Let $\mathcal{P}(n)$ denote the product of all the divisors of n. Show that $\mathcal{P}(n) = n\tau^{n/2}$ and that if $\mathcal{P}(n) = \mathcal{P}(m)$ then $n = m$.

6 Find the least positive integer n for which $\tau(n)$ is equal to: (i) 8; (ii) 9; (iii) 10; (iv) (Mersenne 1644) 60.

7 Find all integers n for which $\sigma(n)$ is equal to: (i) 5; (ii) 14; (iii) 100; (iv) 5611.

8 Identify the set of all integers n for which $\tau(n)$ is equal to: (i) 2; (ii) 3; (iii) 4.

9 Find the smallest integer m for which there exists $n \neq m$ for which $\sigma(n) = \sigma(m)$.

10 Find the smallest integer n for which $\sigma(x) = n$ has: (i) exactly two solutions; (ii) exactly three solutions.

11 (Wallis 1685) In how many different ways can $N = p_1^{\alpha_1} p_2^{\alpha_2} \cdots p_r^{\alpha_r}$ (the p_i being distinct primes) be expressed as a product of two factors? (as a product of *coprime* factors?)

12 Let p be prime. Show that 2^{p-1} is the least integer having p distinct factors. Is the converse true? That is: If 2^{n-1} is the least integer with exactly n factors must n be prime?

13 Show that if $N = 2^{\alpha_1} 3^{\alpha_2} \cdots p_{r-1}^{\alpha_{r-1}} p_r^{\alpha_r}$ where $\alpha_1 \geqslant \alpha_2 \geqslant \cdots \geqslant \alpha_{r-1} \geqslant \alpha_r$ is the least number with $\tau(N)$ divisors then $\alpha_r + 1$ is prime. (Fontene 1902, Chalde 1903).

14 Show that, given $m \in \mathbb{Z}^+$, there exists infinitely many n such that $\tau(n) = m$, but only finitely many n for which (i) $\sigma(n) = m$; (ii) $\phi(n) = m$.

* Jerome Cardan, 24 September 1501 – 21 September 1576.

15 Given distinct primes $p_1, p_2, \ldots, p_r$ and $m \in \mathbb{Z}^+$, show that there are at most finitely many r-tuples $(\alpha_1, \alpha_2, \ldots, \alpha_r)$ for which $\tau(p_1^{\alpha_1} p_2^{\alpha_2} \cdots p_r^{\alpha_r}) = m$. What if the p_i are: (i) primes but not given to be distinct; (ii) distinct but not given to be primes?

16 Show that, given $k \in \mathbb{Z}^+$, there are at most finitely many n such that $n/\tau(n) = k$. Are there values of k for which the number of such n is zero?

17 Find n such that: (i) $\sigma(n)/n = \frac{13}{5}$ (Descartes*); (ii) $\sigma(n)/n = \frac{9}{4}$ (Mersenne, Fermat).

18 Can $\sigma(n)$ be square if $n > 3$?

19 Show that if $m = p^\alpha$ and $n = q^\beta$, p and q being primes, and if $\sigma(m)/m = \sigma(n)/n$, then $m = n$. Show this conclusion can be false if m and n are not prime powers.

20 Show that the number of ordered pairs $\langle a, b\rangle$ of integers for which lcm $[a, b] = n$ is $\tau(n^2)$.

21 Prove the analogue for $\sigma_j(n)$ of Theorem 10.1.5. That is, prove that if $n = p_1^{\alpha_1} p_2^{\alpha_2} \cdots p_r^{\alpha_r}$, then

$$\sigma_j(n) = \frac{p_1^{j(\alpha_1+1)} - 1}{p_1^j - 1} \cdots \frac{p_r^{j(\alpha_r+1)} - 1}{p_r^j - 1}.$$

22 (i) Prove that the only integers not expressible as a sum of (more than one) consecutive positive integers are the powers 2^α of 2.
(ii) Show that the number of distinct ways of writing n as a sum of one or more consecutive positive integers is $\tau(n_0)$, where n_0 is the largest odd divisor of n. [*Hint*: From

$$n = (a+1) + (a+2) + \cdots + (a+b) = \tfrac{1}{2}b(b+2a+1)$$

deduce that b or $b+2a+1$ divides n_0.]

23 Prove that, if $n > 1$ is composite, then $\sigma(n) > n + \sqrt{n}$. [*Hint*: if $d \mid n$ and $d \leqslant \sqrt{n}$ then $n/d \geqslant \sqrt{n}$.]

24 Prove that if $1 < n = p_1^{\alpha_1} p_2^{\alpha_2} \cdots p_r^{\alpha_r}$ then

$$1 > n/\sigma(n) > (1 - 1/p_1) \cdots (1 - 1/p_r).$$

25 Prove that if Goldbach's conjecture is true then, for each positive integer $2n$, there exist positive integers n_1, n_2 such that $2n = \sigma(n_1) + \sigma(n_2)$. (Cf. Exercise 3.3.9.)

26 Find all n such that $2n = \phi(n) + \sigma(n)$. [*Hint*:

$$\frac{p^{\alpha+1} - 1}{p^\alpha(p-1)} \geqslant 1 + 1/p;$$

hence $\sigma(n)/n > \prod_{p_i \mid n} (1 + 1/p_i)$.]

* René du Perron Descartes, 31 March 1596 – 11 February 1650.

27 Show that, in general, for $a, b \in \mathbb{Z}^+$, $\sigma(ab) \leqslant \sigma(a)\sigma(b)$. If $\sigma(ab) = \sigma(a)\sigma(b)$, must $(a, b) = 1$? Can one, for $a \geqslant b \geqslant 2$, have $\sigma(ab) = \sigma(a) + \sigma(b)$? Answer the same question for τ and ϕ.

28 Show that there exist infinitely many pairs m, n such that $m \neq n$ and yet $\sigma(m) = \sigma(n)$. [*Hint*: Try $\sigma(6t) = \sigma(11t)$ if $(t, 66) = 1$.]

Computer problems 10.1

1 Write a program to generate a table of values of $\tau(n)$ and $\sigma(n)$ for $n \leqslant 100$. Do any patterns emerge?

2 For $n \geqslant 2$ define $s^0(n) = s(n) = \sigma(n) - n$, the sum of all divisors of n which are less than n, and set $s^{k+1}(n) = s(s^k(n))$. Meissner (1907) asked if the sequence $\{s^k(n)\}$ always led to a prime, or a perfect or an amicable number. Write a program to explore what happens to $s^k(n)$ as $k \to \infty$.

3 Burton [2] offers 3655 and 4503 as values of n such that $\tau(n) = \tau(n+1) = \tau(n+2) = \tau(n+3)$. Are these the smallest such values? For values within the range of your computer find sequences $n, n+1, \ldots, n+k$ for which $\tau(n) = \tau(n+1) = \cdots = \tau(n+k)$.

4 Given a positive integer n define a sequence of integers $n_1, n_2, n_3, \ldots$ by: $n_1 = \tau(n)$ and $n_{k+1} = \tau(n_k)$ for $k = 1, 2, 3 \ldots$. Use your computer to find, for given values of n, corresponding values of r such that $n_k = 2$ for all $k \geqslant r$.

5 $\sigma(n+2) = \sigma(n) + 2$ if n, $n+2$ are twin primes. Can the equality hold if n, $n+2$ are (i) both odd and composite?; (ii) both even?

6 Write a program to compute, for increasing values of N,

(i) $\displaystyle \frac{\pi^2}{N^2} \sum_{n=1}^{N} \phi(n)$ (ii) $\displaystyle \frac{12}{\pi^2 N^2} \sum_{n=1}^{N} \sigma(n)$

(iii) $\displaystyle \frac{\pi^2}{N} \sum_{n=1}^{N} \frac{\phi(n)}{n}$ (vi) $\displaystyle \frac{1}{N \log N} \sum_{n=1}^{N} \tau(n)$

(v) $\displaystyle \frac{1}{N \log\log N} \sum_{n=1}^{N} \omega(n)$. (See Problem 1.4.3.)

10.2 Multiplicative arithmetic functions

It is immediate from Theorems 10.1.3 and 10.1.5 that τ and σ share, with ϕ, the property attributed to ϕ in Theorem 3.3.7, namely that it is multiplicative—according to the following definition.

Definition 10.2.1
(i) The arithmetic function M is said to be *multiplicative* iff for all $U, V \in \mathbb{Z}^+$ for which $(U, V) = 1$ we have $M(UV) = M(U)M(V)$.
(ii) The arithmetic function A is said to be *additive* iff for all $U, V \in \mathbb{Z}^+$ for which $(U, V) = 1$ we have $A(UV) = A(U) + A(V)$.

Examples 10.2.2 ϕ, τ and σ are multiplicative, ω and Ω are additive.

Notes 10.2.3
(i) Just as with Euler's function the extension of the equalities in Definition 10.2.1 to products of more than two coprime integers is immediate. In particular we clearly have: If $n = p_1^{\alpha_1} p_2^{\alpha_2} \cdots p_r^{\alpha_r}$, the p_i being distinct primes, then

$$M(n) = M(p_1^{\alpha_1})M(p_2^{\alpha_2}) \cdots M(p_r^{\alpha_r})$$

whilst

$$A(n) = A(p_1^{\alpha_1}) + A(p_2^{\alpha_2}) + \cdots + A(p_r^{\alpha_r}).$$

This naturally means that one only needs to evaluate such functions for prime power arguments.
(ii) The important function $\pi(x)$ is, of course, not multiplicative. But note that we only ask π to *count* for us. On the other hand multiplicative functions detect *qualitative*, as distinct from *quantative* properties of the integers that functions like π miss. For example, compare the values of $\pi(x)$ and $\tau(x)$ for $x = 7, 8, 9$ and 10. (π can't distinguish these values of x.)
(iii) Note that if A is an additive function then, for each positive number c, the function $M(n) = c^{A(n)}$ is multiplicative. For this reason we shall restrict our attention here to multiplicative functions.

One way of extending the list of multiplicative functions is to employ the following pleasant surprise.

Theorem 10.2.4 Let f be a multiplicative function and define F by $F(n) = \sum_{d \mid n} f(d)$. Then F is also multiplicative.

Proof Proceeding as naively as possible, let $U, V \in \mathbb{Z}$ with $(U, V) = 1$. Then*

$$F(UV) = \sum_{d \mid UV} f(d) = \sum_{d_1 \mid U, d_2 \mid V} f(d_1 d_2) = \sum_{d_1 \mid U, d_2 \mid V} f(d_1) f(d_2),$$

since $(d_1, d_2) = 1$ and f is multiplicative. But

$$\sum_{d_1 \mid U, d_2 \mid V} f(d_1) f(d_2) = \left(\sum_{d_1 \mid U} f(d_1) \right) \left(\sum_{d_2 \mid V} f(d_2) \right) = F(U)F(V),$$

as required. □

* Using Exercise 1.5.10.

The next to last equality in the above is probably best understood by constructing a specific example. For instance

$$\begin{aligned}\sum_{d|120} f(d) = \sum_{d|8\cdot 15} f(d) \\ &= \quad f(1\cdot 1) \quad +f(2\cdot 1) \quad +f(4\cdot 1) \quad +f(8\cdot 1) \\ &\quad +f(1\cdot 3) \quad +f(2\cdot 3) \quad +f(4\cdot 3) \quad +f(8\cdot 3) \\ &\quad +f(1\cdot 5) \quad +f(2\cdot 5) \quad +f(4\cdot 5) \quad +f(8\cdot 5) \\ &\quad +f(1\cdot 15) +f(2\cdot 15) +f(4\cdot 15) +f(8\cdot 15) \\ &= \quad f(1)f(1) \quad +f(2)f(1) \quad +f(4)f(1) \quad +f(8)f(1) \\ &\quad \vdots \qquad\qquad \vdots \qquad\qquad \vdots \qquad\qquad \vdots \\ &\quad f(1)f(15)+f(2)f(15)+f(4)f(15)+f(8)f(15). \\ &= [f(1)+f(2)+f(4)+f(8)]\cdot[f(1)+f(3)+f(5)+f(15)] \\ &= \left(\sum_{d_1|8} f(d_1)\right)\left(\sum_{d_2|15} f(d_2)\right).\end{aligned}$$

Note 10.2.5 N. V. Bougaief* (1871) called F the *numerical integral* of f and f the *numerical derivative* of F.

From Theorem 10.2.4 we obtain, with very little effort (the effort is all in the proof of Theorem 10.2.4) new proofs of old results together with two new ones.

Corollary 10.2.6 σ, σ_j, σ^* and τ are multiplicative functions.

Proof Rather trivially the functions f and g defined by: $f(k)=1$, $g(k)=k$, for all $k\in\mathbb{Z}^+$ are both multiplicative. Consequently so are the functions F and $G:\mathbb{Z}^+\to\mathbb{Z}^+$ given by

$$F(n)=\sum_{d|n} f(d); \qquad G(n)=\sum_{d|n} g(d).$$

That is, $F=\tau$ and $G=\sigma$ are multiplicative. Similar proofs for σ_j and σ^* are left to the reader. □

To conclude this section we verify one remark and amplify another made in Chapter 2 regarding perfect numbers by giving two results due to Euler. The first is

Theorem 10.2.7 Let n be an *even* perfect number. Then $n=2^{p-1}(2^p-1)$ where 2^p-1 (and hence p itself) is a prime. In other words, every even perfect number is of Euclid's type.

* Nicolai Vasilievich Bougaief, 14 September 1837 - 11 June 1903.

Proof Let $n = 2^{r-1} \cdot m$ where m is odd. Immediately we have

$$2^r m = 2n = \sigma(n) = \sigma(2^{r-1})\sigma(m) = (2^r - 1)\sigma(m).$$

Since $2^r - 1$ is odd we deduce that $2^r | \sigma(m)$, $\sigma(m) = 2^r c$, say. This implies that $m = (2^r - 1)c$. But, now, m and c are divisors of m whose sum is $2^r c$, that is, $\sigma(m)$. This means that m can have no divisors other than m and c and this implies that m is prime (and $c = 1$). Thus $n = 2^{r-1}(2^r - 1)$ where m and hence r are primes—as we claimed. □

Euler was also able to say something about the structure of odd perfect numbers. He proved

Theorem 10.2.8 Let $n = p_1^{\alpha_1} p_2^{\alpha_2} \cdots p_r^{\alpha_r}$, where the p_i are distinct primes, be an odd perfect number. Then, for some i, $1 \leqslant i \leqslant r$, we have $p_i \equiv \alpha_i \equiv 1 \pmod 4$ whilst every other α_i is even.

Proof We know that $\sigma(n) = 2n = \sigma(p_1^{\alpha_1})\sigma(p_2^{\alpha_2}) \cdots \sigma(p_n^{\alpha_n})$. Since n is odd, $2n$ is divisible by 2 but not by 4. Hence just one of the factors $\sigma(p_i^{\alpha_i})$, say, is even, the rest odd. Now, for each k, $\sigma(p_k^{\alpha_k}) = 1 + p_k + \cdots + p_k^{\alpha_k}$. If $p_k \equiv 3 \equiv -1 \pmod 4$ then $\sigma(p_k^{\alpha_k}) \equiv 0$ or $1 \pmod 4$ according as α_k is odd or even. Thus α_k must be even for such p_k since $4 \nmid \sigma(p_k^{\alpha_k})$. Likewise, if $j \neq i$—so that $\sigma(p_j^{\alpha_j})$ is odd—and if $p_j \equiv 1 \pmod 4$ then $\sigma(p_j^{\alpha_j}) \equiv \alpha_j + 1 \pmod 4$. It is then immediate that $\alpha_j + 1$ must be odd, that is, α_j must be even. Finally, since 2—but not 4—divides $\sigma(p_i^{\alpha_i})$, the above shows that $p_i \not\equiv 3 \pmod 4$ and then that $\alpha_i + 1$ must be congruent to 2 (and not 0) modulo 4. Thus $\alpha_i \equiv 1 \pmod 4$ as claimed. □

A corollary which is somewhat easier to swallow is

Corollary 10.2.9 Let n be an odd perfect number. Then n is of the form $p^\alpha m^2$ where p is a prime, $(p, m) = 1$ and $p \equiv \alpha \equiv 1 \pmod 4$. In particular n is of the form $4k + 1$.

Proof Everything follows from Theorem 10.2.8 including the fact that $n \equiv 1 \pmod 4$—because $p \equiv 1 \pmod 4$ and m^2 is the square of an odd integer. □

Further progress has been made since Euler's time. Assuming that $n = p^\alpha q_1^{2\beta_1} q_2^{2\beta_2} \cdots q_r^{2\beta_r}$ is an odd perfect number, it has been shown that not all the β_i can be 1. Nor can they all be 2, nor all 3. And that's not the end of the story! Probing into the size of p, the q_i and r it has been shown that r is at least 8, that n must have a prime divisor in excess of 100 000 and that n itself must be greater than 10^{200}. For references see [5].

Exercises 10.2

1 Show that if f is a multiplicative function defined on $\mathbb{Z}^+$ then, with one exception, $f(1)=1$. What is the exception? What is the corresponding result for additive functions?

2 Prove that, if f and g are multiplicative functions such that $f(p^\alpha)=g(p^\alpha)$ for each prime power p^α, then $f(n)=g(n)$ for each $n\in\mathbb{Z}^+$.

Find an example of multiplicative functions f, g where $f(p)=g(p)$ for each prime p and yet $f(n)\neq g(n)$ for all n.

3 For each $n=p_1^{\alpha_1}p_2^{\alpha_2}\cdots p_r^{\alpha_r}\in\mathbb{Z}^+$ define functions L, Q, V by:

$$L(n)=(-1)^{\alpha_1+\alpha_2+\cdots\alpha_r};$$

$$Q(n)=\begin{cases}0 & \text{if } p\mid n\\ (n/p)^* & \text{if } p\nmid n\end{cases}\quad (p \text{ being a fixed prime});$$

$V(n)$ is the number of incongruent solutions of $x^2\equiv a(\text{mod } n)$, a being a fixed integer. Prove each of L, Q and V is multiplicative.

4 Given multiplicative functions f and g define their *convolution product* to be the function $f*g$ given by $f*g(n)=\sum_{d\mid n}f(d)g(n/d)$. Show that $f*g$ is multiplicative and that if h is a third multiplicative function then $[(f*g)*h](n)=[f*(g*h)](n)$ for each $n\in\mathbb{Z}^+$. If we define $f\cdot g$ by $f\cdot g(n)=\sum_{d\mid n}f(d)g(d)$ is $f\cdot g$ multiplicative? Is $[(f\cdot g)\cdot h](n)=[f\cdot(g\cdot h)](n)$ for each $n\in\mathbb{Z}^+$?

5 Prove that for each positive integer n:

(i) $\sum_{d\mid n}\sigma(d)=\sum_{d\mid n}(n/d)\tau(d)$; (ii) $\sum_{d\mid n}(n/d)\sigma(d)=\sum_{d\mid n}d\tau(d)$;

(iii) $\sum_{d\mid n}\tau(d)^3=\left(\sum_{d\mid n}\tau(d)\right)^2$.

[*Hint*: Prove $F(n)=\sum_{d\mid n}\sigma(d)$, $G(n)=\sum_{d\mid n}(n/d)\tau(d)$ are multiplicative and then that $F(p^\alpha)=G(p^\alpha)$ for each prime power. For (iii) use Theorem 0.4.2.]

6 Show that if $\sum_{d\mid n}f(d)=g(n)$ where f and g are multiplicative, then $\sum_{n=1}^{N}g(n)=\sum_{d=1}^{N}f(d)[N/d]$. [*Hint*: Sum $\sum_{n=1}^{N}(\sum_{d\mid n}f(d))$ by collecting together all terms involving the same $f(d)$.]

7 Let $f(x)$ be a polynomial with integer coefficients and let $\Psi(n)$ denote the number of values $f(0), f(1),\ldots,f(n-1)$ which are coprime to n. Show that $\Psi(ab)=\Psi(a)\Psi(b)$ whenever $(a, b)=1$. For each prime p show that $\Psi(p^\alpha)=p^{\alpha-1}(p-\alpha_p)$, where α_p is the number of $f(0), f(1),\ldots,f(n-1)$ which are divisible by p. Find $\Psi(2001)$ when $f(x)=x^2+3x+5$. [*Note*: if $f(x)=x$, then Ψ is Euler's function.]

* The Legendre symbol. The remaining (n/d) are just ordinary rational numbers.

8 Let $s(n)$ denote the sum of all the positive divisors of n other than n itself. Show that $s(n)$ is not multiplicative (hence the reason for taking $\sigma(n)=s(n)+n$). Show that $s(n)\neq 5$ for any n and that if each even integer greater than 6 is a sum of two *distinct* primes*, then 5 is the only odd number for which $s(x)=m$ has no solutions.

9 (a) (C. de Bouvelles, 1510) Show that each even perfect number n is triangular and that for $n>6$ the sum of the digits of n is congruent to 1 modulo 9.
(b) Show that no integers of the form n^2, p^α, pq (where p, q are odd primes) can be perfect numbers (even or odd).

10 Show that no perfect number can be a divisor of any other. (Cf. Exercise 2.6.4.)

11 (a) Show that if $x=p_1^{\alpha_1}p_2^{\alpha_2}\cdots p_r^{\alpha_r}$ is perfect, then $2=\sigma(n)/n<\prod_{i=1}^{r}(1+1/(p_i-1))$. (b) Deduce that any odd perfect number has at least three prime factors.

12 Show that, given the integer r, there can be at most a finite number of odd perfect numbers n such that n is divisible by no more than r distinct primes.

Computer problems 10.2

1 Use your computer to explore values of n for which $\sigma(n)=2n-1$ (the so called *almost perfect numbers*). Over the same range find all n for which $\sigma(n)=2n+1$, $\sigma(n)=2n-2$ and $\sigma(n)=2n+2$.

2 A *pseudoperfect number n* is one which is the sum of *some* of its (positive) divisors. Write a program to find all such numbers less than 1000. Modify the program to find *primitive pseudoperfect* numbers—pseudoperfects whose proper divisors are not pseudoperfect.

3 Benkoski defines *weird* numbers (see [5] for references) as abundant numbers which are not pseudoperfect. Find the first 24 such numbers.

4 (Catalan 1888) Show that if n is an odd perfect number with $3\nmid n$, $5\nmid n$, $7\nmid n$, then n is divisible by at least 26 different primes.

5 We know (Exercise 3.3.5) that if $m\phi(m)=n\phi(n)$, then $m=n$. Show that $m\sigma(m)=n\sigma(n)$ is possible even if $m\neq n$.

6 Find values of $n<1000$ such that $\tau(n)=\phi(n)$.

* See Problem 2.3.6.

August Ferdinand Möbius *(17 November 1790 – 26 September 1868)*
Born near Naumberg, Germany, Möbius was the only child of a dancing teacher—his father—and a descendant of Luther. He showed an early interest in mathematics but entered the University of Leipzig in 1809 to study law. He soon changed to mathematics and in due course became assistant to the astronomer/mathematician Mollwiede. Subsequently he studied with Gauss before returning to the astronomy section at Leipzig following Mollwiede's appointment to the chair of mathematics there. It took 28 years for the quiet and reserved Möbius to be promoted from 'extraordinary' to 'ordinary' professor—but 4 years later he was made director of the observatory.

His first publications (c.1815) were in astronomy. In 1826 he wrote a famous text on barycentric coordinates. Accordingly Möbius is regarded as one of the originators of the concept of homogeneous coordinates.

In the 1830s he employed continued fractions in two papers on dioptrics, but spent much of his time writing a large text on statics.

Whilst Möbius's name today is attached to certain transformations of the complex plane, he is almost universally known to the public at large for his construction of a one-sided one-edged surface—the Möbius band. This appears in a paper which arose from an essay submitted to the Paris academy which had offered a prize to encourage research on the geometrical theory of polyhedra.

10.3 The Möbius function

Having seen Corollary 10.2.6, natural inquisitiveness will cause the reader to ask immediately: Which 'trivial' function likewise gives rise to our friend ϕ? The answer is not so obvious. A little thought raises the following 'half-way' question: If $\phi(n)=\sum_{d|n} h(d)$ for some function h, need h be a multiplicative function just because ϕ is? Remarkably the answer is 'yes'. And the investigation of *why* this is the case forces the introduction of a new multiplicative function which plays a fundamental role in many areas of number theory.

Let's try to feel our way towards

Theorem 10.3.1 Let $F(n)=\sum_{d|n} f(d)$ for each $n \in \mathbb{Z}^+$ and suppose F is multiplicative. Then so is f. □ (Proof follows that of Theorem 10.3.5.)

Thinking aloud*: Since F is assumed multiplicative, we might consider, at least initially, the value of $F(t)$ when $t=p^\alpha$ is some prime power. Then $F(p^\alpha)-F(p^{\alpha-1})=f(p^\alpha)$, which looks useful since we have a single $f(t)$ expressed in terms of a sum of Fs. This we may write as

$$f(p^\alpha)=\eta(1)F(1)+\eta(p)F(p)+\cdots+\eta(p^{\alpha-1})F(p^{\alpha-1})+\eta(p^\alpha)F(p^\alpha) \tag{*}$$

provided we set $-\eta(p^{\alpha-1})=\eta(p^\alpha)=1$ and $\eta(p^\beta)=0$ for all other powers of p. We soon find that this is not too helpful and find it better to write, instead,

$$f(p^\alpha)=\mu(p^\alpha)F(1)+\mu(p^{\alpha-1})F(p)+\cdots+\mu(p)F(p^{\alpha-1})+\mu(1)F(p^\alpha) \tag{**}$$

where $\mu(1)=1$, $\mu(p)=-1$ and $\mu(p^\beta)=0$ if $\beta \geqslant 2$.

If we now try to extend μ to a *multiplicative* function defined on all of $\mathbb{Z}^+$ we are *forced* into making

Definition 10.3.2 For $n \in \mathbb{Z}^+$

$$\mu(n)=\begin{cases} 1 & \text{if } n=1 \\ 0 & \text{if } n \text{ is not square-free} \\ (-1)^r & \text{if } n=p_1p_2\cdots p_r \text{ where the } p_i \text{ are distinct primes.} \end{cases}$$

This function is now called the *Möbius function*, after an astronomy professor A. F. Möbius, who used it in 1832 in asserting that $\sum_{s=1}^\infty f(sx)/s^n = F(x)$ implies that $f(x)=\sum_{s=1}^\infty \mu(s)F(sx)/s^n$ (cf. Theorem 10.3.5 below). Use of it can also be traced to Euler some 84 years earlier.

The following fundamental property of the μ function was noted by Mertens in 1874. Actually it was Mertens who introduced the symbol μ. He also raised the conjecture below which has been solved only very recently.

Theorem 10.3.3

$$\sum_{d|n} \mu(d)=\begin{cases} 1 & \text{if } n=1 \\ 0 & \text{if } n>1 \end{cases}$$

Proof If $n=1$ the result is trivial. Next set $\mathcal{M}(n)=\sum_{d|n} \mu(d)$ and first suppose that $n=p^\alpha$, where $\alpha \geqslant 1$. Then

$$\begin{aligned}\mathcal{M}(p^\alpha)&=\sum_{d|p^\alpha} \mu(d)=\mu(1)+\mu(p)+\mu(p^2)+\cdots+\mu(p^\alpha)\\ &=1-1+0+\cdots+0=0.\end{aligned}$$

* Or whatever is the written equivalent!

Since μ is multiplicative (Exercise 10.3.1) we know that $\mathcal{M}$ as defined above is also a multiplicative function. In particular if $n = p_1^{\alpha_1} p_2^{\alpha_2} \cdots p_r^{\alpha_r}$, then $\mathcal{M}(n) = \mathcal{M}(p_1^{\alpha_1}) \cdots \mathcal{M}(p_r^{\alpha_r}) = 0 \cdot 0 \cdots 0 = 0$—as claimed. □

Note 10.3.4 In 1897 Mertens, using values of $\mu(n)$ which had been calculated for all $n < 10\,000$, showed that $|\sum_{n=1}^{k} \mu(n)| < \sqrt{k}$ for each k for which $1 \leqslant k \leqslant 10\,000$. Later calculators* took this further and the conjecture was made that this inequality is true for each integer k. In fact Odlyzko and Te Riele have, very recently (see [R]), disproved the conjecture, although it appears to be beyond the capacity of a computer to find the value of k at which the conjecture first fails.

We now obtain a formula, akin to that claimed by Möbius, which will help us solve our problem as to which 'trivial' function gives rise, via summation, to the ϕ function and at the same time prove Theorem 10.3.1. We have

Theorem 10.3.5 (*The Möbius inversion formula*) Let f be any arithmetic function and let F be defined by $F(n) = \sum_{d|n} f(d)$. Then

$$f(n) = \sum_{d|n} \mu(n/d)F(d) = \sum_{d|n} \mu(d)F(n/d).$$

'*Proof*' The equality of the two sums is immediate—for as d runs over all divisors of n so does n/d... backwards!

As for the first equality note that

$$\sum_{d|n} \mu(n/d)F(d) = \sum_{d|n} (\mu(n/d) \sum_{c|d} f(c)) = \sum_{d|n} \left(\sum_{c|d} \mu(n/d) f(c) \right).$$

For clarity we shall proceed by way of a specific example with $n = 12$. We leave a full formal proof† to the reader.

$$\begin{aligned} \sum_{d|12} \left(\sum_{c|d} \mu(12/d) f(c) \right) \text{ is } & \mu(12/1)\ \{f(1)\} \\ & + \mu(12/2)\ \{f(1) + f(2)\} \\ & + \mu(12/3)\ \{f(1) + \qquad + f(3)\} \\ & + \mu(12/4)\ \{f(1) + f(2) \qquad + f(4)\} \\ & + \mu(12/6)\ \{f(1) + f(2) + f(3) \qquad + f(6)\} \\ & + \mu(12/12)\{f(1) + f(2) + f(3) + f(4) + f(6) + f(12)\}. \end{aligned}$$

* Or, as they used to be called, computers!

† What a splendid examination question it would make!

Now counting terms by the columns yields

$$f(1)\left\{\sum_{d|12}\mu(12/d)\right\}+f(2)\left\{\sum_{d|6}\mu(6/d)\right\}$$

$$+f(3)\left\{\sum_{d|4}\mu(4/d)\right\}+f(4)\left\{\sum_{d|3}\mu(3/d)\right\}$$

$$+f(6)\left\{\sum_{d|2}\mu(2/d)\right\}+f(12)\mu(1)$$

$$=0+0+0+0+0+f(12)\text{—by Theorem 10.3.3.} \quad \square$$

We can now give, easily, the

Proof of Theorem 10.3.1 Let $m, n \in \mathbb{Z}^+$ with $(m, n)=1$. From Theorem 10.3.5 we obtain (cf. Theorem 10.2.4)

$$f(mn)=\sum_{d|mn}\mu(mn/d)F(d)=\sum_{\substack{d_1|m\\d_2|n}}\mu\left(\frac{m}{d_1}\cdot\frac{n}{d_2}\right)F(d_1d_2).$$

Since μ and F are multiplicative and since $(d_1, d_2)=(m/d_1, n/d_2)=1$ the previous equality yields

$$\sum_{\substack{d_1|m\\d_2|n}}\mu\left(\frac{m}{d_1}\right)\mu\left(\frac{n}{d_2}\right)F(d_1)F(d_2)=\left(\sum_{d_1|m}\mu\left(\frac{m}{d_1}\right)F(m)\right)\left(\sum_{d_2|n}\mu\left(\frac{n}{d_2}\right)F(n)\right)$$

$$=f(m)f(n),$$

as required. $\square$

We can now attempt to find the mysterious function h which will give us, on summation, Euler's ϕ function. First we recall an old friend:

Theorem 3.3.12 Let $n \in \mathbb{Z}^+$. Then $\sum_{d|n}\phi(d)=n$.

For your entertainment here is

(*Another*) *Proof* Set $T(n)=\sum_{d|n}\phi(d)$. Since ϕ is multiplicative so is T (Theorem 10.2.4). Consequently if $n=p_1^{\alpha_1}p_2^{\alpha_2}\cdots p_r^{\alpha_r}$, where the p_i are distinct primes, then $T(n)=T(p_1^{\alpha_1})T(p_2^{\alpha_2})\cdots T(p_r^{\alpha_r})$. But

$$T(p^\alpha)=\sum_{d|p^\alpha}\phi(d)=\phi(1)+\phi(p)+\cdots+\phi(p^\alpha)$$

$$=1+(p-1)+(p-1)p+\cdots+(p-1)p^{\alpha-1},$$

which tidies up (beautifully!) to p^α. Thus $T(p^\alpha)=p^\alpha$ and $T(n)=n$ follows. $\square$

We then get, immediately, from Theorem 10.3.5

Theorem 10.3.6 $\phi(n)=\sum_{d|n}\mu(d)\cdot(n/d)$ □

In fact Theorem 10.3.6 is unsatisfactory in that what what we were looking for was a formula $\phi(n)=\sum_{d|n}h(d)$, where h is a multiplicative function defined on $\mathbb{Z}^+$. Unfortunately, here, $h(d)$ involves not only the variable d but the quantity n. Of course, one can rewrite Theorem 10.3.6 in the form

$$\frac{\phi(n)}{n}=\sum_{d|n}\frac{\mu(d)}{d},$$

thus expressing $\phi(n)/n$, rather than $\phi(n)$, in the desired form. But, at least, Theorem 10.3.1 does tell us that there is a function h of the required kind which, because it is multiplicative, allows us to restrict our attention to calculating $h(p^\alpha)$ for each power p^α of each prime p. We invite you to do just this in Exercise 10.3.7.

Exercises 10.3

1 Prove that μ is a multiplicative function.

2 (a) Use Theorem 10.3.5 to prove that:

(i) $\sum_{d|n}\mu(d)\tau(n/d)=1$; (ii) $\sum_{d|n}\mu(d)\sigma(n/d)=n$;

(iii) $\sum_{d|n}\mu(d)\log d=-\Lambda(n)$.

(b) Can you find a simple expression for $\sum_{d|n}\mu(d)\phi(n/d)$?

3 Let $p_1^{\alpha_1}p_2^{\alpha_2}\cdots p_r^{\alpha_r}>1$ and let f be any multiplicative function. Prove (A. Berger 1898) that

$$\sum_{d|n}\mu(d)f(d)=(1-f(p_1))(1-f(p_2))\cdots(1-f(p_r)).$$

[*Hint*: The function F defined by $F(n)=\sum_{d|n}\mu(d)f(d)$ is multiplicative. Hence $F(n)=F(p_1^{\alpha_1})F(p_2^{\alpha_2})\cdots F(p_r^{\alpha_r})$.]

4 Using the previous exercise show that:

(i) $\sum_{d|n}\mu(d)\phi(d)=(2-p_1)(2-p_2)\cdots(2-p_r)$;

(ii) $\sum_{d|n}\mu(d)\sigma(d)=(-1)^r p_1p_2\cdots p_r$;

(iii) $\sum_{d|n}\mu(d)\tau(d)=(-1)^r$;

(iv) $\sum_{d|n}(\mu(d))^2=2^r=$ the number of square-free divisors of n;

(v) $\sum_{d|n} \mu(d) \cdot 1/d^k = (1-1/p_1^k) \cdots (1-1/p_r^k)$;

(vi) $\sum_{d|n} (\mu(d))^2/\phi(d) = n/\phi(n)$;

(vii) $\sum_{d|n} (\mu(d))^2/\sigma(d) = \left(\frac{p_1+2}{p_1+1}\right) \cdots \left(\frac{p_r+2}{p_r+1}\right)$

(viii) $\sum_{d|n} (\mu(d))^2/\tau(d) = (3/2)^r$;

5 (Meissel 1850) Show that $\sum_{j=1}^{n} \mu(j)[n/j] = 1$ and that $|\sum_{j=1}^{n} \mu(j)/j| \leq 1$. [*Hint*: See Exercise 10.2.6.]

6 Let $SF(n)$ denote the number of square-free integers less than or equal to n. Show that

$$SF(n) = \sum_{j=1}^{n} |\mu(j)| = \sum_{j=i}^{n} \sum_{d^2|j} \mu(d) = \sum_{j=1}^{n} \mu(j)[n/j^2].$$

7 Let p be a prime. For $\alpha = 1, 2, 3, 4$ find $F(p^\alpha)$, given that $\phi(p^\alpha) = \sum_{d|p^\alpha} F(d)$. Now conjecture what $F(p^\alpha)$ and $F(m) = F(p_1^{\alpha_1} p_2^{\alpha_2} \cdots p_r^{\alpha_r})$ ought to be—and then prove your conjecture correct.

Computer problems 10.3

1 By generating random numbers in the range (1, 100 000) estimate the percentage of integers that are square-free. [One can determine theoretically the probability that a given integer is square-free. See, for example [4], [13], [16].]

2 Write a program to evaluate the Möbius function $\mu(n)$, for any $n \leq 10\,000$, and confirm Mertens' observation that, for all $k \leq 10\,000$, $|\sum_{n=1}^{k} \mu(n)| < \sqrt{k}$. What is the greatest value taken by $(1/\sqrt{k})|\sum_{n=1}^{k} \mu(n)|$ in this range?

10.4 Averaging—a smoothing process

As observed earlier, the arithmetic functions tend to throw light on the *structural* properties of each (positive) integer n rather than reflect the *size* of n. Accordingly it is not too surprising that many of these functions exhibit a rather erratic behaviour when examined from an 'n-strictly-increasing' point of view. To restore order to this different viewpoint we try to find estimates of the 'average size' of the functions we have introduced. In other words, we can look at* $(1/N)\sum_{n=1}^{N} f(n)$ and see what happens as we let N increase

* See Problem 10.1.6.

indefinitely. We shall look at two of our favourite arithmetic functions in that light.

Consider first the divisor function τ. Given the (positive) integer n, $\tau(n)$ is the number of integers $x>0$ to which there corresponds an integer y such that $xy=n$, that is, $\tau(n)$ is the number of points with integer coefficients (so-called *lattice points*) lying in the first quadrant on the hyperbola $xy=n$. We see immediately that $\sum_{n=1}^{N} \tau(n)$ is the number of lattice points in the first quadrant lying *on or below* the hyperbola $xy=N$ (excluding, of course, the points on the axes)—see Figure 10.1.

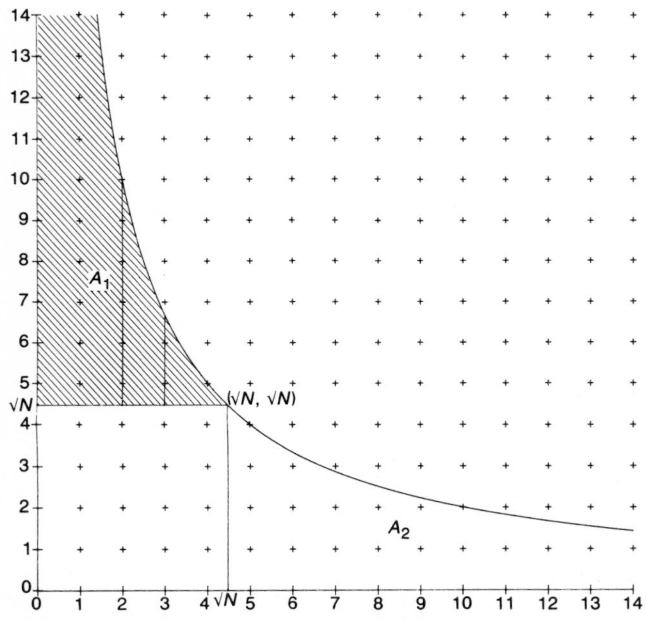

Fig. 10.1 The graph of $xy=N$ (for $N=20$).

From Figure 10.1 it is clear that the number of lattice points contributed to the sum by the square S is $[\sqrt{N}]^2$ whilst, on each line $x=r$, the number of lattice points contributed by area A_1 is $[N/r]-[\sqrt{N}]$. Since area A_2 clearly contributes the same number of points as A_1 we see that

$$\sum_{n=1}^{N} \tau(n)=2\sum_{n=1}^{[\sqrt{N}]}([N/n]-[\sqrt{N}])+[\sqrt{N}]^2$$

$$=2\sum_{n=1}^{[\sqrt{N}]}[N/n]-2[\sqrt{N}][\sqrt{N}]+[\sqrt{N}]^2$$

$$=2\sum_{n=1}^{[\sqrt{N}]}(N/n-\{N/n\})-(\sqrt{N}-\{\sqrt{N}\})^2$$

where we have used the standard symbol $\{t\}$ to indicate, for each real number t the quantity $t-[t]$. We then have

$$\sum_{n=1}^{N} \tau(n) = 2\sum_{n=1}^{[\sqrt{N}]} (N/n) - T_1 - N + 2\sqrt{N}\{\sqrt{N}\} - T_2$$

where $0 \leqslant T_1 < 2[\sqrt{N}] \leqslant 2\sqrt{N}$

and $0 \leqslant T_2 < 1$. We may therefore write

$$\sum_{n=1}^{N} \tau(n) = 2N \sum_{n=1}^{[\sqrt{N}]} (1/n) - N + T_3,$$

where $-2\sqrt{N}-1 < T_3 < 2\sqrt{N}$. Finally, we use a result from calculus to get an estimate for $\sum_{n=1}^{[\sqrt{N}]} (1/n)$. This result says that there is a constant, γ, such that, for all real numbers $M \geqslant 2$,

$$-2/M < \sum_{n=1}^{[M]} (1/n) - \log M - \gamma < 2/M.$$

(For a pictorial proof see Exercise 10.4.1.) Applying this result with $M=\sqrt{N}$ we obtain

$$\sum_{n=1}^{N} \tau(n) = 2N \log \sqrt{N} + 2N\gamma - N + T_4,$$

where $-4\sqrt{N}-2\sqrt{N}-1 < T_4 < 4\sqrt{N}+2\sqrt{N}$ so that, less accurately but more simply, $-7\sqrt{N} < T_4 < 7\sqrt{N}$. We therefore have

Theorem 10.4.1 (Dirichlet 1838) For each $N \in \mathbb{Z}^+$ there exists a quantity T_4, where $-7\sqrt{N} < T_4 < 7\sqrt{N}$, such that

$$\sum_{n=1}^{N} \tau(n) = N \log N + (2\gamma - 1)N + T_4. \quad \square$$

This result can be written more snappily if we introduce the so-called 'big oh' notation, as follows

Definition 10.4.2 Let $f(x)$, $g(x)$ be two functions defined on $\mathbb{R}^+$ (or $\mathbb{Z}^+$ as appropriate) such that $g(x)$ is positive for all $x \in \mathbb{R}^+$. We write $f(x) = O(g(x))$—read '$f(x)$ is big oh of $g(x)$'—if (and only if!) there exists a positive constant K, say, such that $|f(r)| < Kg(r)$ for all r for which f is defined.

Theorem 10.4.1 then becomes

Theorem 10.4.3 For each $N \in \mathbb{Z}^+$,

$$\sum_{n=1}^{N} \tau(n) = N \log N + (2\gamma - 1)N + O(\sqrt{N}). \quad \square$$

Note 10.4.4 It is known that in Theorem 10.4.3 $\sqrt{N}$ can, using more careful analysis, be replaced by $N^{1/3}$. The problem of improving this error estimate further is called *Dirichlet's divisor problem.*

By employing the big oh notation we can also tidy up *proofs* considerably. We show this in

Theorem 10.4.5 $\sum_{n=1}^{N} \sigma(n) = \pi^2 N^2/12 + O(N \log N)$.

*Proof**
$$\sum_{n=1}^{N} \sigma(n) = \sum_{n=1}^{N} \left(\sum_{d|n} d \right) = \sum_{n=1}^{N} \left(\sum_{d=1}^{[N/n]} d \right) = \sum_{n=1}^{N} \tfrac{1}{2}([N/n]^2 + [N/n])$$
$$= \frac{1}{2} \sum_{n=1}^{N} \Big((N/n - \{N/n\})^2 + (N/n - \{N/n\}) \Big)$$
$$= \frac{N^2}{2} \sum_{n=1}^{N} \frac{1}{n^2} + \frac{N}{2} \sum_{n=1}^{N} (1 - 2\{N/n\}) \frac{1}{n}$$
$$+ \frac{1}{2} \sum_{n=1}^{N} (\{N/n\}^2 - \{N/n\}).$$

Now

(i) $-\sum_{n=1}^{N} \frac{1}{n} \leq \sum_{n=1}^{N} (1 - 2\{N/n\}) \frac{1}{n} \leq \sum_{n=1}^{N} \frac{1}{n}$

whilst (more briefly) from Exercise 10.4.1,

(ii) $\sum_{n=1}^{N} (1/n) \leq \log N + \gamma + (1/N) \leq 2 \log N + \gamma$ if $N \geq 2$. Further

(iii) $0 \leq \{N/n\} < 1$ implies $|\frac{1}{2} \sum_{n=1}^{N} \{N/n\}^2 - \{N/n\}| < N/2$.

Finishing the proof in the big oh notation, we have essentially just shown that

$$\sum_{n=1}^{N} \sigma(n) = \frac{N^2}{2} \sum_{n=1}^{N} (1/n^2) + O(N \log N) + O(N).$$

Now, using the well-known result of analysis (see, for example, [28], p. 122†) that $\sum_{n=1}^{\infty} (1/n^2) = \pi^2/6$ we check, fairly easily—see Exercise 10.4.4—that $\sum_{n=1}^{N} (1/n^2) = \pi^2/6 + O(1/N)$.

Hence

$$\sum_{n=1}^{N} \sigma(n) = N^2\pi^2/12 + N^2 O(1/N) + O(N \log N) + O(N)$$
$$= N^2\pi^2/12 + O(N) + O(N \log N) + O(N)$$
$$= N^2\pi^2/12 + O(N \log N)$$

using Exercise 10.4.3. □

* See Exercise 10.4.2.

† For Euler's original 'proof' see [30].

The corresponding result on Euler's ϕ function is:

$$\sum_{n=1}^{N} \phi(n) = 3N^2/\pi^2 + O(N \log N).$$

This result can be used (see [28], p. 122) to show that, provided p is a large enough prime, there will be a quadratic non-residue of p between 1 and $\sqrt{p}$. Since each primitive root of p is necessarily a quadratic non-residue of p (see Exercise 8.2.7), this result throws some (rather dim) light on Artin's problem. (See Heath-Brown's paper referred to on p. 143.)

Of course sums (and averages) of related functions have been calculated. For example, one can show that

$$\sum_{n=1}^{N} \tau(n)/n = (\log N)^2/N + 2\gamma \log N + O(1),$$

that

$$\sum_{n=1}^{N} \phi(n)/n = 6N/\pi^2 + O(N \log N)$$

and that, for example,

$$\sum_{p \leq N} (1/p) = \log \log N + O(1).$$

This latter result, which we first mentioned in Chapter 2, can then be used to establish the equality $\sum_{n=1}^{N} \omega(n) = N \log \log N + cN + O(N/\log N)$, a result which indicates that the average number of distinct prime divisors of an integer n is approximately $\log \log n$. (For more precise information see [29], p. 98 or [13], p. 341.) Clearly this kind of information is not without interest to those who wish to factorise very large numbers—especially in connection with coding problems.

The kind of geometrical analysis used above can also give more information about a problem we considered earlier concerning sums of squares. As before let* $S_2(n)$ denote the number of formally distinct ways in which the non-negative integer n can be expressed as a sum of two squares—so that, for example, $S_2(5) = 8$ as previously noted.

The reason for considering 5 to have eight formally distinct representations as a sum of two squares should be clear from Figure 10.2 where you will see exactly eight lattice points lying on the circle $x^2 + y^2 = 5$.

To tackle the problem of finding the average value $(1/N) \sum_{n=0}^{N} S_2(n)$ (cf. Problem 7.1.4) of the S_2 function taken over the first N integers look again at Figure 10.2. It is clear for each N—the outermost circle in the picture corresponding to $N = 10$—that the number of lattice points lying inside and on the circle of radius $\sqrt{N}$ is precisely $\sum_{n=0}^{N} S_2(n)$.

* Of course S_2 is not a multiplicative function.

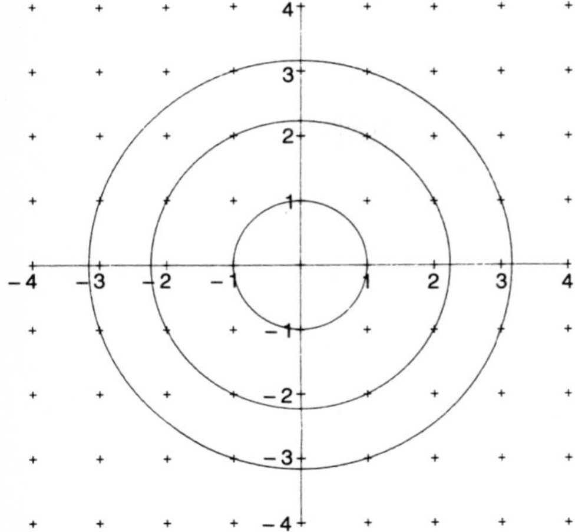

Fig. 10.2 Circles $x^2+y^2=N$ for $N=1, 5$ and 10.

Working now with general N—but keeping the case of $N=10$ in view (see Figure 10.3)—we associate with each lattice point L inside or on the circle $C(N)$: $x^2+y^2=N$, the unit square which has L at its north-west corner. (Each such square—for $N=10$— is shaded in the diagram below.) We get an estimate of the total area shaded by noting that (i) each point *outside* $C(N)$ and in a shaded square lies no more than $\sqrt{2}$ units away from the boundary of $C(N)$ whilst (ii) each point *inside* $C(N)$ and in an unshaded square also lies no more than $\sqrt{2}$ units from the boundary of $C(N)$. It follows that the number

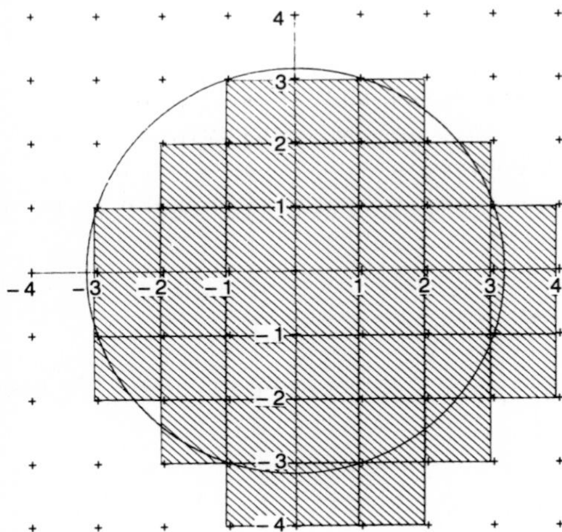

Fig. 10.3 The circle $x^2+y^2=10$ showing the squares associated with each lattice point either inside or on the circle.

$A(N)$ of shaded squares satisfies the equality

$$\pi(\sqrt{N}-\sqrt{2})^2 < A(N) < \pi(\sqrt{N}+\sqrt{2})^2.$$

Since $A(N)$ is also the number of lattice points inside and on $C(N)$ we have

$$\pi(\sqrt{N}-\sqrt{2})^2 < \sum_{n=0}^{N} S_2(n) < \pi(\sqrt{N}+\sqrt{2})^2,$$

that is

$$-2\sqrt{2N}\pi < \sum_{n=0}^{N} S_2(n) - (N+2)\pi < 2\sqrt{2N}\pi$$

or, in our big oh notation,

$$\sum_{n=0}^{N} S_2(n) - N\pi - 2\pi = O(\sqrt{N})$$

and hence we have

Theorem 10.4.6

$$\sum_{n=0}^{N} S_2(n) = N\pi + O(\sqrt{N}).$$

This was Gauss's contribution to the problem of finding the average value of the S_2 function. Subsequent authors have refined the O term—Sierpinski* was able to replace $O(\sqrt{N})$ by $O(N^{1/3})$ in 1906 and $\frac{1}{3}$ was improved to $\frac{27}{82}$(!) by later authors. On the other hand it has long been known that the $\frac{1}{3}$ cannot be replaced by $\frac{1}{4}$.

Exercises 10.4

1 Using Figure 10.4, drawn in the case $M = 4$, show that, for each *integer* $M \geqslant 2$, $\sum_{n=1}^{M} 1/n - \log M$ is equal in value to the total unshaded region $\gamma_1 + \gamma_2 + \cdots + \gamma_{M-1} + 1/M$ in the first column.

Denoting the total area† of the infinitely many similarly defined regions γ_i by γ deduce that

$$0 \leqslant \sum_{n=1}^{M} (1/n) - \log M - \gamma < 1/M.$$

If, for each *real* number $K > 2$ we interpret $\sum_{n=1}^{K} 1/n$ to be the sum $\sum_{n=1}^{[K]} 1/n$ show that

$$-\frac{2}{K} \leqslant -\frac{1}{[K]} \leqslant \sum_{n=1}^{K} 1/n - \log K - \gamma \leqslant \frac{1}{[K]} < \frac{2}{K}.$$

* Waclaw Sierpinski 14 March 1882 – 21 October 1969.
† How do we know that γ exists?

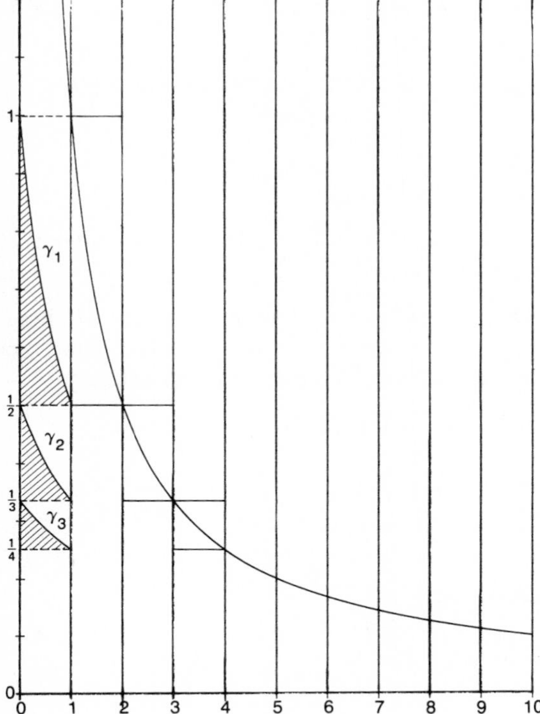

Fig. 10.4

[*Hint*: Apply the first part to the integer $[K]$ and show that $0 \leqslant \log K - \log[K] < 1/[K]$.]

2 Prove, as claimed in Theorem 10.4.5, that

$$\sum_{n=1}^{N}\left(\sum_{d|n} d\right) = \sum_{n=1}^{N}\left(\sum_{d=1}^{[N/n]} d\right).$$

3 Show that if $F(n) = O(n) + \text{constant}$, then $F(n) = O(n)$, and that if $G(n) = O(n) + O(n) + O(n \log n)$, then $G(n) = O(n \log n)$.

4 Prove that from $\sum_{n=1}^{\infty}(1/n^2) = \pi^2/6$ we may write $\sum_{n=1}^{N}(1/n^2) = \pi^2/6 + O(1/N)$ as in Theorem 10.4.4. [*Hint*:

$$\begin{aligned}\sum_{n=1}^{\infty}(1/n^2) - \sum_{n=1}^{N}(1/n^2) = \sum_{n=N+1}^{\infty}(1/n^2) &\leqslant \sum_{n=N+1}^{\infty}(1/(n-1) - 1/n)\\ &= (1/N - 1/(N+1)) + (1/(N+1) - 1/(N+2)) + \cdots\\ &= 1/N.]\end{aligned}$$

5 Prove that $\sum_{m=1}^{t} m = t^2/2 + O(t)$ and that $\sum_{m=1}^{t} m^2 = t^3/3 + O(t^2)$. Is the obvious conjecture valid?

6 Let $T(n)$ denote the number of ordered triples of integers whose product is n. Prove that

$$\sum_{n=1}^{N} T(n) = N \log^2 N + O(N \log N).$$

[*Hint*: Count the lattice points with positive coordinates on or under the surface defined by the equation $xyz = N$.]

7 Let $S_3(n)$ denote the number of representations of n as a sum of three integer squares. Prove that $\sum_{n=0}^{N} S_3(n) = \frac{4}{3}\pi N^{3/2} + O(N)$. [*Hint*: Count the lattice points in and on the sphere of radius $\sqrt{N}$ centred at the origin.]

8 Prove that $\sum_{n=1}^{N} \omega(n) = N \log \log N + cN + O(N/\log N)$. [*Hint*:

$$\sum_{n=1}^{N} \omega(n) = \sum_{p \leq N} \Big(\sum_{n=1}^{[N/p]} 1 \Big) = \sum_{p \leq N} [N/p].$$

Write $[N/p] = N/p + O(1)$ and use

$$\sum_{p \leq N} O(1) = O(\pi(N)) = O(N/\log N)$$

and the formula for $\sum_{p \leq N} (1/p)$ on p. 56.]

11
Continued fractions and Pell's equation

11.1 Finite continued fractions

In this chapter we examine the remarkable fact that the essentially simple ideas used in the Euclidean algorithm, when looked at in a different way, form the basis for solving completely what at first appears to be a rather difficult problem as well as providing a possibly unexpected solution for what seems to be a rather trivial one. The first problem asks, as did Fermat, for solutions of (Diophantine) equations such as $x^2-61y^2=1$ (cf. Problem 0.1.1). The second raises questions of the kind: What is the best rational number approximation a/b to π if we insist that $1 \leqslant b \leqslant 1000$? (The answer is *not* 3142/1000!)

Recall that to find the gcd of 24 769 and 2227 using the Euclidean algorithm we write

$$\begin{aligned} 24\,769 &= 11 \cdot 2227 + 272 \\ 2\,227 &= 8 \cdot 272 + 51 \\ 272 &= 5 \cdot 51 + 17 \\ 51 &= 3 \cdot 17 + 0. \end{aligned}$$

It follows that

$$\frac{24\,769}{2227} = 11 + \frac{272}{2227} = 11 + \cfrac{1}{\cfrac{2227}{272}} = 11 + \cfrac{1}{8 + \cfrac{51}{272}}$$

$$11 + \cfrac{1}{8 + \cfrac{1}{5 + \cfrac{17}{51}}} = 11 + \cfrac{1}{8 + \cfrac{1}{5 + \cfrac{1}{3}}}$$

Such an expression is an example of a (finite) continued fraction. Formally:

Definition 11.1.1 A *finite continued fraction* is a fraction written in the form

$$a_0 + \cfrac{1}{a_1 + \cfrac{1}{a_2 + \cfrac{1}{a_3 + \cdots \; \cdots + \cfrac{1}{a_{n-1} + \cfrac{1}{a_n}}}}}$$

where the a_i are real numbers all, except possibly a_0, being positive. The numbers a_i are called the *partial quotients* (they correspond to the 'quotients' (see Note 0.3.2(i)) in the Euclidean algorithm). The fraction is termed *simple* if all the a_i are integers.

Notes 11.1.2

(i) We write the above continued fraction as $[a_0; a_1, a_2, \ldots, a_n]$ for brevity—so, for example, $24\,769/2227 = [11; 8, 5, 3]$.

(ii) Our main interest will be in simple continued fractions, but it is convenient not to specialise to this case just yet (see Note 11.2.7(ii)).

It is clear that each finite simple continued fraction 'simplifies' to produce a rational number and, conversely, as the above example illustrates, each rational number can be expressed as a finite simple continued fraction.

Identifying the a_i with the quotients in the Euclidean algorithm is slightly misleading, at least as far as the final 'quotient' is concerned. For, since $a_n = (a_n - 1) + 1 = (a_n - 1) + 1/1$, we can clearly rewrite $[a_0; a_1, \ldots, a_{n-1}, a_n] = [a_0; a_1, \ldots, a_{n-1}, a_n - 1, 1]$—provided $a_n - 1$ is positive. On the other side of the coin: if $a_n = 1$, then $a_{n-1} + 1/a_n = a_{n-1} + 1$ and so, in this case, we have

$$[a_0; a_1, \ldots, a_{n-1}, a_n] = [a_0; a_1, \ldots, a_{n-1} + 1].$$

It therefore appears that each rational number has at least two (and, in fact, exactly two—Exercise 11.1.4) representations as a finite simple continued fraction.

Example 11.1.3 $24\,769/2227 = [11; 8, 5, 3] = [11; 8, 5, 2, 1]$.

Program 11.1 converts a rational number (described as t/b) into continued fraction form using the Euclidean algorithm. The quotient (q) at each stage in the iteration is the next term in the finite simple continued fraction.

Program 11.1 *Conversion of a rational number to continued fraction form*

```
10 INPUT t,b
20 PRINT t;"/";b
30 q = INT(t/b)
40 r = t - q * b
```

```
 50 PRINT "(";q;";";
 60    t = b
 70    b = r
 80    q = INT(t/b)
 90    r = t - q * b
100    PRINT ;q;",";
110 IF r > 0 GOTO 60
120 PRINT ;")"
```

To reverse the process the finite continued fraction of n terms is stored in an array a, then (observing the structure in Definition 11.1.1) the rational number is constructed as follows:

(i) set up the last term $a(n)$ so that $t = a(n)$ and $b = 1$.
(ii) then proceed iteratively including each term in the continued fraction (in reverse order) by adding it to the reciprocal of the existing rational number t/b. Thus at each stage the rational number t/b is replaced by $(a(n-i) * t + b)/t$. The algorithm will, of course, produce the rational number in its lowest terms.

Program 11.2 *Conversion of a finite contінued fraction to a rational number*

```
  5 INPUT "Enter the number of terms in the continued fraction ",n
 10 DIM a(n)
 20 PRINT "Enter the terms one at a time"
 30 FOR i = 1 TO n
 40    INPUT a(i)
 50 NEXT i
 60 t = a(n)
 70 b = 1
 80 FOR i = n-1 TO 1 STEP -1
 90    n1 = t*a(i)+b
100    b = t
110    t = n1
120 NEXT i
130 PRINT "The rational number is ";t;"/";b
```

Exercises 11.1

1 Exhibit two finite simple continued fraction representations for each of: (i) 51/11; (ii) 1725/1193; (iii) 1193/1725; (iv) −1193/1725; (v) 30 031/16 579; (vi) (Euler's *Algebra*) 1103/87; (vii) 355/113.

2 Find the simple continued fraction representations of: (i) 2.7182; (ii) 2.7183; (iii) 3.14159; (iv) 3.14160.

3 Determine the rational numbers represented by:
(i) $[0; 1, 2, 3, 4, 5, 4, 3, 2, 1]$;
(ii) $[0; 1, 2, 1, 2, 1, 2, 1, 2]$;
(iii) $[1; 3, 5, 7, 9, 11, 13]$;
(iv) $[1; 3, 5, 7, 11, 13, 17]$;
(v) $[3; 1, 4, 1, 5, 9, 2, 6, 5]$.

4 Prove that each rational number has exactly two representations as a finite simple continued fraction.

5 Let x be a positive real number. Which is bigger: $[a_0; a_1, \ldots, a_n]$ or $[a_0; a_1, \ldots, a_n + x]$?

6 Show that if $r = [a_0; a_1, \ldots, a_n]$ and $r > 1$ then $1/r = [0; a_0, a_1, \ldots, a_n]$.

Computer problem 11.1

1 Modify Program 11.1 so that it produces both possible finite continued fraction representations.

11.2 Infinite continued fractions

Let us now be a little daring with this idea of continued fractions! Surely it would be worthwhile to contemplate representing irrational numbers, especially e, π, $\sqrt{2}$ etc.? If this appears hopeless (after all finite simple continued fractions can only represent rational numbers) what might we do? Answer: drop the word 'finite'. That is, we make

Definition 11.2.1 Let $a_0, a_1, a_2, \ldots$ be an infinite sequence of real numbers (respectively, integers) all except, perhaps, a_0 being positive. The expression

$$a_0 + \cfrac{1}{a_1 + \cfrac{1}{a_2 + \cfrac{1}{a_3 + \cdots}}}$$

is called an *infinite* (respectively, *infinite simple*) continued fraction—which we abbreviate to icf and iscf respectively. Following Note 11.1.2(i), we write the above icf as $[a_0; a_1, a_2, \ldots]$.

Such boldness has to be paid for! We surely have to ask: (A) Does such a 'fraction' have any meaning? (B) If so, can we use it to good effect? (or is it just a definition for definition's sake?) As it happens the answer to (A) is 'yes' whilst the answer to (B) is 'YES' (i.e. 'yes' but emphatically so!)

In fact continued fractions have been put to many uses (see [1], all volumes). Lagrange, in Euler's *Algebra*, describes the theory of continued fractions as 'One of the most useful in arithmetic' (i.e. in the theory of numbers). According to [31] the Indian mathematician Aryabhatta employed continued fractions to solve Diophantine equations of the form $ax + by = c$. So did Lagrange 1200 years later, at the same time asserting that the method was essentially Bachet's. At a slightly deeper level Bombelli's *Algebra* (1572) applied continued fractions to the problem of obtaining good rational approximations to square roots. But even this approach was not new. The Greeks and Indians of c.400 B.C. realised that a/b was a good approximation to $\sqrt{2}$ when $a^2-2b^2=\pm 1$—an equation which, unlike $a^2-2b^2=0$, is solvable in integers. By 130 A.D. Theon of Smyrna had shown how to find infinitely many such approximations (cf. Exercise 8.4.5). In more recent times, Huygens*, around 1615, used continued fractions to find good rational approximations to certain real numbers arising in his construction of a gearing mechanism for a model of planetary motions, whilst in 1767 and 1776 Lagrange used the concept to find approximations to roots of both polynomial and differential equations. Moving to the present, continued fraction expansions have been employed in connection with computer factorisations of very large integers (see Section 11.7.)

Let us begin naively so as to get a flavour of what is going on. For example let us consider the

Problem 11.2.2 What number, if any, is represented by $[1; 1, 1, 1, \ldots]$?

Solution Let the 'number', assuming that there is one, be denoted by α. Then

$$\alpha = 1 + \cfrac{1}{1+\cfrac{1}{1+\cfrac{1}{1+\cfrac{1}{1+\cdots}}}}$$

Since the fraction is 'infinite' it appears that $\alpha = 1 + 1/\alpha$, that is, $\alpha^2 - \alpha - 1 = 0$. In other words $\alpha = (1 \pm \sqrt{5})/2$. Since α is 'clearly' positive it must be that $\alpha = (1+\sqrt{5})/2$.

[We hope this was a pleasant surprise—but do you believe it?]

We now aim to substantiate assertion (A) above. To do this we'll need:

Definition 11.2.3 Let $C = [a_0; a_1, a_2, \ldots]$ be a continued fraction, finite or infinite. For each non-negative integer k the finite continued fraction $[a_0; a_1, a_2, \ldots, a_k]$ is called the *kth convergent of* C and is denoted by C_k.

Example 11.2.4 The first five convergents of $[1; 1, 1, 1, \ldots]$ are

$$1 = \left(=\frac{1}{1}\right), \quad 1+\frac{1}{1}=\frac{2}{1}, \quad 1+\cfrac{1}{1+\cfrac{1}{1}}=\frac{3}{2}, \quad 1+\cfrac{1}{1+\cfrac{1}{1+\cfrac{1}{1}}}=\frac{5}{3}, \quad 1+\frac{1}{5/3}=\frac{8}{5}$$

You will notice, as did Robert Simson† in 1753 that the numerators and denominators are terms of Fibonacci's sequence $1, 1, 2, 3, 5, 8, \ldots$ (see Definition 0.5.1).

* Christian Huygens, 14 April 1629 - 8 July 1695.

† Robert Simson, 14 October 1687 - 1 October 1768.

The whole point of Definition 11.2.3 is that it allows us to make

Definition 11.2.5 Let $C=[a_0; a_1, a_2, \ldots]$ and $C_0, C_1, C_2, \ldots$ be as above. If the sequence $C_0, C_1, C_2, \ldots$ tends to a limit λ, say, that is, if $\lim_{n\to\infty} C_n=\lambda$, then we say that λ is the *value* of the icf C.

Conversely, if λ is a given real number and if an icf C can be found such that $\lim_{n\to\infty} C_n=\lambda$, then we say that C *represents* λ.

We shall frequently, rather casually, identify the icf with its value λ. (The question you should perhaps be asking is answered by Theorem 11.3.2.)

If we write down the first few convergents $C_0, C_1, C_2, C_3, \ldots$ of the icf displayed in Definition 11.2.1 we soon notice that, for $0\leqslant k\leqslant 3$, C_k is equal to the fraction p_k/q_k, where

$$\begin{aligned}
p_0&=a_0 & q_0&=1\\
p_1&=a_1a_0+1 & q_1&=a_1\\
p_2&=a_2(a_1a_0+1)+a_0 & q_2&=a_2a_1+1\\
p_3&=a_3(a_2a_1a_0+a_2+a_0)+a_1a_0+1 & q_3&=a_3(a_2a_1+1)+a_1.
\end{aligned}$$

Consequently, for $k=2$ and 3, we have $C_k=p_k/q_k$, where $p_k=a_kp_{k-1}+p_{k-2}$ and $q_k=a_kq_{k-1}+q_{k-2}$. We claim that such relationships persist for all $k\geqslant 2$, a claim we prove easily by induction.

Theorem 11.2.6 Let the infinite continued fraction $C=[a_0; a_1, a_2, \ldots]$ be given. Set $p_0=a_0$, $q_0=1$, $p_1=a_1a_0+1$, $q_1=a_1$ and for each $k\geqslant 2$ set

$$p_k=a_kp_{k-1}+p_{k-2},\ q_k=a_kq_{k-1}+q_{k-2}.$$

Then, for each $k\geqslant 0$, we have $C_k=p_k/q_k$.

Proof Starting the induction at $k=2$ we see that the first step in the induction works. Now suppose the desired result (i.e. $C_k=p_k/q_k$) holds for some value l of k and consider the convergent C_{l+1}. Now

$$C_{l+1}=[a_0; a_1, \ldots, a_{l+1}]=[a_0; a_1, \ldots, a_l+1/a_{l+1}].$$

By the induction hypothesis we may infer, from the second expression for C_{l+1}, that

$$\begin{aligned}
C_{l+1}&=\frac{(a_l+1/a_{l+1})p_{l-1}+p_{l-2}}{(a_l+1/a_{l+1})q_{l-1}+q_{l-2}}=\frac{a_{l+1}(a_lp_{l-1}+p_{l-2})+p_{l-1}}{a_{l+1}(a_lq_{l-1}+q_{l-2})+q_{l-1}}\\
&=\frac{a_{l+1}p_l+p_{l-1}}{a_{l+1}q_l+q_{l-1}}=\frac{p_{l+1}}{q_{l+1}}
\end{aligned}$$

as required. $\square$

Notes 11.2.7

(i) The formulae for p_k, q_k given in Theorem 11.2.6 are reminiscent of that giving the terms of the Fibonacci sequence—namely $f_1 = 1$, $f_2 = 1$, $f_n = f_{n-1} + f_{n-2}$. Indeed the p_i and q_i are the terms of the Fibonacci sequence when each $a_i = 1$ as we have already seen (Example 11.2.4).

(ii) Having just made full use of allowing the a_i to be rational numbers we, from now on, consider only infinite simple continued fractions (iscfs); that is, where the a_i are assumed to be integers, positive if $i \geqslant 1$.

(iii) When, for $i \geqslant 1$, the a_i are (positive) integers we notice the fact (used frequently below) that $q_i < q_{i+1}$.

Example 11.2.8 The first few convergents of $C = [1; 2, 3, 4, 5, 6, 7, \ldots]$ are obtained from

$$\begin{array}{lllllll} a_i: & 1, & 2, & 3, & 4, & 5, & 6, \ \ldots \\ p_i: & 1, & 3, & 10, & 43, & 225, & 1393, \ \ldots \\ q_i: & 1, & 2, & 7, & 30, & 157, & 972, \ \ldots \end{array}$$

and the $C_k (= p_k/q_k)$ appear to be converging towards . . . what?

To prove our first 'big' result about iscfs we shall need the following corollary of Theorem 11.2.6.

Corollary 11.2.9 Let $C_k = p_k/q_k$ be as above. Then

(i) for $k \geqslant 1$: $p_k q_{k-1} - p_{k-1} q_k = (-1)^{k-1}$; $C_k - C_{k-1} = (-1)^{k-1}/q_{k-1} q_k$

(ii) for $k \geqslant 2$: $p_k q_{k-2} - p_{k-2} q_k = (-1)^k a_k$; $C_k - C_{k-2} = (-1)^k a_k / q_{k-2} q_k$.

Proof By induction: for $k = 1$, $p_k q_{k-1} - p_{k-1} q_k = (a_1 a_0 + 1)1 - a_0 a_1 = 1 = (-1)^0$, as required.

Assuming the desired equality holds for $k = l$ we see that

$$\begin{aligned} p_{l+1} q_l - p_l q_{l+1} &= (a_{l+1} p_l + p_{l-1}) q_l - p_l (a_{l+1} q_l + q_{l-1}) \\ &= p_{l-1} q_l - p_l q_{l-1} = (-1)(-1)^{l-1} = (-1)^l, \end{aligned}$$

as required.

It then follows immediately that

$$C_k - C_{k-1} = \frac{p_k q_{k-1} - p_{k-1} q_k}{q_{k-1} q_k} = \frac{(-1)^{k-1}}{q_{k-1} q_k}.$$

We also deduce (for $k \geqslant 2$) that

$$\begin{aligned} p_k q_{k-2} - p_{k-2} q_k &= (a_k p_{k-1} + p_{k-2}) q_{k-2} - p_{k-2} (a_k q_{k-1} + q_{k-2}) \\ &= a_k (p_{k-1} q_{k-2} - p_{k-2} q_{k-1}) = a_k (-1)^{k-2} = (-1)^k a_k. \end{aligned}$$

The final equality follows on division by $q_{k-2} q_k$. □

One immediate consequence of this corollary is . . . another!

Corollary 11.2.10 Let $C=[a_0; a_1, a_2, \ldots]$ and $C_k = p_k/q_k$ as usual. Then $C_0 < C_2 < C_4 < C_6 < \cdots < C_7 < C_5 < C_3 < C_1$. That is, the 'even' ('odd') C_k form an increasing (decreasing) sequence which is bounded above (below) by each of the 'odd' ('even') C_k.

Proof Since the $a_i (i \geqslant 1)$ are all positive—by assumption—so too are all the $q_i (i \geqslant 0)$ by Note 11.2.7(iii). From Corollary 11.2.9 we deduce that, for $k \geqslant 2$, $C_k - C_{k-2}$ is positive if k is even and negative if k is odd. We therefore have, immediately, $C_2 > C_0$, $C_4 > C_2$, etc. and $C_3 < C_1$, $C_5 < C_3$, etc.

To get the relation between the even and odd C_k we put $k = 2m+2n$ to obtain, from Corollary 11.2.9(i), the inequality $C_{2m+2n} < C_{2m+2n-1}$ and then, from the inequalities just established,

$$C_{2m} < C_{2m+2n} < C_{2m+2n-1} < C_{2n-1},$$

that is, each even C_k is less than each odd C_k. □

Example 11.2.11 In Example 11.2.8 we have

$$1/1 < 10/7 < 225/157 < \cdots < 1.4\,331\,247 < \cdots$$

$$\cdots < 1393/272 < 43/30 < 3/2.$$

We now establish our 'big' theorem.

Theorem 11.2.12 Let $C=[a_0; a_1, a_2, \ldots]$ and C_k be as usual. Then $\lim_{n\to\infty} C_n$ exists.

Proof We call upon a theorem of analysis: *Each increasing (decreasing) sequence of real numbers which is bounded above (below) possesses a limit.*

(A proof of this is given in, for example, [30] and [32].)

Using this result, the sequence $C_0, C_2, C_4, \ldots$ which is bounded above by all the odd C_k (and, in particular by C_1) has a limiting value μ, say: $\lim_{n\to\infty} C_{2n} = \mu$. Similarly the sequence $C_1, C_3, C_5, \ldots$ is a decreasing sequence which is bounded below (by C_0). Hence $\lim_{n\to\infty} C_{2n+1} = \nu$, for some ν.

We claim that $\mu = \nu$. To prove this note that, on the one hand,

$$\lim_{n\to\infty} (C_{2n+1} - C_{2n}) = \lim_{n\to\infty} 1/q_{2n}q_{2n+1} = 0 \qquad \text{(by Note 11.2.7(iii))}.$$

On the other hand

$$\lim_{n\to\infty} (C_{2n+1} - C_{2n}) = \lim_{n\to\infty} C_{2n+1} - \lim_{n\to\infty} C_{2n} = \nu - \mu.$$

Thus $\nu - \mu = 0$ so that $\mu = \nu$ as asserted. This is enough to confirm that $\lim_{n\to\infty} C_n$ exists; it is equal to μ $(=\nu)$. □

Theorem 11.2.6 presents us with a iterative method—used in Program 11.3—for calculating the convergents relating to successive terms of a continued fraction. Note that we can start the iteration by using $p_{-1}=1$ and $q_{-1}=0$, one step before the result presented in Theorem 11.2.6. While this is perhaps artificial from a purist mathematician's point of view it makes the construction of the program slightly easier. The program also displays the relative change between successive convergents. Since a computer stores only a limited number of significant digits of a real number, the decimal representation of any continued fraction as determined by the computer will not change once sufficiently many convergents have been evaluated. Later convergents will only alter the significant figures beyond the reach of the computer unless one uses high-precision arithmetic.

Program 11.3 *Calculation of convergents given the successive terms a_i in the continued fraction $[a_0;a_1,a_2...]$*

```
10 INPUT "ENTER THE FIRST TERM ",A
20 PO=1:P=A
30 Q=1:QO=0
40     INPUT "next term ",A
50     IF A<1 STOP
60 REM Update the numerator of the convergent
70     P1=A*P+PO
80     PO=P
90     P=P1
100 REM Update the denominator
110     Q1=A*Q+QO
120     QO=Q
130     Q=Q1
140 REM calculate the relative error, display the results
150     C=(P/Q-PO/QO)*QO/PO
160     PRINT A;"  ";P;"  ";Q,"  ";P/Q," relative error is";C
170 GOTO 40
```

Exercises 11.2

1 Find the real number represented by:

(i) $[1; 2, 2, 2, 2, 2, 2, \ldots]$; (ii) $[1; 1, 2, 1, 2, 1, 2, \ldots]$;
(iii) $[2; 4, 4, 4, 4, 4, 4, \ldots]$; (iv) $[2; 2, 4, 2, 4, 2, 4, \ldots]$;
(v) $[3; 6, 6, 6, 6, 6, 6, \ldots]$; (vi) $[2; 1, 1, 1, 4, 1, 1, 1, 4, 1, 1, \ldots]$.

2 (a) For parts (iv), (v) of Exercise 11.1.1 determine all the convergents of the continued fractions you obtained; (b) Determine the first six convergents of Exercise 11.2.1(i) above.

3 (a) Prove that if p_k/q_k is the kth convergent of $[a_0; a_1, a_2, \ldots]$, then $q_k \geqslant u_k$, the kth term of the Fibonacci sequence;
(b) Prove that $\lim_{n\to\infty} u_{n-1}/u_n = (\sqrt{5}-1)/2$.

4 Let $x > 1$ be a real number. Show that the nth convergent of $1/x$ is the reciprocal of the $(n-1)$st convergent of x. [Use Exercise 11.1.6.]

5 Show that if $a_0 > 0$ then $p_k/p_{k-1} = [a_k; a_{k-1}, \ldots, a_1, a_0]$ and

$$q_k/q_{k-1} = [a_k; a_{k-1}, \ldots, a_2, a_1].$$

[*Hint*: Find p_k/p_{k-1}, q_k/q_{k-1} from Theorem 11.2.6.]

6 Show that the next to last convergent of the continued fraction expansion of the rational number r/s (where $(r, s) = 1$) solves the equation $rx + sy = 1$ (Huygens 1703).

7 Prove that if p_k/q_k is as above then $(p_k, q_k) = 1$.

8 Use Corollary 11.2.9 to show that, in the Fibonacci sequence $u_1, u_2, \ldots$,

$$u_{k+1}u_{k-1} - u_k^2 = (-1)^{k-1}.$$

9 Check Corollary 11.2.10 on $[1; 2, 2, 2, 2, 2, 2, \ldots]$ at least up to C_7.

Computer problems 11.2

1 Use the result of Exercise 6 above to write a program to solve the Diophantine equation $Ax - By = 1$ where $A, B > 1$.

2 Examine the results from Program 11.3 as you enter longer and longer continued fractions and explain what you observe.

11.3 Computing continued fractions for irrational numbers

Earlier we made the trivial observation that each *finite* simple continued fraction has a rational number value. We now prove that no *infinite* simple continued fraction can have a rational value, that is:

Theorem 11.3.1 The value of each iscf is irrational.

Proof Suppose the value λ of the iscf $C = [a_0; a_1, a_2, \ldots]$ is the rational number $a/b (b > 0)$ For each n we have $C_{2n} < a/b < C_{2n+1}$. It follows that $0 < a/b - C_{2n} < C_{2n+1} - C_{2n} = 1/q_{2n}q_{2n+1}$, from which we may conclude that $0 < aq_{2n} - bp_{2n} < b/q_{2n+1}$. But, for n large enough, $0 < b/q_{2n+1} < 1$ (Note 11.2.7(iii)) whereas $aq_{2n} - bp_{2n}$ is, for all n, a positive integer. This blatant contradiction proves the theorem. □

Two obvious questions arise. (i) Does each irrational number have a representation as an iscf? (ii) If so, how can we compute the (first few terms of the) continued fraction expansion of a given irrational number λ?

Theorem 11.3.2 To each irrational number λ there corresponds a unique iscf which represents λ.

Proof We find the iscf corresponding to λ by successive approximations. If we want to write

$$\lambda = a_0 + \cfrac{1}{a_1 + \cfrac{1}{a_2 + \cdots}},$$

where each $a_i (i \geqslant 1)$ is a positive integer, we see that

$$\cfrac{1}{a_1 + \cfrac{1}{a_2 + \cdots}}$$

is a positive number less than 1 and so we are obliged, if we also want a_0 to be an integer, to set $a_0 = [\lambda]$, i.e. a_0 is the greatest integer not exceeding λ. Then simple arithmetic leads to

$$\frac{1}{\lambda - [\lambda]} = a_1 + \cfrac{1}{a_2 + \cfrac{1}{a_3 + \cdots}},$$

so that, for the same reasons, a_1 is forced to be $[\lambda_1]$, where $\lambda_1 = 1/(\lambda - [\lambda])$. Likewise $a_2 = [\lambda_2]$, where $\lambda_2 = 1/(\lambda_1 - [\lambda_1])$.

Note that $0 < \lambda - [\lambda] < 1$ and, since λ is irrational, λ_1 is also irrational. In a like manner one can show that all the λ_i are irrational numbers greater than 1 where, setting it out formally for clarity; $\lambda_0 = \lambda$ and, for $i \geqslant 0$, $\lambda_{i+1} = 1/(\lambda_i - [\lambda_i])$.

We now claim that $C = [a_0; a_1, a_2, \ldots]$, where $a_i = [\lambda_i]$ for all $i \geqslant 0$, does indeed represent λ.

Clearly

$$\begin{aligned} \lambda_0 = \lambda &= [\lambda_0] + (\lambda_0 - [\lambda_0]) = a_0 + 1/\lambda_1 \\ &= a_0 + \frac{1}{[\lambda_1] + (\lambda_1 - [\lambda_1])} = a_0 + \cfrac{1}{a_1 + \cfrac{1}{\lambda_2}} \end{aligned}$$

etc. so that $\lambda_0 = [a_0; a_1, a_2, \ldots, a_n, \lambda_{n+1}]$ for each $n \geqslant 0$.

Now by Theorem 11.2.6, we may write

$$\lambda_0 = \frac{\lambda_{n+1} p_n + p_{n-1}}{\lambda_{n+1} q_n + q_{n-1}},$$

where, for $k \leqslant n$, we have as always, $p_k/q_k = [a_0; a_1, \ldots, a_k] = C_k$. But then we have

$$|\lambda_0 - C_n| = \left| \frac{\lambda_{n+1}p_n + p_{n-1}}{\lambda_{n+1}q_n + q_{n-1}} - \frac{p_n}{q_n} \right|$$

$$= \left| \frac{p_{n-1}q_n - p_n q_{n-1}}{(\lambda_{n+1}q_n + q_{n-1})q_n} \right| = \left| \frac{(-1)^n}{(\lambda_{n+1}q_n + q_{n-1})q_n} \right|$$

(using Corollary 11.2.9) $= 1/q_{n+1}q_n < 1/q_n^2$.

Since, by Note 11.2.7(iii), the q_i form an increasing sequence of (positive) integers, this shows that $\lambda = \lambda_0 = \lim_{n\to\infty} C_n = [a_0; a_1, a_2, \ldots]$.

With regard to uniqueness, the investigations at the start of the proof suffice. For, as we observed, if $\lambda = [a_0; a_1, a_2, \ldots]$ we are *forced* to take $a_0 = [\lambda]$ and generally $a_i = [\lambda_i]$, where $\lambda_i = 1/(\lambda_{i-1} - [\lambda_{i-1}])$ and where $\lambda = \lambda_0$. Thus, if $[b_0; b_1, b_2, \ldots]$, we have $b_0 = [\lambda]$ and generally, $b_i = [\lambda_i]$—so that $a_i = b_i$ for each $i \geqslant 0$. □

Put another way, the uniqueness part of Theorem 11.3.2 says: Different-looking iscfs represent different irrational numbers.

Theorem 11.3.2 presents, in its proof, an algorithm which we use in Program 11.4 for calculating the continued fraction of any number. If the number entered is rational then the algorithm is identical to Euclid's Algorithm used in Program 11.1. In this case the computation will automatically terminate. However, if the number is irrational (or the continued fraction of the rational number is long) the usual problem of precision of computer arithmetic rears its head again. As each term is calculated the rounding errors that occur in the calculation of the reciprocal of $\lambda_i - [\lambda_i]$ accumulate, so that eventually the next term (and all subsequent terms) are in error. We have shown that the nth convergent C_n is within $1/q_n^2$ of the true value, a distance that decreases with each subsequent term. However, on a computer once the change between successive convergents is less than $(0.5)10^{-d+1}$, where d is the number of significant digits that your computer can handle, we can expect no more correct terms in the continued fraction since we have reached the limits of the computer's accuracy. It is sensible to use this as a means of terminating the computation. We leave the reader to make this modification to the program. Of course if the arithmetic operations are performed using high-precision arithmetic techniques such as those described in Appendix I these problems become less immediate.

Program 11.4 *The continued fraction representation of any positive number*

```
10 INPUT N
20 REM if N contains the number of interest
30 REM  A contains, in turn,
40 REM the successive terms in the continued fraction.
50 REM the program only terminates if it is finite.
```

```
 60 A=INT(N)
 70   PRINT ;A;",";
 80   IF A=N STOP
 90   N = 1 / (N - A)
100 GOTO 60
```

Exercises 11.3

1 Rewriting the equality

$$\lambda = \lambda_0 = \frac{\lambda_{n+1} p_n + p_{n-1}}{\lambda_{n+1} q_n + q_{n-1}},$$

in Theorem 11.3.2, as

$$\lambda - p_n/q_n = \frac{-q_{n-1}}{q_n \lambda_{n+1}} (\lambda - p_{n-1}/q_{n-1})$$

show that, for each $n \geqslant 1$, $|\lambda - p_n/q_n| < |\lambda - p_{n-1}/q_{n-1}|$. This says that 'successive convergents get closer'.

2 Use the same equality to prove that

$$\lambda - p_n/q_n = \frac{(-1)^n}{q_n(\lambda_{n+1} q_n + q_{n-1})}.$$

Computer problem 11.3

1 Modify Program 11.4 to calculate the convergents at each stage and to stop when the calculation is at the limits of your computer's accuracy. Run the program with the following values of N: $\sqrt{2}, \sqrt{3}, \sqrt{8}, \sqrt{13}, \sqrt{29}, \sqrt{35}, \sqrt{4\,729\,494}$; the cube roots of 2, 3, 32; and $(1+\sqrt{5})/2$, $(-4+\sqrt{76})/10$, $(-4+\sqrt{76})/11$, π, e, $(\mathrm{e}-1)/(\mathrm{e}+1)$, $(\mathrm{e}^2-1)/(\mathrm{e}^2+1) = \tanh(1)$, 34/23, 340/230, $1/\sqrt{2}$, $1/\sqrt{4\,729\,494}$. Is there any pattern to your results? How many terms are correctly calculated in each case? [*Note*: Calculating π by 4*ATN(1) and e by EXP(1) will give the values as accurately as possible on your computer.]

11.4 Approximating irrational numbers

An immediate, and yet very interesting, consequence of the results in the last section leads us in a direction which turns out to be most appropriate for studying both of the problems raised at the start of the chapter. The consequence is:

Theorem 11.4.1 Let α be any irrational number. Then there exist infinitely many rationals r/s such that $|\alpha - r/s| < 1/s^2$.

Proof From the proof of Theorem 11.3.2 we see that any of the convergents of α will do! □

Example 11.4.2 Find a rational number within $1/10^6$ of $\alpha = (1+\sqrt{5})/2$.

Solution Using the continued fraction $[1; 1, 1, \ldots]$, Theorem 11.3.2 tells us that $1597/987 = p_{15}/q_{15}$ will certainly do.

Note however that given α, there are fractions r/s for which $|\alpha - r/s| < 1/s^2$ and yet r/s is *not* a convergent of the continued fraction representing α. (Exercise 11.4.3 asks for such an example.)

To ensure that only convergents of α satisfy the inequality we tighten it up somewhat below.

Theorem 11.4.3 Let α be any irrational number and suppose that r/s is a rational number such that $|\alpha - r/s| < 1/2s^2$. Then r/s is a convergent of the continued fraction expansion of α. □ (Proof follows Lemma 11.4.4.)

(This time not all the convergents of α will satisfy the inequality—but see Exercise 11.4.4.)

To prove the theorem we need a technical lemma. Its statement isn't very inspiring but its proof isn't too hard and it *is* just what we shall need to progress.

Lemma 11.4.4 (*Lagrange*) Let $C_n = p_n/q_n$ be the nth convergent of the iscf representing the irrational number α. If $r, s \in \mathbb{Z}$ are such that $1 \leqslant s < q_{n+1}$, then $|q_n\alpha - p_n| \leqslant |s\alpha - r|$.

Proof Let us consider the pair of equations

$$p_n x + p_{n+1} y = r,$$

$$q_n x + q_{n+1} y = s.$$

Since $p_n q_{n+1} - q_n p_{n+1} = (-1)^{n+1} \neq 0$, the equations have a unique solution in integers:

$$x = (-1)^{n+1}(rq_{n+1} - sp_{n+1})$$

$$y = (-1)^{n+1}(sp_n - rq_n).$$

Now $x \neq 0$. For otherwise $q_{n+1}y = s$ so that $q_{n+1}|s$ contrary to the choice of s. On the other hand $y = 0$ *is* possible. However, in this case, since $r = p_n x$, $s = q_n x$ we should have

$$|q_n\alpha - p_n| \leqslant |x| \cdot |q_n\alpha - p_n| = |s\alpha - r|,$$

which is the result we wish to prove.

So, from now on, we shall assume that $x \neq 0$ and $y \neq 0$. We claim that, necessarily, one of x, y is negative, the other positive. For, $q_n x = s - q_{n+1}y$, where s, q_n, $q_{n+1} > 0$. Thus if $y < 0$ then $x > 0$ follows immediately. If, however, $y > 0$, then $s < q_{n+1} \leqslant yq_{n+1}$, the first inequality coming from the hypothesis, the second from the fact that y is a positive *integer*. Thus since $q_n x = s - q_{n+1}y < 0$, so is x.

Now Theorem 11.2.12 shows us that α lies between p_n/q_n and p_{n+1}/q_{n+1}. In each case it follows that $q_n\alpha - p_n$ and $q_{n+1}\alpha - p_{n+1}$ are of opposite signs. But this then implies that $x(q_n\alpha - p_n)$ and $y(q_{n+1}\alpha - p_{n+1})$ are of the *same* sign, from which we can deduce that the absolute values of their sum is the sum of their absolute values. Using these facts shows that

$$\begin{aligned}|s\alpha - r| &= |(q_n x + q_{n+1} y)\alpha - (p_n x + p_{n+1} y)| \\ &= |x(q_n\alpha - p_n) + y(q_{n+1}\alpha - p_{n+1})| \\ &= |x(q_n\alpha - p_n)| + |y(q_{n+1}\alpha - p_{n+1})| \\ &= |x||q_n\alpha - p_n| + |y||q_{n+1}\alpha - p_{n+1}| \geqslant |q_n\alpha - p_n|,\end{aligned}$$

as claimed. □

We can now give the

Proof of Theorem 11.4.3 Suppose that r/s is *not* a convergent of α. Since the q_i form an increasing sequence, there will be an n such that $q_n \leqslant s < q_{n+1}$. By Lemma 11.4.4 and our hypothesis,

$$|q_n\alpha - p_n| \leqslant |s\alpha - r| = |s||\alpha - r/s| \leqslant 1/2s.$$

Because $r/s \neq p_n/q_n$ (by assumption) we can say that $|sp_n - rq_n| \geqslant 1$. It then follows that

$$\begin{aligned}1/sq_n &\leqslant \left|\frac{sp_n - rq_n}{sq_n}\right| = \left|\frac{p_n}{q_n} - \frac{r}{s}\right| \\ &\leqslant \left|\frac{p_n}{q_n} - \alpha\right| + \left|\alpha - \frac{r}{s}\right| < \frac{1}{2sq_n} + \frac{1}{2s^2}.\end{aligned}$$

Since this implies the contradiction $s < q_n$, the proof is complete. □

Exercises 11.4

1 Use the continued fraction expansion of $\sqrt{5}$ in Exercise 11.2.1(iii) to find a rational approximation r/s of $\sqrt{5}$ for which $|\sqrt{5} - r/s| < 10^{-6}$.

2 Use the continued fraction expansion $[2; 1, 2, 1, 1, 4, 1, 1, 6, 1, 1, 8, 1 \ldots]$ of e to find a rational approximation of e correct to four places of decimals.

3 Find an example of α and r/s such that $|\alpha - r/s| < 1/s^2$ and yet r/s is not a convergent for α.

4 Show that not all the convergents p_n/q_n of the irrational number α satisfy the inequality $|\alpha - x/y| < 1/2y^2$—but that at least one out of each successive pair of convergents does. [*Hint*: Use $|p_{n+1}/q_{n+1} - p_n/q_n| = |p_{n+1}/q_{n+1} - \alpha| + |\alpha - p_n/q_n|$.]

5 Deduce from Lemma 11.4.4 that if $1 \leqslant s \leqslant q_n$ then $|\alpha - p_n/q_n| \leqslant |\alpha - r/s|$. That is, amongst all rationals with denominator $\leqslant q_n$, the closest to α is the convergent p_n/q_n.

6 A theorem of Hurwitz* (1891) says that for each irrational α the inequality $|\alpha - x/y| < 1/\sqrt{5}y^2$ has infinitely many solutions x/y. (For a proof see [33].)

* Adolf Hurwitz, 26 March 1859 - 18 November 1919.

Show that if $c(>\sqrt{5})$ is a constant and if $\alpha=(1+\sqrt{5})/2$ then $|\alpha-x/y|<1/cy^2$ has only finitely many solutions x/y. [*Hint*: Suppose $|\alpha-x/y|<1/cy^2$ with $c>\sqrt{5}$. Show that x/y is a convergent of α. Note that $\alpha=[1; 1, 1, 1, \ldots, \alpha_{n+1}]$ where $\alpha_{n+1}=\alpha$. Use Exercise 11.2.3 to show that $\lim_{n\to\infty}(\alpha_{n+1}+q_{n-1}/q_n)=\sqrt{5}<c$. Deduce that $\alpha_{n+1}+q_{n-1}/q_n>c$ for at most finitely many n. Now use Exercise 11.3.2 to deduce that $|\alpha-p_n/q_n|<1/q_n^2c$ is true for at most finitely many n.]

7 Find two rationals r/s such that $|\sqrt{2}-r/s|<1/\sqrt{5}s^2$ and two such that $|\pi-r/s|<1/\sqrt{5}s^2$.

11.5 iscfs for square roots and other quadratic irrationals

Our main interest in continued fractions will concern representations of numbers of the form $\sqrt{N}$, where N is any positive integer other than a perfect square. Let us begin by looking at a specific example, namely with $N=31$. Quite a pleasant surprise awaits us.

Using the notation set up in Theorem 11.3.2 we have

$$\left.\begin{aligned}
\lambda_0&=\lambda=\sqrt{31}. && : a_0=[\lambda_0]=5\\
\lambda_1&=\frac{1}{\sqrt{31}-5}=\frac{\sqrt{31}+5}{6} && : a_1=[\lambda_1]=1\\
\lambda_2&=\frac{6}{\sqrt{31}-1}=\frac{6(\sqrt{31}+1)}{30} && : a_2=[\lambda_2]=1\\
\lambda_3&=\frac{5}{\sqrt{31}-4}=\frac{5(\sqrt{31}+4)}{15} && : a_3=[\lambda_3]=3\\
\lambda_4&=\frac{3}{\sqrt{31}-5}=\frac{3(\sqrt{31}+5)}{6} && : a_4=[\lambda_4]=5\\
\lambda_5&=\frac{2}{\sqrt{31}-5}=\frac{2(\sqrt{31}+5)}{6} && : a_5=[\lambda_5]=3\\
\lambda_6&=\frac{3}{\sqrt{31}-4}=\frac{3(\sqrt{31}+4)}{15} && : a_6=[\lambda_6]=1\\
\lambda_7&=\frac{5}{\sqrt{31}-1}=\frac{5(\sqrt{31}+1)}{30} && : a_7=[\lambda_7]=1\\
\lambda_8&=\frac{6}{\sqrt{31}-5}=\frac{6(\sqrt{31}+5)}{6} && : a_8=[\lambda_8]=10\\
\lambda_9&=\frac{1}{\sqrt{31}-5}
\end{aligned}\right\} \quad (*)$$

and we see that $\lambda_9=\lambda_1$.

In consequence $\lambda_{10}=\lambda_2$, $\lambda_{11}=\lambda_3$, etc., etc. This is the pleasant surprise! The sequence has begun to repeat—in our case

$$\sqrt{31}=[5; 1, 1, 3, 5, 3, 1, 1, 10, 1, 1, 3, 5, 3, 1, 1, 10, 1, 1, \ldots].$$

We write this briefly as $\sqrt{31}=[5; \overline{1, 1, 3, 5, 3, 1, 1, 10}]$ and we say that the continued fraction expansion is *periodic.*

Notes 11.5.1

(i) The pattern seen here is characteristic of continued fraction expansions of square roots, namely: (a) The continued fraction is periodic, the periodic part starting immediately with a_1; (b) The periodic part exhibits symmetry. If $\sqrt{N}=[a_0; \overline{a_1, a_2, \ldots, a_n}]$, then $\sqrt{N}=[a_0; \overline{a_1, a_2, \ldots, a_2, a_1, 2a_0}]$.

(ii) Each λ_n reduces to the form $(\sqrt{N}+r_n)/s_n$. That is, the denominator is always an exact multiple of the multiplier in the numerator. The terms r_n and s_n are given by

$$r_n=a_{n-1}s_{n-1}-r_{n-1} \text{ and } s_n=(N-r_n^2)/s_{n-1}.$$

For proofs of these statements we refer the reader to [33].

Note 11.5.1(i) suggests a simple stopping rule that could be used in conjunction with the algorithm in Program 11.3 for iscfs of square roots. If you have done Computer Problem 11.3.1 you will have seen how the calculation of continued fraction representations is affected by your computer's accuracy. Even for continued fractions corresponding to square roots, the algorithm does not always produce a periodic iscf. (Try $\sqrt{1081}$). However, square roots *are* a special case, so we might expect to find an algorithm more suited to them. Note 11.5.1(ii) suggests an alternative algorithm based on calculating r_n and s_n at each stage and using these to generate the next term.

We can in fact apply this algorithm more widely. If we examine the illustration for $\sqrt{31}$ closely, then for any *quadratic irrational* (an irrational of the form $(p+\sqrt{N})/q$) we can, provided $q|N-p^2$, use the following algorithm with $r(1)=p$ and $s(1)=q$ and $a(1)=\text{INT}((p+\sqrt{N})/q)$.

```
1  set i = 1
2  set i = i + 1
3     r(i) = a(i-1) * s(i-1) - r(i-1)
4     s(i) = (N - r(i) * r(i))/s(i-1)
5     a(i) = INT ((r(i) + √N)/s(i))
6  GOTO 2
```

Then the $a(i)$ are the terms of the continued fraction. (If $q\nmid N-p^2$ then we can replace N by Nq^2, q by $q|q|$ and p by $p|q|$, so that the proviso does hold.)

Since a quadratic irrational has a periodic continued fraction (see Exercise 11.5.6) we can terminate the above algorithm once we have found the complete cycle. Examining the algorithm, this occurs when both $r(i)=r(i-k)$ and $s(i)=s(i-k)$, for some k, since these will generate the next set of a values identical to the set $a(i-k), \ldots, a(i)$.

Program 11.5 uses the above algorithm and stopping rule to compute continued fractions of quadratic irrationals. In the case of simple square roots we could use the alternative (and simpler) stopping rule, which would avoid the need for arrays, suggested by the observation in Note 11.5.1(i)—although we have not, or course, *proved* that that observation always holds.

Program 11.5 *Continued Fractions of Quadratic Irrationals*

```
 10 DIM a(100),r(100),s(100)
 20 INPUT r(1),N,s(1)
 30 IF N-r(1)*r(1) MOD s(1) = 0 GOTO 70
 40    r(1)=r(1)*ABS(s(1))
 50    N=N*s(1)*s(1)
 60    s(1)=s(1)*ABS(s(1))
 70 i=1
 80 a(i)=INT((r(i)+SQR(N))/s(i))
 90    i=i+1
100    r(i)=a(i-1)*s(i-1)-r(i-1)
110    s(i)=(N-r(i)*r(i))/s(i-1)
120    j=i
130    j=j-1
140 IF j=0 GOTO 80
150 IF r(j)<>r(i) GOTO 130
160 IF s(j)<>s(i) GOTO 130
170 P=i-j
180 PRINT "period = ";P
190 FOR k=1 TO j-1:PRINT ;" ";a(k);:NEXT k
200 PRINT ;"  ( ";
210 FOR k=j TO i-1
220    PRINT ;" ";a(k);
230 NEXT k
240 PRINT ;" ) ";
```

Exercises 11.5

1 Determine the iscf representations of: (i) $\sqrt{11}$; (ii) $\sqrt{13}$; (iii) $\sqrt{15}$; (iv) $\sqrt{19}$; (v) $\sqrt{29}$ and, if you've got the patience, $\sqrt{94}$.

2 Determine the iscf representations of: (i) $(1+\sqrt{11})/2$; (ii) $(7+\sqrt{37})/3$; (iii) $(13+\sqrt{20})/2$.

3 Prove that, for each positive integer n: (i) $\sqrt{n^2+1}=[n;\overline{2n}]$; (ii) $\sqrt{n^2+2}=[n;\overline{n,2n}]$. Does $\sqrt{n^2+3}$ always have an iscf representation of length three or less?

4 Find the irrational number represented by: (i) $[3;\overline{1,4,2}]$; (ii) $[2;\overline{7,1,8,2,8}]$; (iii) $[0;\overline{9,3,7,6,5,1,3,9}]$; (iv) $[0;\overline{18,2,1,5,9,18}]$.

5 Let x, y, z be the integers denoting the day, month and year of your birth. Find the real number represented by the continued fraction $[0;\overline{x,y,z}]$.

6 Prove that if the real number a is represented by an iscf which is periodic, then a is of the form $r+s\sqrt{d}$ where r, s are rationals, $s\neq 0$ and d is square-free.

(The converse is also true but too involved to ask you to prove here. See [33], p. 152.)

Computer problems 11.5

1 Write a program to calculate iscf representations of quadratic irrationals using Note 11.5.1(i) to terminate the calculations.

2 Write a program to determine the iscf representations of $\sqrt{n}$ (n not square) for values of $n \leqslant 200$, and display the length of the period. Let n be prime. Does the evidence suggest a conjecture about the length of period? If so can you prove it?

John Pell *(1 March 1611 - 12 December 1685)*
Pell was born in Sussex, the son of the vicar of Southwick. He entered Trinity College, Cambridge at the age of 13, taking his B.A. in 1629 and his M.A. the next year. Not wishing, at that time, to follow his father in to the church, he became a schoolmaster. Having earned a high reputation for both mathematics and languages—in later years both Newton and Leibniz were happy to discuss their latest researches with him—he was invited to take a professorship at the University of Amsterdam. He accepted, moving later, at the request of the Prince of Orange, to the newly founded college at Breda.

In 1654 Pell entered the diplomatic service having earlier been Cromwell's political agent to the protestant cantons of Switzerland. In 1661 he at last took holy orders becoming, in due course, chaplain to the Bishop of London, Gilbert Sheldon, who was appointed Archbishop of Canterbury in 1663.

In 1668 he 'altered and augmented' Brancker's translation of Rahn's *Introduction to Algebra* in which the equivalent of the equation $x^2-12y^2=n$ occurs. Possibly it was this which encouraged Euler's coining the name 'Pell equation'. On the other hand **[21]** reports that in his biography of Pell, Aubrey says that Rahn's *Algebra* is essentially Pell's work—Rahn being, at one time, Pell's student in Zurich.

Aside from writing an immense number of pamphlets and letters, Pell's main publication was his *Idea of Mathematics* written before 1630. Later (1647) his reputation was increased further by an article attacking the alleged squaring of the circle by Longomontanus.

Despite these successes and his election as a Fellow of the Royal Society in 1663, Pell died in London in abject poverty.

11.6 Pell's equation

Early in 1657, Fermat complained, in a letter addressed to the mathematicians of Europe that 'There is hardly anyone who propounds purely arithmetical questions, hardly anyone who understands them.' He added that 'Up to now arithmetic has been treated geometrically rather than arithmetically' whereas 'arithmetic has a special domain of its own, the theory of integral numbers.'

To give impetus to the development of arithmetical methods he proposed the following problem, claiming that 'who discovers the proof will admit that questions of this kind are not inferior in beauty, difficulty or method of proof to the more celebrated theorems of geometry'.

> *Given any number which is not a square, show that there are infinitely many squares which, when multiplied to the given number and unity added, result in a square.*

In brief: Given the non-square integer $d \geqslant 2$ show that there are infinitely many pairs of integers x, y such that $dy^2+1=x^2$.

The problem was probably aimed at Wallis, in England. In 1656 Fermat had received from Wallis a copy of his book *Arithmetica Infinitorum* and Fermat, having failed to interest Pascal and Huygens, perhaps saw Wallis as the most able mathematician whom he might interest in some serious number theory.

Fermat's problem was soon solved in all generality by Wallis and William, Viscount Brouncker* (who was the first president of the Royal Society). Their solution, in rational numbers, is outlined in Exercise 11.6.1. But, of course, Fermat was looking for integral solutions, a condition which Wallis and Brouncker were initially unaware of. On being given fuller details Brouncker and Wallis had, before the end of the year, discovered a method of solving the problem in integers—Brouncker reporting that Frenicle's challenge to solve $x^2-313y^2=1$ had taken him 'an hour or two'. Fermat, too, must have known how to solve the general problem—indeed he claimed a proof 'by descent'—since he specifically asked for the solution in the cases $d=61$ and $d=109$. (Presumably anyone finding these solutions would have found the general method; there seems little chance of finding the least such y (respectively $y=226\,153\,980$, $y=15\,140\,424\,455\,100$) by inspired guesswork! These numbers are delightfully large, especially since the least y for $d=60$, 62, 108 and 110 are, respectively, 4, 8, 130 and 2!)

In his *Algebra* (Part II, Chapter 7), Euler describes the Wallis–Brouncker method, for which no proof of validity had been given. Yet in a paper published in 1767—written in 1759—Euler observes that if $p^2=dq^2+1$ (with $p, q>0$) then p/q is necessarily a convergent of the continued fraction expansion of $\sqrt{d}$ (Theorem 11.6.1). His paper contains all the facts necessary to prove that the equation $x^2-dy^2=1$—which he called the *Pell equation* in the belief that the solution given in Wallis's *Algebra* was due to John Pell—always has an infinity of solutions (for d a positive non-square) and that *all* are obtainable from the continued fraction expansion of $\sqrt{d}$ (Theorem 11.6.2). But Euler never gave a full proof. This was left to Lagrange, first in 1768 and, subsequently, via simpler proof, in his *Additions* to Euler's text book.

In these *Additions* Lagrange attributes to Fermat the authorship of the problem posed above. In fact Fermat was not the first to pose, nor the first to

* William Brouncker, died 5 April 1684.

discover, a general method of solving the problem. As we've already noted (Section 11.2) equations of the form $x^2-dy^2=1$ had been used to find good rational approximations for $\sqrt{2}$ (and, by Archimedes, for $\sqrt{3}$). Furthermore another famous ancient problem (called Archimedes' cattle problem, should you wish to look it up) resulted in the necessity of solving the equation $x^2-4\,729\,494y^2=1$. Diophantus, too, had occasion to derive a second solution of $x^2-3y^2=-11$ given one such, but perhaps the main surprise is that, by the twelfth century, a completely general method, the 'cyclic' method, had been described by the Indian mathematician Bhaskara. This method was, according to Hankel* 'The finest thing achieved in number theory before Lagrange'.

Besides the use of Pell's equation as a means of producing better and better approximations to $\sqrt{N}$, the equation has played a prominent role in number theory. For example Theorem 11.6.5 plainly indicates its relevance to the problem of units in various number systems. Again, Lagrange's solutions of the related equation $x^2-dy^2=n$ led Legendre to his famous theorem on the solutions of the equation $ax^2+by^2+cz^2=0$, using which he *almost* proved the law of quadratic reciprocity. Euler too recognised its value in solving, in integers, the general equation of degree two in two indeterminates. For information on these items and others the reader might profitably consult Volume 2 of Dickson's *History* [1].

As the Wallis–Brouncker method is essentially the continued fraction method we shall not describe what is little more than a difference in presentation, but we do now get on with establishing some of Euler's discoveries.

Theorem 11.6.1 If p, q is a solution of $x^2-dy^2=1$, where $p>0, q>0$, $(p,q)=1$ and d is a positive non-square, then p/q is a convergent of $\sqrt{d}$.

Proof From $p^2-dq^2=1$ we get $(p-q\sqrt{d})(p+q\sqrt{d})=1$, that is, $p/q-\sqrt{d}=1/q(p+q\sqrt{d})$. Since $p>q\sqrt{d}$ [why ?] we have

$$0<p/q-\sqrt{d}<1/q(q\sqrt{d}+q\sqrt{d})<1/2q^2.$$

The proof is then completed by calling on Theorem 11.4.3. □

Of course Theorem 11.6.1 says 'if $p, q>0$ is a solution . . . '. It doesn't claim that there *are* any such solutions! Equally certain is that not *all* the convergents of the continued fraction for $\sqrt{d}$ satisfy $x^2-dy^2=1$. In fact we have (see [33], p. 159/160 for a more general statement.)

Theorem 11.6.2 Let p_k/q_k be the convergents of the continued fraction expansion of $\sqrt{d}$ and let n be the periodic length of the expansion.

(i) If n is even, then all solutions (>0) of $x^2-dy^2=1$ are given by

$$x=p_{kn-1},\ y=q_{kn-1} \qquad (k=1,2,3,\ldots).$$

* Herman Hankel, 14 February 1839 - 29 August 1873.

(ii) If n is odd, then all solutions (>0) of $x^2-dy^2=1$ are given by

$$x=p_{2kn-1},\ y=q_{2kn-1} \qquad (k=1,2,3,\ldots). \quad \square$$

Example 11.6.3 You can check that $\sqrt{14}=[3;\overline{1,2,1,6}]$. It follows that the first ten convergents are 3/1, 4/1, 11/3, 15/4, 101/27, 116/31, 333/89, 449/120, 3027/809, 3476/929. Since the continued fraction representation of $\sqrt{14}$ has length 4, the convergents p_{4k-1}/q_{4k-1} $(k=1,2,3,\ldots)$ provide the solutions of the Pell equation $x^2-14y^2=1$, the first two solutions being $(x,y)=(15,4)$, $(449,120)$.

Example 11.6.4 Likewise you can check that $\sqrt{13}=[3;\overline{1,1,1,1,6}]$ with period length 5. The first few convergents of $\sqrt{13}$ are, therefore, 3/1, 4/1, 7/2, 11/3, 18/5, 119/33, 137/38, 256/71, 393/109, 649/180. By (ii) of Theorem 11.6.2 we see that the first solution $x^2-13y^2=1$ is given by the convergent p_9/q_9, that is $(x,y)=(649,180)$.

(See how long it takes you to work out the second solution and compare the time taken with the alternative method resulting from Theorem 11.6.5.)

The real value of the continued fraction approach to Pell's equation is that it supplies us with the 'first' of the infinitely many solutions. For we can, in fact, avoid the use of continued fractions if we want only to prove that $x^2-dy^2=1$ has a solution other than $x=\pm1$, $y=0$ (see [34], p. 177). Furthermore, given one solution, the following theorem tells us how to generate infinitely many—in particular how to generate them *all*, if the given solution is the smallest.

Let us suppose that $\alpha^2-d\beta^2=1$ and $a^2-db^2=1$, where $\alpha, \beta, a, b>0$ and $\alpha>a$. Then $\beta>b$. Thus, assuming the equation $x^2-dy^2=1$ has a solution, there will always be a 'smallest' positive one—namely that formed by the pair (x_1, y_1), where $x_1^2-dy_1^2=1$, and where $x_1<x_2$ and $y_1<y_2$ for every other positive solution (x_2, y_2) of $x^2-dy^2=1$. Calling (x_1, y_1) the *fundamental solution* we have

Theorem 11.6.5 Let (x_1, y_1) be the fundamental solution of $x^2-dy^2=1$. Then each pair of integers x_n, y_n defined by

$$x_n+y_n\sqrt{d}=(x_1+y_1\sqrt{d})^n \qquad (n=1,2,3,\ldots)$$

is also a positive solution. Furthermore each (positive) solution of $x^2-dy^2=1$ is obtained in this way.

Proof From $x_n+y_n\sqrt{d}=(x_1+y_1\sqrt{d})^n$ we can deduce $x_n-y_n\sqrt{d}=(x_1-y_1\sqrt{d})^n$ (cf. Exercise 9.5.1). Since $x_1, y_1>0$ so too, clearly, are x_n, y_n. Finally

$$\begin{aligned} x_n^2-dy_n^2&=(x_n+y_n\sqrt{d})(x_n-y_n\sqrt{d})\\ &=(x_1+y_1\sqrt{d})^n(x_1-y_1\sqrt{d})^n=(x_1^2-dy_1^2)^n=1^n=1. \end{aligned}$$

To prove the final assertion of the theorem, suppose that (u, v) is any (positive) solution of $x^2 - dy^2 = 1$ not obtainable from some power of $x_1 + y_1\sqrt{d}$. Let n be such that

$$(x_1 + y_1\sqrt{d})^n < u + v\sqrt{d} < (x_1 + y_1\sqrt{d})^{n+1}.$$

Multiplying through by $x_n - y_n\sqrt{d} = (x_1 - y_1\sqrt{d})^n$ we obtain

$$1 < (x_n - y_n\sqrt{d})(u + v\sqrt{d}) = r + s\sqrt{d} < x_1 + y_1\sqrt{d},$$

where $r = x_n u - dy_n v$ and $s = x_n v - y_n u$. Note that

$$r^2 - ds^2 = (x_n^2 - dy_n^2)(u^2 - dv^2) = 1,$$

so we shall obtain a contradiction to the choice of $x_1 + y_1\sqrt{d}$ if only we can show that $r, s > 0$. But, since $1 < r + s\sqrt{d}$ it follows that $0 < r - s\sqrt{d} < 1$. Consequently $1 + 0 < (r + s\sqrt{d}) + (r - s\sqrt{d}) = 2r$, thus showing that $r > 0$. Likewise $r + s\sqrt{d} - (r - s\sqrt{d}) > 1 - 1 = 0$, so that $s > 0$. This contradiction shows that our supposition concerning (u, v) is wrong—and the final sentence of the theorem is proved. □

Example 11.6.6 By inspection $(x, y) = (7, 2)$ is easily seen to be the fundamental solution of $x^2 - 12y^2 = 1$. A second and third solution of this equation is then given by (x_2, y_2), (x_3, y_3) where $x_2 + y_2\sqrt{12} = (7 + 2\sqrt{12})^2$ and $x_3 + y_3\sqrt{12} = (7 + 2\sqrt{12})^3$. Now $(7 + 2\sqrt{12})^2 = 97 + 28\sqrt{12}$ whilst $(7 + 2\sqrt{12})^3 = 1351 + 390\sqrt{12}$. Hence $(x_2, y_2) = (97, 28)$ and $(x_3, y_3) = (1351, 390)$.

Exercises 11.6

1 (Brouncker–Wallis) Show that

$$x = \frac{a^2 + db^2}{a^2 - db^2}, \qquad y = \frac{2ab}{a^2 - db^2}$$

satisfy Pell's equation, $x^2 - dy^2 = 1$ for all $a, b \in \mathbb{Q}$.

2 Find the two smallest solutions of $x^2 - 31y^2 = 1$. (This example was chosen by Euler in a paper of 1773.) Find the smallest solutions of $x^2 - dy^2 = 1$ for $d = 29$ and $d = 30$.

3 (i) Starting with the solution $(3, 2)$ of the equation $x^2 - 2y^2 = 1$, use Theorem 11.6.5 to check that $(17, 12)$ and $(577, 408)$ are also solutions so that $17/12$ and $577/408$ are rational approximations to $\sqrt{2}$—correct to how many places of decimals?

(ii) By the same means Archimedes approximations $265/153$ and $1351/780$ to 3. [*Hint*: Work with equations $x^2 - 3y^2 = 1$ and $x^2 - 3y^2 = -2.1$].

4 (Euler's *Algebra*) Show that if u, v is a solution of $x^2 - dy^2 = n$ and if a, b is a solution of $x^2 - dy^2 = 1$, then $U = ua + dvb$ and $V = va + ub$ is another solution of $x^2 - dy^2 = n$. Show that not *every* solution of the equation $x^2 - 2y^2 = 7$ arises from the smallest one, $x = 3$, $y = 1$, in this way.

5 (Problem 15, Book 6 of Diophantus) Given that $(5, 8)$ is one solution of $3x^2-11=y^2$ find another. [*Hint*: Put $x=X+5$, $y=8-2X$ and solve for X.]

6 (Van Aubel, 1885) Prove that if (p, q) is the least solution to $x^2-dy^2=1$ and if (x_i, y_i), where $i=m-1, m, m+1$, are three successive solutions, then $x_{m+1}=2px_m-x_{m-1}$ and $y_{m+1}=2qy_m-y_{m-1}$.

7 (Euler's *Algebra*) Show how to find triangular numbers which are also square by using the continued fraction expansion of $\sqrt{2}$. [*Hint*: From $m(m+1)=2n^2$ we have $(2m+1)^2-1=2(2n)^2$.]

8 Let d be a non-square positive integer and let p, q be integers such that $p^2-dq^2=n$, where $|n|<\sqrt{d}$ and $(p, q)=1$. Prove that there is a convergent p_n/q_n of $\sqrt{d}$ such that $p=p_n$ and $q=q_n$. [*Hint*: For $0<n<\sqrt{d}$ modify the proof of Theorem 11.6.1 appropriately. If n is negative consider $q^2-(1/d)p^2=-n/d$. Proceed as for $n>0$ and use Exercise 11.2.4.]

9 (a) Show that the equation $x^2-dy^2=-1$ has no solution if $d\equiv 3(\text{mod } 4)$.

(b) Show that $x^2-dy^2=n$ can have no solution unless n is a quadratic residue of each prime divisor of d. The converse is false since -1 is a quadratic residue of 2 and 17 and yet $x^2-34y^2=-1$ has no solution. (See Computer Problem 11.6.2.)

10 (Brahmagupta, 7th C) To Solve $92x^2+1=y^2$ write $CL^2+A=G^2$ where $C=92$, $L(=1)$ is the 'lesser solution', $A(=8)$ is the 'additive', and $G(=10)$ is the 'greater solution'. Now show that

$$A^2=(CL^2-G^2)^2=(CL^2+G^2)^2-4CL^2G^2.$$

Hence $L_1=2LG(=20)$ and $G_1=CL^2+G^2$ are lesser and greater solutions for the additive $A^2(=64)$. Dividing L_1, G_1 by 8 we get a rational solution corresponding to the additive 1. Now repeat the method of the first part to find an *integral* solution corresponding to additive 1.

Computer problems 11.6

1 Using Program 11.5 and the algorithm suggested by Theorem 11.2.6 write a program to find the fundamental solution to Pell's equation for each positive non-square $d<100$.

2 It is known that if the periodic length of the continued fraction expansion of $\sqrt{d}$ is even, then the equation $x^2-dy^2=-1$ has no solution (Theorem 7.25 of [33]). Using this result confirm the statement in the latter part of Exercise 11.6.9).

11.7 Two more applications

We bring this chapter to a close with a very brief look at two other applications, both already mentioned, of continued fractions.

Best rational approximations

It is noted in Lagrange's contribution to Euler's *Algebra* that the expansion

3.14159 26535 89793 23846 26433 83279 50288 ...

of π yields the continued fraction expansion

[3; 7, 15, 1, 292, 1, 1, 1, 2, 1, 3, 1, 14, 2, 1, 1, 2, 2, 2, 2, 1, 84, 2, 1, 1, 15, 3, 13, 1, 4, 2, 6, 6, 1, ...]

of π. The corresponding convergents are 3/1, 22/7, 333/106, 355/113, 103 993/33 102, 104 348/33 215, ... amongst which we note a couple of old favourites, namely the second and fourth. Now Exercise 11.4.5 tells us that for example 333/106 (respectively 355/113, 103 993/33 102, etc.) is the closest rational approximation to π from *amongst those rationals* r/s for which $s \leqslant 106$ (respectively 113, 33 102, etc.). This, of course, yields no information about the closest of *all* rational approximations r/s to π with $s \leqslant 100$, say. (There is no reason to suppose 22/7 may be the closest rational.) In fact, according to Exercise 11.7.2 the closest rational approximations are those of the form $(p_k + ap_{k+1})/(q_k + aq_{k+1})$ where $0 \leqslant a \leqslant a_{k+2}$. Thus, as we can easily check, $(3+14 \cdot 22)/(1+14 \cdot 7) = 311/99$ is a better approximation to π than is 22/7—and yet $99 < 106$. That is, one doesn't have to use denominators $\geqslant 106$ to obtain a better approximation than 22/7. We leave to you (Exercise 11.7.3) the pleasure of finding the solution to the second of the problems with which we opened the chapter.

Computer factorisation of large integers

The idea behind the application of continued fractions to the factorisation of large integers is based on an old idea of Legendre's which was used again in the 1930s, subsequently falling into disuse, until it was restored in the 1960s, by Brillhart and Morrison [S], to yield the factorisation of $F_7 = 2^{2^7} + 1 = 2^{128} + 1$ (in 1970)

59 649 589 127 497 217 · 5 704 689 200 685 129 054 721.

The idea is this: Given the integer N whose factorisation is desired, one may clearly suppose N (composite) to be odd—since one easily spots and removes a factor 2^α. Then there exist positive integers u, v such that $u^2 - v^2 = N$ and hence, certainly, integers x, y such that $x^2 \equiv y^2 \pmod N$ and yet $x \not\equiv \pm y \pmod N$—see Exercise 11.7.6. Then $N \mid x^2 - y^2 = (x-y)(x+y)$ and yet $N \nmid (x+y)$ and $N \nmid (x-y)$. Hence the gcds $(N, x+y)$ and $(N, x-y)$ are proper factors of N which one might hope to find by the Euclidean algorithm.

If we let $[a_0; a_1, a_2, \ldots]$ be the continued fraction expansion of $\sqrt{N}$ with convergents p_k/q_k, then, by Theorem 11.2.6, we have

$$\sqrt{N} = \frac{p_{t-2} + p_{t-1}\lambda_t}{q_{t-2} + q_{t-1}\lambda_t} \quad \text{where} \quad \lambda_t = \frac{\sqrt{N} + r_t}{s_t} \qquad \text{(see Note 11.5.1(ii)).}$$

Substituting for λ_t gives

$$\sqrt{N}=\frac{s_t p_{t-2}+r_t p_{t-1}+p_{t-1}\sqrt{N}}{s_t q_{t-2}+r_t q_{t-1}+q_{t-1}\sqrt{N}}.$$

Tidying up and using the irrationality of $\sqrt{N}$, (recall N is not a square) we get

$$s_t p_{t-2}+r_t p_{t-1}=Nq_{t-1} \qquad \text{and} \qquad s_t q_{t-2}+r_t q_{t-1}=p_{t-1}.$$

Eliminating r_t yields

$$s_t(p_{t-2}q_{t-1}-q_{t-2}p_{t-1})=Nq_{t-1}^2-p_{t-1}^2$$

which, using Corollary 11.2.9 gives* $s_t(-1)^{t-1}=Nq_{t-1}^2-p_{t-1}^2$.

This implies that $p_{t-1}^2\equiv(-1)^t s_t (\text{mod } N)$—so that a solution of the congruence $x^2\equiv y^2(\text{mod } N)$ will have been found if s_t is a square and t is even. If this solution is not one of the trivial ones (i.e. $x=\pm y$), then the factors $(N, x+y)$ and $(N, x-y)$ can be found as mentioned above. The advent of high-speed computing devices has, of course, made the search for such an s_t a more practical proposition.

Program 11.6 shows how the algorithm used in Program 11.5 can be modified to find factors by this method. You might like to test it with $N=197\,209$, which, as Knuth ([6], p. 382) observes, produces the aesthetically pleasing factorisation 199·991.

Program 11.6 *Factorization using Continued Fractions*

```
 10 R=1 : S=1
 20 INPUT "Enter the interger to be factored",N
 30 D=SQR(N)
 40 A=INT((D+R)/S)
 45 I=0
 50 P=A
 60 PDASH=1
 65 REM Find successive values of R,S and A until S is a square
 70 R=S*A-R
 80   S=(N-R*R)/S
 85   IF S=0 THEN PRINT "The integer is a square":STOP
 90   A=INT((D+R)/S)
 95 REM Calculate the next value of P
110   T=P
120   P=(A*P+PDASH) MOD N
130   PDASH=T
135   I=I+1
140 IF INT(SQR(S))<>SQR(S) GOTO 70
145 IF INT(I/2)<>I/2 GOTO 70
150 REM IF I is even and S is a square use S to find the factors
155 REM using the Euclidean Algorithm
160 G=N
170 B=PDASH-SQR(S)
175 IF B=0 GOTO 240
```

* This would prove Theorem 11.6.2 for us if only we could prove $s_t=1$ when and only when $n|t$ and $s_t\neq-1$ for any subscript. See [33].

```
180 RR = G MOD B
190   G=B
200   B=RR
210 IF RR<>0 GOTO 180
215 IF G=1 GOTO 70
220 PRINT G,N/G
230 STOP
240 PRINT "The integer is possibly prime"
```

As is the case with many of the programs we have presented, the above is by no means the most efficient program for producing factorisations of this form. Knuth [6], for example, describes a refinement of the algorithm which finds the factors of 197 209 in 9 steps compared with the 27 required by Program 11.6. (See Problem 11.7.1.) Another refinement which at first glance appears an exceedingly curious move is that, in order to factorise a large number N it is often convenient to factorise, instead, some multiple, say kN, of N—the reason being that the continued fraction representation of $\sqrt{kN}$ is a more pleasant object than that of $\sqrt{N}$ itself. See [6], again!

Exercises 11.7

1 Show that if $a/b<r/s<c/d$ are positive fractions with $bc-ad=1$, then $s>b$ and $s>d$.

2 Show that if r/s is the closest approximation to the irrational number α amongst all fractions u/v with $v\leq s$, then r/s is either a convergent of α or is one of its *secondary convergents*, that is one of the terms of the sequence

$$\frac{p_{n-1}}{q_{n-1}}, \frac{p_{n-1}+p_n}{q_{n-1}+q_n}, \frac{p_{n-1}+2p_n}{q_{n-1}+2q_n}, \ldots, \frac{p_{n-1}+a_{n+1}p_n}{q_{n-1}+a_{n+1}q_n}=\frac{p_{n+1}}{q_{n+1}}$$

other than the two convergents p_{n-1}/q_{n-1} and p_{n+1}/q_{n+1}. [*Hint*: Show that (i) this sequence is increasing if n is odd and decreasing if n is even; (ii) if a/b and c/d are consecutive terms of this sequence then $ad-bc=\pm 1$. Working WLOG with an increasing sequence, use Exercise 1 to deduce that if $a/b<r/s<c/d$, then $s>b$ and $s>d$.]

3 Find the best rational approximation a/b to π when (i) $b<500$; (ii) $b\leq 1000$. Do the same for e, $\sqrt{2}$ and $\sqrt{3}$.

4 Find the best rational approximation a/b to $(1+\sqrt{5})/2$ for which (i) $b<10^6$; (ii) $b<10^{10}$.

5 The Chinese used the approximation $355/113$ to π. Show using Theorem 11.3.2 that the approximation is certainly accurate to 6 places of decimals.

6 Show that, if N is an odd composite integer other than a prime power, then the equation $x^2\equiv y^2 \pmod N$ has solutions (x_0, y_0) for which $x_0\not\equiv \pm y_0 \pmod N$. [*Hint*: Use the Chinese remainder theorem.] (For the case of prime powers see Exercise 4.2.17.)

Computer problems 11.7

1 A modification to Program 11.6 can be achieved as follows (Knuth [6]). Select a set of small primes $p_1=2, p_2=3, \ldots$ up to p_m. (Primes 2 and those for which $N^{(p-1)/2} \not\equiv 1 (\text{mod } p)$ are the only ones which will be factors of the s_t values generated by the program [why?].) Then for each value of s_t perform the extra calculations set out below.

(i) Set an array e into which the exponents of the factors of s_t will be placed, to zero. Store the value of s_t in T.

(ii) Then for each value of $j (1 \leqslant j \leqslant m)$:

If $T \equiv 0 (\text{mod } p_j)$ set $t = t/p_j$ and $e_j = e_j + 1$ and repeat until $T \not\equiv 0 (\text{mod } p_j)$.

(iii) If $T=1$ then s_t factorises and we have a solution

$$p_t^2 \equiv (-1)^t p_1^{e_1} p_2^{e_2} \cdots p_m^{e_m} (\text{mod } N).$$

Once we have pair of non-trivial solutions for which the sum of the exponents for each possible prime factor is even we can combine them to give values of x and y such that $x^2 \equiv y^2 (\text{mod } N)$. We can then find two factors of our number as before.

Write a program using this modification and count the number of iterations it uses compared with that presented in the text.

2 Modify the programs to use kN rather than N and explore the effect of this suggestion.

3 Apply Program 11·6 to the integers

10001; 20002; 30003; 40004; 50050.

12
Sending secret messages

12.1 A cautionary tale

The desire to send secret messages to chosen recipients is one which almost every one of us has felt—probably most keenly between the ages of 7 and 16!—at least once in his or her lifetime.

In this chapter we indicate how, using some of the concepts introduced earlier in this book, you can reawaken your interest in the practice using what are loosely called 'unbreakable codes'. Many ways of enciphering messages have been devised. In order to make a couple of points we shall first consider one of the simplest.

Let us suppose that the two authors of a certain book on number theory with computing—for want of anything better let us call them A and R—have made a fortune from its worldwide sales and are living in luxury on opposite sides of the globe. They now wish to fulfil a vague promise made when writing the book namely that, if it were successful, they would spend much of their ill-gotten gains on meeting at some major world sporting event. They therefore need to communicate with one another but, as their wives can think of better things to do with the money, their communications must be unintelligible to their families. How, then, can A send a message to R's home which only R can understand?

If A follows a method employed by Julius Caesar he will write out his message 'meetmeinstlouis' by shifting each letter of the message by n places in the alphabet. Thus, with $n=7$, say, A would encode his message according to the following scheme:

```
a b c d e f g h i j k l m n o p q r s t u v w x y z
↓ ↓ ↓ ↓ ↓ ↓ ↓ ↓ ↓ ↓ ↓ ↓ ↓ ↓ ↓ ↓ ↓ ↓ ↓ ↓ ↓ ↓ ↓ ↓ ↓ ↓
h i j k l m n o p q r s t u v w x y z a b c d e f g
```

Consequently *m*, for example, is replaced by the letter 7 places further along in the alphabet, namely *t*, and the original message becomes 'tllatlpuzasvbpz'.

Now A expects that, on receiving the encoded message, R will use the above table 'upside down' to decipher the message immediately. However, after sending his message, A realises that R might not be able to decode the message since A and R didn't *really* anticipate sending secret messages to one another and so never agreed on a code to be used should the need arise. Consequently the coded message makes no more sense to R than to Mrs R. And, of course, there is no point in A now sending R the decoding scheme. After all what if it should fall into Mrs R's hands . . . ?

Actually all is not completely lost since R, having studied a little statistics at university, knows that the most frequently occurring letter in (long) passages of English is the letter e. Ignoring the shortness of the message, R notices that the letter l occurs most frequently in the *cipher text* and makes the supposition that l represents the *plain text* letter e. Knowing that A is a simple fellow, R suspects use of a Caesar-type code with a shift of 7 letters (since l is seven letters after e in the alphabet). He then decodes the message easily. Unfortunately, Mrs R, though not a statistician, can also break the code since she, too, knows of this common occurrence of e and, suspecting the simplicity of A and R's minds applies a little common sense and has no difficulty in deciphering the message.

The Caesar method, described here, converts plain text into cipher text using a *shift transformation* (restricting our attention to the 26 letters only) which is conveniently described by the congruence

$$C \equiv P + k \pmod{26} \qquad 0 \leqslant k \leqslant 25$$

There are only 26 such transformations (one of which is clearly of no use). To complicate things a bit, an alternative is to use the *affine transformation* described by

$$C \equiv aP + k \pmod{26}$$

Here we must chose a so that $(a, 26) = 1$ to ensure that the enciphering code can be 'inverted', that is that $C \equiv aP + k \pmod{26}$ can be 'solved' for P. This restricts a to $\phi(26) = 12$ possible values giving $12 \cdot 26 = -1$ sensible transformations.

On a modern computer it is therefore a feasible proposition to try all possibilities, stopping once the message (or the first part of it) makes sense. Codes constructed using affine transformations are also easily broken by a statistical analysis based on the knowledge that the letters e, t, i, n and r are the most commonly occurring letters in the English language. These can be used to set up two possible equations that can then be solved to express P in terms of C to allow us to decode the text.

Computer problems 12.1

1 Write a program to decode a ciphertext by first identifying the most commonly occurring letters in that text. Then use this information to (i) determine the k in a possible shift transformation and (ii) the a and k in a possible affine transformation. In each case determine the reverse transformation expressing P in terms of C and display the decoded message. If it does not make sense try the next most likely possibility.

Test your program on the following two cipher texts.

(a) DPPTY RESPC PTDYZ ESTYR ESLET DDZEC ZFMWP DZXPE ZXLES PXLET NLWAC LNETD PYZCE SLEOZ ESXZC PXZWP DELYD STYOP CNLWN FWWEZ CDESL YESPX FWETA WTNLE TZYDC TGTDT ZYDDB FLCPL YONFM TNWPP IECLN ETZYD ZQRCP LEYFX MPCDH STNSM POTOP DESPE POTZF DPIAP YDPZQ ESPET XPLCP QZCES PXZDE ALCED FMUPN EEZXL YJDWT AAPCJ PCCZC DTMPR LYESP CPQZC PEZWZ YDTOP CTYXJ XTYOP MJHSL ENPCE LTYPL YOCPL OJLCE TXTRS ECPXZ GPESZ DPSTY OPCLY NPDUZ SYYLA TPCDT IEPPY SFYOC POLYO QZFCE PPY.

(b) IHMXF ZVEHX GEXTM JNEZT KXYOM FHMTM JNHOG TKXYW FOGEZ FMZMF HOGYE XGNKX NZMYU ZZKXY MIKGN ENHMG NUFWE TKZON HQMNO YREGI MJJGJ OTMET VEHXG EX

2 Write a program which searches through all possible transformations. For each attempt let the program display the result of decoding the first part of the cipher text to allow you to accept or reject the transformation before proceeding in an appropriate way. Test your program on the ciphertexts given in the previous question.

12.2 The remedy: The RSA cipher system

Having successfully explained to his wife A's penchant for sending meaningless messages to all and sundry, R decides to tell A how to send a message which only he, R, can unravel no matter who sees the cipher text and no matter what statistical analysis is done on the letters appearing in it.

First R selects two large prime numbers—for ease of illustration only we'll take them to be $p=61$ and $q=73$. (In practice p and q would be very much larger.) Their product 4453 he calls 'n'. He then selects an integer e (called the *key*) not too small (see Exercise 12.2.1(ii) for a reason), but such that $(e, \phi(n))=(e, 60 \cdot 72)=1$. For example R might choose $e=97$—a convenient prime.

R now tells *anyone* who wants to listen the values he has taken for n and e (hence the term 'public key encryption' which is applied to this method of communication) but he tells *no-one at all* the values of p and q. He further announces publicly how anyone wishing to communicate with him should encode a message.

A(i) Turn the (plaintext) message to be sent into numbers according to the scheme A = 00, B = 01, C = 02, ... Z = 25. Thus 'meetmeinstlouis' becomes '1204 0419 1204 0813 1819 1114 2008 1823', where the numbers are arranged into blocks so that no block involves an integer larger than n and where a '23'—that is an 'x'—has been slipped in at the end of the message so as to avoid introducing ambiguities into the subsequent decoding.

A(ii) Now send to R the remainders, modulo 4453, of the integers

$$1204^e \quad 0419^e \quad 1204^e \quad 0813^e \quad 1819^e \quad 1114^e \quad 2008^e \quad 1823^e.$$

(The values can be obtained using Program 3.2.) In this case R receives the numbers

4011 1558 4011 1526 1514 3187 0077 4252

(and that's it! The rest is up to R).

Notice that A doesn't have to tell R how to *decode* messages. Rather it is R who tells A—and everyone else—how to *encode* them!

But what does R do with these numbers?

R(i) First R finds the integer d $(1 < d < \phi(n))$ for which $ed \equiv 1(\text{mod } \phi(n))$. Such a d exists since $(e, \phi(n)) = 1$ by choice of e. Furthermore d is easily found using Program 4.1. In fact in our case $d = 3073$.

R(ii) R then finds the remainders, modulo n, of the integers

$$4011^d \quad 1558^d \quad 4011^d \quad 1526^d \quad 1514^d \quad 3187^d \quad 0077^d \quad 4252^d$$

and these turn out to be

1204 0419 1204 0813 1819 1114 2008 1823

as you can easily check using Program 3.2. R then decodes the message easily.

Does this technique always work? Yes: for letting B be any one of the blocks in the original plain text message, B is changed to B^e (mod n) before it is transmitted by A and then further changed to $(B^e)^d$(mod n) on being received by R. But, since $ed \equiv 1(\text{mod } \phi(n))$ we have $ed = 1 + k\phi(n)$ for some suitable positive integer k. Since, by Theorem 3.4.1, we have $B^{\phi(n)} \equiv 1(\text{mod } n)$, it follows that $B^{ed} = B^1(B^{\phi(n)})^k \equiv B(\text{mod } n)$ so that R does retrieve the plain text message as claimed.

But surely Mrs R can decipher the message as quickly as R? After all R has revealed to *everyone* that all messages sent to him are to be encoded, modulo 4453, using the exponent $e = 97$.

The point is that to decode incoming messages both R and Mrs R need to know d. To determine d one needs to know e and $\phi(n)$. (Remember it is n and not $\phi(n)$ which is revealed by R.) Now $\phi(n) = (p-1)(q-1)$ can clearly be determined if the factors p and q of n are known. Conversely, if n and $\phi(n)$ are known then so are p and q. For, assuming n is the product pq of distinct primes p, q, then $n - \phi(n) = p + q - 1$ whilst $(p+q)^2 = (p-q)^2 + 4n$ (see Exercise 12.2.5). Consequently, given n, finding $\phi(n)$ and factoring n are equally easy (or difficult!). And herein lies the reason for the (somewhat exaggerated) statement that we are dealing here with an 'unbreakable' code.

In practice p and q are chosen to be very large primes—say of size 10^{50} or 10^{100}. This doesn't take too long (see table below) on a powerful computer. (One way of finding such p and q is to choose odd numbers at random and apply Theorem 5.4.12. The number of primes with 100 digits is exactly

$\pi(10^{100)}-\pi(10^{99})$. Consequently, by the prime number theorem, the chance that an odd integer with 100 digits is prime is approximately*

$$\frac{2\left(\frac{10^{100}}{\log_e 10^{100}}-\frac{10^{99}}{\log_e 10^{99}}\right)}{10^{99}(10-1)},$$

which is approximately 0·0086. Thus one might hope to come across a 100-digit prime after choosing approximately 115 odd 100-digit numbers.) A product of two such numbers will be a number with 199 or 200 digits. The following table shows the sorts of times presently required (by powerful computers) for factorising and checking the primeness of numbers of various sizes. (Problem 1.3.5 asked you to consider this problem using four digit primes and their product.) Thus, if in our story, R uses a computer to choose p and q as above and with, say, 50 digits, you can see that the same computer is of little use to Mrs R (or anyone else) in trying to discover what little plot A and R are hatching.

Table 12.1 Comparison of approximate computational times to test for primeness and factorise large numbers using some of the fastest known methods. (See Knuth [6].)

Number of digits	Test for Primeness	Factorise
20	10 seconds	24 minutes
50	15 seconds	3.9 hours
100	40 seconds	74 years
200	10 minutes	3.8×10^{9} years
1000	1 week	3.2×10^{43} years

Exercise 12.2.1 and Problem 12.2.1 emphasise restrictions that should be kept in mind when choosing e and n if the possibility of decoding without first factoring n is to be avoided. There are also restrictions to which p and q should be subjected if rapid factorisation of n is to be made less likely. In particular $p-1$ and $q-1$ should have large prime factors whilst $(p-1, q-1)$ should be small (see [7]). One way to ensure this might be to eschew choosing 100-digit numbers at random but rather build up $p-1$ (and $q-1$) by taking $w-1$ to be, say, $2\cdot101\cdot65\,537\ldots$ and checking the resulting w for primeness.

Finally, please note—before rushing off to send secret messages all over the world—that, even excluding the ill-chosen encipherings of Exercises 1 and 2 and Problem 1 below, no-one has yet proved that one *must*, in general, factorise n as a preliminary to decipherment. On the other hand, no general method of proceeding *without* first factoring n has yet been found.

We conclude by presenting two programs, one to convert the letter codes into four-digit blocks raised to the power e modulo n; the other to accept the

* The 2 is due to the consideration of only odd integers.

coded blocks and decode them by raising them to the power d modulo n. The entry of the original message and the display of the final decoded message can be achieved much more efficiently in most BASICs than we have shown here. It should be possible simply to type in the message and let the program convert it to numerical form. The method we illustrate here is based on the standard BASIC that does not have such useful character-handling facilities. We ask readers to explore with their own machines these more efficient ways of entering (and subsequently displaying) the text of the message.

PROGRAM 12.1 *To encode a message using the RSA method*

```
 10 INPUT "N,E",n,E
 20 DIM W(1000),U(500)
 30 C=0
 40 PRINT "enter the codes of the letters ";
 45 PRINT "enter -1 to indicate the end of the message"
 50   INPUT A
 60   IF A=-1 GOTO 110
 70   C=C+1
 80   W(C)=A
 90   GOTO 50
100 REM If the number of letters is not even insert an extra x at the end
110 IF C/2=INT(C/2)GOTO 150
120   C=C+1
130   W(C)=23
140 REM Combine pairs of letters into blocks
150 FOR I=1 TO INT(C/2)
160   U(I)=W(2*(I-1)+1)*100+W(2*(I-1)+2)
170 NEXT I
230 REM raise each block to the power E modulo n
240  FOR I=1 TO INT(C/2)
250    m=E
260    a=U(I)
270    x=a - INT(a/n)*n
280    b=1
290      m=m/2
300      IF m = INT(m) GOTO 320
310        b = x * b - INT(x*b/n) * n
320      m = INT(m)
330      IF m=0 GOTO 360
340        x=x*x-INT(x*x/n)*n
350    GOTO 290
360    PRINT b;
370 NEXT I
380 PRINT
390 END
```

Program 12.2 *To decode a number using the RSA method*

```
10 INPUT "N,D",n,D
20 INPUT "ENTER THE NUMBER OF BLOCKS OF CODE",L
30 DIM W(L),U(L),A(2*L)
40 PRINT "Enter the blocks"
50 FOR I=1 TO L
60  INPUT W(I)
70 NEXT
```

```
 80 C=2*L
100 PRINT
110 REM raise each block to the power d modulo n
120 FOR I=1 TO L
130   m=D
140   a=W(I)
150   x=a - INT(a/n)*n
160   b=1
170     m=m/2
180     IF m = INT(m) GOTO 200
190       b = x * b - INT(x*b/n) * n
200     m = INT(m)
210     IF m=0 GOTO 240
220        x=x*x - INT(x*x/n) * n
230     GOTO 170
240   U(I)=b:PRINT b;
250 NEXT I
260 REM separate into pairs of digits and display the corresponding letters
270 PRINT
290 FOR I=1 TO L
300    A(2*(I-1)+1)=INT(U(I)/100)
310    A(2*(I-1)+2)=U(I) - INT(U(I)/100)*100
320 NEXT I
330 FOR J=1 TO C
340   PRINT CHR$(A(J)+65);
350 NEXT J
360 END
```

We leave you with the following message which was enciphered using the $A = 00$, $B = 01$, $C = 02, \ldots$ correspondence with $e = 109$ and $n = 6499$.

6132 0615 5995 0615 2368 1225 5201 3198 0499 1342 4718 0499 3221
2851 1520 0001 2432 4326 0472 4945 2555 4718 2271 6219 5941 3266
4713 1990 0036 0096 0744 5882 3998 1790 3198 1541 5349 3998 5941
6098 0048 0893 5349 1835 6463 0615 2168 0414 0754 4718 3334 4043
0953 4402 5249 4830 3144 6485 5361 3499 0615 3198 5952 0075 6057
4244 2477 0744 3334 3370 0200 0189 4787 2168 0274 3198 4713 0044
0025 6098 0048 0893 5349 1506 2848 5686 4718 0753 3158 4718 0722
4787 6098 0048 0893 5349 1520 6463 0753 3158 3198 4718 0722 3344
1361 4043 3158 2534 1520 3091 1989 4249 5443 1520 0075 6124 0615
2477 3383 0200 1990 2494 5213 3221 0615 0044 0021 2915 1318 3696
0744 4885 3608 4719 0615 0832 3147 4718

As it contains a question, the authors would be interested to hear your answer.

Exercises 12.2

1 (i) Using $n = 5893$ and $e = 3$ encode the message SE ND AC AR. What do you notice about each of the two final blocks of four digits in the encoded message? [*Hint*: $4913 = 17 \times 17 \times 17$.]
(ii) Using $n = 5893$ and $e = 3$ a certain message, when encoded, becomes 0391 1141 0001 2197 2197 0381. Without factoring n find the name of the fruit being sought. [*Hint*: $2197 = 13^3$.]

2 (i) Show that if a plain text block B is not coprime to the enciphering modulus n $(=p\cdot q)$ then neither is the corresponding cipher text block which is congruent to B^e. Hence deduce that if a single cipher text block is *not* coprime to n, then the coded message can be broken. [*Hint*: n can be factorised.]
(ii) Factorise by hand the enciphering modulus $n=7663$, given that one of the cipher blocks is 4171.

3 Let $n=pq$ as usual. Show that the probability that a plain text block B is *not* coprime to n is $1/p+1/q-1/pq$. Approximately how large will p, q need to be chosen if p, q are required to be within 10^4 of each other, and the probability mentioned above is to be less than $1/10^6$?

4 Having found a *single* large prime p, can you think of any reason why you should not take n to be p^2 (rather than pq where $q\neq p$?).

5 Show that if $n=pq$ where p, q are distinct primes, then $n-\phi(n)=p+q-1$ and $(p+q)^2=(p-q)^2+4n$. Hence find p, q given that $n=14\,933$ and $\phi(n)=14\,688$.

Computer problem 12.2

1 (i) The following coded message was intercepted. It was encoded by the public key method using $n=4819$ and $e=2401$

2003 1582 1917 1968 2038 2038 1968 0467 1350 1158 3679 4203 2076 3335
1968 4560 3801 4767 4615 3977 0418 1935 1881 4686 1319 4358 1670 3917
1206 1574 0937 1582 3716 0937 0630 1189

By repeatedly encoding each of the blocks, i.e. raising to the power e, mod n, show that a sensible message soon results. [The moral is that e should be chosen so that its order modulo $\phi(n)$ is not too small. Otherwise decoding by repeatedly encoding becomes possible.]
(ii) The following messages were encoded

(a) using $n=3901$ and $e=2515$:

0614 2297 2297 1154 2535 0584 1265 1432 1675 0607 3580 1699 3274
0355 3171

(b) using $n=6319$ and $e=1369$:

3490 1820 0484 5926 0221 3194 5661 4597 0418 0797 4799

Try decoding the message by cubing each block, raising each to the fifth power etc. until a sensible message results. [What is the moral of this example?]
(iii) How well do the coded passages in the text stand up to these two lines of attack?

Appendix I

Multiprecision arithmetic

The size of integers that can be handled on any computer is limited by the architecture of the computer. For example the BBC B and many other small microcomputers can only handle integers between -2^{32} ($-2\,147\,483\,648$) and $2^{32}-1$ ($2\,147\,483\,647$). Thus in asking you to prove John Hill wrong (Problem 0.1.3) we are at the limit of such a computer.

If we want to manipulate numbers of larger magnitude than this we must store the digits in an array and use specially written routines to perform the operations of addition, subtraction, multiplication and division. We present these operations as subroutines that can be called by the GOSUB command. After each calculation is completed the program returns to the statement from which the routines are called. Before we consider the arithmetic operations, we need to begin by saying a brief word about the entry, storage and display of such numbers.

It is easier to program the arithmetic if the digits that make up an integer are stored in an array in reverse order. That is, the first value in the array represents the units, the second the tens etc. Entering integers in their natural form means that the order of the digits must be reversed as they are stored in the array. As each digit is entered therefore we must shift the previous digits one place up the array before placing the current digit in the first position. The size of the integer is not known until the last digit is entered. The following program will allow us to enter an integer digit by digit

Subroutine A1 *Entry of long integers*

```
4010 REM n is the number of digits
4020 REM the array x will contain the integer - it must have dimension m
4030 REM the process stops on entry of a negative number or one > 9
4030 n=-1
4040 INPUT d
4050   IF d<0 or d>9 RETURN
4060   n=n+1
4070   FOR i=1 TO n
4080     x(i)=x(i-1)
4090   NEXT i
4100   x(0)=d
4110   IF n<m goto 4040
4120   PRINT "the array is full"
4130 RETURN
```

The integers can then be displayed starting with the largest non-zero position in the array. The following will therefore display a number of n digits stored in an array of size m ($m < n$).

Subroutine A2 *Display of long integers*

```
5000 REM array x contains the integer - it must have dimension m
5010  i=m+1
5020  i=i-1
5030 IF (x(i) = 0 AND i>1) GOTO 5020
5040 FOR j=i TO 0 STEP -1
5050   PRINT x(j);
5060 NEXT j
```

We now move to the arithmetic operations and begin by presenting simple routines which perform the calculations on a computer in essentially the same way as we would carry them out given paper and pencil. These almost certainly will not be the most efficient ways of performing each of the operations but they require no new thought about the way that the numbers are manipulated.

Addition

Suppose we have integers a, b which can be represented as n-tuples. That is

$$a = (a_n, a_{n-1}, \ldots, a_1, a_0) = \sum a_r 10^r$$

$$b = (b_n, b_{n-1}, \ldots, b_1, b_0) = \sum b_r 10^r$$

$$0 \leq 1_r < 10 \text{ and } 0 \leq b_r < 10$$

Their sum $a + b = \sum a_r 10^r + \sum b_r 10^r = \sum (a_r + b_r) 10^r$ can be represented as the $(n+1)$-tuple $\sum s_r 10^r$, where s_r is determined by

$$a_r + b_r + c_{r-1} = c_r 10 + s_r$$

Here c_r ($=0$ or 1) represents the 'carries' that occur in the addition. The following BASIC statements perform addition in this way

Subroutine A3 *Multiprecison addition of two integers*

```
6000 REM arrays x and y contain the two integers to be added
6005 REM s will contain the result x+y
6010 REM n is initially the number of digits in the longer of the integers
6015 REM at the end n contains the number of digits in the result
6020 C = 0
6030 FOR i = 0 TO n-1
6040   T = x(i) + y(i) + C
6060   C = INT(T/10)
6050   s(i) = T - C * 10
6070 NEXT i
6080 IF C = 0 GOTO 6110
6090 s(n)=C
6100 n=n+1
6110 RETURN
```

Subtraction

$$a-b=\sum_{r=0}^{n} a_r 10^r - \sum_{r=0}^{m} b_r 10^r = \sum_{r=0}^{k} (a_r - b_r)10^r = \sum_{r=0}^{k} d_r 10^r,$$

where $k=\max(n, m)$.

A difference $a_r - b_r$ may involve 'borrowing' from the coefficient of the next highest power of 10. This must be 'paid back' by adding one to the next term in b. Thus if $a_r < b_r$ we must increase a_r by 10 and add 1 to the next digit, b_{r+1}, of the integer b. (Note that in doing this we are changing the value of b. To preserve the value of b see the revised method used in the division program A6.)

If $a<b$ then b_{k+1} will be non-zero and the result will be a negative number. To obtain the answer we must subtract each of the digits d_r from 9 and complete the process by adding 1 to d_0.

Subroutine A4 *Multiprecision subtraction*

```
7000 REM Calculates d = a - b
7010 REM n is the number of digits in the longer of the two integers
7020 REM at the end n contains the number of digits in d, s$ its sign
7030 s$ = '+'
7040 FOR i = 0 TO n-1
7050   IF a(i) >= b(i) GOTO 7080
7060    REM borrow 10 and pay back to the next term in b
7060     a(i) = a(i) + 10
7070     b(i+1) = b(i+1) + 1
7080   d(i) = a(i) - b(i)
7090 NEXT
7110 IF b(n) = 0 RETURN
7120 REM if the answer is negative set up the last digit and
7130 REM subtract each term from 9
7140 d(n)=10-b(n)
7150 FOR i = 0 TO n
7160   d(i) = 9-d(i)
7170 NEXT
7180 d(1) = d(1) + 1
7190 s$='-'
7200 n=n+1
7210 RETURN
```

Multiplication

Multiprecision multiplication can be achieved using the technique of long multiplication. We can build this up by first of all considering the result of multiplying an m-digit number $b=(b_m, b_{m-1}, \ldots, b_1, b_0)$ by a 1-digit number a (producing the $m+1$ digit number $(p_{m+1}, p_m, \ldots, p_1, p_0)$). This can be done as follows:

If, by the division algorithm,

$$ab_0 = q_0 10 + p_0, \qquad 0 \leqslant p_0 < 10,$$

then q_0 must then be added to the result of multiplying a_1 by b. Proceeding in this way we have at the $(i+1)$st digit, using the division algorithm $ab_1 + q_{i-1} = q_i 10 + p_i$ where $0 \leqslant p_i < 10$. Since $b_{m+1} = 0$ we obtain $q_m = q_{m+1}10 + p_{m+1}$. Thus $p_{m+1} = q_m$.

If we now want to multiply an m-digit number b by an n-digit number a, then we take each digit in a in turn and multiply b by it as shown above. We then add the result, multiplied by the appropriate power of 10, to the partial result already evaluated. We can achieve this using the following algorithm

Algorithm

```
1.  Zero an array p into which we are going to place the answer
2.  For a fixed digit a(j) in the first number a
      3. set the carry to zero
      4. For each digit b(i) in the second number
           5. calculate t = a(j)*b(i)+carry
           6. add t to the i+j position in the partial product
                calculate s = remainder (mod 10) of t + p(i+j)
                add the remainder (mod 10) of s to p(i+j)
                add the quotient (mod 10) of s to p(i+j+1)
           7. calculate the new carry = quotient of t
```

which is used in Subroutine A5.

Subroutine A5 *Multprecision multiplication.*

```
8000 REM multplies a by b placing the result in p
8001 REM p has dimension n+m+1 where n and m are the dimensions of a,b
8002 FOR i = 0 TO n+m+1
8003   p(i) = 0
8004 NEXT i
8010 FOR j = 0 TO n
8011   c = 0
8020   FOR i = 0 TO m+1
8030     d = a(j) * b(i) + carry
8040     s = p(i+j) + d MOD 10
8050     p(i+j) = s MOD 10
8060     p(i+j+1) = p(i+j+1) + s DIV 10
8070     c = d DIV 10
8080   NEXT i
8090 NEXT j
8100 RETURN
```

Division

Multiprecision division can be performed in essentially the same way as the method of long division you were first taught around the age of 9. We can therefore proceed as follows:

1 Suppose the divisor y has n_y digits. Place in an array r the first n_y digits (starting with the highest power of 10) of the dividend x.

2 Subtract *y* from *r* repeatedly (using multiprecision subtraction) until a negative answer is obtained (counting the number of these subtractions). Add *y* back on to *r* to obtain a positive remainder.

3 The number of subtractions performed less one is the corresponding term in the quotient and is assigned to the appropriate location in the array *q*.

4 If there are still digits in *x* that we have not used, multiply the current value of the array *r* by 10 (that is shift all values in the array up one place) and place the next digit in the dividend in the units position of *r* and go to step 2.

5 If there are no more digits in *x* to be substituted, then already the array *q* contains the quotient and the array *r* contains the remainder.

Subroutine A6 *Multiprecision Division*

```
9000 REM Divides x by y placing the quotient in q and the remainder in r
9005 REM n1 and n2 represent the number of digits in x and y respectively
9010 FOR i=0 TO n2
9020   r(n2-i) = x(n1-i)
9030 NEXT i
9040 t=n2
9050 n3=n2+1
9060   v = 0
9065 REM subtract y from r.   Note that here any borrow is stored in b
9066 REM rather than added to y.   This ensures that the value of y is
9067 REM not changed so that we can use it again
9068 REM v counts the number of subtractions.
9070     v = v + 1
9080     b = 0
9090     FOR i = 0 TO n3
9100       s = r(i) - y(i) + b
9110       b = 0
9120       IF s >= 0 GOTO 9150
9130         b = -1
9140         s = s + 10
9150       r(i)= s - INT(s/10)*10
9160     NEXT
9170   IF b = 0 GOTO 9070
9180   v = v-1
9190   q(n1-t) = v
9200   c = 0
9210   FOR i = 0 TO n3
9220     s = r(i)+y(i)+c
9230     c = INT(s/10)
9240     r(i) = s - c*10
9250   NEXT i
9260   t=t+1
9270   IF t >n1 RETURN
9280 REM Set up the next quotient using the
9290 REM remainder from the previous calculation
9300 REM and the next integer from x
9310 FOR i= 0 TO n2
9320   r(n2-i+1) = r(n2-i)
9330 NEXT
9340 r(0)=x(n1-t)
9350 GOTO 9060
```

Evaluation

The methods presented here, being essentially translations onto a computer of the techniques we use for 'hand' calculation, are perhaps the most natural ones to employ. ('Classroom methods' is a label that is often attached to them.) It should be noted that these methods are not necessarily the quickest way of solving each of the problems on a computer. Their efficiency can be evaluated by determining how the number of operations employed relates to the number of digits in the integers concerned (that is, to the size of those integers)*. For example, the addition operation described clearly involves three additions/subtractions and two multiplication/division operations for each of the digits involved in the longer of the two numbers. Thus we say that the operation depends linearly on n, where n is the number of digits in the larger integer (or $\log_{10} N$, where N is the larger integer itself). Similarly the multiplication method presented depends linearly on the product of the number of digits. Thus if we multiply numbers of approximately the same length (n) the time taken is a function of n^2. The main reason for considering alternative (less naive) methods to the above is to reduce this number of operations, if possible.

We illustrate this by considering an alternative approach to multiplying two $2n$ digit numbers x and y.

Split x into two n-digit numbers (x_1, x_2), x_1 consisting of the first n digits and x_2 the second n digits. Similarly represent y as (y_1, y_2). Then

$$x \cdot y = x_1 \cdot y_1 10^{2n} + x_1 \cdot y_2 10^n + x_2 \cdot y_1 10^n + x_2 \cdot y_2$$

and we have replaced one $2n$-digit multiplication by 4 n-digit multiplications together with three 'cheaper' shifting operations. By recognising that

$$(x_1 - x_2)(y_1 - y_2) = x_1 y_1 + x_2 y_2 - x_2 y_1 - x_1 y_2$$

we can rewrite this as

$$x \cdot y = x_1 \cdot y_1 10^{2n} + x_1 \cdot y_1 10^n - (x_1 - x_2)(y_1 - y_2) 10^n$$
$$+ x_2 \cdot y_2 10^n + x_2 \cdot y_2$$

and we have reduced it to three n-digit multiplications. If we let $T(n)$ represent the time to multiply two n-digit numbers then

$$T(2n) \text{ is approximately } 3T(n) + cn \qquad (*)$$

where c is a constant and cn represents the (linear) time factor attributable to the cost of the additions, subtractions and shifts. We continue in this fashion and perform each of these multiplications by splitting each number into two halves (if at any stage the number of digits is odd we add one before dividing by two) and so on until we eventually end up multiplying pairs of one-digit numbers. This gives us a recursive method for multiplying two numbers. Is it more efficient than the classroom method? Working inductively with (*), and

* For a more detailed discussion see Knuth [6] and Rosen [7], for example.

assuming c is approximately $T(2)$, we can show that $T(2^k)$ is approximately $c(3^k - 2^k)$. Hence

$$T(n) \approx T(2^{\log_2 n}) \approx c \cdot (3^{\log_2 n} - 2^{\log_2 n}) \leqslant c \times 3^{\log_2 n} = cn^{\log_2 3}.$$

Thus $T(n)$ is approximately linearly related to $n^{1.59}$ compared with the n^2 of the classroom method.

Modular arithmetic

To conclude we show how the Chinese remainder Theorem 4.1.5 provides us with another approach to performing arithmetic on large numbers.

We begin by choosing a set of pairwise relatively prime numbers $m_1, m_2, \ldots, m_r$ such that their product $m = m_1 m_2 \cdots m_r$ is larger than any number we wish to handle. By Theorem 4.1.5 any number x can then be represented uniquely by the r-tuple $(x_1, x_2, \ldots, x_r)$ where $x_k \equiv x \bmod m_k$.

How can we perform arithmetic using this approach? Suppose we have two numbers

$$U = (u_1, u_2, \ldots, u_r) \qquad \text{and} \qquad V = (v_1, v_2, \ldots, v_r).$$

Using the obvious notation

$$\begin{aligned} \text{if } S = U + V &\text{ then } s_i \equiv (u_i + v_i) \pmod{m_i} \quad \text{for each } i \\ D = U - V &\text{ then } d_i \equiv (u_i - v_i) \pmod{m_i} \quad \text{for each } i \\ \text{and if } P \equiv U \cdot V &\text{ then } p_i \equiv (u_1 \cdot v_i) \pmod{m_i} \quad \text{for each } i. \end{aligned}$$

Each component of the calculation can be dealt with separately, removing the need to remember 'carries' and 'borrows'.

The m_i should be chosen as large as possible and the largest of the numbers is usually chosen to be the largest odd number that your computer can handle. The remaining numbers can be found by considering the next smallest odd number which is relatively prime to all those so far chosen. This can be done using the Euclidean algorithm but does not really contribute to the (computing) cost of solving the problem since once a suitable set of values has been found they are available for all time.

The individual calculations for each m_i can be performed using the methods described earlier. Recognising that

$$u_i + v_i (\bmod\ m_i) = \begin{cases} u_i + v_i & \text{if } u_i + v_i < m_i \\ u_i + v_i - m_i & \text{if } u_i + v_i \geqslant m_i \end{cases}$$

and

$$u_i - v_i (\bmod\ m_i) = \begin{cases} u_i - v_i & \text{if } u_i \geqslant v_i \\ u_i - v_i + m_i & \text{if } u_i < v_i, \end{cases}$$

these can be achieved by using only addition and subtraction operations whilst at worst the product can be obtained by computing the product $u_i \cdot v_i$ and then dividing by m_i to obtain the remainder. Although high-precision routines may be needed to perform the multiplications, we never have to use more than twice the number of digits that our computer can handle, whatever the size of the integers to which the arithmetic is being applied.

Conversion of modular numbers back into decimal form can be done using the constructive proof of the Chinese remainder theorem (Theorem 4.1.5.). This, however, requires a large amount of high-precision arithmetic, the very thing we are trying to avoid. This problem can be overcome using a algorithm, due to Gardener and described by Knuth [6], which is based on an alternative proof of Theorem 4.1.5.

One problem with this method is that we lose all notion of the relative size of two numbers. Hence the method is not suitable if we need to make a large number of comparisons between the integers involved since this can only be done by converting the r-tuples back into decimal form.

Computer problems

We leave readers to write programs to implement these last two ideas and write multiprecision versions of some of the programs presented in the text.

Appendix II

Table Showing the least prime factor of each odd integer (other than multiples of 5) less than 10 000. * indicates a prime.

	0				10				20				30				40			
	1	3	7	9	1	3	7	9	1	3	7	9	1	3	7	9	1	3	7	9
0		*	*	3	*	*	*	*	3	*	3	*	*	3	*	3	*	*	*	7
50	3	*	3	*	*	3	*	3	*	*	7	*	3	*	3	*	7	3	*	3
100	*	*	*	*	3	*	3	7	11	3	*	3	*	7	*	*	3	11	3	*
150	*	3	*	3	7	*	*	13	3	*	3	*	*	3	11	3	*	*	*	*
200	3	7	3	11	*	3	7	3	13	*	*	*	3	*	3	*	*	3	13	3
250	*	11	*	7	3	*	3	*	*	3	*	3	*	*	7	17	3	*	3	13
300	7	3	*	3	*	*	*	11	3	17	3	7	*	3	*	3	11	7	*	*
350	3	*	3	*	19	3	*	3	7	*	13	*	3	*	3	*	17	3	*	3
400	*	13	11	*	3	7	3	*	*	3	7	3	*	*	19	*	3	*	3	*
450	11	3	*	3	*	*	*	7	3	11	3	*	13	3	*	3	*	17	7	*
500	3	*	3	*	7	3	11	3	*	*	17	23	3	13	3	7	*	3	*	3
550	19	7	*	13	3	*	3	*	*	3	*	3	7	11	*	19	3	*	3	*
600	*	3	*	3	13	*	*	*	3	7	3	17	*	3	7	3	*	*	*	11
650	3	*	3	*	*	3	23	3	11	*	*	7	3	*	3	13	*	3	17	3
700	*	19	7	*	3	23	3	*	7	3	*	3	17	*	11	*	3	*	3	7
750	*	3	*	3	*	7	13	*	3	*	3	19	11	3	*	3	7	13	*	17
800	3	11	3	*	*	3	19	3	*	*	*	*	3	7	3	*	29	3	7	3
850	23	*	*	*	3	*	3	11	13	3	*	3	*	*	*	7	3	19	3	29
900	17	3	*	3	*	11	7	*	3	13	3	*	7	3	*	3	*	23	*	13
950	3	*	3	7	31	3	*	3	*	7	*	11	3	*	3	23	*	3	*	3
1000	7	17	19	*	3	*	3	*	*	3	13	3	*	*	17	*	3	7	3	*
1050	*	3	7	3	*	*	11	*	3	29	3	13	23	3	*	3	*	*	*	7
1100	3	*	3	*	11	3	*	3	19	*	7	*	3	11	3	17	7	3	31	3
1150	*	*	13	19	3	*	3	7	*	3	11	3	*	7	*	29	3	*	3	11
1200	*	3	17	3	7	*	*	23	3	*	3	*	*	3	*	3	17	11	29	*
1250	3	7	3	*	13	3	7	3	31	19	*	*	3	*	3	*	*	3	*	3
1300	*	*	*	7	3	13	3	*	*	3	*	3	11	31	7	13	3	17	3	19
1350	7	3	23	3	*	29	*	37	3	*	3	7	*	3	19	3	13	7	11	*
1400	3	23	3	*	17	3	13	3	7	*	*	*	3	*	3	*	11	3	*	3
1450	*	*	31	*	3	7	3	13	*	3	7	3	*	*	*	*	3	*	3	*
1500	19	3	11	3	*	17	37	7	3	*	3	11	*	3	29	3	23	*	7	*

Table—continued.

	0				10				20				30				40			
	1	3	7	9	1	3	7	9	1	3	7	9	1	3	7	9	1	3	7	9
1550	3	*	3	*	7	3	*	3	*	11	19	*	3	*	3	7	37	3	*	3
1600	*	7	*	*	3	*	3	*	*	3	*	3	7	23	*	11	3	31	3	17
1650	13	3	*	3	11	*	*	*	3	7	3	23	41	3	7	3	19	*	*	*
1700	3	13	3	*	29	3	17	3	*	*	11	7	3	*	3	37	*	3	*	3
1750	17	*	7	*	3	41	3	29	7	3	*	3	13	*	*	*	3	11	3	7
1800	*	3	13	3	*	7	23	17	3	*	3	31	*	3	11	3	7	19	*	43
1850	3	17	3	11	*	3	*	3	*	*	*	*	3	7	3	*	31	3	7	3
1900	*	11	*	23	3	*	3	19	17	3	41	3	*	*	13	7	3	29	3	*
1950	*	3	19	3	37	13	7	11	3	*	3	*	7	3	*	3	11	*	*	*
2000	3	*	3	7	*	3	*	3	43	7	*	*	3	19	3	*	13	3	23	3
2050	7	*	11	29	3	*	3	*	19	3	31	3	*	*	*	*	3	7	3	*
2100	11	3	7	3	*	*	29	13	3	11	3	*	*	3	*	3	*	*	19	7
2150	3	*	3	17	*	3	11	3	13	41	7	*	3	37	3	11	7	3	13	3
2200	31	*	*	47	3	*	3	7	*	3	17	3	23	7	*	*	3	*	3	13
2250	*	3	37	3	7	31	*	*	3	*	3	43	*	3	*	3	29	*	*	11
2300	3	7	3	*	*	3	7	3	11	23	13	17	3	*	3	*	*	3	*	3
2350	*	13	*	7	3	17	3	23	*	3	*	3	*	*	7	*	3	*	3	*
2400	7	3	29	3	*	19	*	41	3	*	3	7	11	3	*	3	*	7	*	31
2450	3	11	3	*	23	3	*	3	7	*	*	37	3	13	3	19	47	3	11	3
2500	41	*	23	13	3	7	3	11	*	3	7	3	*	17	43	*	3	*	3	*
2550	*	3	*	3	13	11	17	7	3	31	3	*	29	3	13	3	*	*	7	23
2600	3	19	3	*	7	3	*	3	*	43	37	11	3	*	3	7	19	3	*	3
2650	11	7	*	*	3	*	3	17	*	3	*	3	7	*	*	*	3	*	3	*
2700	37	3	*	3	*	*	11	*	3	7	3	*	*	3	7	3	*	13	41	*
2750	3	*	3	31	11	3	*	3	17	47	*	7	3	11	3	*	*	3	*	3
2800	*	*	7	53	3	29	3	*	7	3	11	3	19	*	*	17	3	*	3	7
2850	*	3	*	3	*	7	47	19	3	13	3	*	43	3	*	3	7	11	*	13
2900	3	*	3	*	41	3	*	3	23	37	*	29	3	7	3	*	17	3	7	3
2950	13	*	*	11	3	*	3	*	*	3	13	3	11	19	29	7	3	41	3	*
3000	*	3	31	3	*	23	7	*	3	*	3	13	7	3	*	3	*	17	11	*
3050	3	43	3	7	*	3	*	3	37	7	17	*	3	*	3	*	11	3	19	3

3100	7	29	13	*	3	11	3	*	*	3	53	3	31	13	*	43	3	7	3	47
3150	23	3	7	3	29	*	*	*	3	19	3	11	*	3	*	3	*	31	23	7
3200	3	*	3	*	13	3	*	3	*	11	7	*	3	53	3	41	7	3	17	3
3250	*	*	*	*	3	13	3	7	*	3	29	3	17	7	19	11	3	37	3	*
3300	*	3	*	3	7	*	31	*	3	*	3	*	*	3	47	3	13	*	*	17
3350	3	7	3	*	*	3	7	3	*	*	11	31	3	17	3	*	*	3	43	3
3400	19	41	*	7	3	*	3	13	11	3	23	3	47	*	7	19	3	11	3	*
3450	7	3	*	3	*	*	*	*	3	23	3	7	59	3	11	3	*	7	13	*
3500	3	31	3	11	*	3	*	3	7	13	*	*	3	*	3	*	*	3	*	3
3550	53	11	*	*	3	7	3	43	*	3	7	3	*	*	17	37	3	*	3	59
3600	13	3	*	3	23	*	*	7	3	*	3	19	*	3	*	3	11	*	7	41
3650	3	13	3	*	7	3	19	3	*	*	*	13	3	29	3	7	*	3	*	3
3700	*	7	11	*	3	47	3	*	61	3	*	3	7	*	37	*	3	19	3	23
3750	11	3	13	3	*	53	*	*	3	7	3	*	19	3	7	3	17	*	*	29
3800	3	*	3	13	37	3	11	3	*	*	43	7	3	*	3	11	23	3	*	3
3850	*	*	7	17	3	*	3	53	7	3	*	3	*	11	13	*	3	17	3	7
3900	47	3	*	3	*	7	*	*	3	*	3	*	*	3	31	3	7	*	*	11
3950	3	59	3	37	17	3	*	3	11	29	41	23	3	7	3	*	13	3	7	3
4000	*	*	*	19	3	*	3	*	*	3	*	3	29	37	11	7	3	13	3	*
4050	*	3	*	3	31	17	7	13	3	*	3	*	7	3	61	3	*	*	17	*
4100	3	11	3	7	*	3	23	3	13	7	*	*	3	*	3	*	41	3	11	3
4150	7	*	*	*	3	23	3	11	43	3	*	3	37	47	53	59	3	7	3	13
4200	*	3	7	3	*	11	*	*	3	41	3	*	*	3	19	3	*	*	31	7
4250	3	*	3	*	*	3	17	3	*	*	7	11	3	*	3	*	7	3	*	3
4300	11	13	59	31	3	19	3	7	29	3	*	3	61	7	*	*	3	43	3	*
4350	19	3	*	3	7	*	11	17	3	*	3	29	13	3	41	3	*	23	*	53
4400	3	7	3	*	11	3	7	3	*	*	19	43	3	11	3	23	*	3	*	3
4450	*	61	*	7	3	*	3	41	17	3	11	3	*	*	7	67	3	*	3	11
4500	7	3	*	3	13	*	*	*	3	*	3	7	23	3	13	3	19	7	*	*
4550	3	29	3	47	*	3	*	3	7	17	23	19	3	*	3	13	*	3	*	3
4600	43	*	17	11	3	7	3	31	*	3	7	3	11	41	*	*	3	*	3	*
4650	*	3	*	3	59	*	13	7	3	*	3	*	31	3	43	3	*	13	7	37
4700	3	*	3	17	7	3	53	3	*	*	29	*	3	*	3	7	11	3	47	3
4750	*	7	67	*	3	11	3	19	13	3	17	3	7	*	*	*	3	*	3	*
4800	*	3	11	3	17	*	*	61	3	7	3	11	*	3	7	3	47	29	37	13
4850	3	23	3	43	*	3	31	3	*	11	*	7	3	19	3	*	67	3	59	3
4900	13	*	7	*	3	17	3	*	7	3	13	3	*	*	*	11	3	*	3	7

Table—continued.

	0				10				20				30				40			
	1	3	7	9	1	3	7	9	1	3	7	9	1	3	7	9	1	3	7	9
4950	*	3	*	3	11	7	*	*	3	*	3	13	17	3	*	3	7	*	19	*
5000	3	*	3	*	*	3	29	3	*	*	11	47	3	7	3	*	71	3	7	3
5050	*	31	13	*	3	61	3	37	11	3	*	3	*	13	*	7	3	11	3	*
5100	*	3	*	3	19	*	7	*	3	47	3	23	7	3	11	3	53	37	*	19
5150	3	*	3	7	13	3	*	3	*	7	31	*	3	71	3	*	29	3	*	3
5200	7	11	41	*	3	13	3	17	23	3	*	3	*	*	*	13	3	7	3	29
5250	59	3	7	3	*	19	23	11	3	*	3	*	*	3	17	3	11	67	*	7
5300	3	*	3	*	47	3	13	3	17	*	7	73	3	*	3	19	7	3	*	3
5350	*	53	11	23	3	31	3	7	41	3	19	3	*	7	*	17	3	*	3	*
5400	11	3	*	3	7	*	*	*	3	11	3	61	*	3	*	3	*	*	13	*
5450	3	7	3	53	43	3	7	3	*	13	*	*	3	*	3	11	17	3	23	3
5500	*	*	*	7	3	37	3	*	*	3	*	3	*	11	7	29	3	23	3	31
5550	7	3	*	3	67	*	19	*	3	*	3	7	*	3	37	3	*	7	29	11
5600	3	13	3	71	31	3	41	3	7	*	17	13	3	43	3	*	*	3	*	3
5650	*	*	*	*	3	7	3	*	53	3	7	3	13	*	11	*	3	*	3	41
5700	*	3	13	3	*	29	*	7	3	59	3	17	11	3	*	3	*	*	7	*
5750	3	11	3	13	7	3	73	3	29	23	53	*	3	*	3	7	*	3	11	3
5800	*	7	*	37	3	*	3	11	*	3	*	3	7	19	13	*	3	*	3	*
5850	*	3	*	3	*	11	*	*	3	7	3	*	*	3	7	3	43	71	*	17
5900	3	*	3	19	23	3	61	3	31	*	*	7	3	17	3	*	13	3	19	3
5950	11	*	7	59	3	67	3	47	7	3	43	3	*	31	*	53	3	13	3	7
6000	17	3	*	3	*	7	11	13	3	19	3	*	37	3	*	3	7	*	*	23
6050	3	*	3	73	11	3	*	3	13	*	59	*	3	7	3	*	*	3	7	3
6100	*	17	31	41	3	*	3	29	*	3	11	3	*	*	17	7	3	*	3	11
6150	*	3	47	3	61	*	7	31	3	*	3	37	7	3	23	3	41	11	*	*
6200	3	*	3	7	*	3	*	3	*	7	13	*	3	23	3	17	79	3	*	3
6250	7	13	*	11	3	*	3	*	*	3	*	3	11	61	*	19	3	7	3	*
6300	*	3	7	3	*	59	*	71	3	*	3	*	13	3	*	3	17	*	11	7
6350	3	*	3	*	*	3	*	3	23	*	7	*	3	13	3	*	7	3	*	3
6400	37	19	43	13	3	11	3	7	*	3	*	3	59	7	41	47	3	17	3	*
6450	*	3	11	3	7	23	29	*	3	*	3	11	*	3	13	3	*	43	73	67

6500	3	7	3	23	17	3	7	3	*	11	61	*	3	47	3	13	31	3	*	3
6550	*	*	79	7	3	*	3	*	*	3	*	3	*	29	7	11	3	19	3	*
6600	7	3	*	3	11	17	13	*	3	37	3	7	19	3	*	3	29	7	17	61
6650	3	*	3	*	*	3	59	3	7	*	11	*	3	41	3	*	*	3	37	3
6700	*	*	19	*	3	7	3	*	11	3	7	3	53	*	*	23	3	11	3	17
6750	43	3	29	3	*	*	67	7	3	13	3	*	*	3	11	3	*	*	7	13
6800	3	*	3	11	7	3	17	3	19	*	*	*	3	*	3	7	*	3	41	3
6850	13	7	*	19	3	*	3	*	*	3	13	3	7	*	71	83	3	61	3	*
6900	67	3	*	3	*	31	*	11	3	7	3	13	29	3	7	3	11	53	*	*
6950	3	17	3	*	*	3	*	3	*	19	*	7	3	*	3	29	*	3	*	3
7000	*	47	7	43	3	*	3	*	7	3	*	3	79	13	31	*	3	*	3	7
7050	11	3	*	3	23	7	37	*	3	11	3	*	73	3	19	3	7	41	47	31
7100	3	*	3	*	13	3	11	3	*	17	*	*	3	7	3	11	37	3	7	3
7150	*	23	17	*	3	13	3	67	71	3	*	3	43	11	*	7	3	*	3	23
7200	19	3	*	3	*	*	7	*	3	31	3	*	7	3	*	3	13	*	*	11
7250	3	*	3	7	53	3	13	3	11	7	19	29	3	*	3	37	23	3	*	3
7300	7	67	*	*	3	71	3	13	*	3	17	3	*	*	11	41	3	7	3	*
7350	*	3	7	3	17	37	53	*	3	73	3	47	11	3	83	3	19	*	13	7
7400	3	11	3	31	*	3	*	3	41	13	7	17	3	*	3	43	7	3	11	3
7450	*	29	*	*	3	17	3	7	31	3	*	3	*	7	*	*	3	59	3	*
7500	13	3	*	3	7	11	*	73	3	*	3	*	17	3	*	3	*	19	*	*
7550	3	7	3	*	*	3	7	3	67	*	*	11	3	*	3	*	*	3	71	3
7600	11	*	*	7	3	23	3	19	*	3	29	3	13	17	7	*	3	*	3	*
7650	7	3	13	3	47	79	11	*	3	*	3	7	*	3	*	3	*	7	43	*
7700	3	*	3	13	11	3	*	3	7	*	*	59	3	11	3	71	*	3	61	3
7750	23	*	*	*	3	7	3	17	19	3	7	3	31	43	13	*	3	*	3	11
7800	29	3	37	3	73	13	*	7	3	*	3	*	41	3	17	3	*	11	7	47
7850	3	*	3	29	7	3	*	3	17	*	*	*	3	*	3	7	13	3	53	3
7900	*	7	*	11	3	41	3	*	89	3	*	3	7	*	*	17	3	13	3	*
7950	*	3	73	3	19	*	31	13	3	7	3	79	23	3	7	3	61	*	11	19
8000	3	53	3	*	*	3	*	3	13	71	23	7	3	29	3	*	11	3	13	3
8050	83	*	7	*	3	11	3	*	7	3	41	3	*	59	*	*	3	*	3	7
8100	*	3	11	3	*	7	*	23	3	*	3	11	47	3	79	3	7	17	*	29
8150	3	31	3	41	*	3	*	3	*	11	13	*	3	7	3	19	*	3	7	3
8200	59	13	29	*	3	43	3	*	*	3	19	3	*	*	*	7	3	*	3	73
8250	37	3	23	3	11	*	7	*	3	*	3	17	7	3	*	3	*	*	*	43
8300	3	19	3	7	*	3	*	3	53	7	11	*	3	13	3	31	19	3	17	3

Table—continued.

	0				10				20				30				40			
	1	3	7	9	1	3	7	9	1	3	7	9	1	3	7	9	1	3	7	9
8350	7	*	61	13	3	*	3	*	11	3	*	3	17	83	*	*	3	7	3	37
8400	31	3	7	3	13	47	19	*	3	*	3	*	*	3	11	3	23	*	*	7
8450	3	79	3	11	*	3	*	3	43	37	7	61	3	17	3	13	7	3	29	3
8500	*	11	47	67	3	*	3	7	*	3	*	3	19	7	*	*	3	*	3	83
8550	17	3	43	3	7	*	13	11	3	*	3	23	*	3	31	3	11	13	*	*
8600	3	7	3	*	79	3	7	3	37	*	*	*	3	89	3	53	*	3	*	3
8650	41	17	11	7	3	*	3	*	13	3	*	3	*	19	7	*	3	*	3	*
8700	7	3	*	3	31	*	23	*	3	11	3	7	*	3	*	3	*	7	*	13
8750	3	*	3	19	*	3	11	3	7	31	67	*	3	*	3	11	59	3	19	3
8800	13	*	*	23	3	7	3	*	*	3	7	3	*	11	*	*	3	37	3	*
8850	53	3	17	3	*	*	*	7	3	19	3	13	83	3	*	3	17	*	7	11
8900	3	29	3	59	7	3	37	3	11	*	79	*	3	*	3	7	*	3	23	3
8950	*	7	13	17	3	*	3	*	*	3	47	3	7	13	11	89	3	17	3	*
9000	*	3	*	3	*	*	71	29	3	7	3	*	11	3	7	3	*	*	83	*
9050	3	11	3	*	13	3	*	3	47	43	29	7	3	31	3	61	*	3	11	3
9100	19	*	7	*	3	13	3	11	7	3	*	3	23	*	*	13	3	41	3	7
9150	*	3	*	3	*	7	89	53	3	*	3	67	*	3	*	3	7	29	17	*
9200	3	*	3	*	61	3	13	3	*	23	*	11	3	7	3	*	*	3	7	3
9250	11	19	*	47	3	59	3	13	73	3	*	3	*	*	37	7	3	*	3	17
9300	71	3	41	3	*	67	7	*	3	*	3	19	7	3	*	3	*	*	13	*
9350	3	47	3	7	11	3	17	3	*	7	*	83	3	11	3	41	*	3	*	3
9400	7	*	23	97	3	*	3	*	*	3	11	3	*	*	*	*	3	7	3	11
9450	13	3	7	3	*	*	*	17	3	*	3	*	19	3	53	3	*	11	*	7
9500	3	13	3	37	*	3	31	3	*	89	7	13	3	*	3	*	7	3	*	3
9550	*	41	19	11	3	73	3	7	17	3	61	3	11	7	*	43	3	53	3	29
9600	*	3	13	3	7	*	59	*	3	*	3	*	*	3	23	3	31	*	11	*
9650	3	7	3	13	*	3	7	3	19	17	*	*	3	23	3	*	11	3	*	3
9700	89	31	17	7	3	11	3	*	*	3	71	3	37	*	7	*	3	*	3	*
9750	7	3	11	3	43	13	*	*	3	29	3	7	*	3	*	3	*	7	97	41
9800	3	*	3	17	*	3	*	3	7	11	31	*	3	*	3	*	13	3	43	3
9850	*	59	*	*	3	7	3	71	*	3	7	3	41	*	*	11	3	13	3	19
9900	*	3	*	3	11	23	47	7	3	*	3	*	*	3	19	3	*	61	7	*
9950	3	37	3	23	7	3	*	3	13	*	11	17	3	67	3	7	97	3	13	3

Bibliography

The first two lists below include just those books and papers referred to in the text.

Books

[1] Leonard Eugene Dickson, *History of the Theory of Numbers* (Vols. I, II, III). Carnegie Institute of Washington, Washington, D.C., 1920. (Reprinted by Chelsea Publishing Co., 1952.)

[2] David M. Burton, *Elementary Number Theory*, Revised Printing, Allyn and Bacon, Boston, Mass. 1980.

[3] Donald G. Malm, *A Computer Laboratory Manual for Number Theory*, COMPress, Wentworth, N. H., 1980.

[4] M. R. Schroeder, *Number Theory in Science and Communication* (2nd enlarged edn), Springer-Verlag, Berlin, Heidelberg, 1986.

[5] Richard K. Guy, *Unsolved Problems in Number Theory*, Springer-Verlag, New York, 1981.

[6] Donald E. Knuth, *The Art of Computer Programming* (2nd edn), Addison-Wesley Reading, Mass. 1981.

[7] Kenneth H. Rosen, *Elementary Number Theory and its Applications*, Addison-Wesley, Reading, Mass. 1984.

[8] David Wells, *The Penguin Dictionary of Curious and Interesting Numbers*, Penguin Books, London, 1986.

[9] Leonhard Euler, *Elements of Algebra* Springer-Verlag, New York. (Reprinted from the fifth edition published by Longman, Orme and Co, London.)

[10] Keith Devlin, *Microchip Mathematics*; *Number Theory for Computer Users*, Shiva, Cheshire, 1984.

[11] Emil Grosswald, *Topics from the Theory of Numbers* (2nd edn), Birkhauser, Boston, 1984.

[12] Keith Devlin, Micro-maths, Macmillan, Hampshire, 1984.

[13] Harold N. Shapiro, *Introduction to the Theory of Numbers*, Wiley-Interscience, New York, 1983.

[14] *The Guinness Book of Records*, Guinness Superlatives, England (earlier editions).

[15] E. T. Bell, *Mathematics, Queen and Servant of Science*, G. Bell and Sons, London, 1952.

[16] G. H. Hardy and E. M. Wright, *An Introduction to the Theory of Numbers* (4th edn), Oxford University Press, London, 1962.

[17] C. F. Gauss, *Disquisitiones Arithmeticae*, Trans. by A. A. Clarke, Yale University Press, New Haven, Connecticut, 1966; Reprint edition by Springer-Verlag, New York, 1986.
[18] Hans Rademacher, *Lectures on Elementary Number Theory*, Blaisdell, New York, 1964.
[19] Oystein Ore, *Number Theory and its History*, McGraw-Hill, New York, 1948.
[20] Hans Riesel, *Prime Numbers and Computer Methods for Factorisation*, Birkhauser, Boston, 1985.
[21] Sir Thomas L. Heath, *Diophantus of Alexandria*, Cambridge University Press, 1910. (Reprinted, Dover Publications, New York, 1964.)
[22] Harold M. Edwards, *Fermat's Last Theorem. A Genetic Introduction to Algebraic Number Theory*, Springer-Verlag, New York, 1977.
[23] L. J. Mordell, *Diophantine Equations*, Academic Press, London, 1969.
[24] J. V. Uspensky and M. A. Heaslett, *Elementary Number Theory*, McGraw-Hill New York, 1939.
[25] L. E. Dickson, *Modern Elementary Theory of Numbers*, University of Chicago Press.
[26] Andre Weil, *Number Theory. An Approach through History, from Hammurapi to Legendre*, Birkhauser, Boston, 1983.
[27] Kenneth Ireland and Michael Rosen, *A Classical Introduction to Modern Number Theory*, Springer-Verlag, New York, 1982.
[28] William J. LeVeque, *Topics in Number Theory*, Addison-Wesley, Reading, Mass. 1958.
[29] W. Narkiewicz, *Number Theory*, World Scientific Publishing Co., Singapore, 1983.
[30] J. B. Reade, *An Introduction to Mathematical Analysis*, Oxford University Press, New York, 1986.
[31] Morris Kline, *Mathematical Thought from Ancient to Modern Times*, Oxford University Press, New York, 1972.
[32] R. Maude, *Mathematical Analysis*, Edward Arnold, London, 1986.
[33] Ivan Niven and Herbert S. Zuckerman, *An Introduction to the Theory of Numbers*, J Wiley, New York, 1960.
[34] William W. Adams and Larry Joel Goldstein, *Introduction to Number Theory*, Prentice-Hall, Englewood Cliffs, New Jersey, 1976.
[RFG] R. B. J. T. Allenby, *Rings, Fields and Groups, An Introduction to Abstract Algebra*, Edward Arnold, London 1983.

Whilst the present book was in preparation the following text, which updates several of the 'record' numbers mentioned, appeared.

[PR] Paulo Ribenboim, *The Book of Prime Number Records*, Springer-Verlag, New York, 1988.

Papers from journals

In the following *AMM* refers to the *American Mathematical Monthly* and *AHES* to the *Archive for History of Exact Sciences.* In these journals and in the *Mathematical Intelligencer* can be found many articles of either an expository or a historical nature. Indeed there are far too many for us to list them all. We leave to you the pleasure of discovering their existence.

[A] Leon Henkin, On Mathematical Induction, *AMM* **67**, 323–328, 1960.
[B] Unsolved problems section, *AMM*, **93**, 186–190, 1986. (And see the references given there.)
[C] L. E. Dickson, All integers except 23 and 239 are the sums of eight cubes, *Bull. Amer. Math. Soc.*, **45**, 588–591, 1939.
[D] S. W. Golomb. A direct interpretation of Gandhi's formula, *AMM*, **81**, 752–754, 1974.
[E] Mark Templar, On the Primality of $k!+1$ and $2*3*5*\cdots*p+1$, *Math. Comput*, **34**, 303–304, 1980.
[F] Daniel Shanks and John W. Wrench, Jr., Brun's Constant, *Math. Comput.*, **28**, 293–299, 1974.
[G] Erwin Just and Norman Schaumberger, A Curious Property of the Integer 38, *Math. Magazine*, **46**, 221, 1973.
[H] Review, by Claudia Spiro of "The Lore of Prime Numbers" by George P. Loweke, *AMM* **92**, 672–675, 1985.
[I] H. P. Lawther, Jr., An Application of Number Theory to the Splicing of Telephone Cables, *AMM*, **42**, 81–91, 1935.
[J] J. C. Moorhead and A. E. Western, Note on Fermat's Numbers, *Bull. Amer. Math. Soc.*, **16**, 1–6 1909.
[K] R. D. Carmichael, Note on a New Number Theory Function, *Bull. Amer. Math. Soc.*, **16**, 232–238, 1909.
[L] Samuel S. Wagstaffe, The Irregular Primes up to 125 000, *Math. Comput.*, **32**, 583–591 1978.
[M] L. J. Mordell, Reminiscences of an octogenarian mathematician, *AMM*, **78**, 952–961, 1971.
[N] R. Balasubramanian, J-M. Deshouillers and F. Dress, Problème de Waring pour les Bicarrés, I, II, *C. R. Acad. Sc.*, Paris, **303**, 85–86, 161–163, 1986.
[O] W. Ellison, Waring's Problem, *AMM*, **78**, 10–36, 1971.
[P] Mary Joan Collison, The Origins of the Cubic and Biquadratic Reciprocity Laws, *AHES*, **17**, 63–69, 1977.
[Q] A. E. Western, On Lucas's and Pepin's test for the primeness of Mersenne's numbers, *J. London Math. Soc.*, **7**, 130–137, 1932.
[R] A. M. Odlyzko and H. J. J Te Riele, Disproof of the Mertens conjecture, *J. Reine Angew.*, **357**, 138–160, 1985.
[S] John Brillhart and Michael A. Morrison, A Method of Factoring and the Factorisation of F_7, *Math. Comput.*, **29**, 183–205, 1975.
[T] R. L. Rivest, A. Shamir and L. M. Adleman, A method for obtaining digital signatures and public-key cryptosystems, *Communications of the ACM*, **21**, 120–126, 1978.

Other books not specifically referred to in the text, but consulted in the preparation of the present one, include:

1 George E. Andrews, *Number Theory*, W. B. Saunders, Philadelphia, 1971.
2 Roy Atherton *A Structured Approach to BBC BASIC*, Ellis Horwood Publishers, London, 1983
3 E. Bach, *Analytic Methods in the Design and Analysis of Number-theoretic Algorithms*, M. I. T Press, Cambridge, Mass., 1985.

4 E. T. Bell, *Men of Mathematics*, Simon and Schuster, New York, 1962.

5 Carl B. Boyer, *A History of Mathematics*, Wiley, New York, 1968.

6 Florian Cajori, *A History of Mathematics*, Macmillan, London, 1919.

7 Robert D. Carmichael, *Theory of Numbers and Diophantine Analysis*, Dover Publications, New York, 1959.

8 D. E. R. Denning, *Cryptography and Data Security*, Addison-Wesley, Reading, Mass., 1984.

9 Howard Eves, *An Introduction to the History of Mathematics*, Holt, Reinhart and Winston, New York, 1969.

10 Howard Eves, *Great Moments in Mathematics (Before 1650)*, Mathematical Association of America, 1980.

11 Edna E. Kramer, *The Nature and Growth of Modern Mathematics*, Princeton University Press, Princeton, N. J., 1981.

12 D. M. Monro, *Basic BASIC* (2nd edn) Edward Arnold, London, 1985.

13 D. M. Monro, *Interactive Computing with BASIC, A First Course*, Edward Arnold, London, 1974.

14 E. J. Redfern, *An Introduction to PASCAL and Computational Mathematics*, Macmillan, London, 1987.

15 Paulo Ribenboim, *Thirteen Lectures on Fermat's Last Theorem*, Springer-Verlag, New York, 1979.

16 J. Sass, *A Structured Approach to Basic Programming*, Allyn and Bacon, Boston, Mass., 1972.

17 Winfried Scharlau and Hans Opolka, *From Fermat to Minkowski: Lectures on the Theory of Numbers and its Historical Development*, Springer-Verlag, New York, 1985.

18 Daniel Shanks, *Solved and Unsolved Problems in Number Theory*, Spartak Books, Washington DC, 1962.

19 W. Sierpinski, *250 Problems in Elementary Number Theory*, Elsevier, New York, 1970.

20 D. J. Struik (ed.), *A Source Book in Mathematics*, Harvard University Press, Cambridge, Mass., 1969.

21 *Dictionary of Scientific Biography*, Charles Scribner's Sons, New York, 1970–1980.

Index

To help you locate items more readily we have purposely listed many of them under more than one 'key' word. For example, the reference to amicable pairs (of numbers) is made under headings 'amicable', 'pair' and also 'number'.

Abundant number 74
Adam (and Eve) 2
Additive arithmetic function 230
Affine transformation 278
Algebra, Fundamental Theorem of 119
Algorithm 8
  Division 7, 205, 216, 220
  Euclidean 37, 206, 217, 220
Almost perfect number 234
Amicable pair 74, 226
  imperfectly 75
Approximation (of irrationals by rationals) 252, 253, 261*ff*, 273
Archimedean cattle problem 269
  property of $\mathbb{Z}$ 16
Archimedes' approximation to $\sqrt{3}$ 271
Arithmetic functions (=number theoretic functions) 224
  additive 230
  average values of 240*ff*
  multiplicative 230
'Arithmetica' of Diophantus, Problems from (*see* Diophantus's . . .)
Arithmetic, Fundamental Theorem of (*see* Fundamental . . .)
Arithmetic, multiprecision 285*ff*
Arithmetic of remainders 76
Arithmetic progression 26
  primes in an (*see* Infinitude of . . .)
Artin E. 143
Artin's conjecture (problem) 143
Associate Gaussian integers 207
Average value of an arithmetic function 229, 240*ff*

Bachet C. 74
Bachet-Mordell equation ($y \wedge 2 = x \wedge 3 + k$) 165, 166, 169, 195, 196, 203, 214, 215
Barlow P. 71
Bell E. T. 71
Belonging to the exponent e mod n 127
Bernoulli Daniel 179
Bernoulli Jacob 157
Bernoulli numbers 157
Bertrand J. 67
Bertrand's conjecture 67
Big Oh notation 242
Bonse's inequality 69
Bougaiev N. V. 231
Bouniakovsky V. Y. 100
Brahmagupta's solution to Pell's equation 272
Brouncker W. 268
Brun V. 56
Brun's Theorem 56

Caeser-type code 278
Cancellation (division) in congruences 80
Cardan J. 227
Carmichael R. D. 93
Carmichael number 84, 123, 137
  characterisation of 139, 141
Carmichael's conjecture 93
Casting out nines 80, 81
Cataldi P. 21
Cattle problem of Archimedes 269
Cauchy A-L. 94
Chebychev (*see* Tchebychev)
Chinese remainder theorem 105, 106
  use with large numbers 291
Cipher system, RSA 279
  programs for 282
Ciphertext 278
Code
  Caeser-type 278
  'unbreakable' 277, 280
Cole F. N. 71
Collatz' problem 18
Common
  divisor, in $\mathbb{Z}$ 34
    greatest (=highest common factor) 34, 38, 39, 205, 206, 209
  multiple 35
    least 35
Compact prime table 48, 49
Complete residue system (complete set of residues) 89
Composite number(s) 19
  successive 24
Computer factorisation of large integers 273
Computer storage 23, 48

Computing time 23
Congruence(s)
basic properties 76*ff*
division (cancellation) in 80
identical (for polynomials) 115
linear 102*ff*
of higher degree 109*ff*, 118*ff*
quadratic 115*ff*
simultaneous linear 102, 105
solution of linear 102*ff*, (Bachet's version) 108
Conjecture
Artin's 143, 244
Bertrand's 67
Carmichael's 93
de Polignac's 58
Fermat's (Last Theorem) 153
Goldbach's 57, 58, 93, 228
Lagrange's 58
Legendre's 59, 69
Lehmer's 95
Mertens' 237
Mordall's 157
Continued fraction(s) 249*ff*
computation of 260, 266
convergents of 253
expansion of $\sqrt{d}$ 264, 269*ff*
expansion of π 273
finite 250
infinite (simple) 252
method of factorisation 273
of an irrational number 258*ff*
partial quotient of 250
periodic 265
representing an irrational number 254
secondary convergents of 275
simple 250
used to give best rational approximations 273
value of 254
Converse of
Fermat's Little Theorem 123, 125
Wilson's theorem 98
Convergent(s) of a continued fraction 253
secondary 275
Coprime (=relatively prime) 39
Counterexample, concept of 2, 16
Criterion, Euler's 185
Cubes, Sums of (*see* Sums...)

d'Alembert J. le R 119
Decimal expansions, repeating (periodic) 142*ff*
Deficient number 74
Definition by induction 12, 13
de la Vallee Poussin C. 60
version of the prime number theorem 92
de Jonquieres E. J. P. F. 155
de Polignac concecture 58
Descartes R. 228
Descent, Fermat's method of 153, 154, 163, 171, 217, 268
Dickson L. E. 50
Diophantine equations 146, 147
linear, 146*ff* (*see also* p 108, Ex. 4)
$x^2+y^2=z^2$ 148*ff*
$x^3+y^3=z^3$ 217
$x^4+y^4=z^2$ 153
$x^4+y^4=z^4$ 154
$x^3+y^3=z^3+t^3$ 1, 3, 161, 162
$x^4+y^4=z^4+t^4$ 161, 162
others of like type 155, 161
Diophantus 146
identity of 163
Diophantus's 'Arithmetica', Problems from 146, 147, 148, 152, 163, 202, 272
Dirichlet P. G. L. 53
Theorem of 53
Dirichlet's pigeon-hole principle 107
divisor problem 243
'Disquisitiones Arithmeticae' 54, 76, 204
Divides 19, 205
Divisibility; in $\mathbb{Z}$ 19
criteria (tests) 80, 81
Division algorithm in $\mathbb{Z}$ 7; in $\mathbb{Z}[i]$ 205; in E 216; in $\mathbb{Z}[\sqrt{d}]$ $(d=-2,2,3)$ 220
Division (cancellation) in congruences 80
Divisor(s) (*see* factor(s)) 19
(greatest) common 34, 38, 39, 205, 206, 209
proper 1
function $\tau(n)$ (giving number of) 33, 225
function $\sigma(n)$ (giving sum of) 33, 225
average value of 242, 243
problem of Dirichlet 243

Eisenstein F. G. M. 194
Elements (members) of a set 6
'Elements', of Euclid 20
Empty set 6
Encrypton, public key 279
Equation(s) (*see* Linear, Diophantine, Bachet-Mordell, Pell)
Eratosthenes 22
sieve of 22, 23
program for 23
Euclid 20
Euclid's 'Elements' 20
formula for perfect numbers 70, 74, 231
Euclidean Algorithm, in $\mathbb{Z}$ 37; in $\mathbb{Z}[i]$ 206; in E 216
Euler L. 180
pseudoprime 196
Euler's
criterion 185
from Wilson's Theorem 187
form of the Law of Quadratic Reciprocity 182
four square identity 171
ϕ (phi) function 89

average value of 244
computation of 91, 92
(generalisation of Fermat's Little) Theorem 95, 96
Theorem on perfect numbers 231
Eve (and Adam) 2
Expansion(s)
of $\sqrt{d}$ by continued fraction 264, 269*ff*
repeating (periodic) decimal 142*ff*
Exponent
of p (prime) in n (integer) 30
of p (prime) in $n!$ 63
to which a belongs mod n 127
universal, $\lambda(n)$ 138

Factor tables 293
Factor(s) (*see* divisor(s)) 19
highest common (*see* greatest common)
of Mesenne and of Fermat numbers 78, 85, 86, 191
Factorisation
by continued fraction method 273
by Fermat's method 44, 45
examples of non-uniqueness, into primes 31, 117, 156, 216, 220
In $\mathbb{Z}[i]$ 208
uniqueness into primes (*see* Fundamental Theorem of Arithmetic)
Faltings G., 157
Fermat 83
numbers, 72
Pepin's test for 136, 196
prime divisors of 85
for F_7 273
primes 72*ff*
primitive roots for 195, 196
F_5 is composite 78
Fermat's
Conjecture (Last Theorem) 153*ff*
History of 155*ff*
proof for $n=3$ 217; $n=4$ 154
Last Theorem (*see* Conjecture)
Little Theorem 84
converses of 123, 125
equivalent formulation of 86
Euler's generalisation of 95, 96
method of descent 153, 154, 163, 171, 217, 268
method of factorisation 44, 45
Fibonacci (Leonardo of Pisa) 12
numbers (sequence) 13, 58, 82
Lame's use of 39, 42
Fibonacci's rabbits 13
Finite (simple) continued fractions 250
Formula
Legendre's, for $\pi(x)$ 61
Mobius inversion 237
Formulae for generating primes 51*ff*
Four square theorem, of Lagrange 170
Four square identity of Euler 171
Fourth powers, sums of (*see* Sums . . .)
Fraction(s), Continued (*see* Continued fraction(s))
Frenicle B. 82y
Function
arithmetic (=number theoretic) 224
multiplicative, additive 230
divisor $\tau(n)$ 33, 225, 242
Euler's ϕ 89
Mobius' μ 236
for others *see* Notation section
number theoretic (*see* arithmetic)
Fundamental solution of Pell's equation 270
Fundamental Theorem of Algebra 119
Fundamental Theorem of Arithmetic
in $\mathbb{Z}$ 29, 43; in $\mathbb{Z}[\zeta]$ 156; in $\mathbb{Z}[i]$ 212; in $\mathbb{Z}[\sqrt{d}]$ ($d=-2, 2, 3$) 215, 220; in E $(=\mathbb{Z}[(-1+\sqrt{-3})/2])$ 217
failure in $\mathbb{Z}[\zeta]$ 156; $\mathbb{Z}[\sqrt{-3}]$ 216; in $\mathbb{Z}[\sqrt{5}]$ 220

Gaps between primes 24
Gauss C. F. 203
Gauss's
'Disqisitiones Arithmeticae' 54, 76, 204
form of the Law of Quadratic Reciprocity 188
generalisation of Wilson's theorem 132
Lemma 188
theorem on primitive roots 135
version of the Prime Number Theorem 59
Gaussian integer(s) 205
associate 207
factorisation of 208, 215
prime 207
units in the 207
gcd (*see* greatest common divisor)
(=hcf, highest common factor)
Germain S. 158
Germain's Theorem 159
Girard A. 13
Goldbach C. 51
Goldbach's conjecture(s) 57, 58, 93, 228
Greatest common divisor (gcd) 34, 205
as a linear combination 38, 39, 206, 209
computation of in $\mathbb{Z}$ 40, 41; in $\mathbb{Z}[i]$ 210

Hadamard J. 60
Hankel H. 269
Hardy G. H. 1
hcf (*see* greatest common divisor)
Higher degree congruences 109*ff*, 118*ff*
Hilbert D. 32
numbers (H-numbers) 31, 32, 46
failure of unique factorisation in 31
primes (H-primes) 31, 32
Holzman W. (Xylander) 147

Horner W. G. 95
Hurwitz A. 263
  Theorem 263
Huygens C. 253

Identity
  four square, of Euler 171
  two square, of Diophantus 163
if and only if (iff) 18
Imperfectly amicable pair 75
Induction
  definition by 12, 13
  principles of (mathematical) 10
  proof by 10
Incongruent (mod n) 76
Inequality, Bonse's 69
Infinite simple continued fraction(s) 252
Infinitude of primes
  in $\mathbb{Z}$ 25, 75, 94; of forms $4k+1$ 99; $4k+3$ 27; $5k+4$ 188; $6k+1$ 196; $6k+5$ 28; $8k+1$ 132; $8k+3$ 192; $8k+5$ 192; $8k+7$ 191
  of a-pseudoprimes 137
  of strong 2-pseudoprimes 140
INT 8
Integers (*see* also 'numbers')
  Gaussian 203*ff*
  well ordering of 6
Inversion formula, of Mobius 237
Irrational number
  as a continued fraction 258*ff*
  rational approximation to 252, 253, 261*ff*, 269, 271, 273
  quadratic 265
Irregular prime 157
Ivory J. 95

Jacobi C. G. J. 197
  symbol 198
  computation of 201
Jeans J. H. 87
Julis Caesar 277

Key, public 279
Kummer E. E. 156

Lagrange J. L. 117
Lagrange's conjecture 58
  4 square theorem 170
  Theorem on polynomials mod p 119
Lambert J. H. 36
Lame G. 39
Lame's Theorem 39, 42
  'Theorem' 156
Laplace P. S. 96
Last Theorem, of Fermat 153*ff*
Lattice points 194
Law of quadratic reciprocity 179*ff*, 183
  Euler's form 182
  Gauss's form 188

lcm (Least common multiple) 35
Legendre A-M. 126
  symbol 182
Legendre's
  conjecture 69
  formula for $\pi(x)$ 61
  Theorems 128, 170
  version of the Prime Number Theorem 59
Lehmer's conjecture 95
Leibniz G. W. 50
Lemma
  Gauss's 188
  Thue's 107
Leonardo of Pisa (*see* Fibonacci)
Linear congruences 102*ff*
  Diophantine equations 146*ff* (*see* also p 108, Ex. 4)
Little Theorem, of Fermat 84, 86
  converses of 123, 125
Liouville J. 176
Lucas F-E-A. 82
  sequence 14
Lucas's converse of Fermat's Little Theorem 123
  test for Mersenne primes 221*ff*
Lucky numbers 25

Mathematical Induction, Principles of 10
Members (elements) of a set 6
Merten's conjecture 237
'Mersenne M. 44, 70
  numbers 71
    prime divisors of 85, 86
  primes 1, 70*ff*
    Lucas's test for 221*ff*
    table of 72
Mersenne's assertion 71
Miller's primality test 142
Mobius A. F. 235
Mobius's function 236
  inversion formula 237
MOD 8
Modular arithmetic with large integers 291
Modulus, reduction to prime power 109, 110
Mordell L. J. 166
Mordell–Bachet equations: $y^2=x^3+k$ 165, 166, 169, 195, 196, 203, 214, 215
Mordell's conjecture 157
Multiple 19
  (least) common 35
Multiplication, Russian 79
Multiplicative arithmetic function 230
Multiplier 8
Multiplication arithmetic 285*ff*

Natural numbers (positive integers) 6
Nines, Casting out 80, 81
Non-empty set 6

Non-palindromic number 4
Non-residue, quadratic 180
Non-uniqueness of factorisation
  of polynomials mod 8 117
  of Hilbert numbers 31
  in $\mathbb{Z}[\sqrt{-3}]$ 216
  in $\mathbb{Z}[\zeta]$ 156
  in $\mathbb{Z}[\sqrt{5}]$ 220
  in $\mathbb{Z}[\sqrt{7}]$ 220
Norm 205, 214
nth powers, sums of (Waring's problem) 175
Number theoretic function (*see* arithmetic function)
Number(s)
  abundant 74
  almost perfect 234
  amicable 74, 226
  associate 207
  Bernoulli 157
  Carmichael 84, 123, 137, 139, 141
  composite 19
  deficient 74
  Fermat 72
  Fibonacci 13
  Hilbert (=H-numbers) 31, 32, 46
  imperfectly amicable 75
  lucky 25
  Mercenne 71
  natural 6
  palindromic, non-palindromic 4
  pentagonal 175
  perfect 70, 74
    even 231 odd 232
  polynomial 174*ff*
  prime 19, 207
  primitive pseudoperfect 234
  pseudoperfect 234
  pseudoprime 137, 140, 196
  relatively prime (coprime) 39
  square 175
  square free 236
  triangular 175
  wierd 234
  30 1, 69
  239 1, 16, 301
  341 1, 78
  487 1, 136 (Problem 5.3.1)
  945 1, 75 (Problem 2.6.3)
  1093 1, 157
  1729 1, 141, (179)
Number
  of (prime) divisors of an integer, $\tau(n)$ $(\omega(n))$ 224
  of elements in a reduced residue system, $\phi(n)$ 89
  of operations 4
  of primes $\langle = x$, $\pi(x)$ 59*ff*

Odd perfect numbers

Operations, number of 4
'or' 43
Order of a mod(ulo) n 127

Pair
  amicable 74, 226
  prime 2, 56, 100
Palindromic number 4
Partial quotients of a continued fraction 250
Pascal B. 179
Pell J. 267
Pell's Equation 267*ff*
  All solutions of 269, 270
  Brahmagupta's solution of 272
  Fundamental solution of 270
  Rational solution of 271
Pentagonal numbers 175
Pepin's test 136, 196
Perfect number(s) 70, 74
  and Fermat's Little Theorem 82
  early false assertions about 75
  Euclid's formula for 70, 74
    Euler's converse to 231
  form of odd 232
Periodic
  continued fraction 265
  (repeating) decimal expansions 142*ff*
    (length of) period of 143
Phi (ϕ) function of Euler 89
Pigeon-hole principle of Dirichlet 107
π, continued fraction expansion of 273
Plain text 278
Polygonal numbers 174*ff*
Polynomial congruence(s) 109*ff*, 115, 118*ff*
  roots of (Lagrange's Theorem) 119
Polynomials representing primes 51*ff*
Positive integers (=Natural numbers) 6
Primality tests of
  Lucas 123, 221*ff*
  Miller 142
  Pepin 136, 196
  Rabin 142
  Solovay–Strassen 201
Prime(s)
  compact table of 48, 49
  divisors of Fermat and Mersenne numbers 78, 85, 86, 191
  divisors, number of 33, 224
  exponent of, in n 30
  exponent of, in $n!$ 63
  factorisation into (*see* Fundamental Theorem of Arithmetic)
  Fermat 72*ff*
  formulae generating 51*ff*
  gaps between 24
  Gaussian 207
  Hilbert 31, 32
  in arithmetic progression (*see* Infinitude of...)

infinitude of (*see* Infinitude of . . .)
irregular 157
in $\mathbb{Z}[i]$ 207
Legendre's formula for $\pi(x)$ 61
Mersenne 1, 70*ff*
number 19
Number Theorem 60
de la Vallee Poussin's version 92
Gauss's conjecture 59
Legendre's conjecture 59
Tchebychev's version 63
of form x^2+x+41 51
pairs (=twin primes) 2, 56, 100
pseudo (*see* pseudoprime)
questions concerning 1, 2, 19, 20
regular 157, 158
relatively (=coprime) 39
representing polynomials 51
tables of 47, 48, 49
twin (=prime pairs) 2, 56, 100
Wilson 101
Prime power modulus, reduction to 110
Primitive
pseudoperfect number 234
Pythagorean triple 149
Primitive root 126, 191
for F_n 195, 196
Gauss's Theorem 135
mod n 126
mod p^k 133
mod 2^k 134
mod uv 134
mod 2^k 135
Principle, Well ordering 6
Principles of Mathematical Induction 10
Problem
Collatz' 18
Waring's 175
Programming time 3
Progression, primes in arithmetic (*see* Infinitude of . . .)
Proof
by induction 10
bt reductio ad absurdum 15
Proper divisor 1
Pseudoperfect number 234
Pseudoprime
a^- 137
Euler 196
strong a^- 140
Public key encryption 279
Pythagoras, Theorem of 148
Pythagorean
triple 148*ff*, 214
primitive 149

Quadratic
congruences 115*f*
irrational 265
non-residue, residue 180
Reciprocity, Law of (*see* Law of . . .)
Quotient 8
partial, of a continued fraction 250

Rabbits, Fibonacci's 13
Rabin's primality test 142
Ramanujan S. 1
Rational
approximations to irrationals 252, 253, 261*ff*, 269, 271, 273
solution to Pell's equation 271
Reciprocity, (*see* Law of Quadratic)
Recorde R. 74
Reduced residue system 89
modulo 2^k 136
number of elements in (i.e. $\phi(n)$) 90
Reductio ad Absurdum 15
some uses of 15, 25, 43, 51
Regular prime 157, 158
Relatively prime (coprime) 39
Remainder(s) 8
arithmetic of 76
theorem (Chinese) 105, 106, 291
Repeating (=periodic) decimal expansions 142*ff*
periodic length of 143
Repunit 9
Residue(s)
quadratic, quadratic non- 180
systems (reduced, complete) 89
number of elements in 89, 90
Root(s)
of a polynomial congruence (*see* Lagranges Theorem) 119
primitive 126, 191
RSA cipher system 279*ff*
programs for 282
Russian multiplication 79

Secondary convergents of continued fractions 275
Sequence
Fibonacci 13, 58, 82
Lucas 14
Set
elements (=members) of 6
empty, non-empty 6
Shift transformation 278
Sierpinski W. 246
Sieve of Eratosthenes 22, 23
program for 23
Simple continued fraction 250
Simson R. 253
Simpson T. 59
Simultaneous linear congruences (*see* Chinese remainder theorem)
Solovay-Strassen primality test 201
Square free 236
Square numbers 175

Square root, representation as a continued fraction 264, 269*ff*
Squares, sums of (*see* Sums ...)
Storage (on computer) 23, 48
Strong *a*-pseudoprime 140
Sums of
  cubes 1, 3, 16, 161, 162, 176
  divisors 33, 225
  four squares 170*ff*
  fourth powers 5, 161, 176
  *n*th powers (Waring's problem) 175
  three squares 170, 173
  two squares 163*ff*
    number of representations as 214
    primes as 164, 168, 213
Sub-Tsu 102, 105
Symbol
  Jacobi 198
  Legendre 182

Table(s)
  compact prime 48, 49
  of Mersenne primes 72
  of primes 47
Taylor B. 111
Tchebychev P. L. 63
Tchebychev's Prime Number Theorems 63
Theorem(s)
  Brun's 56
  Chinese Remainder 105, 106, 291
  Dirichlet's 53
  Euler's 95, 96, 231
  Fermat's Little 84, 86
  Fermat's Last (Fermat's Conjecture) 153*ff*
  Germain's 159
  Hurwitz' 263
  Lagrange's 119, 170
  Lame's 39, 42 and 'THEOREM' 156
  Legendre's 128, 170
  Lucas's 123, 221
  Prime Number 59, 60
  Pythagoras' 148
  Tchebychef's 63
  Wilson's 97, 100, 121, 131
  Wolstenholme's 122

Thue A. 107
Thue's Lemma 107
Time, computing 23
Transformation
  affine 278
  shift 278
Triangular numbers 175
Triple, (Primitive) Pythagorean 149
Twin primes (=prime pairs) 2, 56, 100

'Unbreakable' codes 277, 280
Unit in $\mathbb{Z}[i]$ 207; in $\mathbb{Z}[\sqrt{d}]$ 219; in E ($=\mathbb{Z}[(1+\sqrt{-3})/2]$) 220
Uniqueness of factorisation into primes
  failure of, (*see* Fundamental Theorem of Arithmetic)
Universal exponent $\lambda(n)$ 138

value
  of a continued fraction 254
  of $\phi(n)$ 91
  of $\tau(n)$ 225
  of $\sigma(n)$ 225

Wallis J. 144
Waring E. 97
Waring's problem 175
Well ordering
  principle 6, 10, 154
  some uses of 7, 29, 38
Wierd number 234
Wilson, Sir J. 97
  prime 101
Wilson's Theorem 97, 100, 121, 131
  converse of 98
  Gauss's generalisation 132
  implies Euler's criterion 187
WLOG 29
Wolstenholme's Theorem 122

x^2+x+41, primes represented by 51
Xylander (W. Holzmann) 147

$y^2=x^3+k$ for various k (*see* Mordell–Bachet equation)

ZZZ Sweet dreams!

Index of notation

[x] 2
n! 4
$\mathbb{Z}$ 5
{ } 5
$\mathbb{Z}^+$ 6
$\mathbb{Q}$ 6
$\mathbb{R}$ 6
$|a|$ 6, 205
ϕ, (three distinct uses) 6, 89, 218
$\mathbb{N}$ 6
ε, $\in$ 6
WO 6
$\mathbb{Q}^+$ 7
DA 7
PMI, PMI2 10
sigmas (five different—list) 11 33, 56, 94, (3.18)
$\binom{n}{r}$ 11
iff 18
$\Rightarrow$, $\Leftrightarrow$ 18
$|$, $\nmid$ 19, 205
$\pi_{a,b}$ 28, 92
WLOG
Π (three exs) 33, 57, (2.17)
σ 33
τ 33, 224
gcd (=hcf) 34
(a, b), (a, b, c), (several distinct meanings) 34, 35; 213, 87, 148
lcm 35
$[a, b]$ 35
EA 37
$\pi(x)$ 59
M_n 71
F_n 72
$\equiv$, $\not\equiv$ (mod n) 76, 217, 221
FLT 82
crs, *rrs* 89
$\equiv_p$ (4.17)
$\text{ord}_n\, a$ 127
a-psp 137
λ 138
FC 153
ζ, (a pth root of 1, usually a cube root) 156, 216
$\mathbb{Z}[\zeta]$ 156
$S_2(n)$ 169
$S_3(n)$ 174
$g(k)$ 175
$G(k)$ 177
q.n, *q.n.r* 180
(a/p) 182
(P/Q) 198
$\mathbb{Z}[i]$ $(=\mathbb{Z}[\sqrt{-i}])$ 205
$N(\lambda)$, $N(\alpha)$ 205, 214
$\mathbb{Z}[\sqrt{d}]$ 214
$\mathbb{Q}[\sqrt{d}]$ 214
E $(=\mathbb{Z}[\zeta]=\mathbb{Z}[(i+\sqrt{-3})/2])$ 216
$\omega(n)$ 224
$\Omega(n)$ 224
$\Lambda(n)$ 224
σ^* 224
σ_j 224
$\mu(n)$ 236
$\{t\}$ 242
$0(g(x))$ 242
$[a_0; a_1, \ldots, a_n]$ 250
$[a_0; a_1, \ldots\ ]$ 252
icf, iscf 252
C_k $(=p_k/q_k)$ 253
$[a_0; a_1, \ldots, a_n]$ 265